# A STUDY OF STANDARD ENGLISH

BY

J. BARCLAY, M.A.

D. H. KNOX, M.A.

and

G. B. BALLANTYNE, M.A.

ROBERT GIBSON & SONS GLASGOW, LTD
Publishers - - - - GLASGOW

1956

First Impression, - September, 1938
Second Impression, - July, 1939
Third Impression, - October, 1939
Fourth Impression, November, 1940
Fifth Impression, - December, 1942
Sixth Impression, - April, 1944
Seventh Impression, February, 1945
Eighth Impression, December, 1945
Ninth Impression, - August, 1946
Tenth Impression, September, 1947
Eleventh Impression, January, 1949
Twelth Impression, - August, 1950
Thirteenth Impression, Jany., 1952
Fourteenth Impression, - July, 1953
Fifteenth Impression, - Jany., 1954
Sixteenth Impression, - Oct., 1954
Seventeenth Impression, Jany., 1956

PRINTED IN GREAT BRITAIN BY J. AND J. GRAY, EDINBURGH

# PREFACE

"A Study of Standard English" aims at providing a course of at least three years' study, leading to University Matriculation, and generally takes for granted a previous knowledge of elementary English. No attempt has been made to plan a course of study, for the teacher of English, more perhaps than the teacher of any other subject, must ultimately present his facts in his own way. For this reason, though the compilers claim that this volume contains an adequate body of facts, suggestions and exercises, they believe that the order and treatment must be left to the teacher.

This book does not pretend to do the work of the teacher. We are convinced that, in these days of over-crowded curricula and widening schemes, pupils should learn for themselves much that teachers at present are at pains to instil; the time thus gained by the teacher may be the more profitably spent in developing and applying the knowledge already acquired by the pupils. It is hoped that the effort that has been made in every chapter to clarify and make significant the various aspects of English may enable pupils to learn or revise for themselves.

All the exercises have been carefully selected on account of their proved usefulness.

Every effort has been made to avoid infringement of copyright; but if, inadvertently, we have transgressed in any way, we desire to offer sincere apologies.

J. B.
D. H. K
G. B. B.

# ACKNOWLEDGMENTS

Acknowledgments for the use of copyright material are due to:—

Mr. Laurence Binyon, for his Poem, "The Road Menders," published by Messrs. MacMillan & Co., Ltd.

Mr. John Buchan and Messrs. Hodder & Stoughton, for an excerpt from "Huntingtower."

Mr. John Buchan and the Proprietors of the "S.M.T. Magazine," for an excerpt from the Scott Centenary Number.

Lord Baldwin and Messrs. Hodder & Stoughton, for an excerpt from "On England—Political Education."

Messrs. Ernest Benn, Ltd., for an excerpt from "If the Blind Lead," by Alderton Pink.

Messrs. Jonathan Cape, Ltd., and The Trustees of "Seven Pillars of Wisdom," by T. E. Lawrence.

Messrs. Chatto & Windus, for an excerpt from "Fiery Particles," by C. E. Montague.

Messrs. Constable & Co., Ltd., for an excerpt from "Curzon, The Last Phase," by Harold Nicholson.

Mrs. Galsworthy and Messrs. Wm Heinemann, Ltd., for an excerpt from "A Portrait" (*ex* A Motley), by John Galsworthy.

Messrs. Longmans, Green & Co., Ltd., for an excerpt from "British History in the 19th Century," by Professor Trevelyan.

Messrs. MacMillan & Co., Ltd., and the Author's Executors, for an excerpt from "Far From The Madding Crowd," by Thomas Hardy.

Mr. John Masefield, for his poem, "The Rider at the Gate" (reprinted from Collected Poems of John Masefield (Wm. Heinemann, Ltd.), by permission of the Author.

Messrs. Methuen & Co., for an excerpt from "Library of Humour," by E. V. Knox.

Messrs. Methuen & Co. and the Author's Executors, for an excerpt from "The Mirror of the Sea," by Joseph Conrad.

Mr. H. G. Wells, for an excerpt from "The War in the Air."

Mr. George Bernard Shaw, for extracts from the Prefaces to "The Doctor's Dilemma" and "Misalliance."

Mrs. Nora M. Myers, for a Sonnet by Ernest Myers.

Lady Watson and Messrs. George G. Harrap & Co., Ltd., for "The Ideal Popular Leader," by Sir William Watson.

# CONTENTS


| CHAPTER | | PAGE |
|---|---|---|
| I. | General Analysis | 7 |
| II. | Synthesis | 28 |
| III. | Grammar (parsing) | 33 |
| IV. | Punctuation | 63 |
| V. | Composition | 69 |
| VI. | Errors in Composition | 110 |
| VII. | Interpretation | 133 |
| VIII. | Direct and Indirect Speech | 173 |
| IX. | Précis | 180 |
| X. | History of the Language | 200 |
| XI. | The Dictionary and its Uses | 221 |
| XII. | Prosody | 257 |
| XIII. | Figures of Speech | 281 |
| XIV. | Style | 312 |
| XV. | Literary Forms | 344 |
| XVI. | Literary Appreciation | 369 |
| XVII. | Common Literary Terms and Phrases | 388 |
| | Index | 399 |

# A STUDY OF STANDARD ENGLISH

## CHAPTER I

### GENERAL ANALYSIS

1. **A Sentence** is a combination of words expressing *complete sense.*

The two principal and necessary parts of a Sentence are the *Subject* and the *Predicate.*

The Subject of a Sentence may be a Noun, a Pronoun, a Noun Phrase, or a Noun Clause.

The Predicate of a Sentence must be a Finite Verb, that is, a Verb in the Indicative, the Subjunctive, or the Imperative Mood. The Verb may require an Object or a Complement to complete the sense.

2. There are **four kinds of Sentences—**

(1) **The Simple Sentence.**
(2) **The Compound Sentence.**
(3) **The Complex Sentence.**
(4) **The Compound-Complex or Multiple Sentence.**

We must assume at this stage a knowledge of Particular Analysis of a clause or simple sentence and in this chapter are concerned with **General Analysis. General Analysis** is the division of a sentence into the clauses of which it is composed. In addition it generally shows the relation of the clauses to one another. It applies therefore to **Compound, Complex and Compound-Complex Sentences.**

3. The **Compound Sentence** consists of *two or more Simple Sentences joined by a Co-ordinating Conjunction* as "He shakes with joy and weeps with tenderness."

The number of *Clauses* in a Compound Sentence will be determined by the number of Predicates expressed or understood.

Compound Sentences are divided into *four classes*—

(1) **Copulative**: as "Then the maiden *clasped* her hands and *prayed*."

(2) **Adversative**: as "*Give* every man thine ear, but few thy voice."

(3) **Illative**: as "He *was* an obedient child, therefore he *became* a good commander."

(4) **Disjunctive**: as "Either he or I *must go*."

*Note.*—i. The Co-ordinate Clauses in a Compound Sentence are equal in grammatical importance, therefore each of them is a Principal Clause.

The *General* Analysis consists in naming each clause separately and describing its function.

4. The **Complex Sentence** consists of *one Principal Clause, and one or more Subordinate Clauses.*

The Principal Clause is the clause that contains the leading idea.

A Subordinate Clause may serve (1) as Subject or as Object or as Complement; (2) as an Adjective; (3) as an Adverb.

There are thus **three leading classes of Subordinate Clauses**—

(1) **Noun Clauses.** | (2) **Adjective Clauses.**
(3) **Adverbial Clauses.**

5. A **Noun Clause** may be the Subject or the Object of a Principal Clause, or it may be Nominative in Apposition to the Subject, or Objective in Apposition

to the **Object**, or it may be the **Complement** of the Predicate, or may be governed by a Preposition which in Analysis goes with the Principal Clause. A Noun Clause stands for a **Noun.**

*Examples* :—(1) *When he will come* is not known.

*When he will come* is a Subordinate Noun Clause, Subject to *is not known.*

(2) He told me *that he was coming.*

*That he was coming* is a Subordinate Noun Clause, Object to *told.*

(3) It was reported *that the ship had come.*

*That the ship had come* is a Subordinate Noun Clause, Nominative in Apposition to *it.* Here *it* stands for the Noun Clause.

(4) His excuse was *that he had forgotten.*

*That he had forgotten* is a Subordinate Noun Clause, the Complement to *was*, or Nominative after *was.*

*Notes.*—i. In the sentence "'But spare your country's flag,' she said," we have the exact words of the speaker (Direct Speech). *But spare your country's flag* ought to be regarded as a noun clause and then analysed separately as a separate sentence, as it does not depend grammatically on the Principal Parenthetical Clause, *she said.* This is more evident when a Compound, Complex or Compound-Complex Sentence is in Direct Speech. (See Table of Analysis for an example of this kind.)

ii. In changing from Direct to Indirect or Reported Speech, Pronouns of the First or Second Person are turned into the Third Personal Pronouns. Thus, "She said that *he* ought to spare *his* country's flag."

## EXERCISE I

**Write out the Noun Clauses in the following sentences, and state their Case :—**

1. I asked him if he was going.
2. He did not know what he was saying.
3. Where she was staying she did not say.
4. It is curious how often mistakes are made.

5. It is hoped that his health will improve.
6. What he intends to do is uncertain.
7. His explanation of the affair was that the letter must have been misdirected.
8. The Norman Conquest completed what the Saxon Invasion had begun.
9. It is to be noted that, in one respect at least, the Norman Conquest checked the development of the system.
10. You would desire the King were made a prelate.
11. The Kentishmen also withdrew to their homes only to find that they could put no faith in princes.
12. What he said was not announced.
13. It is quite clear that too often France used Scotland as a weapon against England.
14. The maxim that a bad title makes a good king finds a notable example in the first of the Lancastrian kings.
15. It is highly probable that the purely intellectual side of the movement had its origin in the East.
16. He was asked to explain why he went there.
17. No one knew how the accident happened.
18. Where the sugar-cane grows is not suitable for European colonists.
19. They gave orders that he should rejoin his regiment.
20. I would I were far away.

## EXERCISE II

**Expand each Simple Sentence into a Complex one containing a Noun Clause :—**

1. One man's meat is another man's poison.
2. He ordered the soldiers to assist their wounded comrades.
3. Never tell a falsehood.
4. I was delighted to hear of your success.
5. He was very anxious to know the result of the competition.
6. His disappearance at this time is highly suspicious.
7. We have nothing but praise for his behaviour.
8. There is no malice in his remarks.
9. He had to admit his insolvency.
10. It is most absurd his forgetting the tickets.
11. Your action is dangerous to others as well as yourself.
12. Her hiding-place has been carefully concealed.
13. The rumour about his accident has not been substantiated.
14. His speedy recovery is now certain.
15. He will be glad to deal with your accusations.
16. This will now sell for its real value.

17. Appearances are often deceptive.

18. He has always believed in immortality.

19. They requested their friends not to desert them in their distress.

20. He was anxious to know the nature of the offence of which he was accused.

6. An **Adjective Clause** is a Clause used as an Adjective. It may be used as an Attribute of the Subject, Attribute of the Object, or Attribute of the Complement. It is introduced by a Relative Pronoun, or the equivalont of a Relative Pronoun.

*Notes.*—i. Adjective Clauses introduced by *where, when,* etc., may be distinguished from Adverbial Clauses by the fact that these words, if introducing an Adjective Clause, will always have *an Antecedent expressed*:—as "I thought of a *mound* in sweet Auburn *where a little headstone stood.*" "Where a little headstone stood" is an Adjective Clause qualifying "mound." Always remember that the kind of clause depends on its function as noun, adjective or adverb.

ii. Sometimes the Antecedent is omitted before the Relatives, *who, which, that.*

iii. The Antecedent is always omitted before *what.*

iv. Sometimes the Relative is omitted.

v. When *that* is a Relative Pronoun it can always be turned into *who, whom,* or *which.*

vi. *As* following *same* or *such* is a relative pronoun introducing an adjective clause.

## EXERCISE III

**Write out the Adjective Clauses in the following sentences, and state what they qualify :—**

1. This is the cat that killed the rat.
2. I am monarch of all I survey.
3. O Solitude, where are the charms that sages have seen in thy face?
4. Beside the bed where parting life was laid, the reverend champion stood.
5. I dare do all that may become a man, who dares do more is none.
6. Who was the thane lives yet.
7. They left behind them a name which was sufficient to convulse Scotland in 1715.
8. Then there came a time when these influences passed away.

9. The silent heart which grief assails treads soft and lonesome o'er the vales.

10. I seek to trace in leaves and flowers that round me lie, lessons of love and earnest piety.

11. Cherish those hearts that hate thee.

12. This was the reason which he gave.

13. And there are some whom a thirst, ardent, unquenchable, fires.

14. I have a mind presages me such thrift.

15. Man is a harp whose chords elude the sight.

16. There are times when to you it doth impart authentic tidings of invisible things.

17. It was not such as I had reason to expect.

18. 'Tis the past that fills the actual world with unreal likenesses of lovely shapes that were and are not.

19. I sigh the lack of many a thing I sought.

20. By Nature's law, what may be, may be now.

21. And they shall strike your children yet unborn, that lift your vassal hands against my head.

## EXERCISE IV

Expand each **Simple Sentence** into a **Complex one** containing an **Adjective Clause** :—

1. The familiar place is always attractive.
2. The horse, the friend of man is invaluable to nim.
3. Is this a place to behave foolishly?
4. The veterans among the soldiers met the attack with great coolness.
5. The hounds baying and leaping, soon killed the fox.
6. You are not a man terrified by threats.
7. He reached the caves so often described to him as a boy.
8. The advantages of his education were utterly thrown away.
9. The dangers and difficulties surrounding a king are not always perceived by the average man.
10. Shakespeare and Jonson were contemporary dramatists.
11. You should not lose heart over trifling misfortunes.
12. He is admired by his intimates.
13. This is the scene of the tragedy.
14. The conqueror of himself is greater than the victorious general.
15. The victor of a hundred fights has never lost a gun.
16. I naturally took the opinion of the expert as reliable.
17. These were tactics not to be pardoned in such a game.
18. Pedestrians crossing a busy street must always watch for the signal.

19. In their new happiness, they soon forgot the sufferings of their youthful days.

20. This monument celebrating the work of the early reformers is to be removed.

7. An **Adverbial Clause** is a Clause that is used as an Adverb, to modify a Verb, an Adjective, or an Adverb in another Clause.

There are **nine kinds of Adverbial Clauses**—

(1) **Time**: as, His father died *before the prince was born.*
(2) **Place**: as, He lay *where he fell.*
(3) **Manner**: as, The tree still lay as it fell.
(4) **Degree**: as, She was as white *as snow* [*is*].
(5) **Cause**: as, He retreated from that position, *because he was so ordered.*
(6) **Purpose**: as, He went slowly to the school, *that he might be late.*
(7) **Consequence** or **Result**: as, He went so slowly to the school, *that he was late.*
(8) **Condition**: as, *If he goes to London* he will see the king.
(9) **Concession**: as, *Though He slay me,* yet will I trust Him.

An Adverbial Clause of Time answers the questions: **When? How long? How often?**

An Adverbial Clause of Place answers the questions: **Where? Whither? Whence?**

An Adverbial Clause of Manner answers the question: **How?**

An Adverbial Clause of Degree answers the questions: **How much? To what extent?**

An Adverbial Clause of Cause answers the question: **Why?**

An Adverbial Clause of Purpose answers the question: **For what purpose?**

An Adverbial Clause of Consequence answers the question: **With what result?**

An Adverbial Clause of Condition answers the question: **On what condition?**

An Adverbial Clause of Concession answers the question: **Despite what?**

*Notes.*—i. Some clauses are elliptical or contracted, especially after *though, when, unless, till, if.* In analysis the missing words should always be supplied. "He acts as if he were king," might be expanded into "He acts as he would act if he were king." We should therefore have two Adverbial Clauses, one of Manner and one of Condition.

ii. Clauses introduced by *when* and *where* may be Noun Clauses, Adjective Clauses, Adverbial Clauses, or Principal Clauses. If they answer the question "What?" they will be Noun Clauses. If *when* and *where* have Antecedents expressed, the clauses will be Adjectival. If *when* and *where* introduce Direct Questions, the clauses will be Principal.

iii. *If* may introduce a Noun Clause or a Conditional Clause. The Noun Clause will answer the question "What?"

iv. Conditional Clauses are introduced by *if* or *unless* expressed or understood. The Conditional Clause is sometimes called the *Protasis;* the Principal Clause, the *Apodosis.*

v. In Conditional Clauses the Subjunctive Mood of the Verb is used when the Condition is unlikely or impossible.

vi. Concessive Clauses are introduced by *though, although,* or *however,* and are so called because they *concede* or grant some argument.

## EXERCISE V

**Point out the Adverbial Clauses in the following sentences, telling the kind of Adverbial Clause and the words they modify or limit:—**

1. He did as he was told.
2. The son is as tall as the father.
3. He came because I sent for him.
4. All would be well if this were done.
5. When he comes, I shall give you the news.
6. Though he was poor, yet was he honest.
7. Fear the Lord lest evil befall thee.
8. The matter fell out just as I expected.
9. He was not so clever as I thought.
10. He did everything in his power that he might secure the prize.
11. The longer I live the more I am convinced of the truth of his statement.
12. Every one listened with attention when the archbishop spoke.
13. His story was not true, because I was absent at the time.
14. Except ye believe, ye cannot be saved.
15. Unless I had seen the affair myself, I would not have believed it.
16. However it falls out, it will not matter to him.
17. Bring me the exercise when it is finished.
18. But that I am forbid to tell the secrets of my prison-house, I could a tale unfold.
19. He is as brave as he is generous.

20. Whithersoever the shepherd went, the dog followed him.

21. Whatever be the consequence, I shall do my duty.

22. Long before the sun had risen, we had climbed the mountain.

23. I shall tarry here till the day break and the shadows flee away.

24. Take heed lest ye fall into temptation.

25. So I lose not honour in seeking to augment it, I shall be counselled.

## EXERCISE VI

Expand each Simple Sentence into a Complex Sentence containing an Adverbial Clause :—

1. We hope to raise the question again at a suitable occasion.
2. In spite of his anger, we decided to stay.
3. We saw the scene of the murder yesterday.
4. His strength is really much greater than mine.
5. I planned this as a surprise for you.
6. Having made a bargain, he has a duty to keep it.
7. The authorities have offered a reward for his capture, dead or alive.
8. He always acts according to expectations.
9. Of all the speakers at the meeting, he is the most convincing.
10. The more, the merrier.
11. But for the welcome arrival of his own supporters, he might have been seriously injured.
12. He obeyed orders.
13. Whatever the outcome, you can rely on my assistance.
14. The longer our life, the greater our patience.
15. Everybody, however, listened carefully to the preacher speaking.
16. Without consent of his parents, he will never leave home.
17. With every effort, the distance between him and his rival diminished.
18. By constant attention to duty, he hopes to gain promotion.
19. The obstacle was too high to be surmounted.
20. In place of a smiling garden, there was now desolation.

## EXERCISE VII

Complete the following sentences on the lines suggested :—

1. He hopes to be present........... Adv. Cl. of Time.
2. You shall have your reward........... Adv. Cl. of Condition.

3. The new playing field is situated............ Adv. Cl. of Place.

4. The ship is as commodious............ Adv. Cl. of Degree.

5. He behaved nobly............ Adv. Cl. of Manner.

6. He is not necessarily a traitor............ Adv. Cl. of Concession.

7. He left his native village............ Adv. Cl. of Purpose.

8. The poor man could offer no defence............ Adv. Cl. of Reason.

9. The responsibility was so great............ Adv. Cl. of Consequence.

10. Diligence makes a man successful............ Adv. Cl. of Condition.

11. It is too hot............ Adv. Cl. of Consequence.

12. He was good enough to suggest............ Adv. Cl. of Consequence.

8. A **Compound-Complex Sentence** consists of *two or more Principal Clauses and one or more Subordinate Clauses.*

*Examples* :—(1) If to do were as easy as to know what were good to do, chapels had been churches and poor men's cottages princes' palaces.

(2) There, at the foot of yonder nodding beech
That wreathes its old fantastic roots so high,
His listless length at noontide would he stretch,
And pore upon the brook that babbles by.

EXAMPLES OF GENERAL ANALYSIS.

(1) If to do were as easy as to know what were good to do, chapels had been churches and poor men's cottages princes' palaces.

(2) There, at the foot of yonder nodding beech
That wreathes its old fantastic roots so high,
His listless length at noontide would he stretch,
And pore upon the brook that babbles by.

(3) He acted as though he were a madman.

(4) The wave rolled on as if it would swamp the boat.

(5) "Though you may not believe it, you are trespassing at the present moment," he answered angrily.

(6) I am certain the weather will be fine.

(1)

| No. | Clause. | Kind of Clause. | Relation. |
|---|---|---|---|
| A | Chapels had been churches | Principal Clause | Independent |
| B | And poor men's cottages [had been] princes' palaces | Principal Clause | Co-ordinate with (A) |
| $b_1$ | If to do were as easy as to know | Subordinate Adverbial Clause of Condition | Modifying *had been* |
| $b_2$ | What were good to do | Subordinate Noun Clause | Object to *to know* |

**Compound-Complex Sentence.**

*Note.—As to know* might be expanded into a Subordinate Adverbial Clause of Degree modifying *easy.*

(2)

| No. | Clause. | Kind of Clause. | Relation. |
|---|---|---|---|
| A | There, at the foot of yonder nodding beech, his listless length at noontide would he stretch. | Principal Clause | Independent |
| B | And [he would] pore upon the brook | Principal Clause | Co-ordinate with (A) |
| $a_1$ | That wreathes its old fantastic roots so high | Subordinate Adjective Clause | Qualifying *beech* |
| $b_1$ | That babbles by | Subordinate Adjective Clause | Qualifying *brook* |

**Compound-Complex Sentence.**

(3)

| No. | Clause. | Kind of Clause. | Relation. |
|---|---|---|---|
| A | He acted | Principal Clause | Independent |
| $a_1$ | As [he would act] | Adverbial Clause of Manner | Modifying "*acted*" |
| $a_2$ | Though he were a madman | Adverbial Clause of Concession | Modifying ["*would act*"] |

**Complex Sentence.**

(4)

| No. | Clause. | Kind of Clause. | Relation. |
|---|---|---|---|
| A | The wave rolled on | Principal Clause | Independent |
| $a_1$ | As [it would roll] | Adverbial Clause of Manner | Modifying "*rolled*" |
| $a_2$ | If it would swamp the boat | Adverbial Clause of Condition | Modifying ["*would roll*"] |

**Complex Sentence.**

(5)

| No. | Clause. | Kind of Clause. | Relation. |
|---|---|---|---|
| A | He answered angrily | Principal Clause | Independent |
| $a_1$ | Though you may not believe it, you are trespassing at the present moment | Noun Clause | Objective by "*answered*" |

**Complex Sentence.**

| No. | Clause. | Kind of Clause. | Relation. |
|---|---|---|---|
| A | You are trespassing at the present moment | Principal Clause | Independent |
| $a_1$ | Though you may not believe it | Adverbial Clause of Concession | Modifying "*are trespassing*" |

**Complex Sentence.**

(6)

| No. | Clause. | Kind of Clause. | Relation. |
|---|---|---|---|
| A | I am certain | Principal Clause | Independent |
| $a_1$ | The weather will be fine | Noun Clause | Complement of "*am certain*" |

**Complex Sentence.**

OR,

| No. | Clause. | Kind of Clause. | Relation. |
|---|---|---|---|
| A | I am certain [of this] | Principal Clause | Independent |
| $a_1$ | [That] the weather will be fine | Noun Clause | Objective in apposition with [" this "] |

**Complex Sentence.**

## EXERCISE VIII

**Give the General Analysis of the following Sentences :—**

1. Though the wind hath fallen, they drift along,
Till the vessel strikes with a shivering shock.

2. The meteor-flag of England
Shall yet terrific burn,
Till danger's troubled night depart,
And the star of peace return.

3. As bends the bark's mast in the gale,
When rent are rigging, shrouds and sail,
It waver'd 'mid the foes.

4. Into the street the piper stept,
Smiling first a little smile,
As if he knew what magic slept
In his quiet pipe the while.

5. You should have heard the Hamelin people
Ring the bells till they rocked the steeple.

6. But now the Mayor was on the rack,
And the wretched council's bosom beat,
As the piper turned from the High Street
To where the Weser rolled its waters
Right in the way of their sons and daughters.

7. Lightly they'll talk of the spirit that's gone,
And o'er his cold ashes upbraid him ;
But little he'll reck, if they let him sleep on
In the grave where a Briton has laid him.

8. And Ardennes waves above them her green leaves
Dewy with nature's tear-drops, as they pass,
Grieving, if aught inanimate e'er grieves
Over the unreturning brave.

9. From my wings are shaken the dews that waken
The sweet birds every one,
When rocked to rest on their mother's breast,
As she dances about the sun.

10. The triumphal arch through which I march
With hurricane, fire, and snow,
When the powers of the air are chained to my chair,
Is the million-coloured bow.

11. And if my standard-bearer fall, as fall full well he may—
For never saw I promise yet of such a bloody fray—
Press where ye see my white plume shine, amidst the ranks of war,
And be your oriflamme to-day, the helmet of Navarre.

12. Still from the sire the son shall hear
Of the stern strife, and carnage drear
    Of Flodden's fatal field,
Where shiver'd was fair Scotland's spear,
    And broken was her shield.

13. When the goodman mends his armour,
  And trims his helmet's plume,
When the goodwife's shuttle merrily
  Goes flashing through the loom:
With weeping and with laughter
  Still is the story told,
How well Horatius kept the bridge,
  In the brave days of old.

14. If I cannot end my life
In the crimson'd battle strife,
Let me die as I have lived,
    On the sea.

15. Though it be sung of old and young
  That I should be to blame,
Theirs be the charge, that speak so large
  In hurting of my name.

16. A bed of roses saw I there,
  Bewitching with their grace,
Besides so wond'rous sweet they were,
  That they perfum'd the place.

17. And bless'd are those
Whose blood and judgment are so well commingled,
That they are not a pipe for Fortune's finger
To sound what stop she please.

18. But were I Brutus,
And Brutus Antony, there were an Antony
Would ruffle up your spirits, and put a tongue
In every wound of Caesar, that should move
The stones of Rome to rise and mutiny.

19. I listened motionless and still;
And, as I mounted up the hill,
The music in my heart I bore,
Long after it was heard no more.

20. O joy, that in our embers
  Is something that doth live,
That nature yet remembers
  What was so fugitive.

21. I love the brooks, which down their channels fret,
Even more than when I tripped lightly as they.

22. When lo, as they reached the mountain side,
A wondrous portal opened wide,
As if a cavern was suddenly hollowed ;
And the piper advanced and the children followed.

23. And just as I became assured
My lame foot would be speedily cured,
The music stopped and I stood still.

24. There came into many a burgher's pate
A text which says that heaven's gate
Opes to the rich at as easy rate
As the needle's eye takes a camel in.

25. But when they saw it was a lost endeavour,
And piper and dancers were gone for ever,
They made a decree that lawyers never
Should think their records dated duly
If, after the day of the month and year,
These words did not as well appear,
"And so long after what happened here
On the twenty-second day of July,
Thirteen hundred and seventy-six."

26. Strike, as thou didst at Caesar ; for, I know,
When thou didst hate him worst, thou lovedst him better
Than ever thou lovedst Cassius.

27. Poor naked wretches, wheresoe'er you are,
That bide the pelting of this pitiless storm,
How shall your houseless heads and unfed sides,
Your looped and windowed raggedness, defend you
From seasons such as these ?

28. He that trusts you,
Where he should find you lions, finds you hares ;
Where foxes, geese ; you are no surer, no,
Than is the coal of fire upon the ice,
Or hailstone in the sun.

29. Me oft has fancy ludicrous and wild,
Soothed with a waking dream of houses, towers,
Trees, churches, and strange visages, expressed
In the red cinders, while with poring eye
I gazed, myself creating what I saw.

30. Drawn from his refuge in some lonely elm
That age or injury has hollowed deep,
Where, on his bed of wool and matted leaves
He has outslept the winter, ventures forth
To frisk a while, and bask in the warm sun,
The squirrel, flippant, pert, and full of play.

31. These, and a thousand images of bliss,
With which kind nature graces every scene,
Where cruel man defeats not her design,
Impart to the benevolent, who wish
All that are capable of pleasure pleased,
A far superior happiness to theirs,
The comfort of a reasonable joy.

32. I will obey, not willingly alone,
But gladly, as the precept were her own:
And, while that face renews my filial grief,
Fancy shall weave a charm for my relief,
Shall steep me in Elysian reverie,
A momentary dream, that thou art she.

33. I feel almost at times as I have felt
In happy childhood; trees, and flowers, and brooks,
Which do remember me of where I dwelt,
Ere my young mind was sacrificed to books,
Come as of yore upon me, and can melt
My heart with recognition of their looks;
And even at moments I think I could see
Some living thing to love—but none like thee.

34. Ye stars! which are the poetry of heaven!
If in your bright leaves we would read the fate
Of men and empires—'tis to be forgiven,
That in our aspirations to be great,
Our destinies o'erleap their mortal state,
And claim a kindred with you; for ye are
A beauty and a mystery, and create
In us such love and reverence from afar,
That fortune, fame, power, life, have named themselves a star.

35. And if I laugh at any mortal thing,
'Tis that I may not weep; and if I weep,
'Tis that our nature cannot always bring
Itself to apathy, for we must steep
Our hearts first in the depths of Lethe's spring,
Ere what we least wish to behold will sleep.

36. I know he would not be a wolf,
But that he sees the Romans are but sheep;
He were no lion, were not Romans hinds.
Those that with haste will make a mighty fire
Begin it with weak straws: what trash is Rome,
What rubbish and what offal, when it serves
For the base matter to illuminate
So vile a thing as Caesar!

37. I cannot tell what you and other men
Think of this life ; but, for my single self,
I had as lief not be as live to be
In awe of such a thing as I myself.

38. Since my young days of passion—joy, or pain,
Perchance my heart and harp have lost a string,
And both may jar ; it may be, that in vain
I would essay as I have sung to sing.
Yet, though a dreary strain, to this I cling ;
So that it wean me from the weary dream
Of selfish grief or gladness—so it fling
Forgetfulness around me—it shall seem
To me, though to none else, a not ungrateful theme.

39. No longer mourn for me when I am dead
Than you shall hear the surly sullen bell
Give warning to the world, that I am fled
From this vile world, with vilest worms to dwell.

40. Kangaroos, it seems, are not hothouse plants to be reared precariously in private parks under permanent threat of chill and lung trouble.

41. When a traveller returneth home, let him not leave the countries where he hath travelled altogether behind him, but maintain a correspondence by letters with those of his acquaintance which are of most worth.

42. At the present moment when powerful forces are trying to divide the world into two antagonistic groups, any move to strengthen the smaller States who do not desire to belong to either camp is a vital contribution to world peace, and would therefore, I am sure, be supported by Great Britain.

43. I knew one, that when he wrote a letter, he would put that which was most material in the postcript, as if it had been a by-matter.

44. There is no question of another world conference, which in all probability would do more harm than good ; but there is a widespread feeling that the time is opportune for the countries which desire greater freedom in the exchange of their goods to get together in an endeavour to promote it.

45. It is a strange thing to observe how high a rate great kings and monarchs do set upon this fruit of Friendship whereof we speak : so great, as they purchase it many times at the hazard of their own safety and greatness.

46. There is a climatic warmth about Scotland which caused the proposal to be put forward, some years ago, that its rivers could probably breed crocodiles as well as salmon.

47. With much better and more liberal judgment, it is the present practice of most of the Scottish clergymen to seize this opportunity of offering a prayer, and exhortations suitable to make an impression upon the living, while they are yet in the very presence of the relics of him whom they have but lately seen such as they themselves, and who now is such as they must in their time become.

48. It was necessary, he admitted, that he should produce more positive testimony of her innocence than what arose out of general character, and this he undertook to do by the mouth of the person to whom she had communicated her situation.

49. When I do myself the honour of speaking to you next on the subject, I shall hope to receive a more favourable answer than you have now given me; but I am far from accusing you of cruelty at present, because I know it to be the established custom of your sex to reject a man on the first application, and perhaps you may have even now said as much to encourage my suit as would be consistent with the true delicacy of the female character.

50. Should anyone interrogate her, how she works, if graciously she vouchsafe to listen and speak, she will reply, " it behoves thee not to disquiet me with interrogatories, but to understand in silence, even as I am silent and work without words."

51. It is not too much to require that what the wisest of mankind, those who are best entitled to trust their own judgment, find necessary to warrant their relying on it, should be submitted to by that miscellaneous collection of a few wise and many foolish individuals, called the public.

52. An encouraging feature of the present efforts is that they are being directed with a far greater sense of reality than was shown a few years ago.

53. The night-smell of bruised grass came up from under her feet as she went towards the saw-pit and carpenter's shed, which, as I have said before, were in a corner of the field near the road, and where one of her informants had told her it was supposed by the police that the murderer had lurked while waiting for his victim.

54. It is difficult to escape the feeling that, if the responsible authorities go on at their present rate, future Royal Processions

will have to wend their way through streets altered out of all recognition.

55. The strain was solemn and affecting, sustained as it was by the pathetic warble of a voice which had naturally been a fine one, and in which, weakness, if it diminished its power, had improved its softness.

56. Curzon Street, where Becky Crawley lived on nothing a year, is to be transformed into a so-called "main artery."

57. I no sooner saw this venerable man in the pulpit, but I very much approved of my friend's insisting upon the qualifications of a good aspect and a clear voice; for I was so charmed with the gracefulness of his figure and delivery, as well as the discourses he pronounced, that I think I never passed any time more to my satisfaction.

58. It is hardly surprising that Lord Crewe, who owns the largest house in the street, has already moved, and that the fate of Crewe House should have become a subject of discussion and rumour.

59. Can it be that those mysterious stirrings of heart, and keen emotions, and strange yearnings after we know not what, and awful impressions from we know not whence, should be wrought in us by what is unsubstantial, and comes and goes, and begins and ends in itself?

60. Built originally by Shepherd, who gave his name to the market opposite, the mansion passed into the possession of Lord Wharncliffe, who, at the time of the Reform Bill, was the leader of that section of the Tory Party, known as "The Waverers."

61. There can be no better illustration indeed, than this, of the utter futility of all those dreams of perfectibility which are founded on a radical ignorance of what it is that constitutes the real enjoyment of human nature, and upon the play of how many principles and opposite stimuli that happiness depends, which, it is absurdly imagined, would be found in the mere negation of suffering, or in a state of Quakerish placidity, dullness, and uniformity.

62. For though *I* had forgotten it, *we* had never forgotten being there together, and we had been talking about Mackery End all our lives, till memory on my part became mocked with a phantom of itself, and I thought I knew the aspect of a place which, when present, O how unlike it was to that which I had conjured up so many times instead of it.

63. It is a strange thing that, in sea voyages, where there is nothing to be seen but sky and sea, men should make diaries; but in land travel, wherein so much is to be observed, for the most part they omit it, as if chance were fitter to be registered than observation.

64. The idea that the public are apathetic at the continued attacks which are being made on historic London is not true.

65. But howsoever these things are thus in men's depraved judgments and affections, yet Truth, which only doth judge itself, teacheth that the inquiry of Truth, which is the love-making or wooing of it, the knowledge of Truth, which is the presence of it, and the belief of Truth, which is the enjoying of it, is the sovereign good of human nature.

66. Men of noble birth are noted to be envious towards new men when they rise, for the distance is altered; and it is like a deceit of the eye that, when others come on, they think themselves go back.

67. Revenge is a kind of wild justice, which the more man's nature runs to, the more ought law to weed it out; for as for the first wrong, it doth but offend the law, but the revenge of that wrong putteth the law out of office.

68. But such was the repulsion of his moral qualities as a writer, and the fundamental unsoundness of most of his speculations, that he no sooner ceased to write, than he ceased to be read or inquired after, and lived to see those erudite volumes fairly laid on the shelf, which he fondly expected to carry down a growing fame to posterity.

69. Only one Power in Europe has deliberately gone to war since 1918, and then only on the calculation which proved accurate, that it would encounter no serious resistance.

70. In truth, the Scottish peasantry are still infected with that rage for funeral ceremonial, which once distinguished the grandees of the kingdom so much, that a sumptuary law was made by the Parliament of Scotland for the purpose of restraining it; and I have known many in the lowest stations who have denied themselves, not merely the comforts, but almost the necessaries of life, in order to save such a sum as might enable their surviving friends to bury them like Christians, as they termed it.

## CHAPTER II

## SYNTHESIS

*Synthesis* is the opposite process from *Analysis*, being the combination of several short sentences into one longer sentence which is generally, but not necessarily, complex. The new sentence must observe the rules of *unity*, *variety* and *order*, and may be formed in one of the following ways :—

1. By the use of a suitable *co-ordinate conjunction.*

(*a*) {The lion is called the king of beasts.
The tiger is a braver animal.

The lion is called the king of beasts but the tiger is a braver animal.

(*b*) {The child desired to please his teacher.
He was always early at school.

The child desired to please his teacher and was always early at school.

2. By the selection of one sentence as the *principal clause* and the conversion of the others into words or phrases qualifying, or in apposition to the *Subject* or *Object*, or modifying the *Predicate.*

(*a*) {The boy looked over the parapet at the stream.
The stream was swollen and muddy.

The boy looked over the parapet at the swollen and muddy stream.

(*b*) {The rider mastered the fiery horse.
He was skilled and fearless.

The skilled and fearless rider mastered the fiery horse.

(*c*) {Parliament refused to grant the king a subsidy.
It was now a body of men in sullen opposition.

Parliament, now a body of men in sullen opposition, refused to grant the king a subsidy.

(*d*) {He advanced into the arena.
He was bold in his manner of advance.

He advanced in a bold manner into the arena.

3. By the selection of one or more sentences as *principal clauses* and connecting the remaining sentences into *parallel* or *subordinate clauses*.

(a) The event was celebrated by great festivities.
All the most important persons in the city were invited to Government House.
His opponents were amazed at his rapid return to power.

But the event was celebrated by great festivities; and all the most important persons in the city were invited to Government House; and his opponents were amazed at his rapid return to power.

*Note*.—Use of semi-colon in this type of sentence.

(b) The stranger opened the door.
He listened intently on the threshold.
He found no cause for suspicion.
He eagerly searched every corner of the room.
He came at last to the curtained alcove.

When the stranger opened the door, he listened intently on the threshold, but as he found no cause for suspicion, he eagerly searched every corner of the room until he came at last to the curtained alcove.

4. By the selection of one or more sentences as *principal clauses* and converting the others into *participial constructions* placed at the *beginning*, or in the *body*, or at the *end* of the new sentence.

(a) He arrived at a gloomy-looking house.
He peered at the nameplate.
He saw it was the house he wanted.
He knocked noisily at the door.

Having arrived at a gloomy-looking house and peered at the nameplate, he knocked noisily at the door, having seen it was the house he wanted.

(b) The stranger threw his battered hat into the ring.
He climbed leisurely over the ropes after it.
He coolly endured the scornful stare of the champion.

Throwing his battered hat into the ring, the stranger climbed leisurely over the ropes after it, coolly enduring the scornful stare of the champion.

5. By a combination of *two* or *more* of the *above* methods.

(*a*) He looked at us angrily.
He looked as if we had taken advantage of him.
We had drawn a confession from him.
He went on quickly with his story.

Looking at us angrily, as if we had taken advantage in drawing a confession from him, he went on quickly with his story.

## EXERCISE I

*Rewrite* the following, *combining* each of the groups of sentences into a *single* sentence :—

*Note.*—Groups I-X contain hints for the necessary changes with the verb of the principal clause in italics.

1. You nodded to him (*participle*). He *failed* to see you. He wishes to apologise to you (*Adverbial Clause*).

2. A very great silence reigned (*Adv. Cl.*). The notes of the organ *were heard*. They rose through the grey aisles (*phrase*).

3. I often re-read his books (*Adv. Cl.*). I *became* conscious of many things. I had not originally perceived them (*Phrase*). I might have added much to my enjoyment and understanding (*Adj. Cl.*).

4. There was no distinguishable tune (*Phrase*). It was simply an enormous noise (*Phrase*). It *stunned* the listener. It was like an explosion (*Phrase*). He heard it while entering the room (*Phrase*).

5. He and his flock *are* just *issuing* from the church. It stands at the base of the hill (*Phrase*). It is wooded to the top (*Adj. Cl.*). The surrounding country is fertile and cultivated land (*Adv. Cl.*).

6. A wind *had got up*. A tiny clicking rustle could be heard (*Phrase*). One of last year's oak leaves was dragging itself on the stone terrace in the twilight (*Phrase*). It had somehow survived the gardener's broom (*Adj. Cl.*).

7. A certain number of men *are set* apart. The method of government has been decided (*Adv. Cl.*). The poor of them are given a sum of money (*Adj. Cl.*). The wealthier are given certain titles (*Phrase*). There is a condition (*Phrase*). They must vote as they are commanded (*Adj. Cl.*).

8. They continued to live at the cottage (*Adv. Cl.*). It was bare and ruinous (*Phrase*). They feared that a purchaser *might be found.* They expected this to happen soon (*Word*). For many years they *heard* of nothing to disturb their peace.

9. His landlady *dragged* him to his room. She summoned a neighbour to her aid (*Phrase*). The charwoman never stayed after noon (*Adv. Cl.*). She *sent for* the parish doctor. He made a brief examination of the patient (*Phrase*). He declared him to be in some danger (*Adj. Cl.*).

10. Here *comes* in the lack of London. London has no high places (*Adv. Cl.*). The Londoner can never have the exaltation of the mountains (*Adv. Cl.*). This joy has no equal (*Phrase*).

11. The members looked at the young orator. They regarded him with interest. He rose opposite them. He was a politician of an unusual type. His appearance and dress were strange in that place. They were anxious to give him a fair hearing.

12. He was distressed at this treatment. He was not discouraged by it. He had to struggle for many months against their hostility. He was at last to find assistance. It consisted of advice and an offer of money. It came from an unexpected quarter.

13. He settled for a time in Edinburgh. Edinburgh was still a centre of national life. It was a centre of national culture. The life of the city was dominated by men of learning. They had a European reputation.

14. We arrived late at the theatre. Our car had broken down. It was a performance of a popular play. We missed the first scene. It was difficult to understand the plot. The stares of some of the audience added to our misery.

15. I am not a highly paid worker. I am not particularly diligent. I am convinced of my ability to pay an extra pound of Income Tax. I spend much time in solving questions. They are asked by the Income Tax commissioners. This time could be spent more profitably.

16. He possessed an independent mind. He refused to conceal his opinions. He had gained a high reputation as the defender of his co-religionists. His writings earned for him a share in the general persecution. His published works were ordered to be publicly burned.

17. I had a high opinion of my own agility. Our path led up a precipitous cliff. It was a formidable and breath-taking climb. The path had been partly hewn by human hands. It

had been partly worn away by the winter storms. The guide out-distanced me without effort. I was very crestfallen at the end of the climb.

18. The Captain did not fail to meet me there. He met me at the appointed hour. He bade Sir Roger fear nothing. He had put on a sword. It was the sword he had made use of at the Battle of Steinkirk. Sir Roger listened attentively to these remarks. He was no longer concerned with the dangers of our journey.

19. I can see him by the pond. He was standing there of a summer evening. He was watching the great flocks of starlings. They visited those fields. He stood with his head a little to one side. He listened rapturously to a skylark. His every movement and rapt attention revealed his deep love of nature.

20. He took off his overcoat. He carried it on his arm. He went back to the gate. He passed through into a field of grass. Far below him was the sea. The air beat in from the sea. It was fresh, strong and salt. Its freshness went to his head. He felt a sense of exhilaration. It recalled the intense delights of youth.

## EXERCISE II

Construct sentences on the following models :—

1. *Princ. Cl.—Noun Cl.—Adv. Cl.* (*Place*).
2. *Adv. Cl.* (*Time*)—*Princ. Cl.—Adj. Cl.—Noun Cl.*
3. *Prin. Cl.—Prin. Cl.—Adv. Cl.* (*Consequence*)—*Adj. Cl.*
4. *Prin. Cl.—Adj. Cl.—Adv. Cl.* (*Reason*)—*Noun Cl.*
5. *Prin. Cl.—Adv. Cl.* (*Purpose*)—*Prin. Cl.*
6. *Prin. Cl.—Adv. Cl.* (*Concession*)—*Adv. Cl.* (*Manner*)—*Noun Cl.*
7. *Prin. Cl.—Prin. Cl.—Prin. Cl.—Prin. Cl.—Adv. Cl.* (*Manner*).
8. *Prin. Cl.—Adv. Cl.* (*Condition*)—*Adv. Cl.* (*Condition*)—*Adj. Cl.—Adj. Cl.*
9. *Adj. Cl.—Prin. Cl.—Noun Cl.—Adv. Cl.* (*Reason*).
10. *Noun Cl.—Prin. Cl.—Adj. Cl.—Adj. Cl.*

# CHAPTER III

## GRAMMAR (PARSING)

This chapter takes for granted that "straight" analysis (particular and general) and parsing have been mastered. It concerns more difficult parsing only and may be used by advanced pupils for revision.

### THE NOUN

The case of a noun or pronoun indicates its relation to some other word or words in the sentence.

**The nominative case is used :—**

(*a*) When the noun is the subject to a finite verb.

(i) The *bird* of dawning singeth all night long.

(ii) Long live the *king*.

(iii) Is not *this* something more than *fantasy* ?

(*b*) When the noun is in apposition to the subject. (Nominative in Apposition.)

(i) The Queen, your *mother*, would speak with you.

(ii) The guest of summer,
The temple-haunting *martlet*, does approve . . .

(*c*) When the noun represents the person or thing addressed—Nominative of Address (sometimes called the Vocative—always used in the second person).

(i) Get thee to bed, *Francisco*.

(ii) My *Lord*, I came to see your father's funeral.

(*d*) When the noun is used in an absolute construction, *i.e.* a construction grammatically independent of any other part of the sentence. The noun is here used with some tense of the participle. It corresponds to the Ablative Absolute in Latin.

(i) The *sun* having set, we decided to go home.

(ii) Yet now, I must confess, that *duty* done,
My thoughts and wishes bend again toward France.

(iii) But you must fear,
His *greatness* weighed, his will is not his own.

Exceptionally, the noun is used with an infinitive, suggesting futurity.

(iv) The examinations are held to-day, the *results* to be announced next week.

Care must be taken to avoid the unrelated and misrelated participle.

(i) *Bearing* in mind the social conditions, it is easy to understand the discontent which led to the Peasants' Revolt.

(ii) *Sailing* up the Thames, Richmond is soon reached.

(*e*) After a verb of incomplete predication, such as be, become, seem.

(i) I am a rich *man*.
(ii) I am reputed a rich *man*.
(iii) I became a rich *man*.
(iv) I seem a rich *man*.

**The Objective Case is used—**

(*a*) When the noun (or pronoun) is the object to a verb, finite or infinite.

(i) There's no art
To find the mind's *construction* in the face:
He was a gentleman on whom I built
An absolute *trust*.

(*b*) When the noun is governed by a preposition: Beware of entrance to a *quarrel*.

(*c*) When the noun is in apposition to the object after a verb or preposition (Objective in apposition).

(i) And wicked murder
Alarmed by his sentinel, the *wolf*.

(ii) Lay a fault on us, your *tribunes*.

(*d*) When the noun is in the indirect object. (The Dative in Latin.)

(i) Give every *man* thy ear.

(ii) My father! *me*thinks I see my father.

(iii) Woe worth the *day*!

The Ethic Dative, or objective of interest, has an emphatic meaning.

(iv) He plucked *me* ope his doublet.

(v) The cloudy messenger turns *me* his back

(vi) Heat *me* those irons hot.

(*e*) When a noun is used after passive verbs of asking, promising or giving. (Retained object.)

(Active): The general promised the soldier the Victoria Cross.

(Passive): The soldier was promised the *Victoria Cross* by the General.

(*f*) When a noun is used as a second object after verbs of "making" (hence the factitive object).

They made (appointed, elected, acclaimed) him *king*.

(*g*) When a noun is used to denote time, value, weight, distance.

(i) I saw him two *nights* ago (Adverbial Object).

(ii) The article cost five *pounds*.

(iii) The goods weighed a *ton*.

(iv) We walked four *miles*.

(*h*) When a noun repeats the meaning of its predicate, it is called a cognate object.

(i) Fight the good *fight*.
(ii) Run a *race*.

**The Possessive Case** is used to denote possession. (The Genitive Case in Latin.) It is used normally only of persons and animals. An apostrophe (') and an "s" are added to singular nouns, an apostrophe only to plural nouns.

(i) *Shakespeare's* plays.
(ii) *Burns's*, *Keats's* and *Yeats's* poems.
(iii) A *lady's* purse; the *ladies'* purse.
(iv) A *man's* game; but the *men's* game.
(v) *Goodness'* sake; *Jesus'* sake; *Moses'* law.
(vi) *Car* park, *gramophone* needle, *window* ledge (being neuter) take no apostrophe.
(vii) Plays of Shakespeare; the ledge of the window.
(viii) Note the difference between—
John's, William's and Henry's estate (sometimes estates),
and John, William and Henry's estate.
(ix) Robert the *Bruce's* crown.
(x) Classical names ending in "s," usually add an apostrophe, but not an "s"—
*Venus'* statue, *Sophocles'* plays.

**Revision Parsing of the Noun.**

**EXERCISE I**

**Classify the following Nouns, that is, tell what kind of Noun each of the following is :—**

Idleness, committee, minute, covey, falsehood, Table Bay, Natal, merchant, shoal, linen, dancing, glory, Cape Colony, depth, Archibald, poet, fleet, rain, summer, mirth, trees, heath, sin, night, anger, Agnes, The Doon, repentance, pleasure, pupil, choice, Bute, slate, colour, map, finger, loaf, weakness, navy, coming, growth, sleep, labour, century, grass, apples, peasantry, coal, solitude, teacher, blackboard, sky, host, bathing, service, taste, crew, Arran, forgiveness, hunting, violence, hedge, fire, grief, watch, pity, table, school-board, Cromwell, Tundra, carpet, escape, dandelion, ostrich, island, skating, iron, diamond, mob, month, popularity, fishing, eagerness, ardour, garden, cape, library, map, contradiction, cavalry, scout, Wellington, vineyard, crowd, clergy, occupation, father, abundance, photograph, poverty, door, Edward, hunger, hardihood, fish, infantry, cruelty, The Tyne, sense, death, winter, grave, fever, Duncan, discontent, parliament, impertinence, cowardice. A Hercules, march, oxygen, A Solomon, majesty.

## EXERCISE II

**Tell the Gender of the following Nouns :—**

Nephew, hero, coachman, history, egg, daughter, infant, Milton, teacher, ewe, class, scholar, tiger, author, niece, lesson, queen, prince, door, river, colt, student, nun, parcel, goose, witch, wall, goat, footman, bear, friend, duke, bride, James, governor, hare, sparrow, widow, parent, companion, lass, belle, songster, spinster, servant, calf, assistant, actress, hind, pen, camp, railway, guard, driver, car, spectator, Dublin, hand, ox, son, baby, neighbour, peeress, surgeon, shepherd, doe, slut, day, autumn, host, hill, Helen, word, deer, fish, elephant, cat, tyrant, giant, gander, turnip, peacock, tune, traveller, lover, pet, stone, mummy, madam, sweetheart, elector, councillor, doctor, marbles, mouse, pencil, lake, executrix, uncle, master, stag, fire, desk, reindeer, ladybird, punster, doe, drone.

## EXERCISE III

1. **Tell the Number of the following Nouns :—**

Peter, chimneys, pains, pence, gallows, eaves, music, scissors, cherries, class, crowd, feet, dice, series, banditti, phenomena, beaux, mice, sheep, fish, wolf, nails, committee, parliament, cargo, tops, marbles, pease, wives, hair, Liverpool, mass, tea, swine, halves, mile, brethren, seraphim, cities, bunch, goose, leech, summons, tidings, small-pox, amends, ashes, roofs, army, crisis, grouse, kine, gross, data, means, measles, stocks, tongs, analyses, ellipses, radii, species, crocus, coals, folk, Cheviots, logic, mathematics, cannon, area, hail, ciceroni.

2. **Write the Plural of the following Nouns :—**

Sky, fox, die, ruby, boy, lady, valley, staff, thief, deer, cow, penny, seraph, beau, ox, cargo, canto, half, pan, sheaf, lass, ally, potato, scarf, class, tooth, Miss Jones, candle, shelf, bunch, sugar, series, grouse, child, dozen, ass, ray, hero, dwarf, reef, Hindoo, piano, man-servant, forget-me-not, cuckoo, bush, grief, topas, arch, jug, spoon, mother-in-law, foe, joy, watch, gas, trout, fly, mouse, house, echo, pea, basis, money, crocus, hiatus, index, cloth, coal, pair, crew, quality, cannon, sail, crisis, horse-soldier, knight-templar, knight-errant, alkali, man-of-war, spoonful, attorney-general, bamboo, calico, maid-servant.

## EXERCISE IV

1. Write the Possessive Singular of :—

Lady, goodness, boy, fly, ass, widow, man, friend, conscience, Socrates, son, wife, Jesus, teacher, father, child, grocer, enemy, scholar, gentleman, nurse, soldier, frog, bee, girl, duty, apostle, farmer, cousin, niece, horse.

2. Write the Possessive Plural of :—

Lady, boy, fly, ass, widow, man, friend, son, wife, teacher, father, child, brother, grocer, enemy, scholar, gentleman, nurse, soldier, frog, bee, girl, duty, apostle, farmer, cousin, niece, horse, prince, princess.

3. Change the Possessives thus formed in (1) and (2) into Objectives after the Preposition "of," inserting suitable Nouns for the things possessed.

4. Write the following in Possessive form :—

The den of the lions. The wings of the flies. The fleece of the sheep. The bodyguard of the Queen. The tears of the widows. The cries of the orphan. The veil of the lady. For the sake of conscience. The wife of Socrates. The love of Jesus. The creed of the Apostles. The books of the scholars. The plough of the farmer. The friend of men. The father of the child. The book of the teacher. The honey of the bee. The works of Burns. The doves of Venus. The reign of Henry the Seventh. The tragedies of Sophocles. The pleasures of Bacchus. The son of Æneas. The premises of Wilson, Wright & Co.

## EXERCISE V

Parse the Nouns in the following sentences :—

1. O Prophet! what dream didst thou dream!
2. To land King Robert lightly sprang.
3. William the Conqueror landed in England in 1066.
4. Rising early is a good habit.

5. You must always speak the truth.
6. The martyr died for conscience' sake.
7. His master promised him his salary.
8. Augustus was called Emperor.
9. Milton! thou should'st be living at this hour!
10. Wisdom is better than riches.
11. I, the King, demand thy sword.
12. Her mother bought Mary a new hat.
13. The master taught the boys Latin.
14. The crew deserted the ship.
15. The people made him a ruler.
16. The soldiers slept the sleep of death.
17. O Death! where is thy sting!
18. The house being destroyed, the children had no shelter.
19. The house having been rebuilt, afforded protection to his family.
20. Every turf beneath our feet
Shall be a soldier's sepulchre.
21. Religion! what treasures untold
Reside in that heavenly word!
22. Sweet are the uses of Adversity.
23. The child Samuel ministered before Eli.
24. Three years ago, John lived in London.
25. The hermit lives a lonely life.
26. Day having dawned, the soldiers struck their tents.
27. They marched seventy miles in two days.
28. Fast before her father's men
Three days we've fled together.
29. Give us each day our daily bread!
30. Ships bring home many cargoes of fruit every year.
31. Give the poor dog a bone.
32. The news of the battle reached London a fortnight ago
33. He took great pains with his work.
34. An epidemic of small-pox caused the death of many people last year.
35. Writing maketh an exact man.
36. Comes the blind Fury with the abhorréd shears
And slits the thin-spun life.
37. Yet you, Pilates, have here delivered me to my sour cross.
38. Not a soldier discharged his farewell shot.
39. He was offered a better appointment.

## THE PRONOUN

The following classes of pronouns may be noted :—

Personal.
Possessive.
Reflexive.
Emphatic.
Relative.
Demonstrative.
Interrogative.
Indefinite.
Numeral.
Distributive.

### Personal Pronoun

(i) It is usual to treat the genitive or possessive forms as if they were either (*a*) possessive pronouns or (*b*) possessive adjectives.

(*a*) Possessive pronouns include mine, thine, his, hers, ours, yours, theirs.

(*b*) Possessive adjectives include my, thy, his, her, its, our, your, their.

(ii) *His* admits of both uses—

His house (possessive adjective).
The house is his (possessive pronoun).

(iii) *Mine* and *thine* were formerly used as adjectives before words beginning with a vowel or "h" mute—*Mine* honest friend.

(iv) *Its* dates from the seventeenth century. It is used once in the "Tempest."

### Reflexive Pronoun

(i) The reflexive pronoun is formed by adding 'self' (singular or plural) to my, thy, him, her, it, our, your, them.

(ii) The reflexive pronoun repeats the subject in the objective case.

(iii) Exceptionally, '*self*' is omitted—He sat him down.

(iv) *Self*, used alone, may be regarded as a noun—Thine own sweet *self*.

### Emphatic Pronoun

(i) The form is that of the reflexive pronoun.

(ii) The emphatic pronoun takes the case of the pronoun it emphasises—

He *himself* said so (nominative).
I saw the man *himself* (objective).

### Relative Pronoun

**(i) It agrees in person, number and gender with its antecedent.**

**(ii) They are—who (whom, whose), which, that, as, but.**

(iii) *As* is used only after such and same: such men *as* these (are).

(iv) *But* is used only after a negative statement:—

There was no one *but* mourned him.

(v) *What* is sometimes called a compound *relative* as it includes both antecedent and pronoun.

(vi) *That* and *which* are not always interchangeable. Compare—

(*a*) The boat *that* Brown built last year is for sale.
Boats, *which* have been known since the dawn of history, are of varied design.

(*b*) The Bible is a book *that* all men read.
The Bible is a book *which* all men should possess.

The adjective clause of the second sentence is non-defining and tells us nothing new; that of **the first defines, in that it ascribes a *quality*.**

## Demonstrative Pronoun

(i) This pronoun points out the person or thing named.

(ii) They are—This, that (these, those), yon, such, same.

(iii) They stand for, and are never accompanied by a noun.

(iv) The 3rd personal pronoun is sometimes used in a demonstrative sense—"They (*i.e.* those) also serve who only stand and wait."

## Interrogative Pronoun

(i) The interrogative pronoun asks a question.

(ii) They are—who ? (whom ? whose ?) which ? what ? whether ? (archaic).

## Indefinite Pronoun

(i) The indefinite pronoun does not point out with precision the person or thing to which it refers.

(ii) They are—one, any, anything, anybody, certain, aught, naught, other, somebody, something, nobody, nothing, no one, else.

(iii) Indefinite numeral pronouns are—all, few, little less, enough, many, much, more, most, several, whole.

(iv) Indefinite quatitative pronouns are—little, much, less ; whole and all (according to context).

## Numeral Pronoun

(Some designate this a numeral adjective)

The number may be cardinal—one, two, three or ordinal—first, second, third.

*Four* set off but a *fifth* overtook them.

## Distributive Pronoun

(i) A distributive pronoun stands for a noun which denotes all the individuals of a class viewed separately—*Each* loves the other.

(ii) They are—each, each one, everyone, either, neither.

(iii) Each other (used only of two) and one another (used of more than two) may be called Reciprocal Pronouns, and may be parsed together.

(iv) Distributive pronouns are followed by singular verbs.

### EXERCISE VI

**Parse the Pronouns in the following sentences :—**

1. That book is mine.
2. We thought of this.
3. The king commanded the army himself.
4. Are you talking ?
5. Such as are careless of themselves can hardly be mindful of others.
6. Who steals my purse, steals trash.
7. Few, few shall part where many meet.
8. Oh ! tell me I yet have a friend !
9. The beasts that roam over the plain my form with indifference see.
10. Thine is the glory.
11. This was the noblest Roman of them all.
12. Each had his appointed place.
13. Who do men say that I am ?
14. What else have you received ?
15. This is the same as that.
16. I laid me down and slept.
17. I shall sing you a song.
18. Which do you prefer ?
19. I have nothing else.
20. Do you remember what he told you ?
21. Neither was right.
22. Such was the aspect which the country presented.
23. He gives twice who gives quickly.
24. That boy does whatever he is told.
25. The girls to whom I gave the present are ill.

26. Tell me who thou art.
27. Nothing else will do.
28. They hurt themselves at football.
29. Such is the man whose conduct you have defended.
30. There is no vice so simple but assumes some mark of virtue in its outward parts.
31. He was asked if he had had enough.
32. A little of this goes a long way.
33. Several of those who were present refused to give him any more.
34. He spoke little though he thought much.
35. Give me a few of those grapes.
36. Whose is the crime the scandal too be theirs.

## THE ADJECTIVE

Some of the above pronoun (or pronominal) forms may be used in an adjectival sense. These are the possessive, demonstrative, interrogative, indefinite (including definite numeral) and distributive.

**Possessive Adjective**—see under Possessive Pronouns.

**Demonstrative Adjective**—see Demonstrative Pronoun.

(i) *a*, (*an*), *the*, sometimes called the indefinite and definite articles, may be called demonstrative adjectives. *a* (= one) may be a numeral adjective.

(ii) Ordinal numbers may be called demonstrative adjectives.

(iii) Yonder (in its poetical use) is demonstrative—*Yonder* nodding elms.

**Interrogative Adjective**

Which ? and what ? are adjectival. Who ? is always a pronoun. Which and what are not interchangeable, *i.e.*

*What* noise is that ? refers to any noise.
*Which* noise is that ? refers to one of a limited number.

**Numeral Adjective**

(i) Definite : Cardinal numbers used as adjectives. Ordinal numbers when not used as demonstratives.

(*a*) The *first* boy is right and the *second* boy is wrong (demonstrative).

(*b*) The boy got the *second* prize (ordinal).

(ii) Indefinite numeral—All, few, many, several, certain.

(iii) Indefinite quantitative—little, much, less.

**Distributive Adjective**

They are—each, every, either, neither.

**Adjectives of Quality or Description**

(i) Describe, limit or qualify a noun or pronoun.

(ii) By the addition of certain noun suffixes, all such adjectives may be expanded into abstract nouns. Note carefully the exceptions.

(iii) Adjectives derived from proper nouns are sometimes called *proper* :—China—*Chinese* ; Christ—*Christian* ; James—*Jacobite* or *Jacobean*.

(iv) Adjectives derived from names of material are sometimes called *adjectives of material*—*copper* wire, *linen* handkerchief, *paper* hat.

(v) Adjectives denoting shape, direction, nationality, and adjectives of material may not be compared.

(vi) *Far* and *farther* are used only of stationary objects and suggest distance.

*Further* and *furthest* suggest time, motion and sometimes precedence.

**Irregular Comparison of Adjectives**

Some Adjectives form the Comparative and Superlative irregularly :—

| *Positive.* | *Comparative.* | *Superlative.* |
|---|---|---|
| Good | better | best. |
| Bad, evil, ill | worse | worst. |
| Little | less, lesser | least. |
| Far | farther | farthest. |
| (Forth) | further | furthest. |
| Much, many | more | most. |
| Late | later, latter | latest, last. |
| Old | older, elder | oldest, eldest. |
| Fore | former | foremost, first. |
| Hind | hinder | hindmost. |
| Nigh, near | nigher, nearer | nighest, next. |
| (Up) | upper | uppermost, upmost. |
| (In) | inner | innermost, inmost. |
| (Out) | outer, utter | outermost, uttermost. outmost, utmost. |
| Top | .. | topmost. |
| Very | .. | veriest. |
| Head | .. | headmost. |
| South | .. | southmost. |

### EXERCISE VII

**Compare (when possible) the following Adjectives :—**

Sad, yon, far, good, wise, useful, heavy, left, dead, thin, free, chief, wooden, green, African, old, gay, coy, superior, green, mad, many, brave, shy, dry, wonderful, easy, red, woollen, triangular, principal, ill, manly, monthly, annual, flighty, round, crude, late, tender, chief, sly.

## VERB

The commoner forms of the verb, finite and infinite, are parsed below.

**Finite verb**

(*a*) He *came* to see me.

came : verb, 3rd person, singular number, strong, active, intransitive, indicative mood, past tense, agreeing with subject " he."

(*b*) She *may have been invited* to come.
may have been invited : verb, 3rd person, singular number, weak, passive, transitive, subjunctive, perfect, agreeing with subject "she."

(*c*) *Be advised* by me.
be advised : verb, 2nd person, singular or plural number, weak, passive, transitive, imperative or subjunctive present, agreeing with subject "you" (understood).

**Infinite verb**

(*a*) I want *to see* you.
(*b*) I came *to see* you.
(*c*) I must *see* you.

to see : verb, strong, active, transitive, infinitive mood, present tense.

(*a*) used as a noun, object to "want."
(*b*) used as an adverb of purpose, modifying "came."
(*c*) used as a complement to "must."

**The Participle** (verb with adjective function)

(*a*) *Having crossed* the stream, we rested.
(*b*) The stream *having been crossed*, we rested.
(*c*) We have *crossed* the stream.

(*a*) having crossed : verb, weak, active, transitive, participle, perfect, describing or qualifying "we."
(*b*) having been crossed : verb, weak, passive, transitive, participle, perfect, describing "stream."
(*c*) crossed : verb, weak, active, transitive, participle, past, qualifying "we."

Exceptionally, the participle is used adverbially : *dripping* wet, *boiling* hot.

**The Gerund** (verb with noun function)

(*a*) He likes *being complimented.*

(*b*) *Writing* is his hobby.

(*c*) He collects *walking*-sticks.

(*d*) The *hearing* of the case was adjourned.

(*e*) He remembered *having given* the man a letter.

(*a*) being complimented: verb, weak, passive, transitive, gerund, present tense, object to "likes."

(*b*) Writing: verb, strong, active, intransitive, gerund, present tense, nominative (or subject) to "is."

(*c*) walking: verb, weak, active, intransitive, gerund, present, object to "for" (sticks for walking).

(*d*) hearing: noun, common, singular, neuter, subject to "was" (*hearing* is sometimes called a verbal noun).

(*e*) having given: verb, strong, active, transitive, gerund, perfect, object to "remembered."

**Strong and Weak Verbs**

(i) Verbs of the strong conjugation form their past tense or past participle by a change of the internal vowel. These are Old-English verbs.

(ii) Verbs of the weak conjugation form their past tense or past participle by adding "d," "ed," or "t" to the present form.

(iii) Verbs which have the same form for all three parts are usually weak, *e.g.*

**burst, cast, cost, cut, hit, hurt, let, put, set, shed, shut, spread, thrust.**

## Some Weak Verbs

*LIST OF WEAK VERBS.*

| *Present.* | *Past.* | *Past Part.* | *Present.* | *Past.* | *Past Part* |
|---|---|---|---|---|---|
| Bend | bent | bent. | Lead | led | led. |
| Bereave | bereaved, bereft | bereaved, bereft. | Leap | leaped, leapt | leaped, leapt. |
| Beseech | besought | besought. | Leave | left | left. |
| Bleed | bled | bled. | Lend | lent | lent. |
| Breed | bred | bred. | Light | lighted, lit | lighted, lit. |
| Bring | brought | brought. | Lose | lost | lost. |
| Build | built | built. | Make | made | made. |
| Buy | bought | bought. | Mean | meant | meant. |
| Catch | caught | caught. | Meet | met | met. |
| Clothe | clad, clothed | clad, clothed. | Pay | paid | paid. |
| Creep | crept | crept. | Read | read | read. |
| Deal | dealt | dealt. | Rend | rent | rent. |
| Dream | dreamt, dreamed | dreamt, dreamed. | Say | said | said. |
| Dwell | dwelt | dwelt. | Seek | sought | sought. |
| Feed | fed | fed. | Sell | sold | sold. |
| Feel | felt | felt. | Send | sent | sent. |
| Flee | fled | fled. | Shoe | shod | shod. |
| Gild | gilded, gilt | gilded, gilt. | Sleep | slept | slept. |
| Gird | girded, girt | girded, girt. | Speed | sped | sped. |
| Have | had | had. | Spend | spent | spent. |
| Hear | heard | heard. | Sweep | swept | swept. |
| Hew | hewed | hewed, hewn. | Swell | swelled | swollen. swelled. |
| Keep | kept | kept. | Teach | taught | taught. |
| Kneel | knelt | knelt. | Tell | told | told. |
| Knit | knitted, knit | knitted, knit. | Think | thought | thought. |
| Lay | laid | laid. | Weep | wept | wept. |
| | | | Wet | wet, wetted | wet, wetted. |
| | | | Work | wrought, worked | wrought, worked. |

All new Verbs admitted to the language adopt the Weak form.

## Some Strong Verbs

| *Present.* | *Past.* | *Past Part.* | *Present.* | *Past.* | *Past Part.* |
|---|---|---|---|---|---|
| Abide | abode | abode. | Bear | bare, bore | born, borne (carried). |
| Arise | arose | arisen. | Begin | began | begun. |
| Awake | awoke | awoke. | | | |

| *Present.* | *Past.* | *Past Part.* |
|---|---|---|
| Behold | beheld | beheld. |
| Bid | bade, bid | bidden, bid. |
| Bind | bound | bound. |
| Bite | bit | bitten, bit. |
| Blow | blew | blown. |
| Break | broke | broken. |
| Chide | chid | chidden, chid. |
| Choose | chose | chosen. |
| Cleave | clove cleft | cloven, cleft (weak). |
| Cling | clung | clung. |
| Come | came | come. |
| Dig | dug | dug. |
| Draw | drew | drawn. |
| Drink | drank | drunk, drunken. |
| Drive | drove | driven. |
| Eat | ate | eaten. |
| Fall | fell | fallen. |
| Fight | fought | fought. |
| Find | found | found. |
| Fling | flung | flung. |
| Fly | flew | flown. |
| Forbear | forbore | forborne. |
| Forbid | forbade | forbidden. |
| Forget | forgot | forgotten. |
| Forsake | forsook | forsaken. |
| Freeze | froze | frozen. |
| Get | got | gotten, got. |
| Give | gave | given. |
| Go | (went) | gone. |
| Grind | ground | ground. |
| Grow | grew | grown. |
| Hang | hung | hanged (weak), hung. |
| Hide | hid | hidden,hid. |
| Hold | held | held. |
| Know | knew | known. |
| Lie | lay | lain. |
| Ride | rode | ridden. |

| *Present.* | *Past.* | *Past Part.* |
|---|---|---|
| Ring | rang | rung. |
| Rise | rose | risen. |
| Run | ran | run. |
| See | saw | seen. |
| Shake | shook | shaken. |
| Shear | shore, sheared | shorn. |
| Shine | shone | shone. |
| Shoot | shot | shot. |
| Shrink | shrank | shrunk. |
| Sing | sang | sung. |
| Sink | sank | sunk. |
| Sit | sat | sat. |
| Slay | slew | slain. |
| Slide | slid | slid. |
| Sling | slung | slung. |
| Slink | slunk | slunk. |
| Smite | smote | smitten. |
| Speak | spoke | spoken. |
| Spin | span,spun | spun. |
| Spit | spat | spat, spit |
| Spring | sprang | sprung. |
| Stand | stood | stood. |
| Steal | stole | stolen. |
| Stick | stuck | stuck. |
| Sting | stung | stung. |
| Stride | strode | stridden. |
| String | strung | strung. |
| Strive | strove | striven. |
| Swear | swore | sworn. |
| Swim | swam | swum. |
| Swing | swung | swung. |
| Take | took | taken. |
| Tear | tore | torn. |
| Thrive | throve | thriven. |
| Throw | threw | thrown. |
| Tread | trod | trodden, trod. |
| Wear | wore | worn. |
| Weave | wove | woven. |
| Win | won | won. |
| Wind | wound | wound. |
| Wring | wrung | wrung. |
| Write | wrote | written. |

**Auxiliary Verbs** are those which **help** *to form the Tense or Voice of another verb* :—as " He *has* come." " Has " helps " come " to form the present perfect tense, and it is therefore called an Auxiliary Verb.

" The window *is* broken by John." " Is " helps " broken " to form the passive voice, and it is therefore called an Auxiliary Verb.

*Notes.*—i. *Shall, will,* and *have* are tense auxiliaries ; *be* is used both as a tense and a voice auxiliary ; *do* is an emphatic, a negative, and an interrogative auxiliary—*e.g.*, " He *does* love," " He *does not* love," " *Does* he love ? "

ii. *May, might, could, would, should,* are Mood Auxiliaries, that is, they help to form the Subjunctive Mood.

ii. Care must be taken to distinguish between these Verbs used as Auxiliaries and the same Verbs used as Principal Verbs. In the sentence, " We *shall* go," *shall* is a Tense Auxiliary, but in " Thou *shalt* not steal," *shalt* is a Principal Verb. In the sentence " He goes to school that he *may* learn," *may* is a Mood Auxiliary ; but in " *May* I go with you ? " *may* is a Principal Verb containing the notion of permission.

**Transitive Verbs** (finite or infinite) govern an object.

(i) As the object in the active becomes the subject in the passive, every passive verb has an implied object in its subject. So it may be said that all passive verbs are transitive.

(ii) Impersonal verbs, *e.g.* It rains, it hails, it thunders are always intransitive.

**Voice** : Active and Passive

(i) Apart from its definition, the passive voice may be recognised by its form which always includes the verb " to be " and a past participle.

(ii) A verb in the passive voice has no object, but those verbs which have two objects in the active have the retained object in the passive.

Active : He promised me a book.

Passive : I was promised a *book* by him.

(iii) " He *is gone* " is not passive because it is equivalent to " he *has gone.*"

(iv) Be, become, seem are called verbs of incomplete predication.

## MOOD

There are four moods—indicative, imperative, subjunctive and infinitive.

In this table the indicative and the subjunctive are compared.

The subjunctive mood usually implies a condition, doubt or wish.

Optative Subjunctive : God *save* the King.

Potential Subjunctive : He *may come* (implying a doubt).

He *may* (*i.e.* is permitted to) come is in the indicative mood.

Conditional : If he *come*, he will be welcomed.

(i) In Modern English the Subjunctive Mood has almost fallen out of use as regards form, the force of the Subjunctive Mood being now expressed by means of the Auxiliary Verbs *should*, *would*, *may*, and *might*.

(ii) Where the Subjunctive Mood occurs, it is generally the Mood of Verbs in Subordinate Clauses. In a sentence, however, containing a Condition, the Verb in the Principal Clause (Apodosis) may be in the Subjunctive Mood, as well as the Verb in the Conditional Clause (Protasis). " If he *were* here, the question *could* be settled." *Were* in the Protasis is Subjunctive, as also *could* in the

Apodosis. Note that *could* is not equal to *was able*, in which case it would be Indicative, but is equal to *would be able.* Principal Clauses, expressing a *wish*, have often the Verb in the Subjunctive Mood (Optative):—as "Thy will *be* done."

The imperative mood implies a command or request.

*Note.*—The Imperative Mood is used only in the Second Person, the subject *thou* or *you* being generally omitted. When we wish to express a *Command*, etc., in connection with the First or Third Person, we use the Second Person of *let* and an infinitive, or we use for the First Person the Subjunctive Mood:—as "*Let* us *pray*." *Let*, 2nd Sing., Imperat.; *pray*, Pres. Infin. "*Turn* we to survey." *Turn*, 1st Plur., Pres. Sub.

The **Infinitive Mood** is that form of the Verb which is used *to express an action that is unlimited by the conditions of* **Person, Number,** *or* **Time**:—as "He was forced *to act*." "They cannot *escape*." "The boy made me *laugh*."

*Notes.*—i. The Infinitive is preceded by *to* unless when it follows *shall, should, will, would, can, could, may, might, must, bid, dare, hear, feel, make, let, need, see*:—as "He will *come*." "She bids me *speak*." "I dare *do* all that may *become* a man."

ii. The Infinitive can be used as the *Subject, Object,* or *Complement* of a Verb; that is, as a Noun, an Adjective, or an Adverb.

iii. The Infinitive preceded by *to* is sometimes called the *Gerundial Infinitive.*

iv. The *Gerundial Infinitive* or *Dative Infinitive*—so called because it was originally the Dative Case of the Simple Infinitive—is used in *three* ways:—

(1) After a Verb to express purpose:—as "I came *to tell* you."

(2) After a Noun to express purpose:—as "A House *to let*."

(3) After an Adjective to express purpose:—as "Easy *to find*."

The Verb "to ask" (1st Person only)

| | Indicative | | Subjunctive | |
|---|---|---|---|---|
| | Active | Passive | Active | Passive |
| Pres. Indefinite | ask | am asked | ask | be asked |
| Continuous | am asking | am being asked | be asking | am being asked |
| Emphatic | I do ask | | | |
| Past Indefinite | asked | was asked | asked | were asked |
| Continuous | was asking | was being asked | were asking | were being asked |
| Fut. Indefinite | shall ask | shall be asked | | |
| Continuous | shall be asking | | | |
| Pres. Perfect | have asked | have been asked | have asked | have been asked |
| Perfect Continuous | have been asking | | have been asking | |

The Verb "to ask" (1st Person only)

| | Indicative | | Subjunctive | |
|---|---|---|---|---|
| | Active | Passive | Active | Passive |
| Past Perfect | had asked | had been asked | had asked | had been asked |
| Past Perfect Continuous | had been asking | | had been asking | |
| Fut. Perfect | shall have asked | shall have been asked | | |
| Fut. Perfect Continuous | shall have been asking | | | |
| Fut. in the Past Indefinite | should ask | should be asked | | |
| Fut. in the Past Continuous | should be asking | | | |
| Fut. in the Past Perfect | should have asked | should have been asked | | |
| Fut. in the Past Continuous | should have been asking | | | |

## TENSE

Tense tells the time of the action, and may be studied on the table of Moods on pages 54-5.

### Sequence of Tenses

*General Rule.*—When one Verb depends upon another, a Present Tense follows a Present Tense ; a Past Tense follows a Past Tense :—as " He *goes* to school that he *may* learn " ; " He *went* to school that he *might* learn." " He *says* that he *will* do this " ; " He *said* that he *would* do this."

*Note.*—The Present Infinitive and *not* the Perfect Infinitive is used when the time of the action of the Infinitive is *contemporary* with or *after* the time of the principal Verb. Thus, " He appears *to be* right," " He appeared *to be* right " ; " He appears *to have been* right," are correct. But " He expected *to have seen*, etc.," is wrong, as the time of the seeing must be *after* the time of the expecting.

### EXERCISE VIII

**Correct or Justify the following Verbs :—**

1. Even if he were to do this, he will not escape punishment.
2. He appears to have been dismissed.
3. No writer would write a book unless he thinks it will be read.
4. You may do what you have done a year ago.
5. The choir practice has now been started for a month.
6. He has gone to the country last week.
7. I expected to have seen your father, but he seems to have gone away early.
8. I would have liked to have invited him to dinner.
9. He said that he will not come, unless you accompany him.
10. Did he not tell me his fault, and entreated me to forgive him. ?
11. I laboured and wearied myself that thou may be at ease.
12. These instances may, it is hoped, be sufficient to satisfy every reasonable mind.
13. Solomon has told us that all is vanity.
14. Two young gentlemen have made the discovery that there was no God.
15. I intended to have cut the grass yesterday.

## THE ADVERB

The adverb, as the name implies, frequently modifies a verb, but it may modify any other word in the sentence except a noun or pronoun.

He walked *slowly*: modifies a verb.

He walked *very* slowly: modifies an adverb.

He walked at a *very* slow pace: modifies an adjective.

He walked *right* over the pass: modifies a preposition.

He walked *even* when he was tired: modifies a conjunction.

The adverb would seem to modify a noun in:—

*Even* Homer nods.

The **simple adverb** may be classified thus—

Adverbs of Time indicate the time of the action—when?

Adverbs of Place indicate the place of the action—where?

Adverbs of Manner indicate the manner of the action—how?

Adverbs of Degree indicate the intensity of the action—to what extent?

Adverbs of Number indicate the frequency of the action—how often?

Adverbs of Affirmation indicate the certainty of the action—how sure?

Adverbs of Negation indicate the denial of the action—how unsure?

Adverbs of Emphasis indicate the importance of a certain noun—how important?

**Examples** of Adverbs classified—

Time—soon, late, now, then, immediately, instantly.

Place—here, there, yonder.

Manner—well, ill, thus, and nearly all adverbs ending in "ly."

Degree—very, too, so, entremely, sufficiently, almost.

Number—seldom, often, frequently, always, again, repeatedly, once, twice.

Affirmation—certainly, undoubtedly, undeniably, surely, probably possibly, yes.

Negation—unlikely, improbably, abnormally, not, no.

Emphasis—even, only, too, also, likewise. (*Even* he, *only* he, he *too*, he *also*.)

**Irregular Comparison of Adverbs—**

| | | |
|---|---|---|
| Far | farther | farthest. |
| Forth | further | furthest. |
| Ill (badly) | worse | worst. |
| Well | better | best. |
| Much | more | most. |
| Late | later | last. |
| Little | less | least. |

## EXERCISE IX

Parse the Adverbs in the following sentences :—

1. Ill fares the land.
2. He acted too cautiously.
3. She looked coldly on the suitors.
4. On they came.
5. The school's lone porch, with reverend mosses grey, just tells the pensive pilgrim where it lay.
6. Oft may the spirits of the dead descend.
7. They blessed the scene they loved in life so well.
8. Let us, while the wind faintly wails, count the echoings of our feet.
9. He will come immediately.
10. Bright shone the lamps o'er fair women and brave men.
11. The cry is, "Still they come."
12. The paths of glory lead but to the grave.
13. What thou would'st highly, that would'st thou holily.
14. How sweet the tuneful bells' responsive peal !
15. Always try to speak plainly.
16. We look before and after.
17. He is somewhat better.
18. A man he was to all the country dear, and passing rich on forty pounds a year.
19. Sweet smells the rose.
20. I shall meet you when the roses come again.

21. There where a few torn shrubs the place disclose, the village preacher's modest mansion rose.
22. 'Tis but a little faded flower.
23. She will not come, charm he never so wisely.
24. I cannot tell why he has not come
25. Here woman reigns supreme.
26. Yonder comes the powerful king of day.
27. So pale grows reason at religion's sight.
28. Ye masters then do not cruelly demand what the all involving winds have swept away.
29. Then prompt no more the follies you decry, as tyrants doom their tools of guilt to die.
30. Yet once more, ye laurels, I come to pluck your berries.
31. It may indeed be phantasy when I essay to draw from nature deep heart-felt joy.
32. There were a great many spectators.

(i) An adverb is often used as (*a*) an adjective, or (*b*) a noun.

(*a*) The *up* train, the *then* king.

(*b*) *Now's* the time—See also Leigh Hunt's essay on "A Now."

(ii) Distinguish between "he fell *off*" and "he fell *off* the train."

(iii) Here: in this place. Hither: to this place.
Hence: from this place.

There: in that place. Thither: to that place.
Thence: from that place.

Where: in what place? Whither: to what place?
Whence: from what place?

(iv) Distinguish—

"This train only stops at Dundee," and
"This train stops at Dundee only."

(v) Many adverbial phrases exist in English, *e.g.* once upon a time, by and by, by the way, of course, by all means, backwards and forwards.

**A Conjunctive Adverb** joins two clauses. The commonest of these are—where, when, how, why and if, *e.g.*—

Tell me *where* you have been.
Tell me *how* you did it.

Do not confuse these with relative pronouns introducing an adjective clause—

This is the place *where* you saw him.
This is the time *when* you saw him.

**An Interrogative Adverb** introduces a question. The commonest of these are, where ? when ? how ? why ? whither ? whence ?

## THE PREPOSITION

The preposition, as the name implies, is placed before a noun or pronoun. It has a conjunctive function in that it shows the relationship between nouns and pronouns (or equivalents) in the same sentence.

(i) The following prepositions show the relationship between " book " and " table."

The book is *on* (*under*, *beside*, *at*, *by*, *behind*, *near*, *above*, etc.) the table.

(ii) The preposition governs the following noun in the objective (or accusative).

(iii) The preposition is often the same in form as the adverb from which it must be distinguished.

There lay nothing *beyond* this (preposition).
There lay nothing *beyond* (adverb).

(iv) Some words, originally participles, now function as prepositions—

*concerning* these matters, *according* to his principles, *past* mid-day.

(v) "*Between*" refers to two persons or things.
"*Among*" refers to more than two.

(vi) Note the forms—

an apple *a* day, *a*'wooing, twelve *o*'clock.

(vii) Sometimes the objective relative pronoun is omitted—

The man you are interested in, has come.

## EXERCISE IX

**Point out the Adverbs, Prepositions, and Conjunctions in the following sentences :—**

1. I waited two hours after he left.
2. None but the brave deserves the fair.
3. Though he slay me, yet will I love him.
4. I have eaten nothing since breakfast.
5. Since that is the case, I shall have nothing to do with the matter.
6. He will come before daybreak.
7. The boy stood on the burning deck, whence all but he had fled.
8. He came down quickly.
9. The boys ran down the street.
10. He fell from the tree.
11. Grant but three to make a new Thermopylæ.
12. There was none there but would have served him.
13. He died for conscience' sake.
14. He was severely punished, for he had been guilty of many crimes.
15. He told me that he did not say that.
16. Notwithstanding his able defence, he was found guilty.
17. As the twig is bent, so is the tree inclined.
18. Since when have you stopped writing to him ?
19. He would have done this for me, but I refused his help.
20. He said nothing finer than that.
21. If he were here, he could speak for himself.
22. It matters little whether he comes or not.
23. Whether of the twain did the will of his father ?
24. Except that his knee was slightly grazed, he was but little the worse.
25. The sooner he finishes the work, the sooner he will be free
26. During the night, there was an exceedingly severe storm.

27. The that that I had spoken of was not the that that that man declared that he had meant.

28. Which when Beelzebub perceived—than whom, Satan except, none higher sat—with grave aspect he rose.

29. Good writing is always to be praised.

30. He told me that that had happened before he came.

31. Obey, or else go.

32. We were wet through.

## THE CONJUNCTION

A conjunction joins words, phrases or sentences together.

*Notes.*—

(i) Co-ordinating conjunctions (and, both, but, either and or, neither and nor) join clauses of equal value. They also join similar parts of speech.

(ii) Subordinating conjunctions (that, after, before, now, since, till, while, became, as, for, lest, if, but, except, unless, whether, without, although though, than) join a principal to a subordinate clause.

(iii) Correlative conjunctions are co-ordinating. They are either—or, neither—nor, not only—but also.

(iv) Conjunctive adverbs are—

where, when, how, why, if, although, however; but these must not be confused with relative pronouns.

(*a*) He asked me *where* (*when*, *why*, *how*) I was going (conjunctive adverb).

(*b*) He asked me the hour *when* the eclipse was due (relative pronoun).

So also "*place where*" and "*reason why*."

## THE INTERJECTION

The interjection is used to express sudden emotion, such as surprise, fear, pain, joy, *e.g.* oh! indeed! hurrah! hail!
rules.

For example of errors in the use of parts of speech, refer to Chapter on "Errors in Composition."

---

# CHAPTER IV

## PUNCTUATION

Punctuation, like spelling, achieved some common acceptance from the invention of the printing press. It is a device to synchronise the written with the spoken word. It is not, however, indispensable, as intelligible prose can be written with no punctuation other than the full stop. Legal documents and some modern poetry, to avoid ambiguity, use punctuation as sparingly as possible. It is usually inserted (*a*) where the human voice would pause to separate one thought from another, and (*b*) under certain other conditions detailed below. Eventually, punctuation must be a matter of taste, and Dickens, Carlyle, Browning and Shaw make many departures from use and wont. A careful consideration of a single printed page will teach the student more than he can learn from any other source.

**The Period** or full stop ( . ) is used to mark the end of completed thought (*i.e.* of a sentence). When the sentence assumes the form of a question, it is followed by a question mark ( ? ), but only when the question registers the actual words of the speaker.

**The Comma** ( , ) indicates a shorter pause than the period. It is commonly used in the following cases :—

(i) To separate the individuals of a class—

(*a*) Assyria, Greece, Rome, Carthage—where are they ?

(*b*) O'er bog or steep, through strait, rough, dense, or rare,
With head, hands, wings, or feet, pursues his way,
And swims, or sinks, or wades, or creeps, or flies.

(ii) Before and after a parenthetical word, phrase or clause—

(*a*) Turn, fortune, turn thy wheel and lower the proud (nominative of address).

(*b*) When, with some encouragement, I first visited your Lordship . . .

(*c*) The notice you have been pleased to take of my labour, had it been earlier, had been kind.

(*d*) At length, Erasmus, that great injured name,
The glory of the priesthood and the shame !

(iii) After an adverbial clause when it precedes the clause it modifies—

(*a*) But when to mischief mortals bend their will,
How soon they find fit instruments of ill !

(*b*) Had not the girths of the saddle burst, he might not have been unhorsed.

(iv) After a participle, or any absolute construction—

(*a*) Just at that instant, anxious Ariel sought
The close recesses of the virgin's thought.

(*b*) But, being ill-used by the above-mentioned widow, he was very serious for a year and a half.

(v) After a verb predicating direct speech—

"Pray, Sir," said Arthur, "what is that place?"
The old man answered, "Sir, the debtor's prison."

**The Colon** ( : ) divides two sentences where the latter illustrates or elaborates the former. Convention omits the capital letter after the colon.

(*a*) God is not mocked: for whatsoever a man soweth, that shall he also reap.

(*b*) Heard melodies are sweet, but those unheard
Are sweeter: therefore ye soft pipes, play on.

(*c*) And on the pedestal these words appear:
"My name is Ozymandias, king of kings:
Look on my works ye mighty and despair."

(*d*) Study also Wordsworth's sonnet on "Westminster Bridge," and the second stanza in Wordsworth's "Solitary Reaper."

A colon may introduce a quotation or an enumeration—

(*a*) As Shelley says: "If Winter comes, can Spring be far behind?"

(*b*) The little bay was dotted with many craft: canoes, punts, yachts, and even barges swung with the tide from their buoys.

**The Semicolon** ( ; ), a more emphatic pause than the comma—

(i) It preserves the unity of thought in a long sentence by momentarily resting the reader's attention. (See any of Scott's novels and Goldsmith's "Deserted Village.")

(ii) It divides phrases and clauses that are antithetical.

(*a*) Go to the ant, thou sluggard; consider her ways and be wise.

(*b*) Willing to wound, and yet afraid to strike;
Just hint a fault and hesitate dislike.

Consider carefully the use of the semicolon in the following instances—

(*a*) The sombre reds and blacks of the room troubled me; even with seven candles, the place was merely dim.

(*b*) They instantly wrested the government out of the hands of Hastings; condemned, certainly not without justice, his late dealings with the Nabob Vizier, recalled the English agent from Ande, and sent thither a creature of their own.

(*c*) We believe that there never was a public man whose temper was so closely tried; not Marlborough, when thwarted by the Dutch Deputies; not Wellington, when he had to deal at once with the Portuguese Regency, the Spanish Juntas, and Mr. Percival.

**The Exclamation Mark** ( ! ) is used after any short expression of deep emotion—

(*a*) But she is in her grave, and oh,
The difference to me!

(*b*) Rarely, rarely, comest thou,
Spirit of Delight!

(*c*) Milton! Thou shouldst be living at this hour.

**The Apostrophe** ( ' ) denotes (i) the absence of a letter, as o'er, don't, 'scape, speak'st, and (ii) possession, by the curtailment of the Old English genitive "es" to "'s"—

"The moones sphere" is now "The moon's sphere."

The apostrophe of possession is placed after a plural ending in " s "—sisters' souls ; blackbirds' nests.

Note the following forms : Theseus' nuptial day ; high Taurus' snow ; Ninus' tomb ; Burns's poems ; Keats's odes ; Yeats's lyrics ; Dickens's novels.

**The Hyphen** ( - ) is used to compound two or more words into a single thought-unit.

The never-to-be-forgotten massacre of Glencoe ; thy hair, soft-lifted ; a half-reaped furrow ; soft-dying day ; hedge-cricket ; deep-browed Homer.

" Crook-kneed, and dew-lapped like Thessalian bulls."

**Inverted Commas** ( " " ) are used before and after a quotation, *i.e.* the actual words used by a speaker or writer.

(*a*) " Don't you think that a very remarkable sky ? " I said to the coachman.

(*b*) " Don't you think that," I said to the coachman, " a very remarkable sky ? "

and (ii) before and after the name of a book, a ship or a house (in print, however, such words often appear in italics).

Shakespeare's " Hamlet " ; the battleship " Hood."

Single inverted commas denote a quotation within a quotation.

(*a*) " I dread hearing ' To be or not to be ' mouthed by school boys," he replied.

The interrogation mark is used only after a direct question and is included in the inverted commas.

(*b*) There is surely no greater gale to be read of than this : from the first words, " ' Don't you think that,' I said to the coachman, ' a very remarkable sky ? ' " to the end of a magnificent chapter.

## PUNCTUATION EXERCISE

Punctuate the following prose passages :—

1. presently tom seized his comrades arm and said sh what is it tom and the two clung together with beating hearts sh there tis again didnt you hear it I there now you hear it lord tom theyre coming sure whatll we do I dono think theyll see us oh tom they can see in the dark same as cats I wish I hadnt come.

*Tom Sawyer.*

2. who goes stand or we fire flag of truce cried silver the captain was in the porch keeping himself carefully out of the way of a treacherous shot should any be intended he turned and spoke to us doctors watch on the look out dr livesey take the north side if you please jim the east gray west the watch below all hands to load muskets lively men and careful and then he turned again to the mutineers.

*Treasure Island.*

3. his head was scarred with the records of old wounds a sort of series of fields of battle all over it one eye out one ear cropped as close as was archbishop leightons fathers the remaining eye had the power of two and above it and in constant communication with it was a tattered rag of an ear which was for ever unfurling itself like an old flag and then that bud of a tail about one inch long if it could in any sense be said to be long being as broad as long the mobility the instantaneousness of that bud were very funny and surprising.

*Rab and his Friends.*

4. ah said holly he wanted to show off he knew a lot about english constitutional history and what is the use of knowledge unless you can display it he began william the conqueror 1066 he was crowned on christmas day to the 9th of september 1087 william rufus or william the second 1087 to 1100 he frowned and taxed his memory william the third prompted lady porlet kindly no maam said holly loudly he wasnt born for hundreds and hundreds of years.

*Poet's Pub.*

5. she had a mans bonnet with a feather in it an unsheathed sword in her hand and a pair of pistols at her girdle its helen campbell robs wife said the bailie in a whisper of considerable alarm and there will be broken heads amang us or its lang what seek ye here she asked again of captain thornton who had himself advanced to reconnoitre we seek the outlaw rob roy macgregor campbell answered the officer.

*Rob Roy.*

6. whats your line mr mccaskie when he heard he was keenly interested dye say so yere from todds man I was in the book business myself till I changed it for something a wee bit more lucrative I was on the road for three years for andrew matheson ye ken the name paternoster row ive forgotten the number if it hadna been for this war I would have been making four figures my pipes out have you one of those rare and valuable curiosities called a spunk mr mccaskie.

*Mr. Standfast.*

---

# CHAPTER V

## COMPOSITION

It is not surprising that the writing of essays is to most pupils something of an ordeal since it requires effort to state clearly what is vague and indefinite in our minds. This effort is of distinct value to us since thereby we define and clarify our knowledge of the subject and come to realise what we actually know. Constant practice of this kind will assist us to acquire an intelligent interest in those objects, incidents and feelings which come within our observation. We learn to take note of what appeals to us, and to gather and set down sufficient details of what we have seen to form a nucleus from which later we may recapture the total impression. The best composition is not merely a haphazard description of what is actually under our eye but is based on a vague mental picture of which we recapture the details by what Wordsworth called "recollection in tranquillity." It is possible to analyse this process and to follow it out step by step.

The first step is the selection of a suitable subject where a choice is permitted. However unattractive the subjects may seem at first glance, there is generally at least one on which not only can we say something but on which we really *want* to say something. It is always advisable to choose the subject about which, after some thought, we feel we know most. It is therefore unwise to plunge into the first subject on the paper, but we should rather scan each title with care before arriving at a decision. Do not despair though the subjects appear quite unknown. Even a subject seeming to demand technical knowledge such as, **A Trip on a Submarine,** or **The Making of a Radio,** may yield sufficient interest to make a good essay if the writer uses his imagination. Few essays demand an accurate knowledge of technical matters, or even a wide range of definite information. On the other hand, it is not enough to say the first thing we think of; we must prepare by observation, reading and conversation. No essay of any value can be written without ideas.

The following exercise will help us to grasp the significance of essay titles.

## EXERCISE I

Arrange the following groups of titles in order, passing from the *general* to the more *particular* :—

1. (*a*) The Housing Problem; (*b*) Labour Saving Devices; (*c*) Town Planning; (*d*) Slum Clearances; (*e*) Garden Cities; (*f*) Discomforts of a Mediæval Castle.

2. (*a*) Giants of the Press; (*b*) The Influence of the Press; (*c*) The Struggle of Press and Parliament in the eighteenth century; (*d*) Great Newspapers; (*e*) Advertising and the Press; (*f*) Journalese.

3. (*a*) The History of Trade; (*b*) Tariff Reform; (*c*) Trade follows the Flag; (*d*) Free Trade and Tariff Reform; (*e*) Trade in Wartime; (*f*) The Trade of Great Britain.

4. (*a*) Early Pioneers in Science; (*b*) Science and the Mediæval Church; (*c*) Development of Modern Science; (*d*) A great modern Scientist; (*e*) Scientists are the greatest benefactors of mankind; (*f*) Teaching of Science in Schools.

5. (*a*) A Day at the Seaside; (*b*) Modern Life and the need for Holidays; (*c*) A Camping Holiday; (*d*) Summer Holidays; (*e*) Holiday Reading; (*f*) How to enjoy a Holiday.

6. (*a*) Dickens as a Social Reformer; (*b*) Sam Weller; (*c*) Humour in Dickens's Novels; (*d*) The Novels of Dickens; (*e*) A Tale of Two Cities; (*f*) The Treatment of History in Dickens's Novels.

Having chosen the subject most suitable, write (unless it is a lengthy quotation) the exact title at the top of the page, and in any case, make a point of referring to it frequently, to make sure that you are keeping to it and are certain of its scope and purpose. To ensure this, whether the title consists of a phrase or sentence, take note of every word so that your outline or plan may cover the whole ground. Should the title consist of one word, be certain that you understand the exact meaning. Where the essay is prescribed, think over it. Consult such books of reference as you can, making notes of the information. In any case select one particular way of treating the subject and the special aspects you consider important. This settled, set about collecting the material, vague and incomplete as it always appears at first. It is possible to clarify this vague material by a systematic approach, based on the use of interrogative words such as the following: **Who? When? Where? What? How? Why?**

**Example:**

**Sport.**

What? Games such as football, cricket, hockey, golf, etc.; boxing, wrestling, running, hurdling; blood sports such as hunting the fox, deer, shooting grouse, pheasants, etc.; exclude card games, draughts, chess, etc.; element of bodily risk.

Who? Ancient Greeks: Olympic games, ancient and modern; gladiatorial displays—participants, slaves, professionals, criminals; modern interest in sport not confined to youth.

**When ?** Use of leisure ; week-end sports.

**Where ?** Sports grounds ; Roman arena ; modern elaborate stadium ; school and university private grounds ; public city parks.

**How ?** Active participation ; the value to spectators ; special training for certain sports ; need for more general participation ; efforts to develop national health by mass exercise and sport.

**Why ?** Inherent pride in strength and activity ; value to nation of strong healthy body ; escape from monotony of modern industry and over development of one part of the body ; increased standard of efficiency, toughening of moral fibre by element of risk absent in ordinary civilised life.

The material obtained in this fashion is generally well arranged and may be used for a number of paragraphs. When some type of definition is required, it is better to start with " What ? " " Who ? " is more suitable otherwise.

Another method, which may seem much less methodical, is to jot down the ideas which suggest themselves, however haphazard and irrelevant they may seem. Suppose your subject is "Travel." Write down the ideas which the word suggests, not in sentences but in words or phrases, arranging them in a column for easy reading.

**Example :**

**Travel.**

Increase of travel in recent years.
Luxury tours.
Hiking in foreign lands.
Language barrier.
What to see—historic buildings, etc.
Customs of the people.
Avoidance of superior attitude.
Travel in the past confined to the wealthy.
Completion of education.
See Bacon's essay on Travel.
Countries I should like to visit.
Battlefields of the Great War.
Attraction of sunshine.

Influence of books we have read.
Vivid descriptions.
Great travellers of the past—Marco Polo, Columbus, Kinglake.
Great modern travellers—Scott, Lawrence.
Pilgrimages, crusades.
Preparations.

This may be a convenient place to stop. Now arrange ideas according to similarity and write out a suitable *topic* sentence or phrase. Thus—

1. Value of travel.
2. Pleasures of travel.
3. Methods of travel.
4. Great travellers, past and present.
5. Why I should like to travel.

Discard any unsuitable ideas then construct five paragraphs.

**The Beginning.**

A good beginning is as important in composition as it is proverbially elsewhere. The opening sentence should go straight to the theme of the essay, give some indication of what is to follow, and be calculated to attract the interest of the reader. There are certain recognised ways of beginning an essay which will help the writer to accomplish this and so avoid those vaguely connected introductory sentences which merely mark time. Note, however, that those who make an outline as suggested above can generally get to grips with the subject at once. The examples given are all chosen from the works of well-known essayists.

(*a*) A **General Statement.**

September is rather a sad month in some ways.

*Septemberitis.* R. S. HOOPER.

(*b*) A **Definition** (use this method when there is obscurity).

A Book in any worthy sense, as I conceive it, is a personal expression of the reader's mind.

*The Artist in Words.* HAVELOCK ELLIS.

(*c*) A **Quotation or Allusion.**

A clerk I was in London gay.

*The Superannuated Man.* LAMB.

(*d*) An **Anecdote.**

My worthy friend Sir Roger, when we were talking of the malice of parties, very frequently tells of an incident when he was a schoolboy which was at a time when the feuds ran high between the Roundheads and Cavaliers.

*Party Strife.* ADDISON.

(*e*) A **Paradox or Apparent Contradiction.**

It is a hard and nice subject for a man to write of himself.

*Of Myself.* COWLEY.

N.B. *Note.*—Do not begin an essay, *e.g.* **Camping,** with a *pronoun* referring to the title, *e.g.* " It is the most . . . " or " This is a very . . . ." The title should in such cases be repeated.

## EXERCISE II

Classify the following beginnings according to the arrangement given above. Consider how far they prepare the reader for the *point of view, scope* and *proposed manner of treatment* :—

1. To my way of thinking, there is no such thing as " amateur acting."

*A Word to the Amateurs.* AGATE.

2. An hour ago, I parted from a little friend who has borne me company for this fortnight past.

*The Malignant Coin.* THE LONDONER.

3. Revenge is a kind of wild justice.

*Of Revenge.* BACON.

4. " What right has that man to have a spaniel ? " said a witty lady, pointing to a bully : " spaniels should be a reward."

*The Lord of Life.* E. V. LUCAS.

5. Travel, in the younger sort, is a part of education ; in the elder, a part of experience.

*Of Travel.* BACON.

6. I have an almost feminine partiality for old china.

*Old China.* LAMB

7. It is commonly said that everybody can sing in the bathroom: and this is true.

*The Art of Drawing*. A. P. HERBERT.

8. From the crowded theatre to the sick chamber, from the noise, the glare, the keen delight, to the loneliness, the darkness, the dullness, and the pain, there is but one step.

*The Sick Chamber*.

9. He possessed too, that which to the heathen philosopher seemed the greatest good—the sound mind in the sound body.

*William of Orange*. MOTLEY.

10. The Champion Cat Show has been held at the Crystal Palace, but the champion cat was not there.

*Cats*. R. LYND.

11. " To carve out dials quaintly, point by point."

*On a Sun-Dial*. HAZLITT.

12. There has crept, I notice, into our literature and journalism a new way of flattering the wealthy and the great.

*The Worship of the Wealthy*. G. K. CHESTERTON.

13. Lying in bed would be an altogether perfect and supreme experience if only one had a coloured pencil long enough to draw on the ceiling.

*On Lying in Bed*. G. K. CHESTERTON.

14. " I would also recommend," said the late Sir Walter Raleigh, talking of the press, " that a photograph of the author be placed at the head of every article. I have been saved from many bad novels by the helpful pictorial advertisements of modern publishers."

*Photographs*. J. B. PRIESTLEY.

15. As often as I survey my bookshelves, I am reminded of Lamb's " rugged veterans."

*My Books*. GISSING.

16. Oliver Wendell Holmes's plutocrat was a little wide of the mark when he fancied that every man represented a trinity of persons and no more.

*The Toy Theatre*. GERALD BULLETT.

**Note.**

At the end of this chapter you will find essay subjects. Choose suitable number and write beginnings of the types described above for *each*.

**Body of the Essay.**

It is essential to make full use of the outline and be certain that each paragraph deals with a definite aspect of the main theme. See that every part of the essay receives the space that its importance demands, giving fullest treatment to such topics as you wish to emphasise. Introduce variety into the structure of sentences and paragraphs. Try to arrange your paragraphs so that they pass by an easy transition from one topic to another, always remembering that you must arrive at a definite conclusion if the essay is to have any real value. Illustrate your points by reference to actual experiences where possible, as this gives the essay a personal note. These may of course be supplemented from your reading in history and literature.

Unless an essay requires direct personal treatment, avoid the use of such expressions as "I *believe*," "*In my opinion*." Instead of these use the more impersonal forms, "Many *people believe*," or "It *is frequently stated*." The use of "*One*" is awkward and should be avoided where possible. Instead of writing, "When *one enters the exhibition* . . ." write, "The *visitor to the exhibition* . . ." or, "*People who pay a visit to the exhibition* . . ." or even "*Anyone who visits the exhibition* . . ." An impersonal phrase may be used, as "*It is interesting to notice*" instead of "*One is interested*." The colloquial use of "*you*" in a general sense should be avoided. Thus for "*When you go for a walk*" write "*When we go for a walk*."

**The Ending.**

The ending is almost as important as the beginning for on it depends the final impression. There must be a sense of completeness, with no suggestion of new or contradictory ideas. The ending should not seem forced or unnatural, but simple and clear, proceeding naturally from the earlier treatment of the subject. The last paragraph, and especially the final sentence, should receive special consideration. The final sentence should be neither abrupt nor drawn out. The following methods of concluding an essay are derived from the work of great essayists.

1. **A simple statement summing up the previous statements.**
These are my ordinary companions.
*The Spectator Club.* STEELE.

2. **Brief summary of previous arguments and statements with reflections.**
It has force enough to light the world and grind the world's bread beside. *Niagara.* MASEFIELD.

3. **A quotation which sums up the subject matter or bears upon it.**
" I don't suppose I shall do it again for months and months and months." *On Moving a Library.* J. C. SQUIRE.

4. **A sentence arranging ideas in form of a climax.**
I suspect it is at least ten per cent. of why Lord Beaconsfield and Mr. Gladstone have debated so much in the House of Commons, and why Burnaby rode to Khiva the other day, and why the Admirals courted war like a mistress.
*The English Admirals.* R. L. STEVENSON

5. **A sentence which recalls the initial paragraph of the essay.**
I found myself quietly seated in my bachelor armchair where I had fallen asleep. *Dream Children.* LAMB.

## EXERCISE III

**Classify the following endings according to the arrangement given above. Consider how far they give a sense of completeness :—**

1. The still night held us all.
*London in August.* A. WAUGH.

2. Go to the garden and see, in the shadow of a cedar, the apple blossom glow.
*Rain.* E. THOMAS.

3. I roll up my magic carpet and bless the man who invented maps for the solace of men.
*On a map of the Oberland.* ALPHA OF THE PLOUGH.

4. And yet—what a long time off it all seemed, both in space and time, to me yet lingering on the threshold of that old-world chamber!

*The Secret Drawer.* K. GRAHAME.

5. Such is the allegory, or morality, of the Lost Train.

*Losing One's Train.* VERNON LEE.

6. These are the chaotic depths of that dreaming nature out of which humanity has to grow.

*War.* G. SANTANYANA

7. But instead of the rolling tide, the arched bridges and the happy islands, I saw nothing but the long, hollow valley of Bagdad, with oxen, sheep and camels grazing upon the sides of it.

*The Vision of Mirza.* ADDISON.

8. He daily sees and daily considers God's wonders in the deep.

*The Good Sea Captain.* FULLER.

9. A youth of misery was concluded with an old age of elegance, affluence and ease.

*An Eastern Tale.* GOLDSMITH.

10. These several adventures, with the Knight's behaviour in them, gave me as pleasant a day as ever I met with in any of my travels.

*Sir Roger at the Assizes.* ADDISON.

11. To love the glory of virtuous deeds is a sure proof of the love of virtue.

*Of Human Nature.* HUME.

12. "To travel hopefully," says he, "is better than to arrive."

*Travellers' Tales.* MARY COLERIDGE.

13. Creepers are good; but their beauty must not be taken as any excuse for bad architecture.

*The Roses round the Door.* TIMES LEADER.

14. Let us rejoice then that the mainland life of these boys dedicated to her service should be so blithe.

*Admirals All-to-be.* E. V. LUCAS.

15. This would not only be more easy to themselves, but more edifying to the people.

*Sir Roger at Home.* ADDISON.

16. Reader if you wrest my words beyond their fair construction, it is you and not I, that are the *April Fool.*

*All Fools' Day.* LAMB.

### EXERCISE IV

At the end of this chapter you will find essay subjects. Choose a suitable number and write *endings* of the kinds described above for *each* of them.

## TYPES OF COMPOSITION.

(*a*) Narrative.
(*b*) Descriptive.
(*c*) Expository.
(*d*) Reflective.
(*e*) Argumentative.

### (*a*) Narrative.

We are not at this stage concerned with the simplest form of narrative composition which ranges from the account of a single incident in a single paragraph to longer narratives telling a short and easy story such as a fable or anecdote and consisting of several paragraphs. Nor are we concerned here with the story developed from a given introductory or final paragraph. The narrative essay with which we are to deal is a kind of chronicle essay which not only narrates the incidents, but gives space to comment on the feelings and thoughts aroused by them. It is much wider in scope than the ordinary narrative and much more difficult to write. Some narratives may be founded on some personal narrative such as a visit to the seaside, others may tell the story of a person's life, others again may give an account of some period from history or even of a series of events. The facts may be imaginary.

Many pupils think that narrative is the easiest form of composition, since they convert any and every subject given into this form. They generally find that narrative has its difficulties and pitfalls. The following hints are offered for the preparation of such essays.

(1) *Collect* the material by one of the methods suggested. Incidents may be imaginary but must be

true to common experience and neither improbable nor, what is generally worse, impossible.

(2) *Arrange* the material in a natural order, usually based on time sequence, though this may occasionally be disregarded. The selection of material must be relevant and significant. Excess of detail may obscure important ideas.

(3) Obtain a definite *point of view* by deciding who is telling the story, a chief actor, a minor actor, or a spectator interested or disinterested.

(4) Choose such incidents as will reveal the *point of view* of the *characters*, but little freedom is possible in dealing with a historical narrative.

(5) *Avoid* a selection of *commonplace incidents* linked by such phrases as "I went next," "Then I saw."

(6) Make the background of *time* and *place* as clear and definite as the characters. This is necessary if the story is to carry conviction and the characters are to be consistent with the action. The usual method, and the least satisfactory is to give an introductory paragraph of straightforward information. To avoid holding up the action, it is better to build up the setting and characterisation by short, telling, descriptive passages in the course of the story. So we may learn of the feelings and motives of the characters by their sayings or by short descriptive phrases indicative of their feelings. Thus "He bit his lip," "He laughed sardonically," "They shook hands cordially."

(7) Use dialogue carefully for it may develop the action of the story or reveal the nature of the speakers. Properly used it is worth more than pages of description. It should be natural but avoid the excessive use of colloquial or slang expressions, which are natural enough when heard, but strange when read only.

(8) Begin generally with an *exciting episode* or an interesting conversation to attract and hold attention.

(9) Do not obtrude *irrelevant* incident, however interesting, nor personal tastes or opinions to excess.

(10) The *narrative* should conclude with the point or crisis towards which the story moves. It may break off with a striking situation which finally unravels the plot, or with some form of comment on the story, ranging from an abrupt exclamation to a quiet reflective statement. Whatever form it takes, it should maintain the feeling of suspense as long as is natural.

(11) Use *verbs* denoting *action* or *movement.* Avoid the use of the *passive voice* ; excessive use of *conjunctions* such as—and, but, then ; phrases such as—of course, after that, the next thing. Sacrifice *adjectives* unless they describe *actions* or reveal *character.*

## EXERCISE V

1. Write a short story dealing with *one* of the following :—
   (*a*) A great storm.
   (*b*) My unluckiest day.
   (*c*) My master (told by a dog).
   (*d*) A day with the boy scouts.

2. Write an account of some *plot, battle* or other *historical event.*

3. Write an account of the adventures (in the first person) of *one* of the following :—
   (*a*) A policeman.
   (*b*) An airman.
   (*c*) A tramp.
   (*d*) A soldier..
   (*e*) A football player.
   (*f*) A nurse.

4. Write a short story dealing with *one* of the following :—
   (*a*) A coal mine.
   (*b*) The sea.
   (*c*) The railway.
   (*d*) Air travel.
   (*e*) A shipyard.
   (*f*) School life.

5. Invent a story to illustrate any *one* of the following :—

(*a*) Misery acquaints a man with strange bed fellows.
(*b*) A rolling stone gathers no moss.
(*c*) It never rains but it pours.
(*d*) While the grass grows, the steed starves.
(*e*) Rome was not built in a day.
(*f*) A burnt child dreads the fire.

6. Invent a story to fit any *one* of the well known pictures with the following titles :—

(*a*) The Fighting Téméraire.
(*b*) The Roll Call.
(*c*) Ah, Bisto !
(*d*) When did you last see your father, boy ?
(*e*) Bubbles.
(*f*) Since then I've used no other.

**Descriptive.**

The power to describe a thing clearly and accurately is constantly necessary. It is seldom that people possess it naturally, but it can be acquired to some extent by practice. The aim of the descriptive writer is to show things, events or persons as they are, or were, or will be, so as to produce in the mind of the reader a clear mental picture of what the writer has himself seen or imagined. He must also decide for himself the order of his description whereas in writing a narrative the events arrange themselves naturally in order of time. So, in describing a person's appearance, he must decide whether the head or feet or some other part of the body is to be dealt with first.

(*a*) Strive for unified treatment by choosing some *central theme*, and filling in appropriate details derived from careful observation.

(*b*) Select what is peculiar to *object*, *event* or *person* described in order to give concreteness and vividness. Thus, omit such facts as that, a dog barks, or a carriage has wheels, or a building, windows.

(*c*) Avoid *over-emphasis* of salient feature, as the description is thereby distorted, and becomes a caricature.

(*d*) When a writer has reached this stage, he may embellish his description by *personal reflections* and *comparisons* arising from the associations excited by the ideas in his own mind.

(*e*) Avoid vague or general *reflections*.

(*f*) Early practice should begin with description of simple *familiar objects* from direct observation. Later, describe similar objects from *memory*. The next stage will deal with more complicated things.

*Note*.—The ***pen portrait*** or ***personal description*** is treated later

## EXERCISE VI

1. Write a description of *one* of the following :—
   (*a*) A fountain pen.
   (*b*) A thermometer.
   (*c*) An electric bell.
   (*d*) A bicycle.
   (*e*) A football.
   (*f*) A dog or other pet.

2. Write a description of *one* of the following :—
   (*a*) A shop window.
   (*b*) A motor car.
   (*c*) The school library.
   (*d*) A well-known picture.
   (*e*) A country lane.
   (*f*) A locomotive.

3. Write a description of *one* of the following :—
   (*a*) A highland glen.
   (*b*) A famous river.
   (*c*) The moors in Autumn.
   (*d*) A suburban garden.
   (*e*) The harvest field.
   (*f*) A waterfall.

4. Write a descriptive essay on *one* of the following :—
   (*a*) The Signing of Magna Charta.
   (*b*) The Battle of Bannockburn.
   (*c*) The Spanish Armada.
   (*d*) The Black Hole of Calcutta.
   (*e*) The Relief of Lucknow.
   (*f*) The Retreat from Mons.

5. Write a descriptive essay on *one* of the following :—
   (*a*) My favourite film.
   (*b*) My favourite newspaper.
   (*c*) My favourite play.
   (*d*) My favourite piece of music.
   (*e*) My favourite picture.
   (*f*) My favourite novel.

6. Write a descriptive composition on *one* of the following :—
   (*a*) A crowd at a railway station.
   (*b*) A crowd at a football match.
   (*c*) A crowd at a street accident.
   (*d*) A crowd at a band performance.
   (*e*) A crowd at a political meeting.
   (*f*) A crowd at sheep-dog trials.

**Expository Essay.**

This type of essay may explain a process, a direction, a machine or some device more or less simple. To do this is not at all simple as any attempt to define even a football, a pencil, a golf club, or any other familiar object in a manner free from obscurity soon shows. It is then we find how hard it is to free the essential from the irrelevant, yet to do so is imperative if every detail selected is to contribute to the accuracy of the description. The writer, therefore, must have a clear and systematic grasp of his facts.

The expository essay is *objective,* that is, the writer is not concerned with stating his own opinions but with giving definite information to the reader. He must not write of subjects in which his information is inaccurate or incomplete, but must choose a subject with which he is familiar, and prepare a statement written in a fashion intelligible to readers with little or no knowledge of the subject.

(1) State, in the first sentence, what the thing discussed is or is not, or what it is like or is unlike.

(2) State the same fact, where it is difficult, from different *points of view*, and provide concrete illustrations of particular statements, especially of those which are abstract.

(3) *Summarise* the conclusions reached at different stages, generally at the end of paragraphs.

(4) Pay special *attention* to simplicity, clearness and orderly arrangement.

## EXERCISE VII

1. Write a clear account of *one* of the following :—
   (*a*) How to bandage a cut finger.
   (*b*) How to operate a vacuum cleaner.
   (*c*) How to locate and mend a puncture.
   (*d*) How to use the telephone.
   (*e*) How to darn a hole in a stocking.
   (*f*) How to make a letter-rack.

2. Give clear instructions on how to perform *one* of the following operations :—
   (*a*) Pitching a tent.
   (*b*) Laying and lighting a fire, either in a grate or in the open.
   (*c*) Making a wireless set.
   (*d*) Learning to swim.
   (*e*) Looking after a pet.
   (*f*) Playing football, cricket, hockey.

3. Write a composition showing *one* of the following :—
   (*a*) How to become a doctor.
   (*b*) How to become a chartered accountant.
   (*c*) How to become a detective.
   (*d*) How to become a nurse.
   (*e*) How to become a civil servant.
   (*f*) How to become a film-star.

4. Write a clear account of *one* of the following :—
   (*a*) The uses of books.
   (*b*) The uses of physical training.
   (*c*) The uses of electricity in the home.
   (*d*) The uses of aeroplanes in times of peace.
   (*e*) The uses of travel.
   (*f*) The uses of drugs.

5. Explain clearly and with full detail *one* of the following :—
   (*a*) The making of a film.
   (*b*) The growth of a bean or a pea.
   (*c*) The making of jam.
   (*d*) Running a school library.
   (*e*) Preparing a school magazine.
   (*f*) The preparation of a gas.

6. Give clear and full instructions on *one* of the following :—
   (*a*) How to prepare for the school sports.
   (*b*) How to prepare for a hiking holiday.
   (*c*) How to prepare for the term examinations.
   (*d*) How to prepare a speech for the School Debating Society.
   (*e*) How to prepare a three-course dinner.
   (*f*) How to prepare for a holiday at the coast.

### Reflective Essay

So far, the various types of composition have been concerned with definite objects visible to the eye and under observation at one time or another. The reflective essay, however, deals with the abstract and for that reason most candidates avoid it as likely to lead to vague and generalised statements. Others, as a matter of tactics, choose this type believing, and probably rightly, that since it is less popular, there is an opportunity of excelling in it. As the writer of the reflective essay is expressing not a matter of fact but rather a matter of opinion, it is much more difficult to lay down a method of treatment, since the essay is bound to be much more personal. Until the writer gains by practice a method of his own, the following hints may be studied with advantage.

**Treatment**

(1) Let the *introduction be brief*, and attempt in it to arouse the interest and sympathy of the reader.

(2) State clearly (especially where it is an abstract word such as, Benevolence, Monotony, Folly) what *meaning* you attach to the title. Do not define it in terms of itself, *e.g.* Fear is a state of being afraid.

(3) State clearly what you intend to *prove* in the light of this definition.

(4) Express your *opinion* definitely, and substantiate it by the *arguments* or by relevant applications of your point of view.

(5) Avoid a mere *catalogue* of facts, but vary and enforce them by the uses of comparison and analogy, of quotation or proverbial saying, or by reference to history or literature. Make a rule of allocating one concrete illustration to each statement of opinion.

(6) Do not let the essay become a mere *narrative* illustrative of the writer's point of view.

(7) Use *freedom* in the statement of opinions provided that they are relevant and backed by proof.

(8) The *conclusion*, on the lines suggested in the general section on essay writing, should be brief.

## EXERCISE VIII

1. (*a*) Make a list of all the *nouns*, *adjectives*, *verbs* and *phrases* connected with the following *abstract* ideas :—

| | |
|---|---|
| Benevolence. | Industry. |
| Noise. | Charity. |
| Curiosity. | Leisure. |
| Monotony. | Vanity. |
| Humility. | Ignorance. |
| Pride. | Self Satisfaction. |

(*b*) Write a composition on any *one* of the subjects given in Exercise VIII, 1 (*a*).

2. Write a composition on any *one* of the following :—

(*a*) Revenge.
(*b*) Education.
(*c*) Insularity.
(*d*) Humour.
(*e*) Self-discipline
(*f*) Jingoism.

3. Write a composition on any *one* of the following :—

(*a*) Is progress an illusion ?
(*b*) The joys of speed.
(*c*) The good old times.
(*d*) The force of example.
(*e*) The value of competition.
(*f*) Playing the game.

4. Write a composition on any *one* of the following :—

(*a*) "Where ignorance is bliss, 'tis folly to be wise."
(*b*) "The best laid schemes o' mice and men gang aft agley."
(*c*) "Our sweetest songs are those that tell of saddest thought."
(*d*) "Give every man thine ear, but few thy voice."
(*e*) "As the twig is bent, the tree's inclined.
(*f*) "There is a tide in the affairs of men, which taken at the flood, leads on to fortune."

5. Write a composition on *one* of the following :—

(*a*) Procrastination is the thief of time.
(*b*) Too many cooks spoil the broth.
(*c*) Penny wise, pound foolish.
(*d*) Birds of a feather flock together.
(*e*) Necessity knows no law.
(*f*) Time and tide wait for no man.

6. Write a composition on *one* of the following :—

(*a*) The wise use of leisure.
(*b*) The wisdom of proverbs.
(*c*) When and how to be lazy.
(*d*) Modern superstitions.
(*e*) Freedom in modern civilisation.
(*f*) Pleasure is the chief end of life.

**Argumentative Essay.**

The **argumentative** like the reflective essay makes use of reasoning, but unlike the latter attempts definitely to persuade and convince. In doing this, the writer may use any one of the other forms of composition, to state his opinions so as to recommend and justify them to others, or to define a thing and then justify the definition, or to compare two things, consider their merits and give reasons for the preference.

**Treatment**

(1) State clearly the *points at issue* so as to gain the consideration, if not the sympathy, of the reader.

(2) Give definite statements of *fact*, supported by experience, history or literature, and arrange them in paragraphs.

(3) Let each paragraph end with a *conclusion* drawn from the facts.

*Note.*—Sections (2) and (3) above are called the Proof.

(4) State the *opposite* arguments clearly and fully and then prove their inaccuracy (Refutation).

(5) *Link* the various points of the proof together, and having drawn a *final conclusion*, refer the matter to the judgment of the reader.

(6) Avoid—

(*a*) the use of words or phrases that *assume* what you wish to prove, *e.g.* "It is clear to everyone . . ."

(*b*) the device of attributing to your imaginary opponent arguments which are erroneous or absurd or irrelevant.

## EXERCISE IX

*Note.*—All the essays should be treated as *controversial* subjects

1. Write an essay on *one* of the following themes :—

(*a*) On forgetting.
(*b*) On advertising.
(*c*) On rambling.
(*d*) On keeping one's temper.
(*e*) On speaking one's mind.
(*f*) On keeping a diary.

2. Write an essay on *one* of the following subjects :—
   (*a*) New Year resolutions.
   (*b*) Fears and scruples.
   (*c*) Day-dreams.
   (*d*) Divine discontent.
   (*e*) Bad manners.
   (*f*) Practical jokers.

3. Write a composition on *one* of the following :—
   (*a*) The penalties of popularity.
   (*b*) Thoughts on Spring cleaning.
   (*c*) Force of habit.
   (*d*) In praise of birds.
   (*e*) The importance of roads.
   (*f*) The problems of disarmament.

4. Write a composition on *one* of the following themes :—
   (*a*) Pocket money, and the lack of it.
   (*b*) Parents and the careers of their children.
   (*c*) Loyalty to the State.
   (*d*) The qualities of a good leader.
   (*e*) The barriers between nations.
   (*f*) The injustice of oblivion.

5. Write an essay on *one* of the following :—
   (*a*) Keeping fit as a patriotic virtue.
   (*b*) The difficulties you have had to face.
   (*c*) One's duty to live dangerously.
   (*d*) Occupations I should not like.
   (*e*) History repeats itself.
   (*f*) Safety razors.

6 Write a composition on *one* of the following quotations :—
   (*a*) He prayeth best who loveth best
   All things both great and small.
   (*b*) Grow old along with me!
   The best is yet to be.
   (*c*) A primrose by the river's brim
   A yellow primrose was to him
   And it was nothing more.
   (*d*) A man, Sir, should keep his friendship in constant repair.
   (*e*) All who joy would win
   Must share it—Happiness was born a twin.
   (*f*) And God fulfils Himself in many ways,
   Lest one good custom should corrupt the world.

## Letter Writing.

Letter writing is a form of composition subject to the general rules of composition; we demand accurate spelling and good English, as well as legible writing. There are in addition certain rules peculiar to letter writing and each type of letter—whether it is the personal letter between friends or intimates, the formal letter in the third person, or the business letter—demands a different method of approach.

The *personal* or *familiar* letter gives more freedom than the others and is intended not only to give information but also to develop personal intimacy between the writer and the recipient.

**Treatment.**

(*a*) Aim at an ideal *conversational* style, both simple and natural, but avoid slovenly treatment or an excessive use of colloquial expressions.

(*b*) Aim at *grammatical expression* and careful *punctuation*.

(*c*) Select a few *topics* to be illustrated with *significant* detail rather than enumerate a mere *catalogue* of events.

(*d*) Introduce *personal* details and references, little personal touches but avoid mere gossip.

(*e*) Begin with *one* or more friendly paragraphs displaying suitable interest in the recipient before introducing the main theme.

(*f*) Avoid the excessive use of "*I*," the use of such apologetic phrases as "*sorry I can't think of anything else to say*," or "*I must hurry to catch the post*," etc.

(*g*) Let the letter consist of the *heading*, which contains the *address* and *date*, the *salutation*, the *body* of the *letter*, and the *conclusion* or *subscription*.

## EXERCISE X

*Correct* the following errors :—

(*a*) The Rev. Smith ; Mr. John Brown, Esq. ; James Jones, M.A., Esq.
(*b*) Dear Brown, Esq. ; Yours respectively ; Yrs sin'ly ; Your's sincerely.
(*c*) Dear Sir . . . I remain, Sir.
(*d*) Will you go to see us when you have time ?
(*e*) I will thank you to lend me the use of your dictionary.
(*f*) Thanking you in anticipation.
(*g*) I shall have much pleasure in accepting your invitation.

## EXERCISE XI

(*a*) Write a letter to a friend describing a recent holiday tour.
(*b*) Write a letter to a colonial cousin describing any recent films or plays you have seen.
(*c*) Write a letter to a friend who left school a year ago describing any school news of interest.
(*d*) Write a letter to your favourite novelist or film star or broadcaster.
(*e*) Write a letter to an intimate friend describing your hobbies.
(*f*) Write a letter in reply to one from an elderly relative in which he complained of the lack of responsibility and politeness in modern youth.

**Business Letter.**

The first aim of the business letter is to give definite *information*, and all information should be clear and relevant. Remember it is not your purpose to entertain but to inform the reader.

**Treatment.**

(*a*) In addition to the parts of the ordinary letter, include the *name* or official description of the person or persons addressed, inserting this *before* the salutation.

(*b*) Give the full *date*, which may be necessary for reference.

(*c*) Avoid "*to-day*" or "*to-morrow*," giving the exact day of the week and month, thus, "*Tuesday*, 17*th May*."

(*d*) If the letter is in answer to another, first acknowledge *receipt* and then answer the *matters* referred to in it.

(*e*) Avoid what is called *Commercial English*, which includes certain hackneyed expressions.

(*f*) In letters of application, give such *information* as may enable the reader to assess the capabilities of the writer.

(*g*) It is better to give *particulars* of *qualifications* or certificates of efficiency than to make statements of one's loyalty or willingness, *e.g.* "*I shall be a faithful employee* . . ."

(*h*) The writer should always sign his name in full.

**1. Letter of Application.**

37 Moreland Road,<br>
Glasgow, W. 2,<br>
*1st August*, 193-

Messrs. Brown and Wilson,<br>
94 Bath Street,<br>
Glasgow, C. 1.

Dear Sirs,

In reply to your advertisement in the issue of Tuesday, 31st July, of the *Glasgow Guardian* for an apprentice chartered accountant, I beg to offer myself as a candidate for the post.

I am seventeen years of age, and after seven years' attendance in the primary department of Murray Hill School, entered the Secondary department of Regent Park High School where I have just completed the full course for the Higher Leaving Certificate, having passed in English, French, German and Mathematics on the Higher standard. During the last three years of the Secondary course, I gained three prizes in Mathematics and this session I also gained a prize in English.

I have taken an active share in several school activities, having been for two years a member of the 1st XV of the football team, of which I was secretary during the last season. I have also taken a keen interest in the school debating society.

Mr. Williamson, the headmaster of Regent Park High School and my Form Master, Mr. Macpherson, have kindly consented to act as referees.

I shall be glad to supply any further information either by letter, or personally, should you see fit to grant me an interview.

Yours faithfully,

WILLIAM MARSHALL.

## EXERCISE XII

*Correct* and comment on the errors which you find in the following :—

(*a*) Messrs. John Smith ; p.p. Brown Brothers ; Gents. ; Messrs. William Allen & Sons . . . Dear Sir.

(*b*) Your letter of Monday's date ; Yours of the 14th inst. to hand ; Yours of even date ; Adverting to yours of 5th ult.

(*c*) Hoping for the favour of an early reply ; Thanking you in anticipation ; Please let me know soon if I am to get the post ; If you give me the post you will never regret it.

(*d*) Replying to your favour of the 15th inst., you will be glad to know . . .

(*c*) I am to inform you that you have to kindly remit the amount by to-morrow.

(*f*) In reply to your advert. in last night's paper . . .

## EXERCISE XIII

(*a*) Write a letter to your landlord asking him to carry out specified repairs and improvements in the house.

(*b*) Write a letter to the editor of a local newspaper complaining of some local grievance or nuisance.

(*c*) Write a letter ordering a costume of your own design for a fancy-dress ball. Fix a limit to the cost.

(*d*) Write a letter to your school fellows proposing the foundation of a new school society and giving your ideas for its constitution.

(*e*) Write a letter enquiring for board and lodgings during your holiday.

(*f*) Write a letter to a tradesman regarding repairs at your house, complaining of poor workmanship and high cost.

## Formal Letters.

These are generally invitations to some function, or the replies to such. They are usually written in the third person and are full of pitfalls. The following hints should be noted.

(*a*) Retain the use of the *third person* not only for pronouns but for possessive adjectives and the tenses and auxiliaries of verbs.

(*b*) The letter begins with the *name* of the writer; there is no *signature* and the *address* and *date* are put at the *end*.

No. 1. Formal Letter of Invitation.

Mr. and Mrs. Walker present their compliments to Mr. Donaldson, and request the pleasure of his company at a party on Thursday, November 9, at 7.15 p.m. to celebrate the coming of age of their daughter, Margaret.

Woodville,
Churchill Drive,
Stirling.

R.S.V.P.

### EXERCISE XIV

*Correct* the errors which occur in the following:—

5, John Street,
Glasgow,
*Tuesday*.

(*a*) Dear Sir,

Mr. Smith wishes to inform Mr. Brown that your dog has destroyed some valuable plants in my garden, and if you do not stop this nuisance I have no option but to inform the police who will deal with you as I feel you have long deserved.

Yours faithfully,
JOHN SMITH.

(*b*) I shall have great pleasure in accepting your invitation.

(c)

5 Leith Walk,
Edinburgh,
*Tuesday, 7th.*

Dear Mr. and Mrs. Bruce,

Mr. Allan Young has much pleasure in receiving your kind invitation to dinner but I regret that I shall be unable to accept it as I am going to London on business on that night.

Yours faithfully,
ALLAN YOUNG.

EXERCISE XV (All in *third*-person)

(*a*) An invitation to a dinner.
(*b*) A reply to the above (*a*) accepting.
(*c*) A reply to the above (*a*) declining.
(*d*) An order to a local dealer.
(*e*) A letter of complaint to a farmer whose cattle have strayed into your garden.
(*f*) A letter to a stranger who has threatened you with legal proceedings for some offence.
(*g*) An invitation to a wedding from the parents of the bride.

## Dialogue

Most of us realise that the dramatist depends on dialogue to express his ideas, but it is less fully understood how much all forms of fiction and many other forms of composition depend for their success upon its skilful use. Consider how the novelist and short story writer use it to characterise, to develop the action and to explain past action. Note also that it adds to narrative an interest and vividness that reported speech lacks.

To define dialogue as conversation or talk is not sufficient. Literary dialogue is not merely talk, but talk in character condensing and heightening the talk of real people, by eliminating all superfluous, trivial and irrelevant ideas. At its best, it represents the best talk of clever people at their best moments. Such dialogue is of course the work of experienced writers.

**Treatment.**

(*a*) Use the language of easy, natural *conversation*—that is, simple words instead of pretentious words, and abbreviations such as *I'm*, *can't*, *don't*, instead of *I am*, *cannot*, *do not*, and significant interjections.

(*b*) Use *short* sentences in preference to long ones; long speeches should be avoided.

(*c*) Language and sentences should be *true* to the *character*, *calling* and *social standing* of the speaker, *e.g.* a navvy should not speak like a clergyman. *Colloquialisms*, and even slangy or technical terms, may be introduced cautiously, but only if they reveal the *character* of the speaker.

(*d*) Avoid mere slavish *imitation* in dialogue as a word written carries more weight than one spoken, since the latter is emphasised and illuminated by the facial expressions, gestures or movements of the speaker, who may smile, frown, move about restlessly, etc.

(*e*) Use short *parenthetical* phrases, *e.g.* he *glared menacingly*, he *glanced contemptuously*, etc. This device should not be overworked.

(*f*) Avoid the *excessive* use of explanatory passages linking the speeches of the different characters. This should generally be done by the dialogue.

(*g*) Avoid the needless *repetition* of the colourless phrase, "*he said*." It may be modified by a word or phrase, or be replaced by a more telling verb, thus—*retorted*, *sneered*, *grinned*, etc.

(*h*) *Insert* the *name* of the speaker at intervals and avoid confusion of pronouns by the occasional use of "*the former*," "*the latter*."

**Outline :—**

(i) A *short* descriptive passage indicating the *time*, *place* and *speakers*.

(ii) The dialogue proper on the lines suggested (*a-h*) reaching a definite *crisis* or *turning point* which should control the trend of the dialogue.

(iii) The conclusion should be in the form of some *event* generally more or less unimportant which breaks up the meeting and dialogue in a natural fashion. At times a *sudden* ending may be desired and the less expected the ending, the more striking or exciting the terminating incident.

## EXERCISE XVI

A novel has been described as a "play with the stage directions written out." Continue the following passage on the lines suggested for the first speech. (*The Tempest, Act III, scene* 2.)

*Stephano.* [In drunken good nature.] Tell not me; when the butt is out, we will drink water; [With an emphatic gesture.] not a drop before; therefore bear up and board 'em. [Holding the bottle to Caliban's mouth and speaking with good-natured contempt.] Servant-monster, drink to me!

*Trinculo.* Servant-monster! the folly of this island! They say there's but five upon this isle; we are three of them; if th' other two be brained like us the state totters.

*Ste.* Drink, servant-monster, when I bid thee: thy eyes are almost set in thy head.

*Trin.* Where should they be set else? He were a brave monster indeed, if they were set in his tail.

*Ste.* My man-monster hath drown'd his tongue in sack; for my part the sea cannot drown me; I swam ere I could recover the shore, five and thirty leagues off and on, by this light, thou shalt be my lieutenant, monster, or my standard.

*Trin.* Your lieutenant, if you list; he's no standard, etc.

## EXERCISE XVII

1. Pick out the *word* or *words* which reveal the *mood* of the speaker. State the mood expressed :—

(*a*) The devil damn thee black thou cream-faced loon !
(*b*) Seems, madam ! nay, it is ! I know not " seems."
(*c*) This is no answer, thou unfeeling man,
To excuse the current of thy cruelty.
(*d*) How now, daughter ! what makes that frontlet on ?
Methinks you are too much of late i' the frown.
(*e*) What is't ? a spirit ?
Lord, how it looks about ! Believe me, sir,
It carries a brave form.
(*f*) Alas, poor Richard ! where rode he the whilst ?

## EXERCISE XVIII

1. Write a dialogue between a football player and a cricket player on the merits of their favourite games.
2. Write a dialogue between a coast landlady and a prospective tenant for the holidays.
3. Write a dialogue between one who believes in the good old days and a modernist.
4. Write a dialogue between a highwayman and the occupants of a coach he has stopped.
5. Write a dialogue between a gamekeeper and a " hiker " on the moors in August.
6. Write a dialogue between you and a famous man.
7. Write a dialogue between two cinema " fans " on the relative merits of British and American films.
8. Write a dialogue between a gramophone and a wireless set, on their respective merits.
9. Write a dialogue between a Fascist and a Communist.
10. Write a dialogue between a lover of Dickens and a lover of Scott.
11. Write a dialogue between a cat and a dog on which is the more intelligent.
12. Write a dialogue between a colonial and an intending emigrant.

## Character Sketch or Pen Portrait.

The character sketch or pen portrait, though it is a form of descriptive composition, is important enough to be treated separately. Few of us have a clear mental picture of the people we are in the habit of meeting, and we would find it extremely difficult, perhaps impossible, to describe them to others. It is not enough to say that most people we know are so commonplace that they possess no distinctive features or qualities to stir the memory; rather it is that we do not exercise our powers of observation. Let the reader imagine that one of his closest friends is missing and try to write a useful description. It is almost certain that he will fail to select from memory such significant details as help to individualise his friend. Yet our first assessment of character (which generally determines our attitude to strangers) is based on such vague impressions founded only on looks, impressions that unfortunately we are very unwilling to change. Moreover no permanent valuation is possible without a study of speech and action extending over a lengthy period, and some would say that only a crisis of some kind reveals the fundamental qualities. There are indeed few more salutary, and generally humiliating exercises to test one's powers of observation, to exercise one's descriptive abilities, and to discipline one's judgment, than making character sketches of our closest friends and of ourselves. To secure accuracy of detail, there must be close and faithful observation of the subject; to be effective the writer must select only significant details.

**Treatment**

(*a*) Begin with people you have actually met; next describe living people of whom you have heard or read; then people from history and, finally, imaginary people to be found in works of fiction, etc.

(*b*) Try to recall your mental image of the person concerned by such questions as, Is he tall or short, fat or thin, strong or weak, dark or fair, handsome or plain ? What is the colour of his eyes, hair, etc. ? Has he any physical peculiarities or mannerisms of speech or action ? Does he wear a distinctive dress ? Is he weak or strong-willed, mean or generous, cheerful or gloomy, talkative or taciturn, brave or cowardly, rash or cautious ? On what remarks or actions do you base your opinion of him ? What do his friends and his enemies say of him ? What are his private thoughts ?

(*c*) Let each statement of opinion be illustrated by *reference* or *quotation*.

(*d*) Arrange material according to the following method which is based upon the usual way that we become acquainted with people, and proceeds from the outward *physical* aspects, to the inner *mental* and *moral* qualities.

(1) *Appearance*, (age, build, height, face, eyes, colouring, dress) with special emphasis on what is distinctive.

(2) *Habits*, mental and moral qualities, fully illustrated by reference to speeches and actions of the character under consideration.

(3) *Opinions* held of him by others, both *friends* and *enemies*.

(4) If character in literature, part played in plot.

(5) Your final opinion. This should follow naturally from the ideas of the preceding paragraphs.

(*e*) If the character described is imaginary, or intended to represent a *type*, try to draw material from a *number* of examples and mould them into a consistent picture.

(*f*) The *caricature* method—that is, the emphasising of one or more characteristics, physical or mental, by repetition, is effective, but as this method may lead to a false distortion it should be used with caution.

(*g*) The *outline* method adds unity by an introductory statement of the general impression and method shown under (*d*) may be used to fill in the detail.

(*h*) Make use of ***comparison*** and ***contrast*** with other people.

(*i*) Select words carefully, especially ***adjectives*** and ***verbs*** ; the latter may seem less essential but a proper choice of verbs gives that sense of movement associated with a living person ; a wrong choice produces a still-life portrait.

## EXERCISE XIX

What do you learn of the appearance, dress and qualities of the characters described in the following extracts? Note any other information as to *occupation, past life,* etc. :—

**(*a*) The Artful Dodger.**

"Hallo! my covey! what's the row?"

The boy who addressed this inquiry to the young wayfarer, was about his own age; but one of the queerest-looking boys that Oliver had ever seen. He was a snub-nosed, flat-browed, common-faced boy enough; and as dirty a juvenile as one would wish to see; but he had about him all the airs and manners of a man. He was short for his age; with rather bow-legs, and little, sharp, ugly eyes. His hat was stuck on the top of his head so lightly, that it threatened to fall off every moment—and would have done so, very often, if the wearer had not had a knack of every now and then giving his head a sudden twitch, which brought it back to its old place again. He wore a man's coat, which reached nearly to his heels. He had turned the cuffs back, half-way up his arm, to get his hand out of the sleeves, apparently with the view ultimately of thrusting them into the pockets of his corduroy trousers; for there he kept them. He was, altogether, as roystering and swaggering a young gentleman as ever stood four feet six, or something less, in his bluchers.

*Charles Dickens.*

**(*b*) Beatrix Esmond.**

She was a brown beauty; that is, her eyes, hair, and eyebrows and eyelashes were dark; her hair curling with rich undulations, and waving over her shoulders; but her complexion was as dazzling white as snow in sunshine; except her cheeks, which were a bright red, and her lips, which were of a still deeper crimson. Her mouth and chin, they said, were too large and full, so they might be for a goddess in marble, but not for a woman whose eyes were fire, whose look was love, whose voice was the sweetest low song, whose shape was perfect symmetry, health, decision, activity, whose foot as it planted itself on the ground was firm but flexible, and whose motion, whether rapid or slow, was always perfect grace—agile as a nymph, lofty as a queen—now melting, now imperious, now sarcastic, there was no single movement of hers but was beautiful.

*William Makepeace Thackeray.*

(*c*) Frederick the Great.

The man is not of god-like physiognomy, any more than of imposing stature or costume; close-shut mouth with thin lips, prominent jaws and nose, receding brow, by no means of Olympian height; head, however, is of long form, and has superlative grey in it. Not what is called a beautiful man; nor yet, by all appearance, what is called a happy. On the contrary the face bears evidence of many sorrows, as they are termed, of much hard labour done in this world; and seems to anticipate nothing but more still coming. Quiet stoicism, capable enough of what joy there were but not expecting any worth mention; great unconscious and some conscious pride, well tempered with a cheery mockery of humour, are written on that old face, which carries its chin well forward, in spite of the slight stoop about the neck; snuffy nose, rather flung into the air, under its old cocked hat, like an old snuffy lion on the watch; and such a pair of eyes as no man, or lion, or lynx of that century bore elsewhere.

*Thomas Carlyle.*

(*d*) Marmion.

Well by his visage you might know
He was a stalworth Knight, and keen,
And had in many a battle been;
The scar on his brown cheek revealed
A token true of Bosworth field;
His eyebrow dark, and eye of fire,
Showed spirit proud, and prompt to ire:
Yet lines of thought upon his cheek
Did deep design and counsel speak.
His forehead, by his casque worn bare,
His thick moustache, and curly hair,
Coal-black, and grizzled here and there,
    But more through toil than age;
His square-turned joints, and strength of limb,
Showed him no carpet knight so trim,
But in close fight a champion grim,
    In camps a leader sage.

*Sir Walter Scott.*

(*e*) **Staff Nurse.**

Experienced ease
And antique liveliness and ponderous grace;
The sweet old roses of her sunken face;
The depth and malice of her sly, grey eyes;
The broad Scots tongue that flatters, scolds, defies,
The thick Scots wit that fells you like a mace.
These thirty years has she been nursing here,
Some of them under Syme, her hero still.
Much is she worth, and even more is made of her.
Patients and students hold her very dear.
The doctors love her, tease her, use her skill.
They say "The Chief" himself is half-afraid of her.

*William Ernest Henley.*

(*f*) **Achitophel.**

A fiery soul which, working out its way,
Fretted the pigmy body to decay,
And o'er-informed the tenement of clay,
A daring pilot in extremity,
Pleased with the danger, when the waves went high
He sought the storms; but for a calm unfit,
Would steer too nigh the sands to boast his wit.
Great wits are sure to madness near allied,
And thin partitions do their bounds divide.
Else why should he, with wealth and honour blest,
Refuse his age the needful hours of rest?
Punish a body which he could not please;
Bankrupt of life, yet prodigal of ease?

*John Dryden.*

(*g*) **Macbeth.**

*Sergeant.* For brave Macbeth—well he deserves that name—
Disdaining fortune with his brandish'd steel,
Which smoked with bloody execution,
Like valour's minion carved out his passage
Till he faced the slave.

*Macbeth.* If chance will have me king, why chance may crown me
Without my stir.

*Duncan.* True, worthy Banquo; he is full so valiant,
And in his commendation I am fed.

*Lady Macbeth.* I do fear thy nature;
It is too full o' the milk of human kindness
To catch the nearest way; thou would'st be great;
Art not without ambition, but without
The illness should attend it

*Macbeth.* I dare do all that may become a man
Who dares do more is none.
*Macduff.* Not in the legions
Of horrid hell can come a devil more damn'd
In evils to top Macbeth.
*Macbeth.* Blow wind! come wrack!
At least we'll die with harness on our back.

*Shakespeare.*

(*h*) Falstaff.

*Prince.* Death hath not struck so fat a deer to-day
Though many dearer in this bloody fray.

*Falstaff* (accused of running away from the Prince).
Thou know'st I am as valiant as Hercules; but beware instinct; the lion will not touch the true prince.

*Falstaff* (accused of robbing the hostess).
Thou seest I have more flesh than another man, and therefore more frailty.

*Falstaff* (who has pretended to be dead).
The better part of valour is discretion; in the which better part I have saved my life.

*Hostess* (whom he has often cheated).
Well fare thee well; I have known thee these twenty-nine years come peascod time; but an honester and truer-hearted man—well, fare thee well.

*Falstaff* (an old man).
Bacon-fed knaves! they hate us youth.
I am not only witty but the cause that wit is in other men. *Shakespeare.*

(*i*) Viola (disguised as a man).

*Duke.* They shall yet belie thy happy years,
That say thou art a man; Diana's lip
Is not more smooth and rubious.

*Malvolio* (of Viola). Not yet old enough for a man, nor young enough for a boy; as a squash is before 'tis a peascod . . . he is very well-favoured and he speaks very shrewishly.

*Sir Andrew.* That youth's a rare courtier.

*Viola.* I am one that had rather go with sir priest than sir knight.

*Viola* (challenged to a duel). Pray God defend me! A little thing would make me tell them how much I lack of a man.

*Viola.* I hate ingratitude more in a man
Than lying vainness. *Shakespeare.*

## EXERCISE XX

Write character sketches of the following :—

1. A young brother or sister.
2. People (at least three) I meet in the bus or car.
3. Boys who don't play games.
4. A film hero or heroine or villain.
5. A pavement artist.
6. The "funny-man" of the class.
7. An old boat-hirer.
8. Who is it? Describe a member of your class without giving his name.
9. Any famous character in fiction or drama.
10. A great historical character.
11. The clown in the pantomime.
12. Your mental picture of your favourite broadcaster.
13. People who nag.
14. A football enthusiast.
15. A night watchman.
16. My pet aversion.

## EXERCISE XXI

**Write a Short Essay on the following :—**

1. A Country Twilight Scene ; or, A Country Walk.
2. The Advantages of Travel.
3. Summer and Winter Amusements.
4. A Walk by the Seashore.
5. Your Favourite Hero or Heroine in Fiction.
6. Your Favourite Hero or Heroine in History.
7. A Sea Voyage.
8. The Pleasures and Uses of a Garden ; or, Wild Flowers.
9. A Storm.
10. School Friends.
11. The Seasons.
12. A Visit to a Cathedral or some Historic Building.
13. Reading.
14. The Use and Abuse of Novels.
15. The Influence of Music.
16. The Biography of some Famous Statesman, Warrior, or King.
17. The Advantages of Colonies.
18. Imperial Federation.

19. True and False Patriotism.
20. Courage, Moral and Physical.
21. The Characteristics of a Good Biography.
22. Conscription.
23. A British Academy.
24. Rural Depopulation : its Cause and Cure.
25. Free Libraries.
26. Education.
27. Newspapers.
28. Free Trade and Protection.
29. A State Theatre.
30. "Sweet are the Uses of Adversity."
31. The Place of Modern Languages in the School Curriculum
32. The Education of Women.
33. National Peculiarities and Prejudices.
34. Competition.
35. Arbitration.
36. The Decimal System in Weights and Coins.
37. The French Revolution and its Influence upon Britain.
38. "Procrastination is the Thief of Time."
39. The Effects of Wealth on a Nation.
40. The Women of Shakespeare—Which You Prefer and Why?
41. Public Opinion.
42. Party Government : its Advantages and Disadvantages
43. Thrift.
44. The Power of Habit.
45. The Growth of Empires.
46. Wit and Humour.
47. Your Favourite Poem.
48. The Effects of Invention on the Nation.
49. Character.
50. The Tyranny of Fashion.
51. A British Zollverein or Customs Union.
52. The Influence of Sea Power on History.
53. Gambling and its Influence on Athletics.
54. The Effect of City Life on Character.
55. Books.
56. "Wisdom is better than Riches."
57. Poetry—its Influence on the Life of a Nation.
58. The Geographical Conditions that have the Greatest Effect upon Commerce.
59. Byron's and Scott's romantic poems.
60. "Every great poet is a teacher."
61. The principal humorous creations of Shakespeare or Scott, or Dickens or Thackeray.

62. The History of the Drama or Novel.
63. The Division of Labour.
64. The Study of History.
65. Peace and War.
66. The Characteristics of the Nineteenth Century.
67. The Leading Factors in the Formation of Character.
68. The modern craze for Speed.
69. Thoughts on Armistice Day.
70. The advantages and disadvantages of Boarding Schools.
71. Should we have a State-Supported Theatre ?
72. Books I have read more than once.
73. "Happiness depends on temperament more than on surroundings."—*Goldsmith*.
74. What use has Britain made of her natural advantages ?
75. Should Hospitals be supported by the State or by Voluntary Contributions ?
76. A Holiday spent at a Farm.
77. Our Public Parks.
78. The Lure of the Sea.
79. Suitable Occupations for a Rainy Day.
80. School Friendships.
81. A Night Out of Doors.
82. The qualities of Character required to make an ideal School Captain.
83. Changes made in Rural Scotland through the use of the Motor Car.
84. How Schools could be improved.
85. The advantages of being a Member of the School Debating Society.
86. My opinion of Compulsory Training.
87. Which Foreign Country are you most interested in and why ?
88. Our Climate.
89. My Suggestions for an Evening Wireless Programme.
90. Shorts *versus* Plus-Fours.
91. "We look before and after<br>And pine for what is not."
92. Is Comfort the end of Science ?
93. The Evils of Party Government in Municipal and National Administration.
94. An Address to an audience condemning Blood Sports.
95. Chemical Discoveries are both a Boon and a Curse to Mankind.
96. Your Ideal Schoolmaster.
97. A Fire at Sea.
98. November in a large city.

99. Early Navigators.
100. My best Friend.
101. You are left in charge of your Aunt's Shop for a day; describe your Experiences.
102. A Day in the Life of a Policeman.
103. A Jumble Sale.
104. My Dog.
105. "Peace hath her Victories no less renowned than War."
106. Which do you prefer—the Theatre or the Picture House?
107. People I dislike.
108. "The good old days."
109. Reading in Bed.
110. Aunts and Uncles.
111. Lost in the Fog.
112. Scotland's possibilities as a Holiday Centre.
113. A Wet Day in Camp.
114. Discuss the Statement:—"The Master of the Sea is no longer the Master of the World."
115. The Career I should like to follow.
116. Even in these enlightened days Superstition is by no means dead.
117. Are attempts to conquer Mount Everest worth while?
118. Faces in a crowd.
119. My Dream-Room.
120. Roman Remains in Scotland or England.
121. Life's little ironies.
122. The Charm of old things.
123. National characteristics.
124. Spirit of Adventure in the 20th Century.
125. Musings in Glencoe, Iona, Westminster Abbey (etc.).
126. "Long glories of the Winter Moon."
127. On being alone.
128. The Clyde's Busy Day. (Or other river.)
129. Natural Beauties of Scotland and their preservation.
130. Scott Country or Burns Country or Lake District or Hardy's Wessex.
131. "The trouble about miracles is—they happen."
132. "Only the busy man finds time."
133. "The backbone of a Nation is the middle-class on the rise."
134. "A thing of beauty is a joy for ever."
135. "To understand all is to forgive all."
136. "One crowded hour of glorious life<br>Is worth an age without a name."
137. "There is a tide in the affairs of men<br>Which, taken at the flood, leads on to fortune."

138. "East is east and west is west,
And never the twain shall meet."
139. The pen is mightier than the sword.
140. "A man's reach should exceed his grasp."
141. The world becomes smaller every day.
142. Reading is a lost art.
143. Education should fit us for our leisure.
144. Live dangerously.
145. To form habits is to fail.
146. "The old order changeth, yielding place to new."
147. This little world.
148. Dress is an indication of character.
149. The sonnet in English literature.
150. The ballad in English literature.
151. The elegy in English literature.
152. What is a gentleman?
153. Co-education.
154. Do Wireless and Cinema destroy initiative?

---

# CHAPTER VI

# ERRORS IN COMPOSITION

It is widely accepted that the surest method of learning to write good English is to speak carefully and correctly. This, unfortunately, is a counsel of perfection that few of us obey consistently and, as a result, we fall into careless habits of speech which soon creep into our composition where they constitute a serious defect. It is necessary therefore for us to beware of such errors whether in grammar or in style. We shall now consider the various rules which must be observed.

## I.—LAWS OF GRAMMAR

### (*a*) Rules of Agreement

(1) **A Verb** agrees with its subject in number and person:—as "I love, thou lovest, he loves."

(2) A **Composite Subject,** consisting of two or more nouns or pronouns in the singular number, joined by

the conjunction *and*, takes a plural verb :—as "William and Mary *were* sovereigns of England."

(3) A **Composite Subject,** consisting of two or more nouns or pronouns in the singular number, joined by *either—or*, or *neither—nor*, takes a singular verb :—as "Neither teacher nor pupil *was* present."

(4) When a **Composite Subject** consists of two or more nouns or pronouns in different numbers and of different persons, joined by *and*, the verb is in the plural number, and agrees with the first person rather than the second and the second person rather than the third :—as "John and I *were* there."

(5) When a **Composite Subject** consists of two or more nouns or pronouns in different numbers and of different persons, joined by *either—or*, *neither—nor*, the verb agrees with the last noun or pronoun :—as "*Neither* John *nor* you *are* right."

(6) When the **Composite Subject** consists of two singular nouns, joined by *along with*, *as well as*, the verb is in the singular number :—as "Homer, as well as Vergil, was studied on the banks of the Rhine."

(7) When the **Subject** is a Collective Noun or a Distributive Pronoun, or *none*, or *many a*, the verb is in the singular number :—as "*Each loves* the other better than *himself*." "The congregation *was* greatly moved."

(8) **Pronouns** agree in *gender*, *number*, and *person* with the nouns for which they stand. The *Case* of Pronouns depends on their relation to their own clauses :—as "John went to school, although *he* had not prepared *his* lessons." "I, *who have* always helped *you*, *am* still *your* friend."

*Notes.*—i. When a Relative Pronoun has two Nouns or Pronouns of different Persons, either of which might be the Antecedent, it agrees with the Noun or Pronoun on which the greater emphasis is placed :—as "I am a plain blunt man *who loves* his friends," "I am a plain blunt man *who love* my friends," the latter of which is equal to "I am a plain blunt man and I love my friends."

ii. The Relative Pronoun should be placed as close as possible to the Antecedent to prevent ambiguity.

iii. *And who, and which,* should never be used unless preceded by *who* or *which.*

iv. *That* is restrictive and cannot be used when the Antecedent is a Proper Noun.

(9) *This* and *that* agree in Number with the nouns which they qualify :—as "*This* boy" (sing.), "*These* boys" (plur.).

(10) Two **negatives** make an affirmative :—as "*Nor* shall I utter *nothing* more" would mean "I shall utter *something* more."

## EXERCISE I

Re-write the following sentences correctly and explain the error in *each* :—

1. Neither you nor I were there.
2. None of us were present.
3. Here have there always been a faithful remnant.
4. Neither of you have told the truth.
5. Each of them were occupied with their own cares.
6. John as well as James have gone.
7. Many a soldier have been killed.
8. Neither the farmer, nor you, nor I were to blame for this.
9. What work has these men been doing ?
10. The new distribution of parcels are being carried out successfully.
11. Twice one are two.
12. Every man, woman and child have been granted mercy.
13. The farmer as well as the townsman have to be considered.
14. The crowd in the enclosure were quiet and orderly.
15. None of the speakers in the debate have dealt with the most important question.
16. Liquid and solid refreshment is to be supplied.
17. Tell them it is I, who, in your extremity has come to your aid.
18. Keeping a dog chained up makes them very fierce.
19. Everyone have to be the judge of their own actions.
20. Those sort of arguments will never convince me.
21. This is where you and him had the accident.

22. The builder along with the architect have come to help one another to plan the new church.

23. I didn't pay no attention to their rude remarks.

24. He forbade me in angry tones not to trespass on his estate.

25. The answer to the question and which you should have realised long ago is not to be found by dreaming.

### (*b*) The Noun and Pronoun—*Case, etc.*

(1) A **Noun** in the possessive singular is marked by an apostrophe *s* ('s) ; in the possessive plural it is marked by *s* apostrophe (s') :—as "Lady's, ladies'."

*Note.*—i. *Nouns* not monosyllabic the last syllable of which begins and ends with "s," Classical Names, certain idiomatic phrases mark the possessive by an apostrophe only : as Moses' laws, Achilles' heel, for goodness' sake.

ii. Nouns which mark the plural by internal change of vowel have an apostrophe *s* ('s), for both possessive singular and possessive plural :—as "Man's, men's."

(2) When two or more **Nouns** in the possessive case are in apposition, the sign of the possessive is placed after the last word only :—as "In His Majesty the King's name" ; "Messrs. Brown, Jones & Walker's premises."

(3) **Possessive Pronouns** take no apostrophe—"This book is hers," "these books are theirs."

(4) **Nouns or Pronouns** with a following Gerund are in the possessive case :—as "I heard of *his* running away."

(5) *Each other* is used of two persons, *one another* of more than two.

(6) *Each* can be used of *two*, or more than *two* persons ; *one another* is only used of more than *two* :—"Each of the two men has been ransomed" ; "Each of the party is an experienced climber" ; "The members of the class are loyal to one another."

(7) *One* should be followed by *one's*, not *his*, *her*, etc. :—"One should pay attention to one's appearance."

## EXERCISE II

Re-write the following sentences correctly and *explain* the error in *each* :—

1. I remain, your's sincerely.
2. Leave the gardener and I to clear away the rubbish.
3. Who is the damage due to ?
4. Let each choose companions like themselves.
5. Here is the one what did it.
6. Him and his brother, I think should be punished.
7. Let you and I decide what is to be done.
8. The parcel is to be taken to Brown's the baker's shop.
9. The ambition of Macbeth was his Achilles's heel.
10. Two members of the same family should help one another.
11. The girl who this book belongs to is absent to-day.
12. A soldier and scholar play different parts in the life of the country.
13. When one is in a position of responsibility, they should avoid any reckless action.
14. Give the horse it's head and trust to luck.
15. Each of the lads in the class have to be examined.
16. I was delighted to hear of him winning the prize.
17. You must put a mark between each lamp-post to guide us to the hall.
18. It was either a lark or a pewit's nest we found.
19. The crew of the fishing boat, five in all, were very fond of each other.
20. It was him shouting out that betrayed the party.

### (c) The Verb—*Tense, etc.*

(1) **Transitive Verbs** govern the objective case :—as "They brought *him* home."

(2) The **Verbs** *to be, seem, appear, become, remain, grow*, etc., along with passive verbs of *making, naming, appointing, electing, crowning, calling, creating*, etc., take the same case after them as before them :—as "Edward was crowned *king*." *King* is in the nominative case.

(3) *Bid, can, dare, feel, hear, let, make, see, may, must, need, shall, will*, are followed by the infinitive mood without *to* :—as "He bade me *come*."

*Notes.*—i. The past of *ought* and *must* is expressed by a following perfect infinitive :—as " He must go," " He must *have gone* " ; " He ought to go," " He ought *to have gone.*"

ii. Verbs of *expecting, hoping, intending,* etc., are followed by the Present Infinitive, not by the Perfect Infinitive :—as " He intended *to go,*" not " He intended *to have gone.*"

(4) The **Past Participle** and not the Past Tense is used after the auxiliary *have* :—as "I have *begun,*" not "I have *began.*"

(5) A **Present** or **Future Tense** should follow a Present Tense ; a **Past Tense** should follow a Past Tense ; thus :— " He hopes that he *would* arrive in time " ought to be " He hopes that he *will* arrive in time."

(6) **Shall, will.**

(*a*) As Auxiliaries **with the Infinitive to form the** Future Tense use,

*Shall* for the 1st person,
*Will* for the 2nd and 3rd person.
"I *shall* ask," " you *will* ask," " he *will* ask."

*Note.*—For a **Question** *Shall* as well as *Will* may be used in the **Second Person**—

" *Will* (or *shall*) you ask him to come ? "

(*b*) When the idea of *command* or *permission* is intended, these uses are *reversed*—

" I *will* ask him, although he has already refused."
" They *shall* not go without my permission."

(7) The ellipsis of the **Principal Verb** in contracted clauses or in answers, after the auxiliaries *may, can, shall, will, have, be,* is permissible only *when the form understood is the same as the form expressed* :—thus, " *I did not and I do not* **believe** *the report* " is correct, as the same form follows *did* as that which follows *do*. But " *no promotion money has or will* **be** *paid* " is wrong, as we require to supply *been* after *has*.

(8) A **Participle** should qualify the *subject* of the nearest *finite* verb.

"Walking down the street I saw the accident."

*Note*.—Inattention to this rule produces the Unrelated Participle:—as "*Sailing* down the river, the whole town came into view." In syntax *sailing* agrees with *town*, in sense *sailing* agrees with *we* understood. "While we were sailing," etc.

(9) A **Gerund** must be qualified unless it has the same *subject* as the *finite verb*.

"Through *their* being on holiday, the house was easily burgled."

"Through being on holiday they had no knowledge of their loss."

### EXERCISE III

**Re-write** the following sentences correctly and ***explain*** the error in *each*:—

1. He has often went to town for me.
2. We shall drain our dearest veins but they will be free.
3. No writer would write a book unless he thinks it will be read.
4. They have ran a good race.
5. You may do what you have done a year ago.
6. He ought to write his exercise yesterday.
7. I expected to have seen your father but he seems to have gone away early.
8. I would have liked to have invited him to dinner.
9. Did he not tell me his fault and entreated me to forgive him!
10. Two young gentlemen have made the discovery that there was no God.
11. I intended to have cut the grass yesterday.
12. It seemed to be him that they disliked.
13. Trusting you are all well, believe me, etc.
14. He, they elected their leader because of his great courage.
15. I have carefully broke the news to his father.
16. On asking for help, a loud laugh was heard.
17. Turning the corner rapidly, a deep ravine suddenly yawned before them.
18. I, after many weary years, they released and sent home.
19. Being deeply attached to his pets, his house was not always too pleasant to visit.
20. I will come to see you to-morrow, if I may.

### (*d*) The Adjective—*Comparison, etc.*

(1) The **Comparative Degree** of the adjective is used when two things or two sets of things are compared :—as "John is *taller* than James."

*Notes.*—i. Comparatives are generally followed by *than*. Exceptions—*superior, inferior, exterior, interior*. The Comparatives of Latin form and origin are followed by *to*.

ii. The thing compared must be always *excluded* from the class with which it is compared when we use the Comparative Degree :—thus, "*John is taller than any boy in the class*" ought to be "*John is taller than any* other *boy in the class.*"

(2) The **Superlative Degree** of the adjective is used when more than two things are compared :—as "John is the *tallest* boy in the class."

*Note.*—When we use the Superlative Degree the thing compared must be *included* in the class with which the comparison is made :—thus "*John is the tallest of all the* other *boys*" ought to be "*John is the tallest of all the boys.*"

(3) The Articles are repeated before two or more connected nouns or adjectives which apply to different persons or things :—as "*A* white and *a* blue flag" means two flags ; "*A* white and blue flag" means *one* flag.

(4) *Like* is an **adjective,** not a **conjunction** :—as "He was a man *like* you and me."

*Note.*—Do *not do* like *I do but do* like *I tell you* ought to be "*Do not do* as *I do but do* as *I tell you.*"

(5) A **Past Participle** purely *adjectival* in function may be modified by *very*, but when *verbal* in function is modified by *much* :—as "He was *very* tired," but "He was *much* irritated."

### (*e*) The Preposition

(1) A **Preposition** governs the *objective* **case** :—as "*To* whom shall I give this book ?"

(2) *Without*, *except* are **prepositions** and not **conjunctions** :—as "He did this *without* my permission.

(3) *Between* refers to two persons or things; *among* refers to more than two :—as " Divide the apple *between* the twins "; " The Treasure was divided *among* the crew."

### (*f*) The Conjunction

(1) *Whether or not* is used rather than *whether or no.*

(2) *Neither* must be followed by *nor*, *either* by *or*, *not only* by *but also* :—as " *Neither* he *nor* his brother is present "; " *Either* the boy *or* his father must sign the agreement "; " They gave him ***not only*** food ***but also*** shelter."

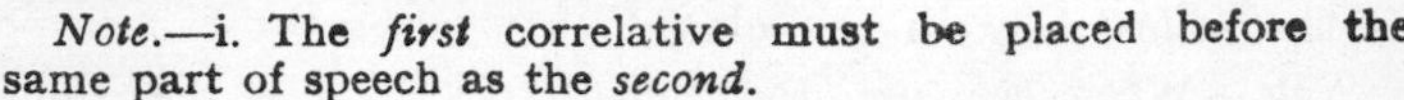

*Note.*—i. The ***first*** correlative **must be** placed **before the** same part of speech as the ***second.***

#### EXERCISE IV

Re-write the following sentences correctly and ***explain*** the error in ***each*** :—

1. We were very limited in our choice of rooms.
2. Of all other men I would have avoided thee.
3. Jim was suddenly confronted with the marooned men.
4. He had less opportunities than most people to educate himself.
5. I can buy it at less than a shilling at least.
6. Who shall I give this valuable article to?
7. Divide it between all the members without you intend to keep it for yourself.
8. The insult is even more gratuitous than I expected
9. You have both done so well that I have decided to divide the prize among you.
10. A boy finds himself at a disadvantage when he is elder than his schoolmates.
11. He is not a favourite of mine but I deny that I have any prejudice to him.
12. He was very averse from accepting what he considered a bribe.
13. He enjoined me not to break the rules of the college again.
14. Many believe him to be the wiser of all the older statesmen.
15. The idea of the extent of the universe is the most infinite we can think of.
16. I cannot concur with the statement you made.

17. You do your exercise much too quick to please me.
18. Firstly, read the passage and secondly, write down what it means.
19. Divide this apple between the four smallest of the children.
20. He is adept at leaping the hurdles.

## EXERCISE V

Correct or Justify the following :—

1. He hoped to have accomplished the work before he left.
2. Looking westward, the scene was a striking one.
3. None of the boys were present.
4. John and I am coming.
5. He has wrote no essay for some time.
6. Everyone likes to hold their own opinions.
7. These kind of people are always despised.
8. That boy is the tallest of the two.
9. She loves me better than him.
10. The two sisters love one another dearly.
11. Whether he comes or no matters little.
12. Whom do men say that I am ?
13. If he had gone to London he will see the king.
14. Will you go to London ?
15. I shall tell him the whole truth that he might not be alarmed.
16. He ought to prepare his lessons yesterday.
17. Thou art the man who has done the deed.
18. I did not hear of you coming till yesterday.
19. In the bestowing favours, care should be taken to offend none.
20. It is me whom he accuses.
21. He died in William's and Mary's reign.
22. A hot and cold spring was found.
23. The father as well as the mother were in the room.
24. Neither he nor I were to blame.
25. Each of them had their reward.
26. He was sent to Paterson's the grocer's.
27. This is the man whom he said was your brother.
28. He is older than me.
29. I know not who to blame.
30. She seems coldly this morning.
31. O Thou who poured the patriot-tide !
32. He obtained his father and his mother's permission.
33. This boy was not attentive to his parents nor his teachers.
34. He wrote to his father that was in America.

35. Please send me a copy of your latest work, and for which I enclose a postal order for five shillings.
36. The number of names together were about one hundred and twenty.
37. I am the Lord that maketh all things: that stretch forth the heavens alone.
38. By this means, they are happy in each other.
39. This noble nation hath, of all others, admitted fewer corruptions.
40. He who is blessed naturally with a good memory, continually exercise it.
41. The climate of Pau is perhaps the most genial of any other spot in France.
42. He was more popular, but not so much respected as his father.
43. They were both fond of one another.
44. A larger circulation than any of the Liberal newspapers.
45. But the problem is one which no research has hitherto solved, and probably never will.
46. There is no use in asking him for he never knows nothing.
47. We were very injured by his sneering comments.
48. Not one of the oranges which he gave us were really ripe.
49. It is a path not easy to follow and which few people know about.
50. Any remission of your sentence is contingent with your good behaviour.

## II.—LAWS OF STYLE

Style depends on (*a*) **the selection of words**; (*b*) **the forms of words**; and (*c*) **the arrangement of words.**

### (*a*) Selection of Words.

The words selected must be: (1) sanctioned by the best writers; (2) used in their proper sense.

(I) A **Barbarism** is the use of a word not found in classic English.

The leading forms of this fault are—

1. The use of **Archaic** or **Obsolete** words:—as *yclad, hight.*

2. The use of **Colloquial, Slang** or **Vulgar Terms**:—as *get even, awfully, rotten, that ugly, step on the gas, doss, boss.*

3. The unnecessary **use of Scientific, Legal** or **Technical Terms** :—as *leitmotif, a complex, epidermis.*

4. The use of foreign words or phrases :—as *café, kudos.*

5. The use of **New Words, Coinages** or **Neologisms** :—as *burglarize, enthuse, merger, pelmanize.*

6. The use of **Scotticisms** :—as *gigot, sort* (arrange), *the cold, canny.*

*Note.*—It must be remembered that the subject matter will determine whether any of the above classes of words may be used or not. In dialogue, for example, it may happen that any of these may be used quite appropriately.

(II) An **Impropriety** is the use of a word in its wrong sense. Impropriety arises from—

1. The use of good English words in a slang sense :—as *tough (of persons), pinch (to steal).*

2. The excessive use of **Ellipsis** in which the correct word cannot be implied from the words given. Thus, "He was as brave or braver than the soldier" ought to be "He was as brave *as* or braver," etc.

*Notes.*—a. This is one of the most common causes of error in English Composition. The best mode of discovering this mistake is to expand the elliptical sentence by supplying the words that are wanting.

b. Note the different uses of the following Prepositions :—

(1) Agree with persons ; to proposals.
(2) Angry with persons ; at things.
(3) Attend upon a person ; to an order.
(4) Call on a person ; for a thing.
(5) Correspond with persons ; to things.
(6) Disappointed in things ; by persons.
(7) Martyr for a cause ; to a disease.
(8) Part from a person ; with a thing.
(9) Reconcile to a person ; with a statement.
(10) Taste (noun) for ; taste (verb) of.
(11) Tired of a thing ; with an action.
(12) Wait for a person or thing ; upon a person only.

(III) Confusion between words closely related in sound (**Malapropism**) or in meaning :—as *discover, invent* ;

*luxury, luxuriance*; *credulous, credible*; *compliment, complement*; *wave, waive*; *whether, whither*; *custom, habit*.

"If there is a child of this marriage, he will be the heir *presumptuous*."

*Note*.—Anachronism (Gk. *ana*, up; and *chronos*, time) is an error in time. By this mistake things are mentioned as if belonging to an age earlier or later than that to which they really belong. Thus Shakespeare makes *the clock strike three* in *Julius Caesar*, and in *Macbeth* he makes reference to *cannon*.

(IV) **Ambiguity** arising from the use of (*a*) **the same word in different senses,** (*b*) **confusion of pronouns,** (*c*) **lack of orderly arrangement** :—as "The love *of* God is beyond all understanding"; "There is a *certain* truth in what you say"; "When he stopped the fugitive, he was amazed at *his* courage."

(V) **Pedantry,** which gives us words of "learned length" for simple words, or general terms for particular terms, or remote allusions for direct statements:—"*Palladium* of our liberties"; *wild beast* for *lion*; the *Maecenas of our day* for *patron of literature*; the *wearer of the strawberry leaf* for *duke*.

*Note*.—The same qualities are often found in what is called **Fine Writing, Johnsonese** or **Journalese.**

## EXERCISE VI

**Re-write** the following sentences in good English **and** ***explain*** the error in *each* :—

1. We have a terrible amount of work to do and very little time to ourselves.
2. This individual declares that you gave him permission to call.
3. Sure, if I reprehend anything in this world, it is the use of of my oracular tongue, and a nice derangement of epitaphs.
4. I am afraid that if he goes on like this, he will meet a sticky end.
5. He was acutely aware of certain well defined effluvia from the open sewer near the hut.
6. The train came to a halt and stood stationary at the platform.

7. I shall be frightfully bucked if you manage to come.

8. My father is well and my mother is quite all right too.

9. We are going home to get our dinner now.

10. The ointment is guaranteed to produce a luxurious growth of hair in a fortnight.

11. Despite its cheapness, the quality of the tea is almost phenomenal.

12. I can offer you three alternatives, one is safe, one is audacious, and the third is cowardly.

13. He is a jolly good player and sure to be capped.

14. I will stop at my cousin's house if I get the chance.

15. You must try and please your father if you can.

16. I am not opposed to democracy, but I detest the *hoi polloi*.

17. No doubt you will mind that, the next time you are tempted to misbehave.

18. The cook also went on strike, and refused to function in the kitchen.

19. The way he has been treating us is too thick and I, for one, refuse to stand for it.

20. There is a something, a *je ne sais quoi* about that tune, which fascinates me.

21. Every civilian is to be issued with a gas mask within the next month or so.

22. The dentist declared that, as he had a shot-out bite, his upper lip would always protrude.

23. That is a very funny question to ask an innocent man.

24. Will you come through to Glasgow and see me on Monday first ?

25. I assume, by your appearance, that you have been in an accident.

26. I spoke to the man, and then waited to see what would transpire.

27. A bazaar is to be held in the course of a month or two in the town hall which the minister is to open.

28. I only had a glass of milk in the morning.

29. The police have orders to prevent excessive speeding through the narrow and tortuous village street which the people dislike very much.

30. He said his brother was prepared, and he had no fears of the test.

31. The meals are certainly appetising, but too fragile to satisfy a hungry man.

32. He soon became notorious for his kindly behaviour in the village.

33. I shall not give you verbal instructions as I think it better for you to have them in writing.

34. His performance on the piano was so brilliant as to be somewhat unique.

35. Forget this fellow; illiterate him from your memory.

36. If you order me from your house, you infer that you think I am the thief.

37. She suits that new hat, I saw the difference on her at once.

38. He has taken the medicine which the doctor has sent with the greatest regularity.

39. He suddenly turned upon the beggar who had been following him in a very threatening manner.

40. It was a nice day and we thought we might have enjoyed a nice game or a nice book at home; we went instead for a nice walk with my cousin who is a very nice man to a nice house which we reached by a nice long avenue which in spite of the morning rain was nice and dry, or my nice new shoes might have been in a nice mess.

### (*b*) The Forms of Words.

The leading faults under this heading are:—

(I) **Solecisms,** or grammatical inaccuracies. These mistakes have been fully considered in the section dealing with the Parts of Speech.

(II) **Redundancy, Verbosity or Wordiness is the use of** unnecessary words and may be classified as follows:—

(*a*) **Tautology,** or the repetition of the *same* meaning in words which are *synonymous*:—as

1. "To all intents and purposes you have answered the question." *Omit "and purposes."*

(*b*) **Pleonasm**—or the repetition of the *same* meaning in words which are *not synonymous*:—as

1. "I am honestly, seriously and unalterably of opinion that nothing can possibly be more incurably and emphatically destructive, or more decisively fatal to a kingdom, than the introduction of thoughtless dissipation and the pomp of lazy luxury."

*Rewrite*: "I am of opinion that nothing is more ruinous to a kingdom than luxury and dissipation."

2. "In the Attic commonwealth it was the privilege and birthright of every citizen and poet to rail aloud and in public."

*Rewrite*: "In the Attic commonwealth it was the privilege of every citizen to rail aloud."

(*c*) **Prolixity**—or the *excessive use of details* :—as "I have parted with the plate myself," said Mrs. Micawber, "Six tea, two salt, and a pair of sugars. I have at different times borrowed money on, in secret, with my own hands."

(*d*) **Circumlocution** or **Periphrasis** is the *talking round* the subject instead of describing it directly and exactly :—as

1. "At no period in the history of mankind has there ever appeared a greater exponent of the glorious art of self-defence."

2. "The ploughman poet, the effulgent luminary of the heavens."

## EXERCISE VII

*Name the error* and *re-write* the sentences in good English :—

1. Bisect the given line into two equal parts.
2. She was in a towering rage and stamped her foot upon the ground.
3. Gradually, step by step, the cunning Uriah gained control of the business.
4. The ornament was cruciform in shape.
5. The boy ran down the stairs two at a time, rushed breathlessly to the booking office, purchased a third-class ticket for the city, and with only a few coppers in his pocket leaped into a crowded compartment, as the train slowly glided from the station with its passengers immersed in their morning papers.
6. A conquered nation cannot but feel such indignities too intolerable to be borne.
7. Boys take great pleasure in football, and generally find it an enjoyable game.
8. The medicine he prescribed is of course not a universal panacea.

9. As a consequence, it follows that we must accept his judgment.

10. This country cannot hope to have the sole monopoly of the African trade.

11. As a rule, he frequently travels in the noon train.

12. We must show our preference whether it be for the ploughman bard, the sweet swan of Avon, the learned sock of Jonson, or the triumphal car of Dryden.

13. He must be permitted to carry on his work without any let or hindrance save and except a formal supervision by his tutor.

14. From the autobiography of his own life, we learn still more about this remarkable man.

15. Personally, speaking for myself, I have no desire to take part in the procession.

16. After sampling the culinary efforts of the cook with gusto, he paid his customary matutinal visit to the tonsorial artist whom he invariably patronised without fail.

17. Simultaneously they broke into a shout at exactly the same moment.

18. His statement may seem far-fetched and extravagant, but it does not lack clearness and lucidity.

19. This fight was a triumph for the British boxer who came out of it with flying colours.

20. He burns the midnight oil night after night, and seems to find ample refreshment in the cup that cheers but not inebriates.

## The Arrangement of Words.

(I) Follow when possible the **normal** order of words, viz. **Subject—Predicate—Object** :—as "The rich should assist the poor."

*Note.*—i. The **complement** follows the *object* if the verb is *transitive* :—

as "They appointed him king."

ii. The **indirect object** when used *without a preposition* precedes the *direct object* :—

as "John gave me the book."

(II) All **qualifying** or **modifying words, phrases** and **clauses** should be placed as *close* as possible to the *words* they *qualify* or *modify* :—as

"When Mr. Chamberlain entered the House, the Members waved their hats *filled with enthusiasm.*"

The last phrase should be placed beside *Members.*

" The emperor was so intent on the establishment of his absolute power in Hungary that he exposed the empire doubly to desolation and ruin *for the sake of it.*" Place the italicised words after *that.*

" It is folly to pretend to arm ourselves against the *accidents* of life, by heaping up treasures *which* nothing can protect us against but the good providence of our Creator." Place *by heaping up treasures* after *pretend.*

" Erected to the memory of John Smith accidentally shot as a mark of affection by his brother." The miscollocation of this last sentence is obvious.

*Note.*—i. Do not split the **infinitive.** *e.g.* You are to once and for all realise that this must stop.

*Re-write* : You are to realise once and for all that this must stop.

(III) **Relative Pronouns** should be placed close to their *antecedents* :—as " The man told me the story whom I met last night."

*Rewrite* : " The man whom I met last night told me the story."

(IV) **Subordinate phrases** and **clauses** should be placed as near as possible to the *beginning* of the sentence :—as " He prepared for the attack, seizing the nearest weapon and hurling back his chair."

*Rewrite* : " Hurling back his chair and seizing the nearest weapon, he prepared for the attack."

(V) Sentences should be completed as they are planned, balancing *word* with *word*, *phrase* with *phrase* and *clause* with *clause.* This should be carefully observed in the use of the *correlatives*, either—or, neither—nor, not only—but also :—as

(i) " He prefers to travel in a stuffy car to tramping in the rain."

(ii) " He not only showed kindness to them but also to their friends."

*Rewrite* :

(i) " He prefers travelling in a stuffy car to tramping in the rain."

(ii) " He showed kindness not only to them but also to their friends."

## EXERCISE VIII

Improve the construction of the following sentences and state what *rules have been broken* :—

1. This medicine should be taken fasting and mixed with an equal quantity of hot water.
2. The girl sat at a very elaborate comptometer with a merry smile.
3. He was anxious to in every way possible assist his less fortunate friends.
4. The two first chapters are the least interesting of the book.
5. The patient was discharged but only came home to die.
6. For sale or exchange, a motor car by a private owner with several spare parts.
7. At that moment, a fanatic fired a shot in the crowd which mortally wounded the prince.
8. He drove away as quickly as possible from the scene of the accident where his best friend had been killed in his car.
9. Boys wanted to sell programmes of smart appearance.
10. It was hardly fair for us to quite lose sight of him after all he had suffered for us.
11. The chair was one of the jealously guarded treasures of a well known dealer that she sat on.
12. I and my friend often pay him a visit.
13. The match was played last night, when younger men were sitting huddled over fires in the steady downpour of a June storm.
14. The politician left the platform at last without a hearing, angry at the constant interruptions of the local worthies.
15. I went down to look at the sea staggering along the streets and holding on by people I met at angry corners.
16. This is the whitest, the purest and the flour that will prove most palatable.

17. The travellers could see an ancient church nestling at the foot of the hill at the door of which stood the aged sexton.

18. I never remember to have experienced such a crushing.

19. He seldom filled the pipe, which he frequently did, without remarking on the quality of the wood.

20. He declared that physical training was good both for body and mind.

21. I was rather surprised by his delivery than by his matter.

22. A prince can never even be certain of his friends.

23. He is as much remarkable for his skill as for his bodily strength.

24. He will not only purchase a house but also a car.

25. The dog is the friend of man but if treated unkindly, he will not do so.

## EXERCISE IX

Correct the following sentences, and *give reasons* for any *alterations* you make :—

1. This generous action greatly increased his former services.

2. Gregory favoured the undertaking, for no other reason than this, that the manager, in countenance, favoured his friend.

3. You must not consider that I am wishing to deteriorate in the slightest degree from the merits of the great and the good man who carried out the treaty.

4. There are principles in man, which ever have, and ever will incline him to offend.

5. When a string of such sentences succeed one another, the effect is disagreeable.

6. The person, who I travelled with, has sold the horse.

7. He is not as diligent and learned as his brother.

8. The first proposal was essentially different and inferior.

9. What can be the reason of the committee having delayed this business.

10. A variety of pleasing objects charm the eye.

11. In him were happily blended true dignity with softness of manners.

12. Not one of them whom thou sees clothed in purple, are completely happy.

13. The variety of the productions of genius, like that of the operations of nature, are without limit.

14. " I am sure I would if I could," agreed both of the literary ladies.

15. The swimmers did not, as was to be expected, lack a numerous or enthusiastic audience.

16. Ninety persons were present embracing the invited guests.

17. To thee the world its present homage pays—
The harvest early, but mature the praise.

18. In unity consists the welfare and security of every society.

19. Never did Atticus succeed better in gaining the universal love and esteem of all men.

20. Theism can only be opposed to Polytheism.

21. One may have an air which proceeds from a just sufficiency and knowledge of the matter before him, which may naturally produce some motions of his head and body which might become the bench better than the bar.

22. Patience and diligence, like faith, removes mountains.

23. In a short time he commenced his career as a shipowner in conjunction with his father, who had risen from being a seaman, to be the captain of his own ship and his uncle.

24. Few of his friends except myself felt aggravated by his absence.

25. He always read Lord Byron's writings as soon as they were published with great avidity.

26. The report of her death originated from her having been despaired of in September.

27. There are many faults in spelling, which neither analogy nor pronunciation justify.

28. Thou who has been a witness of the fact, can give an account of it.

29. Something like what have been here premised, are the conjectures of Dryden.

30. I am happy in the friend which I have long proved.

31. There is not a single view of human nature that is not enough to extinguish the seeds of pride.

32. As for such animals as are mortal or noxious, we have a right to destroy them.

33. I should have been happy to have come, but I am pre-engaged.

34. Few ladies, except Her Majesty, could have made themselves heard.

35. I hoped to procure the original placard which was posted on the walls of Grenoble on that occasion, but which I have been unable to do.

36. From the character of those who you associate with, your own will be estimated.

37. Of whom were the articles bought? Of a mercer; he who resides near the mansion house.

38. Each of them, in their turn, receive the benefits to which they are entitled.

39. Cowper was as indisputably the most virtuous man, as Rousseau the greatest intellectual power.

40. He was very dexterous in smelling out the views and designs of others.

41. He is our mutual benefactor, and deserves our respect and obedience.

42. We have enlarged our family and expenses ; and increased our garden and fruit orchard.

43. Not to exasperate him, I only spoke a very few words.

44. We do those things frequently, which we repent of afterwards.

45. The fear of shame, and desire of approbation, prevent many bad actions.

46. Peter's, John's, and Andrew's occupation, was that of fishermen.

47. I will not for David's thy father's sake.

48. If we alter the situation of any of the words, we shall presently be sensible of the melody suffering.

49. He so much resembled my brother, that, at first sight, I took it to be he.

50. Whom do the people say that we are ?

51. I should be obliged to him, if he will gratify me in that particular.

52. He was greatly heated, and drunk with avidity.

53. Neither riches nor honours, nor no such perishing goods, can satisfy the desires of an immortal spirit.

54. We should entertain no prejudices to simple and rustic persons.

55. The matter was no sooner proposed, but he privately withdrew to consider it.

56. The more I see of his conduct, I like him better.

57. The court of France, or England, was to have been the umpire.

58. No person was ever so perplexed, or sustained the mortifications, as he has done to-day.

59. There are principles in man, which ever have, and ever will incline him to offend.

60. He resembles one of those solitary animals, that has been forced from its forest, to gratify human curiosity.

61. Celia is a vain woman, whom, if we do not flatter, she will be disgusted.

62. To be patient, resigned, and thankful under afflictions and disappointments, demonstrate genuine piety.

63. To despise others on account of their poverty, or to value ourselves for our wealth, are dispositions highly culpable.

64. He charged me with want of resolution, in the which he was greatly mistaken.

65. The great storm wave which passed up the lower Hooghly, is said to have been of the height of a man at a distance of ten miles from the bed of the river.

66. To our mind, it was impossible to entertain any doubt on the subject, at least not since the intimation conveyed by the American Minister.

67. Must I wage war with this race alone for so many years?

68. Common sense is what we want.

69. It will invariably be found to be the case as a rule that when a fine sentiment comes from his pen, it is not his own.

70. Father Mathew in Ireland effected the reform of temperance.

71. Lost: a large Spanish blue gentleman's cloak.

72. His servant being ill, he had consented to allow his brother, a timid youth from the country, to take his place for a short time, and for that short time he was a constant source of annoyance.

73. He preferred to know the worst than to dream the best.

74. They were both agreed in the future not to accept these kind of excuses.

75. If Providence clothe the grass of the field, and shelters and adorns the flowers that everywhere grows wild amongst it, will he not clothe and protect his servants and children much more?

76. The rise and fall of the tides in this place makes a difference of about twelve feet.

77. Entering the drawing-room, the conviction came to him that he was in the dwelling of an individual of refined taste.

78. Not a creature is there that moves, nor a vegetable that grows, but what, when minutely examined, furnished materials of pious admiration

79. He has destroyed his constitution by the very same errors that so many have been destroyed.

80. What is the reason that our language is less refined than those of Italy, Spain, or France?

81. Will martial flames for ever fire thy mind,
And never, never be to Heav'n resigned?

82. The prisoners are allowed to receive food from their friends outside, an indulgence which has been in many instances abused by the secretion of tobacco and written communications in the food sent in.

83. The *Queen*, without exception, is one of the best transport ships afloat.

84. I bridle in my struggling muse with pain,
That longs to launch into a bolder strain.

85. He divided his property between his four sons.

86. That was the universal opinion of all.

87. I saw several dead men riding over the plain.

88. Wellington was not only renowned as a warrior but as a statesman.

89. I wrote in order that you may not be alarmed.

90. The fleet threw shells into the town which did great damage.

91. The sad faces and joyous music formed an incongruous sight.

92. Bacon was the great father and inventor of common sense, as Ceres was of the plough, and Bacchus of intoxication.

93. Hope, the balm of life, darts a ray of light through the thickest gloom.

94. What passes in the hearts of men is generally unknown to the public eye.

95. The ends of a divine and human legislator are vastly different.

96. The French writers of sermons study neatness in laying down their heads.

97. The hand of industry may change, in a few years, the face of a country; but to alter the sentiments and manners of a people, requires often as many generations.

98. While pursuing his avocation, the electric fluid penetrated the unhappy man's person.

99. There is no need to name the copyists, since neither pleasure nor duty is performed in depreciating by comparison.

100. Some years after, being released from prison, by reason of his consummate knowledge of civil law, and of military affairs, he was exalted to the supreme power.

---

# CHAPTER VII

## INTERPRETATION

An important part of most modern examination papers in English consists of interpretation. This forms a most comprehensive test of a candidate's ability to understand a passage, and to render the meaning of it (or parts of it) in his own words. In addition, he is frequently asked to explain allusions, to select passages containing figures of speech, to give the precise meanings of words and phrases as they are used in the passage, to criticise the style and to do any other task, that the examiner can base on the passage, which comes within the scope of English as a school subject.

The first essential is to understand the passage. Read the passage carefully; keep on reading it until you have given yourself an opportunity to understand the meaning thoroughly. **Then, and only then,** should you attempt the answers.

Unless otherwise requested, you should give your meaning of the passage—or parts of it—**in your own words.** This does not mean that you have to avoid using single words that occur in the passage, provided that the words are in general use and likely to be understood at the present time. *e.g.* If the word "imagination" occurs in the passage set, you are entitled to use it in your answer unless you are asked to define the meaning of the word. If the word is unusual, or archaic, or only in limited currency, a substitute in general use should be used.

If the passage set is **in direct speech,** do not turn it into indirect speech unless you are specially requested to do so. Otherwise you are making your task more difficult and you will find yourself awkwardly beginning each sentence with some such words as, "The author states."

When asked to give the meaning of certain words and phrases, first of all write down the words or phrases you are defining and make sure that you give their exact meaning **as they are used in the passage.** Most words have a great variety of meanings and it is essential to choose the one in which it is used in the passage. Substitute the meaning you think the word (or phrase) has for the word (or phrase) in the passage in order to test its correctness.

Remember to answer the questions **in sentences**; exercises in interpretation are also tests in composition.

Sometimes the name of the author is given. You may know something about him from your knowledge of literature, *e.g.* that he lived in the sixteenth century. Here you may have a clue to look for archaic words and constructions. If the name appended is that of Burke or Bright or Pitt, it at least is possible that the passage is from a speech, and your knowledge of the part played by the author in history may help you to a better understanding of the passage.

In Interpretation questions, you should always ensure that you have authority for your answers in the original passage. Do not leave out any meaning that is explicit or implied; and do not add any meaning for which you have no warrant in the original.

On some occasions, you may be asked to summarise or make a précis of the passage. You may be informed of the approximate number of words in which you have to give your summary. If you are given no definite instruction, you will have to use your own judgment, always remembering that your answer should be a précis, *i.e.* an abridged version. It must contain the most important ideas expressed in the passage.

Candidates are frequently asked for derivations of words. Those who study Latin and Greek undoubtedly have the best chance in this question but those who study a modern language, or modern languages, should not despair of gaining some marks. Frequently words asked have prefixes and/or suffixes; if you know their meaning, put them down. If you can derive the word from French, you have a good deal of justification for assuming that the word is from Latin, since French is a Romance tongue. Do what you can with the question. Even although you do not study Latin or Greek, you may know some of the commoner roots and prefixes in these languages, *e.g.* *arch*bishop, *arch*angel—you may at least know that *arch* means *chief*. It is worth while putting down a bit of an answer rather than leave a blank. You will get recognition for whatever you do.

### Example 1

Read the following passage carefully, and then, in your own words, answer simply these questions :—

General propositions respecting the working of climate and physical agencies upon character are indeed treacherous; for our knowledge of the globe is now sufficient to teach us that heat and cold, mountain and plain, sea and land, moist and dry atmosphere, are all *consistent* with the greatest diversities of resident men; moreover, the contrast between the population of Greece itself, for the seven centuries preceding the Christian era, and the Greeks of more modern times, is alone enough to inculcate reserve in such *speculations*. Nevertheless, we may venture to note certain improving influences connected with their geographical position, at a time when they had no books to study, and no more *advanced* predecessors to imitate. We may remark, first, that their position made them at once mountaineers and mariners, thus supplying them with great variety of objects, sensations, and adventures; next, that each petty *community*, nestled apart amid its own rocks, was sufficiently severed from the rest to possess an individual life and *attributes* of its own.

" *History of Greece* "—GROTE.

1. What is the topic discussed in the paragraph ?
2. Give Grote's reasons for distrusting the general propositions he refers to.
3. State clearly the benefits which Grote says came to the Greeks, and explain to what influence he ascribes each benefit.
4. What important improving influences does Grote say the Greeks did not experience ?
5. Give accurately the meanings of the words in italics.

**N.B. All your information should be derived from the passage.**

(1) General statements about the influence of climatic conditions and environment on the character of a people form the topic of discussion.

(2) Our knowledge enables us to state that men of very different types are to be found in countries which vary greatly in climate and in configuration. In addition, the contrast afforded by considering the type of Greek who lived during the seven centuries before Christianity, and the modern Greek, should make us chary of drawing any general conclusions about this influence.

(3) The Greeks, owing to their country being mountainous and sea-girt, were mountaineers and sailors and consequently had a great variety of experiences and opportunities for adventure. Furthermore, since the mountainous nature of their country divided them into small groups of inhabitants, each group had an opportunity to develop an individuality of its own.

(4) They had no books to study; nor any forefathers more learned than themselves.

(5) *Consistent*: in keeping with: existing at the same time as. *Speculations*: general conclusions or theories. *Advanced*: more learned than themselves: more educated. *Community*: a group of people having equal rights. *Attributes*: qualities.

### Example 2

Read the following passage carefully, then answer these questions:—

MILTON'S ATTITUDE TO THE PUBLIC.

Various *ingredients, constitutional or circumstantial,* concurred to produce this repellent or unsympathetic attitude in Milton. His *dogmatic Calvinism,* from the effects of which his mind never recovered—a system which easily disposes to a cynical abasement of our fellow-men—counted for something. Something must be set down to habitual converse with the classics—a converse which tends to impart to character "a certain grandeur and generosity, removed from the spirit of *cabal* and mean cunning which prevail among men of the world." His blindness threw him out of the competition of life, and back upon himself, in a way which was sure to foster egotism. These were constitutional elements of that aloofness from men which characterised all his utterance. These disposing causes became *inexorable fate*, when, by a turn of the political wheel of fortune, he found himself alone amid the mindless dissipation and reckless *materialism* of the Restoration. He felt himself then at war with human society as constituted around him, and was thus driven to withdraw himself within a poetic world of his own creation.

1. Set down, in order, numbering them, the ingredients which caused Milton to be unsympathetic towards his fellow-men: and after each ingredient, state, in one sentence, in your own words, the effect of it on his character.

2. State what is meant in the passage by:—" ingredients constitutional or circumstantial": "dogmatic Calvinism": "cabal": "egotism": "inexorable fate": "materialism."

3. Quote a line from a sonnet by Wordsworth which supports this view of Milton's attitude to the public.

1. The ingredients which caused Milton to be unsympathetic towards his fellow-men were: (*a*) His dogmatic Calvinism. This religious doctrine was prone to make those who believe in it think meanly of others. (*b*) His unremitting study of the classics. This is inclined to influence the character of a man in such a way that he is somewhat aloof from the petty considerations that often occupy men's minds. (*c*) His blindness. This prevented his competing with others who were not blind, throwing him back on his own mental resources and rendering him self-centred.

2. *Ingredients, constitutional or circumstantial*: those component parts of his character which belonged to his nature or those which arose with circumstances.

*Dogmatic Calvinism*: the religious doctrine of John Calvin, the believers in which admitted no other view.

*Cabal*: plotting.

*Egotism*: self-exaltation.

*Inexorable fate*: unalterable destiny.

*Materialism*: condition of living in which matters of the spirit are ignored or neglected.

3. " Thy soul was like a Star, and dwelt apart."

### Example 3

Read the following passage through and then answer the questions *in your own words*.

MR. LLOYD GEORGE AND THE PEACE CONFERENCE AFTER THE GREAT WAR.

One of the most constant traditions of British Diplomacy is that *alliance loses its validity as soon as common victory has been achieved.* In the days when we were still governed by a *territorial aristocracy*, that repudiation (of an alliance) was disguised under the formula of chivalry towards a stricken foe. In 1919 so *palliative* a formula was difficult to proclaim. Chivalry, at such a date, would have been regarded by our Press and public as *reactionary*, " pro-German," high-brow and out-of-date. The balance of power, owing to the mistaken theories of prominent publicists, was not a principle which by then could openly be *invoked*. There was in fact no *popular* principle to which Mr. L. George could at the moment appeal. He decided to appeal to no principle. The tide of tradition pulled him away from France and towards Germany and Russia. *The tide of public opinion was still set against Germany and in the wake of France.* He decided to go in one direction while pretending that he was going in another. He realised that if his right hand were allowed to know what his left hand was doing, his right hand might begin to interfere. He saw that to provoke a conflict of principle would end by provoking parliamentary opposition. He readily concluded that he could only attain his objectives by creeping through *devious* paths. And in so doing, he strayed sadly among the hedgerows, and wasted valuable months of time.

Lord Curzon, at such a *juncture*, should have helped him with historical knowledge, *patrician detachment*, and extended views. He failed to help him. He, also, possessed the traditional British instinct for the balance of continental power. He also realised that it was not a British interest to leave France isolated, and supreme upon the continent. Yet being a man of academic aptitudes rather than of constructive vision—being a historian rather than a man of action—he was seldom able to transmute his knowledge of the past, his analysis of the present, into any proposals for the future. Again and again would Curzon quote *recondite* precedents, and summarise with astonishing mastery the elements as well as the antecedents of the problem before him; yet when asked what future action he suggested, he would lean back in his chair, *petulantly* disconcerted, and gaze with injured indignation at the realist who had dared to advance so material an inquiry.

"*Curzon—the last phase.*"—HAROLD NICOLSON.

(1) With what difficulties was Mr. Lloyd George confronted when he was inclined to support Germany after the War?

(2) What course of action did he decide to adopt to attain his end?

(3) Why is his policy condemned by the writer?

(4) What qualities did Lord Curzon possess which might have helped Mr. Lloyd George in deciding his post-war policy?

(5) Why was Lord Curzon not a very suitable Foreign Secretary to help the Premier in his task?

(6) Give one instance from British history of the truth of the statement "that alliance loses its validity as soon as common victory has been achieved."

(7) Explain and criticise the metaphor in the sentence beginning, "The tide of public opinion, etc."

(8) Give the meaning of the following words and phrases (in italics) as they are used in the passage:—territorial aristocracy; palliative; reactionary; invoked; popular; devious; juncture; patrician detachment; recondite; petulantly.

(9) Give the derivation of four of the following:—territorial: antecedents: reactionary: invoked: popular: transmute: parliamentary: juncture.

1. If Mr. Lloyd George had openly expressed his desire to be lenient towards Germany after the War, the Press and the public would have condemned him as doing something contrary to contemporary opinion. He would have been accused of being in favour of the Germans, of assuming an intellectual attitude superior to that generally held and regarded as out-of-date. He could not claim as support for his attitude that he would be maintaining the balance of power in Europe because this principle had been condemned, mistakenly, by prominent writers on politics. Mr. Lloyd George could

not appeal to any doctrine which would find favour with the public.

2. Since he could get no public support for his lenient attitude towards Germany, he decided to be lenient and yet to appear exacting.

3. His policy is condemned by the writer because in adopting it, he wasted valuable months of time.

4. The qualities which Lord Curzon possessed, which might have helped Mr. Lloyd George, were his knowledge of history, his capacity for judgment apart from personal considerations and his wide knowledge of world affairs. He knew that to leave France isolated and supreme on the continent was not to the advantage of Britain.

5. Since Lord Curzon was more of a student and historian than a man who could suggest constructive proposals, he was not a very suitable Foreign Secretary to help the Premier. He liked to theorise, and was annoyed when asked to make concrete suggestions.

(6) Britain was allied with Austria in the war of the Austrian Succession in 1748. By 1756, in the Seven Years War, Britain was fighting against Austria.

(7) The metaphor is that of the tide (public opinion) running against Germany and helping France, as if Germany and France were vessels, trying to go in opposite directions.

The metaphor is clear and adequate. The point of similarity between public opinion and tide, *i.e.* their ability to help or hinder, is easily discernible. The metaphor is effective and clearly illustrates the meaning the author desires to convey.

(8) *Territorial aristocracy*: a government of people of noble birth who can claim the right to govern because they own land.

*Palliative*: which could afford an excuse for.

*Reactionary*: opposed to the opinion of such as considered themselves progressive.

*Invoked*: appealed to: called upon to aid.

*Popular*: pleasing to the people.

*Devious*: round-about: indirect.

*Juncture*: critical point of time.

*Patrician detachment*: ability to judge with that impartiality characteristic of the Roman Senators.

*Recondite*: abstruse: difficult to comprehend.

*Petulantly*: in a peevish manner.

(9) *Antecedent*: Latin, *ante*—before: *cedere*—to go.

*Invoked*: Latin, *invocare*—to call upon.

*Popular*: Latin, *popularis, populus*—the people.

*Transmute*: Latin, *trans*—across: *mutare*—to change.

**Example 4.**

**Read this sonnet carefully and explain the allusions in it to the life and works of Milton.**

MILTON.

He left the upland lawns and serene air
Wherefrom his soul her noble nurture drew,
And reared his helm among the unquiet crew
Battling beneath; the morning radiance rare
Of his young brow amid the tumult there
Grew grim with sulphurous dust and sanguine dew;
Yet through all soilure they who marked him knew
The signs of his life's dayspring, calm and fair.
But when peace came, peace fouler far than war,
And mirth more dissonant than battle's tone,
He, with a scornful sigh of his clear soul,
Back to his mountain clomb, now bleak and frore,
And with the awful Night he dwelt alone,
In darkness, listening to the thunder's roll.

ERNEST MYERS.

Milton, before the Civil War, spent his time in quiet study and contemplation, his mind taken up with noble thoughts which improved it. After the outbreak of the Civil War he supported the cause of the Commonwealth by writing pamphlets in its favour and, as these pamphlets were often low and abusive, it was degrading work for Milton. Yet, during this pamphleteering war, those who watched Milton closely realised that his purpose in life remained with him.

Peace came, but it was a peace that to Milton seemed worse than the previous years of struggle, as all the ideals he had fought for were lost. The public rejoicing at the Restoration grated on his nerves worse than the noise of battle. He retired to his lofty thoughts, alone and now blind, listening to, but no longer taking part in, the affairs of the world.

### Example 5.

Read carefully the following passage and then answer the questions below :—

By *constitutional law*, the Crown can refuse its assent to any Act of Parliament, and can appoint to office and maintain in it any minister, in opposition to the remonstrances of Parliament. But the *constitutional morality* of the country nullifies these powers, preventing them from being ever used ; and, by requiring that the head of the Administration should always be virtually appointed by the house of Commons, makes that body the real sovereign of the State. These unwritten rules, which limit the use of lawful powers, are, however, only *effectual*, and maintain themselves in existence, on condition of harmonising with the actual distribution of real political strength. There is in every constitution a strongest power—one which would gain the victory if the *compromises* by which the Constitution habitually works were suspended and there came a trial of strength. Constitutional maxims are adhered to, and are practically operative, so long as they give the predominance in the Constitution to that one of the powers which has the preponderance of active powers out of doors. This, in England, is the *popular power*. If, therefore, the legal provisions of the British Constitution, together with the unwritten maxims by which the conduct of the different political authorities is in fact regulated, did not give to the popular element in the Constitution that substantial supremacy over every department of the government which corresponds to its real power in the country, the Constitution would not possess the stability which characterises it; either the laws or the unwritten maxims would soon have to be changed. The British government is thus a representative government in the correct sense of the term; and the powers which it leaves in *hands not directly accountable to the people* can only be considered as precautions which the ruling power is willing should be taken against its own errors. J. S. Mill.

1. What powers does the Crown possess?
2. Why are those powers not used?
3. What is the strongest power in England?
4. What gives the British Constitution stability?
5. Explain accurately what is meant in the passage by these words and phrases: constitutional law; constitutional morality; effectual; compromises; popular power; hands not directly accountable to the people.

1. The Crown possesses the power (*a*) of refusing assent to any Act of Parliament, (*b*) of appointing and maintaining in office any minister even in spite of any objections from Parliament.

2. These powers of the Crown are not used because the legal practice adopted by this country has made them inoperative: the custom has been for the head of the government to be appointed by the House of Commons so that it is really the supreme power of the state.

3. The strongest power in England is that possessed by the people of England (through their voting power).

4. The British Constitution is given stability through the fact that the power of the people is paramount over every department of the government. Such powers as are given to those who are not directly under the power of the people are granted to them voluntarily by the people to safeguard their interests lest they should err.

5. *Constitutional law*: the laws—written and unwritten —by which the country is governed.

*Constitutional morality*: the legal custom or practice used in the governing of the country.

*Effectual*: successful in attaining the desired result.

*Compromises*: settlements of differences by arrangement between parties at variance.

*Popular power*: power possessed by the people.

*Hands not directly accountable to the people*: officials of the government who are not directly or immediately responsible to the people.

### Example 6

Read the following passage carefully and then answer the questions.

Cobden's new position (of commercial traveller) was *peculiarly* suited to the turn of his character. Collecting accounts and soliciting orders for muslins and calicoes gave room in their humble sphere for those high inborn qualities of energy and sociability which in later years produced the most active and the most persuasive of popular statesmen. But what made the life of a traveller so specially welcome to Cobden was the gratification that it offered to the master-passion of his life, an insatiable desire to know the affairs of the world. Famous men, who became his friends in the years to come, agree in the admission that they never knew a man in whom this trait of a sound and rational desire to know and to learn was so strong and so inexhaustible. It was not the curiosity of the *infantile* dabbler in all subjects, *random* and superficial; and yet it was as far removed from the dry parade of the mere *tabulist* and statistician. It was not bookish, for Cobden always felt that much of what is best worth knowing is never written in books. Nor was it the curiosity of a *speculative* understanding; yet, as we shall presently see, there soon grew up in his mind a body of theoretic principles, and a philosophic conception of modern society, round which the knowledge so strenuously sought was habitually grouped, and by which the desire to learn was gradually directed and configured.

MORLEY'S "*Life of Cobden*"

1. Why was Cobden's new position particularly suited to his character?

2. In your own words, describe fully and lucidly Morley's analysis of Cobden's insatiable desire to know the affairs of the world.

3. Give the meaning of the following words as they are used in the passage :—peculiarly ; infantile ; random ; tabulist ; speculative .

1. Cobden had great energy and liked to mix with his fellow-men.

2. His desire to know the affairs of the world was very sane. It was not the childish, shallow interest of one who trifles aimlessly with all subjects : on the other hand it was not merely the interest in facts and figures such as would attract a statistician. His was not the interest of a mere theorist, because Cobden believed that a great deal of knowledge well worth having is not contained in books. His interest in his fellow-men was not exercised only for the purpose of working out theories about society, but through his study of society, he did evolve in his mind certain general principles with which he combined the practical knowledge he had obtained through mixing with his fellow-men.

3. *Peculiarly* : singularly, particularly suitable to him as an individual.

*Infantile* : childish.

*Random* : aimless or haphazard.

*Tabulist* : one interested professionally in tables of facts and figures.

*Speculative* : prone to deduce theories.

## EXERCISES IN INTERPRETATION.

### SECTION 1—Passages suitable for Forms III and IV

1. Read the passage carefully and then answer the questions that follow.

LOCOMOTION.

The chief cause which made the fusion of the different elements of society so imperfect was the extreme difficulty which our ancestors found in passing from place to place. Of all inventions, the alphabet and the printing press alone excepted, those inventions which abridge distance have done most for the civilisation of our species. Every improvement of the means of locomotion benefits mankind morally and intellectually as well as materially, and not only facilitates the interchange of the various productions of nature and art, but tends to remove national and provincial antipathies, and to bind together all the branches of the great human family. In the seventeenth century, the inhabitants of London were, for almost every practical purpose, farther from Reading than they now are from Edinburgh, and farther from Edinburgh than they now are from Vienna.

LORD MACAULAY.

1. Put the first sentence into your own words.
2. What three inventions or groups of inventions have done most for the "civilisation of our species"?
3. How does improved locomotion benefit mankind

 (i) materially, (ii) intellectually?

4. Suggest any unfortunate result of improved locomotion.
5. Derive fully inventions, alphabet, cunning, biology, locomotion, antipathies.

**2. Read the following passage carefully and then answer the questions.**

The better one civilised country is acquainted with another, the more it will find to respect and to imitate. For of all the causes of national hatred, ignorance is the most powerful. When you increase the contact, you remove the ignorance, and thus you diminish the hatred. This is the true *bond of charity*; and it is worth all the lessons which *moralists* and *divines* are able to teach. They have pursued their *vocation* for centuries, without producing the least effect in lessening the frequency of war. But it may be said without the slightest exaggeration, that every new railroad which is laid down, and every fresh steamer which crosses the Channel, are additional guarantees for the preservation of that long and unbroken peace which, during forty years, has knit together the fortunes and the interests of the two most civilised nations of the earth.

1. State *in your own words* all that the writer has to say in support of his theory that "The chief cause of national hatred is ignorance."
2. Why does the author state that "every fresh steamer

which crosses the Channel . . . is worth all the lessons which moralists and divines are able to teach" ?

3. What does the writer mean by :—This is the true bond of charity ; moralists ; divines ; vocation ?

3. Read carefully the following passage, then answer the questions below.

THE AMERICAN INDIAN.

Of the Indian character, much has been written foolishly, and *credulously* believed. By the rhapsodies of poets, the cant of sentimentalists, and the *extravagance* of some who should have known better, a *counterfeit* image has been tricked out, which might seek in vain for its likeness through every corner of the habitable earth. The shadows of his wilderness home, and the darker mantle of his own inscrutable reserve, have made the Indian warrior a wonder and a mystery. Yet to the eye of rational observation, there is nothing unintelligible in him. He is full, it is true, of contradiction. He deems himself the centre of greatness and renown ; his pride is proof against the fiercest torments of fire and steel ; and yet the same man would beg for a dram of whisky, or pick up a crust of bread thrown to him like a dog, from the tent door of a traveller. At one moment, he is wary and cautious to the verge of cowardice ; at the next he abandons himself to a very insanity of recklessness ; and the habitual self-restraint which throws an impenetrable veil over emotion is joined to the wild, *impetuous* passions of a beast or a madman.

PARKMAN.

*The information for 2, 3, 4 should be derived from the passage and expressed in your own words.*

1. How does it come about that the natives (aborigines) of America are called Indians ?

2. What does the writer blame for our having a false idea of the Indian character ?

3. What has made the Indian a mystery to us ?

4. State in your own words what the writer considers to be the true character of the Indian.

5. Give the meanings of the following words as they are used in the passage ; credulously ; extravagance ; counterfeit ; impetuous.

6. Choose a metaphor from the passage and write the words containing it.

4. Read the following poem carefully, then answer the questions below :—

THE IDEAL POPULAR LEADER.

He is one who counts no public toil so hard
As idly glittering pleasures ; one controlled
By no mob's haste; nor swayed by gods of gold
*Prizing*, not courting, all just men's regard ;
With none but Manhood's ancient Order starred,
Nor crowned with titles less *august* and old
Than human greatness ; large-brained, *limpid-souled*
Whom dreams can hurry not, nor doubts retard ;
Born, nurtured of the People ; living still
The People's life ; and though their noblest flower,
In nought removed above them, save alone
In loftier virtue, wisdom, courage, power,
The ampler vision, the serener will,
And the fixed mind to no light dallyings prone.

WM. WATSON.

1. Describe accurately all the qualities with which an Ideal Popular Leader should be endowed. (All the information should be taken from the poem and expressed in your own words.)

2. Give the meanings of the following, as they are used in the poem ; prizing, august, limpid-souled.

3. Choose an illustration of metaphor from the passage and give its literal meaning.

5. Read carefully the following poem and then answer the questions below.

COLERIDGE.

With him there often walked in friendly guise,
Or lay upon the moss by brook or tree,
A noticeable Man with large grey eyes,
And a pale face that seemed undoubtedly
As if a blooming face it ought to be ;
Heavy his low-hung lip did oft appear,
Deprest by weight of *musing Phantasy ;*
*Profound* his forehead was, yet not severe ;
Yet some did think that he had little business *here.*

Sweet heaven *forfend !* his was a lawful right ;
Noisy he was, and gamesome as a boy :
His limbs would toss about him with delight,
Like branches when strong winds the trees annoy.

Nor lacked his calmer hours, device or toy
To banish *listlessness* and irksome care;
He would have taught you how you might employ
Yourself; and many did to him repair,—
And certes not in vain, he had inventions rare.

*Expedients* too of simplest sorts he tried:
Long blades of grass, plucked round him as he lay,
Made, to his ear attentively applied,
A pipe in which the wind would deftly play;
*Glasses* he had, that little things display,
The beetle *panoplied* in gems and gold,
A mailed angel on a battle-day;
The mysteries that cups of flowers unfold,
And all the gorgeous sights that fairies do behold.

WORDSWORTH.

1. Note that "a noticeable Man" (line 3) is Coleridge.
In your own words give the impression you get of Coleridge from Wordsworth's description (remember "impression" includes appearance and the kind of man he was).

2. Explain, accurately, the meaning of the following words as they are used in the passage:—musing Phantasy; profound; here; forfend; listlessness; expedients; glasses; panoplied.

3. Write out the words from the poem that contain an example of simile; metaphor; personification.

6. Read this passage carefully, and answer the questions that follow it:—

THE RIDER AT THE GATE.

(A ghostly messenger demands to speak with Cæsar.)

"Speak your word," said the guard at the gate;
"Yes, but bear it to Cæsar straight;
Say, 'Your murderers' knives are *honing*,
Your killers' gang is lying in wait.'

"Out of the wind that is blowing and moaning,
Through the city palace and the country *loaning*
I cry, 'For the world's sake, Cæsar, beware,
And take this warning as my atoning.'

"'Beware of the court, of the palace stair,
Of the downcast friend who speaks so fair,
Keep from the Senate, for Death is going
On many men's feet to meet you there.'

"I, who am dead, have ways of knowing,
Of the *crop of death* that *the quick* are sowing,
I, who was Pompey, cry it aloud,
From the dark of death, from the wind blowing.

"I, who was Pompey, once so proud,
Now I lie in the sand *without a shroud*,
I cry to Cæsar out of my pain,
'Cæsar, beware, your death is vowed.'"

The light grew grey on the window-pane,
The windcocks swung in a burst of rain,
The window of Cæsar flung unshuttered,
The horse-hoofs died into wind again.

Cæsar turned in his bed and muttered,
With a struggle for breath the lamp-flame *guttered*,
Calpurnia heard her husband moan:
"The house is falling,
The *beaten men come into their own*."

MASEFIELD.

1. What warning does the messenger send to Cæsar?
2. Of what is Cæsar to beware?
3. Who is the messenger? What does he say of himself?
4. What sounds are heard in the early morning?
5. What suggests that it is all a dream?
6. Give the meaning of the following words and phrases as used in the passage:—

   honing; loaning; the crop of death; the quick; without a shroud; guttered; the beaten men come into their own.

7. Give two examples of antithesis.
8. Make a general analysis of the fifth stanza.

7. Read this passage carefully and **then answer the** questions which follow it:—

The Highlanders, in particular, are masters of this difficult trade of driving, which seems to suit them as well as the *trade of war*. It affords exercise for all their habits of *patient endurance and active exertion*. They are required to know perfectly the drove-roads, which lie over the wildest tracts of the country, and to avoid as much as possible the highways which distress the feet of the bullocks, and the *turnpikes*, which annoy the spirit of the drover; whereas, on the broad green or grey track, which leads across the pathless moor, the herd not only moves at ease and without taxation, but, if they mind their business, may pick up a mouthful of food by the way. At night, the drovers usually sleep along with their cattle, let the weather be what it will; and many of these hardy men do not once rest under a roof during a journey on foot from Lochaber to Lincolnshire. They are paid very highly, for the trust reposed is *of the last importance*, as it depends on their *prudence*, *vigilance*, and *honesty*, whether the cattle reach the final market in good order, and afford a profit to the grazier.

SCOTT.

1. What physical qualities make the Highlanders good drovers?
2. Enumerate the advantages of the drove-roads over the highways.
3. Why do the turnpikes annoy the spirit of the drover?
4. What proof is given that the drovers are hardy men?
5. What moral qualities must the successful drover possess? What depends upon them?
6. Give the meaning of the following words or phrases as used in the passage:—trade of war; patient endurance and active exertion; turnpikes; of the last importance; prudence, vigilance and honesty; grazier.
7. Make a general analysis of the sentence:—

"At night........................it will."

8. Read the passage carefully and **then answer the** questions that follow:—

Matthiolus notices the *incombustibility* of this wood; but it is known that the larch timber will resist water in a still stronger degree than it is able to endure the fire; as, when employed under water, it remains almost to eternity without rotting The *piles* of this timber on which the houses of Venice were built many hundred years ago are still found as fresh as when first put in. Dr. Pallas discovered several *tumuli* in *Kamchatka* reared at a remote period, of which the mound of earth was raised upon platforms of larch wood, which wood was found to be *uncorrupted*. It is said, moreover, that planks of larch are superior to those of oak for many purposes in shipbuilding, especially in the lighter parts of the upper works, but not where many pieces of timber are required, on account of its weight. On account of its bitter nature, worms will not attack it, and it is not subject to *warp* like most other panels of wood; it is therefore particularly adapted for artists to paint on The artist not only finds his palette and his panels in the larch, but this tree also *bleeds freely* to furnish him with turpentine and varnish for his paint, and lends its assistance also in furnishing a material for the frame.

1. What two illustrations are given to prove that larch does not rot rapidly?
2. Enumerate, without illustration, the merits claimed for the wood of the larch;
3. What defect is there in larch as a timber for ship-building?
4. Why is larch wood suitable for making panels on which to paint?
5. Explain the words and phrases italicised.
6. Analyse into clauses :—" It is known . . . fire."

9. Read the passage carefully and then answer the questions that follow :—

Night is a *dead monotonous period* under a roof; in the open world it passes lightly, with its stars and dews and perfumes. The man who sleeps afield can hear Nature breathing deeply and freely, but even as she takes her rest, she turns and smiles; for there is one stirring hour unknown to those who dwell in houses, when a wakeful influence goes abroad over the *sleeping hemisphere*. It is then that cattle awake on the meadows, cocks crow, and houseless men who have lain down with the fowls, open their dim eyes and behold the beauty of the night. At what *inaudible summons* are all those sleepers thus recalled in the same hour to life? Even shepherds have not a guess as to the purpose of this nightly resurrection; towards two in the morning it takes place. It is pleasant to reflect that we have escaped out of the *Bastille of civilisation* and have become temporarily a *kindly animal of Nature's flock*. When that hour came to me among the pines, there was no sound save the indescribable quiet talk of the runnel over the stones.

(*Abbreviated from " Travels with a Donkey "*) STEVENSON.

1. This paragraph may be divided into (*i*) theme or subject (*ii*) illustration of theme, (*iii*) thought arising from illustration, (*iv*) author's final comment. Show these divisions by quoting the first and last word of each section.
2. Explain the words and phrases italicised.
3. Quote examples to show how the author has personified nature.
4. Write the meaning of the passage in your own words, reducing the length by a half.
5. Derive as many as you can :—influence, hemisphere, inaudible, resurrection, reflect, civilisation, temporarily, animal, indescribable.

**10. Read the passage carefully and then answer the questions that follow :—**

" My Lords ! His Majesty's Government are the *trustees* of the British Empire. That empire was formed by the enterprise of your ancestors. No Cæsar ever presided over a dominion so *peculiar*. Its flag floats on many waters ; it has provinces in every zone which are inhabited by persons of different races, religions, laws, manners and customs. Some of these are bound to us by ties of loyalty, fully conscious that without their connection with this *metropolis*, they have no security for public freedom; others are bound by flesh and blood ; millions are bound to us by our military sway to which they bow because they know they are indebted to it for justice. All these *communities* agree in recognising the commanding spirit of these islands. That empire is no mean *heritage*, it can only be maintained by the same qualities as created it—by courage, discipline, patience, determination and by a *respect for national rights*."

1. To whom was this speech addressed ?
2. What three types of British possessions are mentioned ?
3. Explain the words or phrases italicised.
4. Write a significant sentence on " Its flag floats on many waters."
5. Derive as many as you can :—empire, dominion, inhabited, metropolis, security, indebted, courage, discipline, patience.
6. Analyse into clauses—" Millions are bound to us........ for justice."

## SECTION 2—Passages suitable for Forms IV and V

1. Read the passage carefully and then answer the questions that follow.

Dr. Johnson shows the need for commenting on the difficulties of Shakespeare's works:—

It is to be lamented, that such a writer should want a commentary ; that his language should become obsolete, or his sentiments obscure. But it is vain to carry wishes beyond the condition of human things ; *that which must happen to all, has happened to Shakespeare, by accident and time* ; *and more than has been suffered by any other writer* since the use of types, *has been suffered by him through his own negligence of fame, or perhaps by that superiority of mind, which despised its own performances, when it compared them with its powers,* and judged those works unworthy to be preserved, which the criticks of following ages were to contend for the fame of restoring and explaining.

Among *these candidates of inferior fame,* I am now to stand the judgment of the publick and wish that I could confidently produce my commentary as equal to the encouragement which I have had the honour of receiving. Every work of this kind is by its nature deficient, and I should feel little solicitude about the sentence, were it to be pronounced only by the skilful and the learned.

1. Why has the need for a commentary on Shakespeare's works arisen?

2. Contrast the points of view of Shakespeare and his critics towards his plays.

3. What is Johnson's opinion of his commentary and what will be his attitude towards any criticism of it?

4. Explain "since the use of types", "these candidates of inferior fame."

5. Give general Analysis of passage from "that which must happen"...... to "powers."

**2. Read the following passage carefully and then answer the questions below :—**

The division of the English Parliament into two parties originally grew up on account of a very real division of opinion concerning the powers to be assigned to the monarch. The issues of that conflict have long been settled, but the arrangement by which the government is always confronted by His Majesty's Opposition has become fixed. Every question must be made a party-matter, even although it is one which demands *impartial scientific treatment.* The House of Commons is nowadays concerned chiefly with highly complicated social and economic problems, yet it retains the methods that were effective only when discussion dealt mainly with broad matters of principle and *the routine business of supply.* Moreover, the influence of the existing institution is so strong that *political theorists* argue that it should be perpetuated. They tell us that in actual practice, no better means of conducting public affairs can be devised. In other words, we are asked to acquiesce in a system that repels the best minds, that is failing more and more conspicuously to arouse the interest of the masses ; and that degrades practical politics to a wretched business of manœuvring for position, of gambling on election chances, and of pursuing always the second best and *the expedient.* In this way *the prestige* of a long tradition cramps our thinking and prevents us from even attempting to devise machinery by which public questions can be raised from the mire of party-bickering to the plane of scientific discussion.

ALDERTON PINK.

1. Why was Parliament originally divided into two parties?

2. Why should it not continue to be so divided?

3. Enumerate all the evils which, the author states, result from a continuation of the original division in modern times.

4. Explain accurately the meaning of the following as they are used in the passage: "impartial scientific treatment"; "the routine business of supply"; "political theorists"; "the expedient"; "prestige."

5. Choose a metaphor from the passage and criticise its appropriateness.

3. Read carefully the following passage and then answer the questions that follow.

### COBDEN AS ORATOR.

Though he abounded in matter, Cobden can hardly be described as copious. He is neat and pointed, nor is his argument ever left *unclenched*; but he permits himself no large excursions. What he was thinking of was the matter immediately in hand, the audience before his eyes, the point that would tell best then and there, and would be most likely to remain in men's recollections. For such purposes, copiousness is ill-fitted; that is for the stately leisure of the pulpit. Cobden's task was to leave in his hearer's mind a compact answer to each current *fallacy*, and to *scotch* or kill as many protectionist *sophisms* as possible within the given time. What is remarkable is that while he kept close to the matter and substance of his case, and resorted comparatively little to *sarcasm, humour, invective, pathos*, or the other elements that are catalogued in manuals of rhetoric, yet no speaker was ever farther removed from prosiness, or came into more real and sympathetic contact with his audience. His speaking was thoroughly business-like, and yet it was never dull. It was not, according to the old definition of oratory, *reason fused in passion*, but reason fused by the warmth of personal geniality. No one has ever reached Cobden's pitch of success as a platform speaker, with a style that seldom went beyond the vigorous and animated conversation of a bright and companionable spirit. MORLEY'S "*Life of Cobden.*"

1. Describe accurately, in your own words, the style of Cobden's oratory.

2. "Sarcasm, humour, invective, pathos." Define each of these in one sentence. If possible, state where an illustration of each of these qualities may be found in speeches which you have read in Shakespeare's plays.

3. Give the meaning of—unclenched, fallacy, scotch, sophisms.

4. Write a paragraph giving your opinion of "the old definition of oratory, reason fused in passion."

4. Read carefully the following passage and answer the questions below :—

"Promise was that I
Should Israel from Philistian *yoke* deliver!
Ask for this great deliverer now, and find him
Eyeless in Gaza, at the mill with slaves,
Himself in bonds under Philistian yoke.
Yet stay; let me not rashly call in doubt
*Divine prediction*. What if all foretold
Had been fulfilled but through mine own default?
Whom have I to complain of but myself,
Who this high gift of strength committed to me,
In what part lodged, how easily bereft me,
Under the seal of silence could not keep,
But weakly to a woman must reveal it,
O'ercome with *importunity* and tears?
O *impotence* of mind in body strong!
But what is strength without a double share
Of wisdom? Vast, unwieldy, burdensome,
*Proudly secure*, yet liable to fall
By weakest subtleties; not made to rule,
But to subserve where wisdom bears command.
God, when he gave me strength, to show *withal*
How slight the gift was, hung it in my hair."

SAMSON AGONISTES.

1. Give the meaning of the passage in your own words. (Keep in direct speech.)
2. Give a general analysis of lines 9-14 inclusive. (Whom have . . . and tears?)
3. Give the exact meaning of the following words and phrases as they are used in the passage: yoke; divine prediction; but (line 8); importunity; impotence; proudly secure; withal.
4. Comment on Milton's use of cæsura and enjambment in this passage.

5. Read this passage carefully, and then answer the questions that follow it :—

Studies serve for delight, for ornament, and for ability. Their chief use for delight, is in privateness and retiring; for ornament, is in discourse; and for ability, is in the judgment and disposition of business; for expert men can execute, and perhaps judge of particulars one by one; but the general counsels, and the plots and marshallings of affairs come best from those that are learned. To spend too much time, is sloth; to use them too much for ornament, is affectation; to make judgment wholly by their rules, is the humour of a scholar; they perfect nature, and are perfected by experience; for natural abilities are like natural plants, that need pruning by study; and studies themselves do give forth directions too much at large, except they be bounded in by experience. Crafty men condemn studies; simple men admire them, and wise men use them; for they teach not their own use; but that is a wisdom without them and above them, won by observation. Read not to contradict and confute, nor to believe and take for granted, nor to find talk and discourse, but to weigh and consider. Some books are to be tasted, others to be swallowed, and some few to be chewed and digested; that is, some books are to be read only in parts; others to be read but not curiously; and some few to be read wholly, and with diligence and attention. BACON.

1. What are the three ends of study? Express in your own words.

2. These three ends easily lend themselves to abuse. In what ways?

3. What are the different attitudes to study, of crafty men, simple men and wise men?

4. "Some books are to be tasted . . . chewed and digested." Express this sentence in your own words.

5. Give the derivation of the following :—ornament, particulars, affectation, contradict, attention.

6. Privateness, humour, curiously. What do these words mean as used here? What is the modern meaning of each?

6. Read this passage carefully and then answer, from it, the questions which follow :—

In natural courage and intelligence both the nations which now became connected with England ranked high. In perseverance, *in self-command, in forethought*, in all the virtues which conduce to success in life, the Scots have never been surpassed. The Irish, on the other hand, were distinguished by qualities which tend to make men interesting rather than prosperous. They were an *ardent and impetuous race*, easily moved to tears or to laughter, to fury or to love. Alone among the nations of Northern Europe they had the *susceptibility*, the vivacity, the *natural turn for acting and rhetoric*, which are *indigenous* on the shores of the Mediterranean Sea. In mental cultivation Scotland had an *indisputable superiority*. Though that kingdom was then the poorest in Christendom, it already vied in every branch of learning with the most favoured countries. Scotsmen, whose dwelling and whose food was as wretched as those of the Icelanders of our time, wrote Latin verse with more than the delicacy of Vida, and made discoveries in science which would have added to the renown of Galileo. MACAULAY.

1. What qualities did both nations possess?

2. State three qualities which are likely to promote success in life.

3. Give one adjective to describe the races dwelling on the shores of the Mediterranean (not Mediterranean).

4. What are the qualities which distinguish such races?

5. What two statements illustrate the poverty of the Scots?

6. How does Macaulay illustrate the mental superiority of the Scots?

7. Give the meaning of the following words or phrases as used in the passage: in self-command, in forethought: ardent and impetuous race; susceptibility; natural turn for acting and rhetoric; indigenous; indisputable superiority.

8. Give one example of antithesis, inversion.

7. Read this passage carefully and then answer the questions which follow it :—

Whatever reproach may, at a later period, have been justly thrown on the indolence and luxury of religious orders, it was surely good that, in an age of *ignorance* and violence, there should be quiet cloisters and gardens in which the arts of peace could be safely cultivated, in which gentle and contemplative natures could find an asylum, in which one brother could employ himself in transcribing the Aeneid of Vergil, and another in meditating the Analytics of Aristotle, in which he that had a genius for art might *illuminate* a martyrology or carve a crucifix, and in which he who had a turn for natural philosophy might make experiments on the properties of plants and minerals. Had no such retreats been scattered here and there, among the huts of a miserable peasantry, and the castles of a ferocious *aristocracy*, European society would have consisted of beasts of burden and beasts of prey. The Church has many times been compared by divines to the ark of which we read in the Book of Genesis; but never was the resemblance more perfect than during that evil time when she alone rode, amid darkness and tempest, on the deluge beneath which all the great works of ancient power and wisdom lay entombed, bearing within her that feeble germ from which a second and more glorious *civilisation* was to spring. BUCKLE.

1. To what period of European history does this passage refer? Express in your own words the picture of the condition of the people.

2. State briefly what purpose the religious orders served in the community, noting the arts they studied.

3. What were the religious orders referred to?

4. Give the meanings of—cloister, asylum, martyrology. Who were Vergil and Aristotle?

5. What charge was made against the religious orders at a later date?

6. Explain the metaphor of the last sentence.

7. Give three examples of antithesis.

8. Give the derivation of the following:—ignorance, illuminate, aristocracy, civilisation.

## 8. Read the passage carefully and then answer the questions that follow:—

DISRAELI'S SPEECH TO HIS CONSTITUENTS, *May 9th*, 1843.

"There is no phrase more *glibly* used in the present day than "the barbarism of the feudal system." Now, what is the fundamental principle of the feudal system, gentlemen? It is that the *tenure* of all property shall be the performance of its duties. Why, when the conqueror carved out parts and introduced the feudal system, he said to the *recipient*, 'You shall have that estate, but you shall do something for it: you shall feed the poor; you shall endow the church; you shall defend the land in case of war; you shall execute justice and maintain truth to the poor for nothing.' It is all very well to talk of the barbarities of the feudal system and to tell us that in those days when it flourished, a great variety of gross and grotesque circumstances and great miseries occurred; but these were not the result of the feudal system: they were the result of the barbarism of the age. The principle of the feudal system, was the noblest principle, the grandest, the most magnificent and benevolent that was ever conceived by sage, or ever practised by patriot. Why, when I hear a *political economist*, or an *Anti-Corn-Law Leaguer*, or some conceited Liberal reviewer come forward and tell us, as a grand discovery of modern science—*twitting* and taunting, perhaps some unhappy squire who cannot respond to the alleged discovery—when I hear them say, as a great discovery of modern science, that 'Property has its duties as well as its rights,' my answer is that that is but a feeble *plagiarism* of the very principle of that feudal system which you are always reviling."

1. In what points of diction and style does a speech (oratory) differ from an essay (exposition)? Illustrate by examples drawn from this passage.

2. Explain fully Disraeli's definition of "the fundamental principle" of the feudal system.

3. Give the substance of this passage (about 100 words) in indirect or reported speech. Begin—"Disraeli said to his constituents in May, 1843, that . . ."

4. Give the meaning of the following words and insert, where you can, their root meaning—glibly, tenure, recipient, political economist, Anti-Corn-Law Leaguer, twitting, plagiarism.

9. Read the passage carefully and then answer the questions that follow:—

"THE ROAD MENDERS."

How solitary gleams the lamp-lit street
Waiting the far-off morn!
How softly from the unresting city blows
The murmur borne
Down this deserted way!
Dim loiterers pass home *with stealthy feet*;
Now only, *sudden at their interval*,
*The lofty chimes awaken* and let fall
*Deep thrills of ordered sound*;
*Subsiding* echoes gradually drowned
In a great stillness, that creeps around,
And darkly grows
Profounder over all
Like a strong frost, hushing a stormy day.
But who is this, that by the brazier red,
Encamped in his rude hut,
With many a sack about his shoulder spread
Watches with eyes unshut?
The burning brazier flushes his old face,
Illuminating the old thoughts in his eyes.
Surely the Night doth to her secrecies
Admit him, and the watching stars *attune*
To their high patience, who so lightly seems
To bear the weight of many thousand dreams,
(Dark hosts around him sleeping numberless);
He surely hath unbuilt all walls of thought
To reach an air-wide wisdom, past access
Of us who labour in the *noisy noon*,
The noon that knows him not.

L. BINYON.

1. Write the rhyme scheme of the first fourteen lines.

2. Collect the word-pictures and the sound-pictures in the above lines and write two short descriptive paragraphs, one on each.

3. Explain the phrases italicised.

4. Express in your own words the thoughts of the last nine lines, beginning "Surely the night . . ."

5. Quote from the passage one example of each—simile, metaphor, personification, metonymy, rhetorical question, onomatopœia.

## 10. Read the passage carefully and then answer the questions that follow :—

He stood *confessed* a botanist—he had the large green cylindrical can of the tribe, oval in section and hung by a strap from the shoulder, like the *traditional* vivandière cask in French art. He was also, I found while we smoked through that evening together, a good fellow. He had, too, a good leg, if one only. The other was stiff and unbendable at the knee. He had broken it last year, he said, and the bones seem to have set only too *hard*, or else Nature had gracelessly grudged to the mended knee-joint of her lover a proper supply of whatever substitute she uses for *ball*-bearings.

His name was Darwin. "*No relation, really*," he humbly assured me. . . . One lure alone had drawn him to these out-works of Snowdon. Some *eccentric* flower grew on these heights, and a blank page in one of his books of squashed specimens ached for it. Was it so lovely ? I asked, like a goose. He was too gentle to snub me. But all that fellow's thoughts shone out through his face. Every flower that blew—to this effect did his soul mildly rebuke mine—was beauteous *beyond Helen's eyes*. All he said was : "No, not fair, perhaps, to outward view as many roses be ; but, just think !—it grows on no patch of ground in the world but these *crags* !"

From "*Fiery Particles*," by C. E. MONTAGUE.

1. On what enterprise was the botanist bent and how was he handicapped ? Why was the enterprise so important to him ? Write a character sketch of such a person in half a dozen lines.

2. Quote one or two phrases to show that the author does not wholly share the enthusiasm of Darwin. What adjectives might be used to express this attitude ?

3. Annotate the phrases in italics.

4. Does the prose style of this passage suggest the date of its composition ?

5. Parse "confessed," "hard," "ball," "relation," "crags."

## SECTION III

The following passages are suitable for Form V.

1. Read the following passage carefully and then answer the questions below :—

J. S. MILL ON "THE EXTENSION OF THE SUFFRAGE."

It may, perhaps, be said, that a constitution which gives equal influence, man for man, to the most and to the least instructed, is nevertheless *conducive* to progress, because the appeals constantly made to the less instructed classes, the exercise given to their mental powers, and the exertions which the more instructed are obliged to make for enlightening their judgment and ridding them of errors and prejudices, are powerful stimulants to their advance in intelligence. That this most desirable effect really attends the admission of the less educated classes to some, and even to a large share of power, I admit, and have already strenuously maintained. But theory and experience alike prove that a counter current sets in when they are made the possessors of all power. Those who are supreme over everything, whether they be One, or Few, or Many, have no longer need of the arms of reason : they can make their *mere* will prevail ; and those who cannot be resisted are usually far too well satisfied with their own opinions to be willing to change them, to listen without impatience to any one who tells them that they are in the wrong. The position which gives the strongest stimulus to the growth of intelligence is that of rising into power, not that of having achieved it ; and of all resting-points, temporary or permanent, in the way to ascendancy, the one which develops the best and highest qualities is the position of those who are strong enough to make reason prevail, but not strong enough to prevail against reason. This is the position in which, according to the principles we have laid down, the rich and the poor, the much and the little educated, and all the other classes and *denominations* which divide society between them, ought as far as practicable to be placed. And by combining this principle with the otherwise just one of allowing superiority of *weight* to superiority of mental qualities, a political constitution would realise that kind of *relative* perfection which is alone *compatible* with the complicated nature of human affairs.

1. Enumerate the powerful stimulants to the advance in intelligence of the less instructed classes.
2. Give reasons why the less instructed classes should not be made possessors of all power.

3. What conditions produce the most intellectually alive government?

4. What are the two principles that should be combined to realise the best type of government?

5. Express, clearly and briefly, in your own words, the meaning of the passage.

6. Give, accurately, the meanings of these words, as they are used in the passage:—conducive; mere; denominations; weight; relative (perfection); compatible.

7. Distinguish between stimulant and stimulus. Are these words correctly used in this passage?

## 2. Read this passage carefully and then answer the questions that follow:—

A portion of mankind may be said to constitute a Nationality if they are united among themselves by common sympathies which do not exist between them and any others—which make them co-operate with each other more willingly than with other people, desire to be under the same government, and desire that it should be government by themselves or a portion of themselves exclusively. This feeling of nationality may have been generated by various causes. Sometimes it is the effect of identity of race and descent. Community of language, and community of religion greatly contribute to it. Geographical limits are one of its causes. *But the strongest of all is identity of political antecedents: the possession of a national history and consequent community of recollections; collective pride and humiliation, pleasure and regret, connected with the same incidents in the past.* None of these circumstances, however, are either indispensable, or necessarily sufficient by themselves. Switzerland has a strong sentiment of nationality, though the cantons are of different races, different languages, and different religions. Sicily has, throughout history, felt itself quite distinct in nationality from Naples, notwithstanding identity of religion, almost identity of language, and a considerable amount of common historical antecedents. The Flemish and the Walloon provinces of Belgium, notwithstanding diversity of race and language, have a much greater feeling of common nationality than the former have with Holland, or the latter with France. On the other hand, identity of language, literature, and, to some extent, of race and recollections, have maintained the feeling of a nationality in considerable strength among the different portions of the German name, though they have at no time been really united under the same government; but the feeling has never reached to making the separate states desire to get rid of their autonomy.

1. Divide this paragraph into three sub-paragraphs. Give the subject of each.

2. What, in your own words, does the author understand by "nation"?

3. Enumerate the causes of the development of a sense of nationality as detailed in the passage.

4. Explain fully the meaning of the sentence beginning "But the strongest of all . . . ." (lines 11 to 15). Illustrate from Scottish or English history the truth of each point dealt with in the latter part of the sentence (collective pride, etc.).

5. Can this passage be dated from the historical reference?

**3. Read this passage carefully and then answer the questions that follow:—**

The Englishmen in the Middle East could be divided into two classes. Class one, *subtle and insinuating*, caught the characteristics of the people above him, their speech, their *convention of thought*, almost their manner. He directed men secretly, guiding them as he would. In such *frictionless* habit of influence, his own nature lay hid, unnoticed.

Class two, *the John Bull of the books*, became *the more rampantly English* the longer he was away from England. He invented an Old Country for himself, a home of all remembered virtues, so splendid in the distance that, on return, he often found a sad falling off and withdrew his muddle-headed self into *fractious advocacy of the good old times*. Abroad, through his armoured certainty, he was a rounded sample of our traits. He showed the complete Englishman. There was friction in his track and his direction was less smooth than that of the intellectual type; yet his stout example *cut wider swathes*.

Both sorts took the same direction. Each assumed the Englishman a chosen being, inimitable, and the copying of him *blasphemous* or *impertinent*. In this conceit they urged on the people the next best thing. God had not given them to be English; a duty remained for them to be good of their type.

Consequently we admired native customs; studied the language; wrote books about their architecture, *folklore*, and dyeing industries. Then one day we woke up to find this national spirit turned political, and shook our heads with sorrow over its ungrateful *nationalism*—truly the fine flower of our innocent efforts.

The French, though they started with a similar doctrine of

the Frenchman as the perfection of mankind, went on, contrarily, to encourage their subjects to imitate them; since, even if they could never attain the true level, yet their virtue would be greater as they approached it. We looked upon imitation as a *parody*, they as a compliment.

"*Seven Pillars of Wisdom.*"

1. Where is the Middle East?

2. What, according to the passage, is the attitude of (*a*) Englishmen, (*b*) Frenchmen to the people of the Middle East? Which type do you consider would make the more successful administrator? Why?

3. Explain the phrases in italics.

4. Write antonyms for advocacy, admired, native, similar, encourage.

5. Make a grammatical analysis of the last paragraph as far as "approached it."

6. Select an example of metaphor, antithesis, irony.

4. Read the following passage carefully and then answer the questions below:—

No *unbiassed* observer, who derives pleasure from the welfare of his species, can fail to consider the long and uninterruptedly increasing prosperity of England as the most beautiful *phenomenon* in the history of mankind. Climates more *propitious* may impart more largely the mere enjoyments of existence; but in no other region have the benefits that political institutions can confer been *diffused* over so extended a population; nor have any people so well reconciled the discordant elements of wealth, order, and liberty. These advantages are surely not owing to the soil of this island, nor to the latitude in which it is placed; but to the spirit of its laws, from which, through various means, the characteristic independence and industriousness of our nation have been derived. The constitution, therefore, of England must be to *inquisitive* men of all countries, far more than to ourselves, an object of superior interest; distinguished, especially as it is from all free governments of powerful nations which history has recorded, by its manifesting, after the lapse of several centuries, not merely no symptom of irretrievable decay, but a more expansive energy. Comparing long periods of time, it may be justly asserted that the administration of government has progressively become more equitable, and the privileges of the subject more secure; and though it would be both *presumptuous* and unwise to express an unlimited confidence as to *the durability of liberties, which owe their greatest security to the constant suspicion of the people*, yet, if we calmly reflect on the present aspect of this country, it will probably appear that whatever perils may threaten our constitution are rather from circumstances altogether unconnected with it than from any *intrinsic* defects of its own. It will be the object of the ensuing chapter to trace the gradual formation of this system of government. Such an investigation, impartially conducted, will detect errors diametrically opposite; those intended to impose on the populace, which, on account of their *palpable* absurdity and the ill faith with which they are usually proposed, I have seldom thought it worth while to repel; and those which better informed persons are apt to entertain, caught from *transient* reading, and the misrepresentations of late historians, but easily refuted by the genuine testimony of ancient times. H. HALLAM.

1. To what does the writer principally attribute the prosperity of the English people?
2. What is a remarkable feature of the constitution of England?
3. Explain what is meant by the statement, "durability of liberties which owe their greatest security to the constant suspicion of the people?
4. Describe fully the two types of errors diametrically opposite which the author proposes to deal with.
5. What do you understand by the constitution of England?
6. Show that "unbiassed" is really a decayed metaphor.
7. Give the meaning of "inquisitive" as it is used in the passage; give its more usual meaning.
8. Give the meaning of each of the following as it is used in the passage: phenomenon; propitious; diffused; presumptuous; intrinsic; palpable; transient.

5. Read the following passage and then answer the questions that follow :—

In 1834 Macaulay was sent out to India as the first legal member of the Council of India. He drew up the Indian *Penal Code*, and he persuaded the Indian government to adopt English instead of any oriental language as the medium of instruction in the scheme of state-aided higher education. The present position of India and the possibilities of its future have been deeply *affected by* this decision.

On the one hand, the bringing up of *orientals* on an alien literature, largely devoted to the love of liberty in forms natural to an advanced Western democracy, has had many unhappy results. It has been said that "we attempted to raise a race of administrators on the literature of revolt." Another class of critic has pointed out that the contempt expressed by Macaulay for oriental learning was in large measure the result of ignorance and want of imaginative sympathy.

It must be remembered on the other side, that only the English language was capable of giving the races of India a common tongue for communication with each other and with the British. And it is arguable that, in spite of present dangers, the sense of Indian national unity which has resulted from this new '*lingua franca*' may in the end *subserve* the *political and administrative welfare* of the peninsula. The revival of Indian science, philosophy and literature in our own day is due in no small degree to the Indians' knowledge of the literature and science of Europe.

The teaching of English *has effected* what we may, by *historical analogy*, call the '*renaissance*' of Indian thought. It is at least possible that, although the decision of 1835 has hastened the peculiar troubles of India as we know them, it has prevented the growth of worse trouble that must eventually have arisen from a deliberate policy of *segregating* the British and the Indians in water-tight compartments of thought and knowledge, and endeavouring to prevent the spread of Western science and literature in a country governed by a progressive Western power. Such an attempt would largely have failed. Many natives were determined to obtain the educational key to Western learning both for its own sake, and because it was also the key to advancement in the Anglo-Indian world.

G. M. TREVELYAN.

1. What are the criticisms levelled against Macaulay's policy of making English the language of high schools and universities in India ?

2. What arguments does the author bring forward in defence of Macaulay's action ?

3. What do you understand by the words and phrases in italics ? Give the derivation, if you can, of sympathy ; renaissance ; segregating.

4. Give a grammatical analysis of the sentence in the last paragraph beginning—" It is at least possible. . . ."

## 6. Read this passage carefully, and then answer the questions asked :—

At the time of which we write, statesmen were surrounded by the *incessant* din of *theological controversy*. Opinions were still in a state of *chaotic anarchy*, intermingling, separating, advancing, receding. Sometimes the *stubborn bigotry* of the Conservatives seemed likely to prevail. Then the *impetuous* onset of the Reformers for a moment carried all before it. Then again the resisting mass made a desperate stand, arrested the movement, and forced it slowly back. The vacillation which at that time appeared in English legislation and which it has been the fashion to attribute to the *caprice* and to the power of one or two individuals, was truly a *national vacillation.* It was not only in the mind of Henry that the new theology obtained the *ascendant* one day, and that the lessons of the nurse and of the priest regained their influence on the morrow. It was not only in the House of Tudor, where agreement might have provided an example to the nation, had not the controversy been so violent and fundamental, that dissension and persecution existed. The principles of Conservation and Reform carried on their warfare in every part of society, in every congregation, in every school of learning, round the hearth of every private family, in the recesses of every *reflecting* mind.

MACAULAY.

1. With what particular period in English history does the passage deal?

2. What do you understand by the Conservatives and the Reformers?

3. Using about half the number of words in the passage, express in simple language the meaning conveyed to us by the author.

4. Explain the following phrases :—theological controversy; chaotic anarchy; stubborn bigotry; a national vacillation.

5. Give the meaning of :—incessant; impetuous; caprice; ascendant; reflecting; and the derivation of :—theological; obtain; persecution; congregation; recesses.

6. Why does the author use the expression "the lessons of the nurse and of the priest"?

7. Explain the metaphor used in the fourth and fifth sentences. In what word is the metaphor continued in the last sentence?

8. Give a general analysis of the sentence beginning: "It was not only in the House of Tudor . . ."

## 7. Read the following passage carefully and then answer the questions that follow :—

The doctor whose success blinds public opinion to medical poverty is almost completely demoralised. His promotion means that his practice becomes more and more confined to the *idle rich*. The proper advice for most of their ailments is typified in Abernethy's "Live on sixpence a day and earn it." But here, as at the other end of the scale, the right advice is *neither agreeable nor practicable* and *every hypochondriacal rich lady* or gentleman who can be persuaded that he or she is a lifelong invalid means anything from fifty to five hundred pounds a year for the doctor. Operations enable a surgeon to earn similar sums in a couple of hours; and if the surgeon also keeps a nursing home, he may make considerable profits at the same time by running what is the most expensive type of hotel. These gains are so great that they undo much of the moral advantage which the absence of grinding *pecuniary anxiety* gives the rich doctor over the poor one. It is true that the temptation to prescribe a sham treatment because the real treatment is too dear for either patient or doctor does not exist for the rich doctor. He always has plenty of genuine cases which can afford genuine treatment; and these provide him with enough *sincere scientific professional work* to save him from the *ignorance, obsolescence, and atrophy of scientific conscience* into which his poorer colleagues sink. But on the other hand, his expenses are enormous. Even as a bachelor, he must at London west-end rates make over a thousand a year before he can afford even to insure his life. His house, his servants, and his equipage must be on the scale to which his patients are accustomed, though a couple of rooms with a camp bed in one of them might satisfy his own requirements. Above all, the income which provides for these outgoings stops the moment he himself stops working.

G. B. SHAW.

1. What demoralising influences affect the successful doctor or surgeon?
2. From what disadvantages does the poor doctor suffer?
3. State the disadvantages of the successful doctor or surgeon.
4. Explain briefly the following phrases:—idle rich; neither agreeable nor practicable; every hypochondriacal rich lady; pecuniary anxiety; sincere scientific professional work; ignorance, obsolescence and atrophy of scientific conscience.
5. Give the derivations of—demoralised; promotion; considerable; prescribe; pecuniary; obsolescence.
6. Make a general analysis of the sentence:—"Operations enable . . . kind of hotel."

8. Read the following passage through, and then answer the questions that follow it:—

Scott's mood is not the contemporary mood—at any rate what was recently the contemporary mood. Ever since the beginning of the century, the world has been going through a period of conflict and confusion. It began before the War, but the War and our *subsequent difficulties* intensified the turmoil.

It has been an *age of sceptical disillusionment.* The solid framework of society has seemed to be dissolving, and many of the *secular landmarks of thought* have been removed. This spirit has been at work in every *domain of human activity,* in literature, in politics, in economics, in art, in philosophy, in ethics, in science—most of all, perhaps, in science.

The consequence is that we have been living in an *era of dilapidation and disintegration* ; dilapidation which is the breakdown of shape and line ; disintegration, which means the dissolving of things into minute elements. It has been an age not so much of iconoclasts as of anatomists. Old bonds have been loosened and new ones have yet to be forged. In fiction, in poetry, in statecraft, in conduct, there has been a movement towards reducing life to its elements and remaining content with these elements. This means that we renounce those working conventions which give law and order to human society, and ignore that world under the rule of law which Scott represents.

BUCHAN.

1. Write a suitable title for the passage.
2. State in your own words the attitude of the present generation towards established conditions of society.
3. What changes have taken place in the modern world as a result of this attitude ?
4. With what kind of world was Scott concerned ?
5. Give the meaning of the following phrases :—subsequent difficulties ; age of sceptical disillusionment ; secular landmarks of thought ; domain of human activity ; era of dilapidation and disintegration.
6. Give the meaning (as used in the passage) and the derivation of *five* of the following :—contemporary, conflict, philosophy, consequence, dissolving, iconoclasts, anatomists.
7. Make a general analysis of the sentence :—" The consequence . . . into minute elements."

**9. Read the passage carefully and then answer the questions below :—**

*Integrity* of understanding and *nicety of discernment* were not allotted in a less proportion to Dryden than to Pope. The *rectitude* of Dryden's mind was sufficiently shown by the dismission of his poetical prejudices, and the rejection of unnatural thoughts and *rugged numbers.* But Dryden never desired to apply all the judgment that he had. He wrote, and professed to write, *merely* for the people ; and when he pleased others, he contented himself. He spent no time in struggles to rouse *latent* powers ; he never attempted to make that better which was already good, nor often to mend what he must have known to be faulty. He wrote, as he tells us, with very little *consideration*; when occasion or necessity called upon him, he poured out what the present moment happened to supply, and, when once it had passed the press, ejected it from his mind; for when he had no pecuniary interest, he had no further *solicitude*.

1. Give the meaning of the passage in simple words.

2. Give precisely the meaning of :—integrity; nicety of discernment; rectitude; rugged numbers; merely; latent; consideration; solicitude.

3. Enumerate the chief features of the style in which the passage is written. Who do you think wrote it? Give reasons for your opinion.

10. Read carefully the following passage and then answer the questions below :—

" Powers and Dominions, *Deities of Heaven* !—
For, since no deep within her gulf can hold
Immortal vigour, though oppressed and fallen,
I give not Heaven for lost: from this descent
Celestial Virtues rising will appear
More glorious and more dread than from no fall,
And trust themselves to fear no second fate !—
Me though just right, and the fixed laws of Heaven,
Did first create your leader—next free choice,
With what besides in council or in fight
Hath been achieved of merit—yet this loss,
Thus far at least recovered, hath much more
Established in a safe, unenvied throne,
Yielded with full consent. The happier state
In Heaven, which follows dignity, might draw
Envy from each inferior; but who here
Will envy whom the highest place exposes
Foremost to stand against the Thunderer's aim
Your bulwark, and condemns to greatest share
Of endless pain? Where there is, then, no good
For which to strive, no strife can grow up there
From faction: for none will claim in Hell
Precedence; none whose portion is so small
Of present pain that with ambitious mind
Will covet more! With this advantage, then,
To union and firm faith, and firm accord,
More than can be in Heaven, we now return
To claim our just inheritance of old,

Surer to prosper than prosperity
Could have assured us ; and by what best way,
Whether of open war or covert guile,
We now debate. Who can advise may speak."

1. (*a*) Why does Satan still call his companions " Deities of Heaven."
   (*b*) On what grounds does he claim supremacy in Hell ?
   (*c*) What contrast does he draw between leadership in Heaven and leadership in Hell ?
   (*d*) What encouragement for future success does he offer his legions ?

2. State briefly in the third person the points in Satan's argument.

3. Analyse, generally, from " Where there is then no good . . . Will covet more."

---

# CHAPTER VIII

## DIRECT AND INDIRECT SPEECH

### (Sometimes termed Direct and Indirect Narration)

A speech is said to be *direct* or in *direct narration* when the actual words used by the speaker are put down without any change being made, *e.g.* the words of a character in a play.

*Duke Senior* : Now, my co-mates, and brothers in exile,
Hath not old custom made this life more sweet
Than that of painted pomp ?

When this speech is given indirectly, *i.e.* when it is reported by some one, the words originally spoken are given, but *with some change in construction.*

In Direct Speech, the words spoken are usually preceded by a verb indicating the fact that they are spoken, *e.g. said, remarked, replied,* etc.

The Indirect or Reported form of Duke Senior's words would be :—Duke Senior inquired of his co-mates and brothers in exile if old custom had not made that life more sweet than that of painted pomp.

Unless speeches delivered in public are made by very important people and are of great public concern, they are not given fully or in direct form. The reporter usually alters the original speech by making a précis of it and reporting it indirectly.

**Changes which are necessary when converting direct into indirect narration.**

1. The conjunction **that** is inserted before the reported words.

2. The rules governing sequence of tenses must be observed. Briefly stated these are :—

(*a*) If the *reporting* verb (*said, observed,* etc.) is in the **past** tense, then the verbs that follow must also be in the past tense.

(*b*) If the *reporting* verb (*says, observes,* etc.) is in the **present** or **future** tense, then the verbs that follow may be in any tense.

Examples :—

Direct : He said, "I *am* hungry."
Indirect : He said *that* he *was* hungry.
Direct : He *says*, "I *am* hungry."
Indirect : He *says that* he *is* hungry.
Direct : He *says*, "I *shall be* hungry."
Indirect : He *says that* he *will be* hungry.
Direct : He *will say*, "I *am* hungry."
Indirect : He *will say that* he *is* hungry.

*N.B.*—If the words spoken state *a universal truth* then the present tense is used *even after a reporting verb in the past tense.*

Example :—

Direct : He said, " Two and two make four."

Indirect : He said that two and two *make* four.

As a result of the Sequence Rules, when converting direct into indirect speech, when the reporting verb is in past tense, make the following changes :—

| | |
|---|---|
| *is* into *was* ; | *shall* into *should* ; |
| *are* into *were* ; | *will* into *would* ; |
| *has, have* into *had* ; | *may* into *might* ; |
| | *can* into *could*. |

3. Special attention must be given to *pronouns*, *adjectives* conveying information about position (*e.g.* demonstrative), and *adverbs* of time and place.

Accordingly :—

1*st* and 2*nd* personal pronouns become 3rd person.

*I*, *me* become *he* (*she*), *him* (*her*).

*We*, *us* become *they*, *them*.

*You* becomes *him*, *her*, *they*, *them*.

| **Adjectives.** | **Adverbs.** |
|---|---|
| *this* becomes *that*. | *now* becomes *then*. |
| *these* „ *those*. | *hither* „ *thither*. |
| | *hence* „ *thence*. |
| | *to-day* „ *that day*. |
| | *to-morrow* „ *the next day*. |
| | *yesterday* „ *previous day, day before*. |
| | *ago* „ *before*. |

Words denoting *nearness* in time or place *in direct speech* become words denoting *distance in indirect speech*.

Study the following notes carefully.

1. When changing from indirect to direct speech, special attention must be given to punctuation. The

reporting verb is followed by a comma and then inverted commas enclose the actual words spoken. If a quotation is made within the words spoken, a single set of inverted commas is used; or if a single set of inverted commas is used for the words spoken then a double set is used for the quotation, *e.g.* :—

He remarked, "I definitely heard James say, 'I cannot accept these terms.'"

He remarked, 'I definitely heard James say, "I cannot accept these terms."'

2. The reporting verb, especially when the words spoken are numerous, is best inserted within the words spoken, *e.g.* :—

"After all," he said, "it is not often we are so fortunate. The weather looks like holding, the going is good, we are all in fine fettle, so why not tackle the summit?"

rather than :—

He said, "After all, etc."

3. When reporting questions, use a verb that indicates that a question has been asked, *e.g.* :—

He said, "May I have some water?"

He *inquired* if he might have some water.

Likewise, in dealing with sentences such as follow, indicate by means of the verb you use the emotion or feeling, *e.g.* approval, disapproval, disappointment; commands also must be indicated by the verb used. Exclamations are either omitted or recast in the form of a statement.

Direct: "I am surprised," said James, "that the receipts are so low."

**Indirect:** James expressed surprise that the. etc.

Direct: "You're a fine time keeper!" he said, consulting his watch.

Indirect: Consulting his watch, he ironically complimented him on being a fine time keeper.

Direct: The spectators shouted, "Shot, sir!"

Indirect: The spectators showed their admiration by shouting that it was a capital shot.

Direct: "Give me the duster at once!" said the angry teacher to the pupil.

Indirect: The angry teacher commanded the pupil to give him the duster at once.

4. You should vary your reporting verb to avoid monotony, *e.g.* :—suggested, admitted, replied, affirmed, told, reminded, explained, etc.

5. Try to avoid confusion and ambiguity by making quite clear the identity of the person denoted by your pronoun, *e.g.* :—

Direct: He said, "He will arrive presently."

Indirect: He (the speaker) said that he (name the person referred to) would arrive soon afterwards.

6. Note that sometimes in indirect speech the reporter may, for some special reason, such as emphasis, desire to retain some of the original words; such words are included within inverted commas, *e.g.* :—

Direct: In his evidence at the trial James said, "I assure you that I had nothing to do with the dastardly crime. I can prove that the deed was committed *when I was in my sister's house.*"

Indirect: In his evidence at the trial James assured them that he had nothing to do with the dastardly crime. He actually stated that he could prove the deed was committed "*when I was in my sister's house.*"

## EXERCISES

Convert the following passages into indirect speech :—

1. " Am I not taller," he asked, " than I was several years ago ? "

2. " We shall depart now," he remarks, with a touch of disappointment in his voice. " I am sorry to-morrow comes so soon."

3. " This house," he said, pointing at it with his stick, " is now an eyesore. It seems but yesterday that this was open country, unspoiled by man's interference."

4. " Are you going out again to-night ? " he stormed at his daughter. " If you persist in this stupid conduct, you can depart hence and your parents will not break their hearts."

5. He remarked to me, " I am so pleased you are going to be able to come to-morrow."

6. He said to her, " You are too proud. Give me your promise to obey me at once and I'll not tell your father."

7. *Goldsmith* : " I think, Mr. Johnson, you don't go near the theatres now. You give yourself no more concern about a new play, than if you had never had anything to do with the stage."

*Johnson* : " Why, Sir, our tastes greatly alter. The lad does not care for the child's rattle. But as we advance in the journey of life we drop some of the things which have pleased us : whether it be that we are fatigued and don't choose to carry so many things any farther, or that we find other things which we like better."

8. " In the present situation of affairs, His Majesty thinks it indispensably necessary to make a further augmentation of his forces by sea and land, for maintaining the security and rights of his dominions, for supporting his allies, and for opposing views of aggrandisement and ambition on the part of France."

9. " But what is the constitutional state of the question ? It is competent, undoubtedly, to any gentleman to make the character of an ally the subject of consideration : but in this case it is not to the Emperor of Russia we vote a subsidy, but to his Majesty."

10. Neither cousin spoke for a minute or two. At last Amyas—
" Well, Cousin Hide-and-seek, how long have you added horse-stealing to your other trades ? "

" My dear Amyas," said Eustace very meekly, " I may surely go into an inn stable without intending to steal what is in it."

"Of course, old fellow," said Amyas mollified, "I was only in jest. But what brings you here? Not prudence certainly."

"I am bound to know no prudence save for the Lord's work."

11. *Lord Dufferin*: "All ready, sir!"

*Wilson* to Doctor (*sotto voce*): "Sir!"

*Doctor*: "Eh?"

*Wilson*: "Do you know, Sir?"

*Doctor*: "What?"

*Wilson*: "Oh, nothing, Sir;—only we're going to the hicy regions, Sir, ain't we? Well, I've just seen that ere brig as is come from there, Sir, and they say there's a precious lot of ice this year! [Pause.] Do you know, Sir, the skipper showed me the bows of his vessel, Sir? She's got seven feet of solid timber in her for'ard: *we've* only two inches, Sir!" [Dives below.]

*Voice of French Captain* (with a slight accent): "Are you ready?"

*Lord Dufferin*: "Ay, ay, Sir! Up anchor!"

Convert the following indirect statements into direct speech:—

1. He admitted that he ought not to have failed in his examination the previous week.

2. They said to him that they were greatly disappointed in his report from school the previous term.

3. He assured them that his sister was honest and that she would justify their faith in her when she returned.

4. Alcibiades told Tissaphernes to say to the Peloponnesians that the Athenians, whose maritime experience was of an older date than their own, only gave their men three obols, not so much from poverty as to prevent their seamen being corrupted by being too well off, and injuring their condition by spending money upon enervating indulgences, and also paid their crews irregularly in order to have a security against their deserting in the arrears which they would leave behind them. He also told Tissaphernes to bribe the captains and generals of the cities, and so to obtain their connivance—an expedient which succeeded with all except the Syracusans, Hermocrates alone opposing him on behalf of the whole confederacy.

5. The whole situation, said Mr. Lansbury, referring to the Central European position, had arisen because of the folly of those who broke up systems in the peace treaties and took no care to deal with what they must have known would be the results.

He was no apologist for Hitler. He thought a crime had been committed in the invasion of Austria, but if France and Britain, when there was a Republican Government in Germany and in Austria, had allowed the union to take place Hitler might never have come into power.

They could have been assisted then, and there would have been a strong, powerful, democratic Germany instead of a dictatorship. One could not do evil without reaping the results of evil.

6. Moving the resolution, Dr. T——, Glasgow University, said they were opposed to war of every description whether engaged in by the League of Nations or through an alliance of peace-loving nations. An engagement of that kind would in no way resemble police action on an international scale, because what would happen would be that the innocent would suffer and the guilty escape.

---

# CHAPTER IX

## PRÉCIS

The writing of a précis forms a very important test in many examinations, and, whether it is required for a certain examination or not, it gives practice in a great many things that a student of English ought to be able to do.

### WHAT IS A PRÉCIS ?

**1.** A précis ought to be shorter than the original passage—usually about *one third* of it.

(Often you are given a definite number of words to aim at ; do not exceed the number.)

A **Summary** is usually very much shorter than a précis.

**2.** A précis should contain the most important points in an argument, debate, narrative, description, series of letters or despatches. That which is subsidiary should be left out.

3. A précis should be coherent and intelligible. (Remember it should be *coherent and intelligible to one who has not read the original.*)

4. A précis should be written in your own words, *i.e.* in simple words (*original words may be retained for official arguments, speeches. etc.*).

5. A précis should be a piece of good composition, written usually in the past tense and in the third person.

Let us examine each of these requirements in turn.

1 and 2. Since a précis must be shorter than the original passage, condensation must take place. This necessitates the ability to discriminate between the essential and the unessential in meaning. This discrimination can be exercised *only after reading the original passage very carefully several times.* Retain what you consider important and essential, leave out what is subsidiary in your précis.

This process of condensation must also apply to the **expression** of the thought, as the original passage is expressed too fully for our purpose. Comparisons and illustrations should either be omitted or, where significant, brought together in one sentence. A catalogue of similar ideas may be summarised in a general statement. Having got rid of the unessential in the *thought,* we must express the essential meaning *in concise terms.* Accordingly, all verbose, tautological constructions, and all circumlocutions must be ruthlessly cut out. The exercise of a judicious economy of words is necessary.

3. The thought of your précis should be *connected,* leaving no gaps. Aim at brevity and precision, but do not omit connecting words or give a series of disjointed statements. Try to bring related ideas into one sentence but avoid excessively long sentences. The test you should apply to your own précis is this :—" Would some

one, who has not the time to study the original passage, get all the essential meaning of the original from my précis?" We are often inclined to think that what is clear to ourselves must necessarily be clear to others.

4. Your précis should be "in your own words." Here a difficulty occurs. If the diction of the original passage is simple and current, then you are entitled to keep original words in your version. But although you may use the actual words of the passage, you will require to alter the expression of them, *i.e.* the composition of the original.

5. Remember that when making a précis you cannot throw overboard the laws that apply to composition. It should be free from all faults in writing.

## SOME GENERAL HINTS.

The number of words in the original passage may be found by jotting down the total in each line in the right-hand margin and adding; alternatively, by counting the words in a few lines, taking the average, and multiplying it by the total number of lines.

Read over the passage carefully, and sum up the general impression in a short and comprehensive title. This is often asked, and, in any case, is invaluable for forcing you to grasp the meaning.

Underline or jot down on a sheet of paper what you consider the essential thoughts, *using your own concise choice of words*. Remember that the principal clauses of sentences, the topic sentences of paragraphs, and sentences containing the conclusion are of prime importance. An elementary form of précis or note-taking may be practised when the passage consists of several paragraphs. Write down a concise title for the passage as suggested above, then sub-headings or topics for each paragraph. These are often directly expressed in the paragraph, generally near the beginning.

After having satisfied yourself that you have missed nothing important, connect the ideas in a coherent piece of composition. If the passage has been accurately scrutinised and understood, *your précis should be made from your notes without reference to the passage.* Since the object of the précis is to give an exact summary, do not add anything of your own to amend or develop the original. It is also generally profitable to retain **the order** of the original ideas.

Note the number of words you use at the end of each line, then check the length of your version.

Unless warned to the contrary, write a précis of a speech ***indirectly***, *i.e.* use indirect speech or narration. See Chapter VIII. This entails changing pronouns, tenses, adverbs. demonstrative adjectives, etc. Do your utmost to avoid a needless and monotonous repetition of " He said ", " he next said ", then he said " etc. By taking thought, you can easily vary your verbs and so convey the manner in which the words were spoken, *e.g.* he expostulated, cajoled, appealed, insisted, emphasised, deprecated, etc.

After much practice, you may find it convenient to discard the outline, but always take time for the study of the passage, for only thus can you avoid a possible misunderstanding of the meaning. Always mark the important ideas if they are brief, by underlining, or if lengthy, by side-lining.

## EXERCISE I

1. Give one word which could be substituted for :—
   that cannot be avoided.
   ,, ,, ,, placated.
   ,, ,, ,, rooted out.

that cannot be expressed.
" " " understood.
" " " wounded.
equally clever with both hands.
one's life story written by oneself.
without having made a will.
to feign illness to avoid doing a duty.
a hater of his fellow men.
an office with salary but without work.
a cure for all diseases.
not having any backbone.
happening one after the other.
happening at the same time.

## EXERCISE II

Rewrite the following sentences substituting a single word or shorter phrase for each group of words italicised.

1. He is *one of those people who cannot distinguish between what is their own and other people's.*
2. Our watches must be *set at the same time.*
3. His story of a robbery is *too strange to be believed.*
4. A judge must *have no leanings towards either of the parties* at a trial.
5. He is a suitable room-mate: he rises *with the lark* and *makes not the slightest noise.*
6. He is looking for a situation which is *highly paid and entails little work.*
7. He writes *in such a fashion that his writing can be easily read.*
8. Such an invention *exists in possibility but not in reality.*
9. The *short note, added to the will,* deprived him of the prospects of a fortune.
10. He is fond of expressing himself *in concise and pointed sayings.*

## EXERCISE III

Give a general expression to denote each of the following passages (selected from standard authors); then condense each passage into one short sentence.

1. He was a small, meagre man much below the middle height, with thin legs, a narrow chest and the shrinking, timid air of an habitual invalid.

2. They (the Persians) made use of gloves when they walked out in the sun; they no longer hunted except in battues, slaughtering without danger or fatigue the lean, mangy creatures of the park. They painted their faces and pencilled their eyebrows, and wore bracelets and collars.

3. Early debauchery had unnerved his body and mind. He indulged immoderately in the use of ardent spirits, which inflamed his weak brain almost to madness. His chosen companions were flatterers sprung from the dregs of the people, and recommended by nothing but buffoonery and servility.

4. The wound in the skull is behind, and above the left ear, is roughly circular, measures one inch and seven-sixteenths at most, and a ragged scalp-wound runs from it towards the left eye. On the right cheek is a linear, contused wound three and a quarter inches long.

5. Since the coming of the railroad, the mamma rushes sixty miles in two hours to the aching finger of her conjugating and declining grammar-boy. The early Scotsman scratches himself in the morning mists of the north, and has his porridge in Piccadilly before the setting sun.

6. The curfew tolls the knell of parting day,
The lowing herd winds slowly o'er the lea,
The ploughman homeward plods his weary way,
And leaves the world to darkness and to me.

7. He was a tall, strong, heavy, nut-brown man; his tarry pigtail falling over the shoulders of his soiled blue coat; his hands ragged and scarred, with black, broken nails; and the sabre cut across one cheek, a dirty, livid white.

8. A good deal of the leisure of the modern man is taken up with theatres, cinemas, football, cricket, greyhound and horse racing, private amateur games, etc.

9. While he from forth the closet brought a heap
Of candied apples, quince, and plum, and gourd;
With jellies soother than the creamy curd;
And lucent syrups, tinct with cinnamon;
Manna and dates, in argosy transferr'd
From Fez; and spiced dainties, every one,
From silken Samarcand to cedar'd Lebanon.

10. Toilet soap is made by adding fat to ordinary washing soap in order to remove any caustic soda which would irritate the skin. Soft soap is another kind of soap, but it is made with caustic potash instead of caustic soda. Carbolic soap is made by adding disinfectant to ordinary soap.

## EXERCISE IV

Select the essential sentences (not more than *two*) in the following paragraphs.

1. He carefully scrutinised the passengers as they trooped along the platform. They were indeed of a type seldom seen by a confirmed city-dweller like himself. Here were apple-cheeked

farmers and their wives with their baskets, bound for the market. There came an angler or two, thick-booted, carrying rods and creels, their hats wreathed with many-coloured flies. Nowhere was anyone like the man he sought.

2. Bohun saw the tragedy in one glance, flat underneath him like a plan. In the yard of the smithy were standing five or six men mostly in black, one in an inspector's uniform. They included the doctor, the Presbyterian minister, and the priest from the Roman Catholic chapel to which the blacksmith's wife belonged.

3. The appearance of the place through which he walked in the morning was not calculated to raise the spirits of the young surgeon, or to dispel any feeling of anxiety or depression which the singular kind of visit he was about to make had awakened. Striking off from the high road, his way lay across a marshy common, through irregular lanes, with here and there a ruinous and dismantled cottage fast falling to pieces with decay and neglect. A stunted tree, or pool of stagnant water roused into a sluggish action by the heavy rain of the preceding night, skirted the path occasionally.

4. I had resolved to speak to him, but when I looked into his face, I felt as if it were impossible to do so. That eye—the eye of a serpent—fixed and held me spellbound. And withal, about the man's whole person was a dignity—there was an air of pride and station and superiority that would have made anyone, habituated to the usages of the world, hesitate long before venturing upon a liberty or impertinence.

5. He (Cæsar) was singularly careful of his soldiers. He allowed the legions rest, though he allowed none to himself. He rarely fought a battle under a disadvantage. He never exposed his men to unnecessary danger, and the loss by wear and tear in the campaigns in Gaul was exceptionally and even astonishingly slight. When a gallant action was performed, he knew by whom it had been done, and every soldier, however humble, might feel assured that if he deserved praise he would have it. The army was Cæsar's family . . . .

## EXERCISE V

Express in one sentence the meaning of each of the following passages.

1. "We are prisoners," says she; "in everything but chains, we are prisoners. Let them come, let them consign me to dungeons, or strike off my head from this poor little throat" (and she clasped it in her long fingers). "The blood of the Esmonds will always flow freely for their kings. We are not like the Churchills—the Judases who kiss their master and betray him.

We know how to suffer, how even to forgive in the royal cause." (No doubt it was to that fatal business of losing the place of Groom of the Posset to which her ladyship alluded, as she did half a dozen times in a day.) "Let the tyrant of Orange bring his rack and his odious Dutch tortures—the beast! the wretch! I spit upon him and defy him. Cheerfully will I lay this head upon the block; cheerfully will I accompany my lord to the scaffold: we will cry 'God save King James!' with our dying breath, and smile in the face of the executioner."

2. "Under the impression," said Mr. Micawber, "that your peregrinations in this metropolis have not yet been extensive, and that you might have some difficulty in penetrating the arcana of the modern Babylon in the direction of the City Road—in short," said Mr. Micawber, in another burst of confidence, "that you might lose yourself—I shall be happy to call this evening, and instal you in the knowledge of the nearest way."

3. (Falstaff has asked what he owes the speaker, Dame Quickly.)

Marry! if thou wert an honest man, thyself and the money too. Thou didst swear to me upon a parcel-gilt goblet, sitting in my Dolphin-chamber, at the round table, by a sea-coal fire, upon Wednesday in Wheeson week, when the prince broke thy head for liking his father to a singing-man of Windsor—thou didst swear to me then, as I was washing thy wound, to marry me and make me my lady, thy wife.

4. "It would be very wrong to suppose that this sum has not been expended for the benefit of the community. The point which your lordships are required to decide has never been decided before, and, if your lordships are able to decide it now, it need never be decided again, nor can it be decided otherwise. It is never likely to rise again, but that is another matter. Your lordships' house is almost the only authority in this mortal world whose word on any subject is the last word for ever. Your pronouncements have the unalterable force of a law of nature; and if we are able by taking pains to add a single grain of certitude to the shifting sands of human affairs, is there any one who is prepared pedantically to count the cost?"

5. He felt no deleterious effects from his nocturnal adventure; and after a hearty matutinal meal, he gave his friend a valedictory warning to avoid similar escapades in the future, paid his accustomed visit to the tonsorial artist, and, refreshed once more, sought his own far-from-palatial domicile.

**Model passage for Précis :—**

Clive was in a painfully anxious situation. He could place no confidence in the sincerity or in the courage of his confederate; and, whatever confidence he might place in his own military talents, and in the valour and discipline of his troops, it was no light thing to engage an army twenty times as numerous as his own. Before him lay a river over which it was easy to advance, but over which, if things went ill, not one of his little band would ever return. On this occasion, for the first and last time, his dauntless spirit, during a few hours, shrank from the fearful responsibility of making a decision. He called a council of war. The majority pronounced against fighting; and Clive declared his concurrence with the majority. Long afterwards, he said that he had never called but one council of war, and that, if he had taken the advice of that council, the British would never have been masters of Bengal. But scarcely had the meeting broken up when he was himself again. He retired alone under the shade of some trees and passed near an hour there in thought. He came back determined to put everything to the hazard, and gave orders that all should be in readiness for passing the river on the morrow.

## METHOD

1. Underline in the passage :—

Clive in anxious situation
no confidence in confederate
no light thing. . . . .
engage an army
river
spirit shrank. . . . .
making decision
council of war
pronounced against fighting
taken advice
never masters of Bengal
himself again
an hour in thought
determined to put everything to hazard
orders . . . for passing the river

2. Make an outline in your own words:

Clive realises danger of situation . . . Clive's Indecision

since (*a*) No confidence in ally
(*b*) Opposed by superior army
(*c*) Perilous crossing of river
} Causes of indecision

He calls a council of war
Majority against a battle
Clive accepts their verdict
} Decision of Council

Clive goes apart to think
He decides upon attack
} His final decision

3. Précis.

Clive realised the dangers of an attack: he could not rely on his ally, the enemy vastly outnumbered him, and to cross the river was to incur grave risks. For once in his life he threw responsibility upon a council of war and agreed with the majority whose decision against a battle might have meant the loss of Bengal. Later, his fortitude returned, and after much thought, he gave orders to prepare for an attack.

*Note.*—The original passage contains 218 words, the précis, 75. The usual proportion is 1 to 3, and a margin of 5 per cent either way is permissible.

## EXERCISE VI

Make a précis of each of the following passages, reducing it to about one-third of its present length.

Their infantry was divided into three lines. The first, tolerably provided with fire-arms, were advanced almost close to the verge of the bog, so that their fire must necessarily annoy the royal cavalry as they descended the opposite hill, the whole front of which was exposed, and would probably be yet more fatal if they attempted to cross the morass. Behind this first line was a body of pikemen, designed for their support in case the dragoons should force the passage of the marsh. In their rear was their third line, consisting of countrymen armed with scythes set straight on poles, hay-forks, spits, clubs, goads, fish-spears, and other such rustic implements as hasty resentment had converted into instruments of war. On each flank of the infantry, but a little backward from the bog, as if to allow themselves dry and sound ground whereon to act in case their enemies should force the pass, there was drawn up a small body of cavalry, who were in general but indifferently armed, and worse mounted, but full of zeal for the cause, being chiefly either land-holders of small property or farmers of the better class, whose means enabled them to serve on horseback. A few of those who had been engaged in driving back the advanced guard of the Royalists, might now be seen returning slowly towards their own squadrons. These were the only individuals of the insurgent army which seemed to be in motion. All the others stood firm and motionless, as the gray stones that lay scattered on the heath around them. SCOTT.

With a view to these considerations, it seems advisable that, when examining the different civilizations into which the great countries of Europe have diverged, I should also give an account of the way in which history has been commonly written in each country. In the employment of this resource, I shall be mainly guided by a desire to illustrate the intimate connexion between the actual condition of a people and their opinions respecting the past; and, in order to keep this connexion in sight, I shall treat the state of historical literature, not as a separate subject, but as forming part of the intellectual history of each nation. The present volume will contain a view of the principal characteristics of French civilization until the great Revolution; and with that there will be incorporated an account of the French historians, and of the remarkable improvements they introduced into their own departments of knowledge. The relation which these improvements bore to the state of society from which they proceeded, is very striking, and will be examined at some length; while, in the next volume, the civilization and the historical literature of the other leading countries will be treated in a similar manner. Before, however, entering into these different subjects, it has occurred to me, that a preliminary inquiry into the origin of European history would be interesting, as supplying information respecting matters which are little known, and also as enabling the reader to understand the extreme difficulty with which history has reached its present advanced, but still very imperfect, state. The materials for studying the earliest condition of Europe have long since perished; but the extensive information we now possess concerning barbarous nations will supply us with a useful resource, because they have all much in common; the opinions of extreme ignorance being, indeed, everywhere the same, except when modified by the differences which nature presents in various countries. BUCKLE.

For some time past, the subject of barges had occupied a great deal of our talk, and we had projected an old age on the canals of Europe. It was to be the most leisurely of progresses, now on a swift river at the tail of a steamboat, now waiting horses for days together on some inconsiderable junction. We should be seen pottering on deck in all the dignity of years, our white beards falling into our laps. We were ever to be busied among paintpots; so that there should be no white fresher, and no green more emerald than ours, in all the navy of the canals. There should be books in the cabin, and tobacco jars, and some old Burgundy as red as a November sunset and as odorous as a violet in April. There should be a flageolet whence the Cigarette, with cunning touch, should draw melting music under the stars; or perhaps, laying that aside, upraise his voice—somewhat thinner than of yore, and with here and there a quaver, or call it a natural grace note—in rich and solemn psalmody.

All this simmering in my mind, set me wishing to go aboard one of these ideal houses of lounging. I had plenty to choose from, as I coasted one after another, and the dogs bayed at me for a vagrant. At last I saw a nice old man and his wife looking at me with some interest so I gave them good day and pulled up alongside. I began with a remark upon their dog, which had somewhat the look of a pointer; thence I slid into a compliment on Madame's flowers, and thence into a word in praise of their way of life.

STEVENSON.

What are the essential characteristics of the spirit of our nation? Not, certainly, an open and clear mind, not a quick and flexible intelligence. Our greatest admirers would not claim for us that we have these in a pre-eminent degree; they might say that we had more of them than our detractors gave us credit for; but they would not assert them to be our essential characteristics. They would rather allege, as our chief spiritual characteristics, energy and honesty; and, if we are judged favourably and positively, not invidiously and negatively, our chief characteristics are no doubt these: energy and honesty, not an open and clear mind, not a quick and flexible intelligence. Openness of mind and flexibility of intelligence were very signal characteristics of the Athenian people in ancient times; everybody will feel that. Openness of mind, and flexibility of intelligence are remarkable characteristics of the French people in modern times; at any rate, they strikingly characterise them as compared with us; I think everybody, or almost everybody, will feel that. I will not now ask what more the Athenian or the French spirit has than this, nor what short-comings either of them may have as a set-off against this; all I want now to point out is that they have this, and that we have it in a much lesser degree. Let me remark, however, that not only in the moral sphere, but also in the intellectual and spiritual sphere, energy and honesty are most important and fruitful qualities; that, for instance, of what we call genius, energy is the most essential part. So, by assigning to a nation energy and honesty as its chief spiritual characteristics—by refusing to it, as at all eminent characteristics, openness of mind and flexibility of intelligence—we do not by any means, as some people might at first suppose, relegate its importance and its power of manifesting itself with effect from the intellectual to the moral sphere. ARNOLD.

One could say about this barn, what could hardly be said of either the church or the castle, akin to it in age and style, that the purpose which had dictated its original erection was the same with that to which it was still applied. Unlike and superior to either of those two typical remnants of mediævalism, the old barn embodied practices which had suffered no mutilation at the hands of time. Here at least the spirit of the ancient builders was at one with the spirit of the modern beholder. Standing before this abraded pile, the eye regarded its present usage, and dwelt upon its past history, with a satisfied sense of functional continuity throughout—a feeling almost of gratitude, and quite of pride, at the permanence of the idea which had heaped it up. The fact that four centuries had neither proved it to be founded on a mistake, inspired any hatred of its purpose, nor given rise to any reaction that had battered it down, invested this simple grey effort of old minds with a repose, if not a grandeur, which a too curious reflection was apt to disturb in its ecclesiastical and military compeers. For once mediævalism and modernism had a common stand-point. The lanceolate windows, the time-eaten arch-stones and chamfers, the orientation of the axis, the misty chestnut work of the rafters, referred to no exploded fortifying art or worn-out religious creed. The defence and salvation of the body by daily bread is still a study, a religion, a desire.

HARDY.

"See here, then. You're daft about the working-class and have no use for any other. But what in the name of goodness do you know about working men? . . . I come out of them myself, and have lived next door to them all my days. Take them one way and another, they're a decent sort, good and bad like the rest of us. But there's a wheen daft folk that would set them up as models—close to truth and reality, says you. It's sheer ignorance, for you're about as well acquaint with the working-man as with King Solomon. You say I make up fine stories about tinklers and sailor-men because I know nothing about them. That's maybe true. But you're at the same job yourself. You idealise the working-man, you and your kind, because you're ignorant. You say that he's seeking for truth, when he's only looking for a drink and a rise in wages. You tell me he's near reality, but I tell you that his notion of reality is often just a short working day and looking on at a footba'-match on Saturday . . . . And when you run down what you call the middle-classes that do three-quarters of the world's work and keep the machine going and the working-man in a job, then I tell you you're talking havers. Havers!" BUCHAN.

He who lets the world, or his own portion of it, choose his plan of life for him, has no need of any other faculty than the ape-like one of imitation. He who chooses his plan for himself, employs all his faculties. He must use observation to see, reasoning and judgment to foresee, activity to gather materials for decision, discrimination to decide, and when he has decided, firmness and self-control to hold to his deliberate decision. And these qualities he requires and exercises exactly in proportion as the part of his conduct which he determines according to his own judgment and feelings is a large one. It is possible that he might be guided in some good path, and keep out of harm's way, without any of these things. But what will be his comparative worth as a human being? It really is of importance, not only what men do, but also what manner of men they are that do it. Among the works of man, which human life is rightly employed in perfecting and beautifying, the first in importance surely is man himself. Supposing it were possible to get houses built, corn grown, battles fought, causes tried, and even churches erected and prayers said, by machinery—by automatons in human form—it would be a considerable loss to exchange for these automatons even the men and women who at present inhabit the more civilised parts of the world, and who assuredly are but starved specimens of what nature can and will produce. Human nature is not a machine to be built after a model, and set to do exactly the work prescribed for it, but a tree, which requires to grow and develop itself on all sides, according to the tendency of the inward forces which make it a living thing. MILL.

Thus the Puritan was made up of two different men, the one all self-abasement, penitence, gratitude, passion; the other proud, calm, inflexible, sagacious. He prostrated himself in the dust before his Maker: but he set his foot on the neck of his king. In his devotional retirement, he prayed with convulsions, and groans, and tears. He was half maddened by glorious or terrible illusions. He heard the lyres of angels or the tempting whispers of fiends. He caught a gleam of the Beatific Vision, or woke screaming from dreams of everlasting fire. Like Vane, he thought himself entrusted with the sceptre of the millennial year. Like Fleetwood, he cried in the bitterness of his soul that God had hid his face from him. But when he took his seat in the council, or girt on his sword for war, these tempestuous workings of the soul had left no perceptible trace behind them. People who saw nothing of the godly but their uncouth visages, and heard nothing from them but their groans and their whining hymns, might laugh at them. But those had little reason to laugh who encountered them in the hall of debate or in the field of battle. These fanatics brought to civil and military affairs a coolness of judgment and an immutability of purpose which some writers have thought inconsistent with their religious zeal, but which were in fact the necessary effects of it. The intensity of their feelings on one subject made them tranquil on every other. One over-powering sentiment had subjected to itself pity and hatred, ambition and fear. Death had lost its terrors and pleasure its charms. They had their smiles and their tears, their raptures and their sorrows, but not for the things of the world. Enthusiasm had made them Stoics, had cleared their minds from every vulgar passion and prejudice, and raised them above the influence of danger and of corruption. It sometimes might lead them to pursue unwise ends, but never to choose unwise means. They went through the world, like Sir Artegal's iron man Talus with his flail, crushing and trampling down oppressors, mingling with human beings, but having neither part nor lot in human infirmities insensible to fatigue, to pleasure, and to pain, not to be pierced by any weapon, not to be withstood by any barrier.

MACAULAY.

The firm of Grubb and Smallways, formerly Grubb, had indeed been persistently unlucky in the last year or so. For many years the business had struggled along with a flavour of romantic insecurity in a small dissolute-looking shop in the High Street, adorned with brilliantly coloured advertisements of cycles, a display of bells, trouser-clips, oil-cans, pump-clips, frame-cases, wallets, and other accessories, and the announcement of "Bicycles on Hire," "Repairs," "Free Inflation," "Petrol," and similar attractions. They were agents for several obscure makes of bicycles, two samples constituted the stock, and occasionally they effected a sale; they also repaired punctures and did their best—though luck was not always on their side—with any other repairing that was brought to them. They handled a line of cheap gramophones, and did a little with musical boxes. The staple of their business was, however, the letting of bicycles on hire. It was a singular trade, obeying no known commercial or economic principles—indeed, no principles. There was a stock of ladies' and gentlemen's bicycles in a state of disrepair that passes description, the hiring stock, and these were let to unexacting and reckless people, inexpert in the things of this world, at a nominal rate of one shilling for the first hour and sixpence per hour afterwards. But really, there were no fixed prices, and insistent boys could get bicycles and the thrill of danger for an hour for so low as threepence, provided they could convince Grubb that that was all they had. The saddle and handle-bar were then sketchily adjusted by Grubb, a deposit exacted, except in the case of familiar boys, the machine lubricated, and the adventurer started upon his career. Usually he or she came back, but at times, when the accident was serious, Bert or Grubb had to go out and fetch the machine home. Hire was always charged up to the hour of return to the shop and deducted from the deposit.

WELLS.

His attitude towards the poor, for instance, was essentially that of man to man. Save that he could not tolerate impostors (one of his favourite words), and saw through them with almost startling rapidity, he was compassionate to any who had fallen on evil fortune, and especially to those who had been in any way connected with him. But in these almonary transactions he was always particularly secretive, as if rather doubting their sagacity, and the wisdom of allowing them to become known—himself making up and despatching the parcels of old clothes, and rather surreptitiously producing such coins and writing such cheques as were necessary. But "the poor," in bulk, were always to him the concern of the Poor Law pure and simple, and in no sense of the individual citizen. It was the same with malefactors; he might pity as well as condemn them, but the idea that the society to which he and they belonged was in any way responsible for them, would never have occurred to him. His sense of justice, like that of his period, was fundamentally based on the notion that every man had started with equal, or at all events, with quite sufficient opportunities, and must be judged as if he had. But, indeed, it was not the custom in his day to concern oneself with problems outside one's own class. Within that class, and in all matters domestic, no man was ever born with a nicer sense of justice. It was never overridden by his affections; very seldom, and that with a certain charming naïveté, by his interests.

GALSWORTHY.

Now, surely, when we want to educate ourselves for the purpose of citizenship, whatever the immediate course of study may be, whether it be history or economics, whether it be humane letters, whether it be mathematics, the object of such education must always be the same, and to my mind the purpose of such education —a purpose which we try to put in our mind—is always twofold; it is, in the first place, to clear the mind of cant, and in the second place, not to rest content with having learnt enough to follow the syllogism, knowing perfectly well that to follow the syllogism alone is a short-cut to the bottomless pit, unless you are able to detect the fallacies that lie by the wayside. If you can clear the mind of cant and detect the fallacy, whatever guise it may be wearing, I think you have made a long step forward in the education that every citizen in a democracy that may hope to endure must have. I think that we all of us realize to-day that no civilized community is bound necessarily and by an inscrutable fate to progress, that there are such things in civilization as checks, that there is such a thing as retrogression, and that the mere existence of a civilized community is no guarantee either for its continuance or for its progress—in other words, that unless we are the faithful guardians of such civilization as we have already attained to, we run the risk of seeing the whole of the progress that has been made with such infinite labour up to our own time gradually slipping back and back and back.

EARL BALDWIN.

It was flood tide when Daniel Quilp sat himself down in the wherry to cross to the opposite shore. A fleet of barges were coming lazily on, some sideways, some head first, some stern first; all in a wrong-headed, dogged, obstinate way, bumping up against the larger craft, running under the bows of steamboats, getting into every kind of nook and corner where they had no business, and being crunched on all sides like so many walnut shells; while each, with its pair of long sweeps struggling and splashing in the water, looked like some lumbering fish in pain. In some of the vessels at anchor, all hands were busily engaged in coiling ropes, spreading out sails to dry, taking in or discharging their cargoes; in others, no life was visible but two or three tarry boys, and perhaps a barking dog running to and fro upon the deck or scrambling up to look over the side and bark the louder for the view. Coming slowly on through the forests of masts, was a great steamship, beating the water in short impatient strokes with her heavy paddles, as though she wanted room to breathe, and advancing in her huge bulk like a sea-monster among the minnows of the Thames. On either hand, were long black tiers of colliers; between then, vessels slowly working out of harbour with sails glistening in the sun, and creaking noise on board, re-echoed from a hundred quarters. The water and all upon it was in active motion, dancing and buoyant and bubbling up; while the old grey Tower and piles of building on the shore, with many a church-spire shooting up between, looked coldly on, and seemed to disdain their chafing neighbour. DICKENS.

In school, he finds himself in a dual world, under two dispensations. There is the world of the boys, where the point of honor is to be untameable, always ready to fight, ruthless in taking the conceit out of anyone who ventures to give himself airs of superior knowledge or taste, and generally to take Lucifer for one's model.

And there is the world of the masters, the world of discipline, submission, diligence, obedience, and continual and shameless assumption of moral and intellectual authority. Thus the schoolboy hears both sides, and is so far better off than the home-bred boy who hears only one. But the two sides are not fairly presented. They are presented as good and evil, as vice and virtue, as villainy and heroism. The boy feels mean and cowardly when he obeys, and selfish and rascally when he disobeys. He loses his moral courage just as he comes to hate books and languages. In the end, John Ruskin, tied so closely to his mother's apron-string that he did not escape even when he went to Oxford, and John Stuart Mill, whose father ought to have been prosecuted for laying his son's childhood waste with lessons, were superior, as products of training, to our schoolboys. They were very conspicuously superior in moral courage ; and though they did not distinguish themselves at cricket and football, they had quite as much physical hardihood as any civilized man needs. But it is to be observed that Ruskin's parents were wise people who gave John a full share in their own life, and put up with his presence both at home and abroad when they must sometimes have been very weary of him ; and Mill, as it happens, was deliberately educated to challenge all the most sacred institutions of his country. The households they were brought up in were no more average households than a Montessori school in an average school.

SHAW.

Twice had the trees let fall
Their leaves, as often Winter had put on
His hoary crown, since I had seen the surge
Beat against Albion's shore, since ears of mine
Had caught the accents of my native speech
Upon our native country's sacred ground.
A patriot of the world, how could I glide
Into communion with her sylvan shades,
Erstwhile my tuneful haunt ? It pleased me more
To abide in the great City, where I found
The general air still busy with the stir
Or that first memorable onset made
By a strong levy of humanity
Upon the traffickers in Negro blood ;
Effort which, though defeated, had recalled
To notice old forgotten principles,
And through the nation spread a novel heat
Of virtuous feeling. For myself, I own
That this particular strife had wanted power
To rivet my affections ; nor did now

Its unsuccessful issue much excite
My sorrow ; for I brought with me the faith
That, if France prospered, good men would not long
Pay fruitless worship to humanity,
And this most rotten branch of human shame,
Object, so seemed it, of superfluous pains,
Would fall together with its parent tree.
What, then, were my emotions, when in arms
Britain put forth her freeborn strength in league,
Oh, pity and shame ! with those confederate Powers
Not in my single self alone I found,
But in the minds of all ingenuous youth,
Change and subversion from that hour.

WORDSWORTH.

Peace to all such ! but were there One whose fires
True Genius kindles, and fair Fame inspires ;
Blest with each talent and each art to please,
And born to write, converse, and live with ease :
Should such a man, too fond to rule alone,
Bear, like the Turk, no brother near the throne,
View him with scornful, yet with jealous eyes,
And hate for arts that caus'd himself to rise ;
Damn with faint praise, assent with civil leer,
And without sneering, teach the rest to sneer ;
Willing to wound, and yet afraid to strike,
Just hint a fault, and hesitate dislike ;
Alike reserv'd to blame, or to commend,
A tim'rous foe, and a suspicious friend ;
Dreading e'en fools, by Flatterers besieg'd,
And so obliging, that he ne'er oblig'd ;
Like Cato, give his little Senate laws,
And sit attentive to his own applause ;
While Wits and Templars ev'ry sentence raise,
And wonder with a foolish face of praise—
Who but must laugh, if such a man there be !
Who would not weep, if Atticus were he !

POPE.

Nigh on the plain, in many cells prepared,
That underneath had veins of liquid fire
Sluiced from the lake, a second multitude
With wondrous art founded the massy ore,
Severing each kind, and scummed the bullion-dross.
A third as soon had formed within the ground
A various mould, and from the boiling cells
By strange conveyance, filled each hollow nook ;

As in an organ, from one blast of wind,
To many a row of pipes the sound-board breathes.
Anon out of the earth a fabric huge
Rose like an exhalation, with the sound
Of dulcet symphonies and voices sweet—
Built like a temple, where pilasters round
Were set, and Doric pillars overlaid
With golden architrave; nor did there want
Cornice or frieze, with bossy sculptures graven;
The roof was fretted gold. Not Babylon
Nor great Alcairo such magnificence
Equalled in all their glories, to enshrine
Belus or Serapis their gods, or seat
Their kings, when Egypt with Assyria strove
In wealth and luxury. The ascending pile
Stood fixed her stately highth; and straight the doors,
Opening their brazen folds, discover, wide
Within, her ample spaces o'er the smooth
And level pavement: from the arched roof,
Pendent by subtle magic, many a row
Of starry lamps and blazing cressets, fed
With naphtha and asphaltus, yielded light
As from a sky.

MILTON.

. . . . . . . . . . . . . . . —there to wander far away,
On from island unto island at the gateways of the day.

Larger constellations burning, mellow moons and happy skies,
Breadths of tropic shade and palms in cluster, knots of Paradise.
Never comes the trader, never floats an European flag,
Slides the bird o'er lustrous woodland, swings the trailer from the crag;
Droops the heavy-blossom'd bower, hangs the heavy-fruited tree—
Summer isles of Eden lying in dark-purple spheres of sea.
There methinks would be enjoyment more than in this march of mind,
In the steamship, in the railway, in the thoughts that shake mankind.
There the passions cramp'd no longer shall have scope and breathing-space;
I will take some savage woman, she shall rear my dusky race.
Iron-jointed, supple-sinew'd, they shall dive, and they shall run,
Catch the wild goat by the hair, and hurl their lances in the sun;
Whistle back the parrot's call, and leap the rainbows of the brooks,
Not with blinded eyesight poring over miserable books—

Fool, again the dream, the fancy but I know my words are wild,
But I count the grey barbarian lower than the Christian child.
I, to herd with narrow foreheads, vacant of our glorious gains,
Like a beast with lower pleasures, like a beast with lower pains
Mated with a squalid savage—what to me were sun or clime ?
I the heir of all the ages, in the foremost files of time—
I that rather held it better men should perish one by one,
Than that earth should stand at gaze like Joshua's moon in Ajalon.

TENNYSON.

---

# CHAPTER X

## HISTORY OF THE LANGUAGE

Man became articulate more than 20,000 years ago and it is unlikely that there was ever one original speech. We do not know how words originally came to be formed, but the process in operation in the 20th century may be a guide. The motor car provides us with (1) chassis, garage, chauffeur—words transferred deliberately from another living tongue; (2) synchro-mesh, terminal, ignition—coined from dead languages; (3) wind-screen wiper, tail-light, front-wheel brake—hyphenated words awaiting contraction; (4) gadget, bumper, jay-walker—words in course of admission. These are all young words with a long ancestry. Language therefore is not an arbitrary selection of sounds, but a growth. The "emotional" origin of words is widely accepted.

The important literary languages of the world to-day are English, French, German, Italian and Spanish, and they are all based on the one alphabet. They are derived from Aryan, a tongue or tongues of which there is no written record. With the exception of the old Testament and the Koran, the world's greatest literature is written in this Aryan medium.

The English tongue is the most widely spoken and written. It is composite, that is, it is composed of many other dialects besides Old English. Chief among these may be mentioned Celtic, Greek and Latin, Norse, Norman and some modern languages.

**Celtic**: The original Celts emerged from the head waters of the Rhône and Rhine and gradually spread over France, Spain and Britain. They were a warrior race and disinclined to settle, consequently the body of pure Celtic literature is slight, their ballads having been almost entirely lost. Malory probably got some inspiration from 6th century Druidical poems, and "*Fingal*" and "*Temora*," believed to have been written by Ossian, were translated by Macpherson in 1762 into English. To-day, the influence of Celtic is stronger than it has ever been in the past.

**Greek**: Greeks were the first Aryans to settle in Southern Europe and the siege of Troy, about 1200 B.C., may have been a clash between Aryan and Semitic. It was from the Phœnicians—the dark Iberians of the "Scholar Gipsy"—the earlier occupants of the Peninsula, that the Greeks learned the alphabet, which was passed to Italy and thence to Northern Europe. It is difficult to isolate the Latin from the Greek debt, but the influence of Greek on Milton, Gray, Keats, Arnold and Tennyson is clear. The New Testament was originally found in a Greek dialect.

**Latin**: The accident that conferred an Aryan dialect on a few scattered bands of peasants near the mouth of the Tiber, gave to the world its most widely-spread language. There are more Latin than English words in an English dictionary; Europe, west and south of the Rhine and Danube, speaks in Latin dialects; missionaries of the Roman Church carried it everywhere,

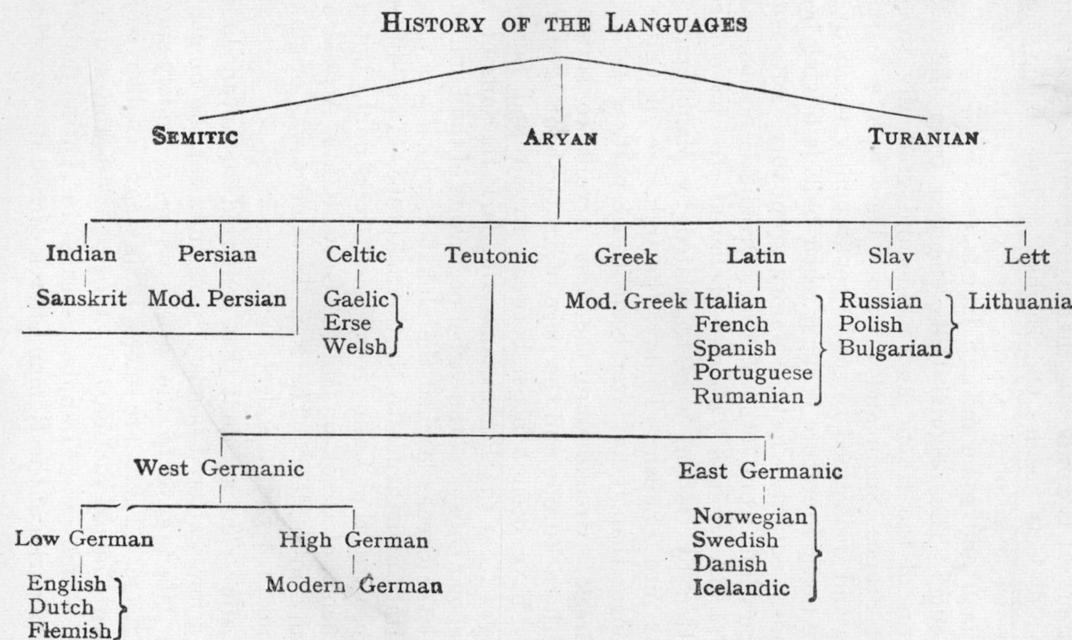
History of the Languages
Semitic
Aryan
Turanian
Indian
Persian
Celtic
Teutonic
Greek
Latin
Slav
Lett
Sanskrit
Mod. Persian
Gaelic
Erse
Welsh
Mod. Greek
Italian
French
Spanish
Portuguese
Rumanian
Russian
Polish
Bulgarian
Lithuanian
West Germanic
East Germanic
Low German
High German
Norwegian
Swedish
Danish
Icelandic
English
Dutch
Flemish
Modern German

and when the classical tongue was no longer spoken the vernacular Latin, *lingua Romana rustica,* continued to live in France, Spain and Italy.

**Teutonic**: The Teutons emerge from obscurity as a collection of related tribes inhabiting South Scandinavia. They were never as a race colonised by the Romans, while their love of freedom, coupled with a splendid physique, made them troublesome neighbours to their more civilised relations. It is conjectured that the Aryan element must originally have been a dominant minority for the Teutonic tongue shows a wider variation from the parent Aryan than Celtic or Slavonic. By the sixth century, Teuton migrations were at an end and already the Germans in the low-lying north spoke a different dialect from those in the high lands. (The Roman Empire was now disintegrated.) Gibbon assigned the fall of Rome to Bishops within and Barbarians without. It is significant that the Barbarians, having destroyed Rome, continued to carry on its best traditions and use its language.

**The English Invasion**: Mr. Trevelyan, speaking of the Anglo-Saxon invasion of England, uses the term, "History's blank page." No Roman annalist lived to tell the story of King Arthur (if he ever lived), and of the long struggle between the Celts and English. Nearly all the documentary evidence we possess till the time of King Alfred, consists of the Beowulf, which seems to have been committed to writing about 750, the works of Bede (673-735) and the Anglo-Saxon Chronicles, the earlier parts of which are not well authenticated. It appears that about the middle of the fifth century, Angles, Saxons and Jutes, speaking different dialects of Low-German, left their homes in north-west Germany and Denmark to plunder the Romanised provinces of what we now call England. No one knows why they came, but the Teuton seems to have shared the wanderlust of other barbarous peoples of Europe during the fifth and sixth centuries. Their attacks were confined to the east and south-east. At first, they seem to have been unwilling or unable to occupy the land they pillaged, but, supplemented by later bands of immigrants who came to settle rather than to destroy, they gradually spread over all England and Lowland Scotland except the mountainous parts to the west and north. It is not possible to estimate the number of the conquerors nor do we know to what extent the native Britons were enslaved or massacred. There is no doubt, however, that the conquest was thorough and that the original Celts who remained were insufficient to influence the Anglo-Saxon tongue which in its early stages contained no Celtic and few Latin borrowings. The wide area of conquest, and the substitution of English for Celtic place names are further evidence that, henceforth, a new race had assumed complete control in England. Nothing could have been more complete than the Nordic Invasion. The battles of Deorham in 577 and Chester in 613 divided the Celts and confined them to the western areas. The Celtic people, the Celtic tongue and Celtic Christianity disappeared from England.

While for convenience of study, history may be divided into periods, no such periods really exist. Language is a continuous growth—a dead language like Latin or Sanskrit is one which has ceased to grow. For fifteen centuries, English has continued to grow, though naturally the greatest changes have taken place during the youth of the language, *i.e.* before the Invention of Printing. A 20th century dictionary contains over 100,000 words; the *Beowulf* contains barely a thousand.

**Old English or Anglo-Saxon** was a highly inflected language. The relation between words was expressed by means of inflections rather than by separate words. On this account it is called a *Synthetic Language*, whereas Modern English is an *Analytic Language*, the relation between words being expressed by means of separate words rather than by inflections. A simple illustration of these methods may be seen in the two expressions: "the eagle's wing" (synthetic), "the wing of the eagle" (analytic). Anglo-Saxon is a loose term to describe the language and literature which was spoken and written between the 6th and 11th centuries. There is no doubt that the English brought with them from the Continent a large body of pagan legend, myths and stories, some of which may even have been transcribed in runic characters. Most of these have been lost, and many, like the *Beowulf*, have been recast to conform with the new Christian teachings. The Jutes who took possession of Kent and the Isle of Wight were early absorbed and there is no record of their written tongue. The Angles, occupying the land between the Forth and Lower Midlands, later divided into two sects, the Northumbrians and Mercians, while the Saxons occupied the Thames Valley and Southern Coast. A long rivalry terminated in the political supremacy of Wessex, but Northumbria was first to produce a literature, Caedmon writing his *Paraphrases* and Bede his Church *History*.

**Early English**: 1100-1250.—During the Early English period, English almost ceased to be a written language on account of Norman ascendancy. When Latin was the language of the Church, and French of the nobles, English became that of the serf (vernacular). It was during this century and a half, when English was speech only, that it lost those grammatical inflections which it had in common with the classical languages. *The Peterborough Chronicles* belongs to the first part of this period and *Layamon's Brut* to the latter part.

**Middle English** (1250-1485)

In this period, English reappeared as a written language in three main dialects :—(*a*) the Northern Dialect, a corrupt form of Northumbrian, (*b*) the Midland Dialect, corrupted from Mercian, and (*c*) the Southern Dialect, corrupted from Wessex. Eventually, the Midland Dialect, holding an intermediate position between north and south, became Standard English. The loss of Normandy under the Plantaganets and the Hundred Years' War brought French into contempt and the mother tongue into repute, while the growth of national feeling stimulated a new interest in all things English, including the language. In 1362, Parliament enacted that English be used for pleading at law, and by 1385, school Latin was translated into English, not French. The Court and Universities of Oxford and Cambridge adopted it while Wiclif and Chaucer wrote it. By 1400 the "King's English" was standard, and a century later, Caxton printed it. The Northern Dialect lived on in Scotland to be revived by Burns and Scott, and to flower in the 20th century (Mr. M'Diarmid's experiment in synthetic Scots is remarkable), while Old Wessex has still its equivalent in the Somerset dialect to-day.

**Modern English** (1485 onwards)

While there have been some changes during this period, these changes have been comparatively slight and unimportant, the invention of printing and the ever-increasing means of communication tending to bring about this result.

The invention of printing has, so to speak, stereotyped the forms of the language. It gave to the people of

Britain, in the translation of the Bible, a standard of English. This fixing of the forms of our language has not prevented the addition to its vocabulary of hundreds of words, from every language in the world, so that *modern English differs from Anglo-Saxon not only in its* **accidence** *but also in its* **vocabulary.** But while orthography has been fixed by the printing press, not only has the sound of individual words undergone change (as may be noted by comparing the rimed sounds of a careful poet like Pope with their 20th century equivalent), but it is believed that the basis of articulation itself may have gradually altered. It has been suggested that late 17th century English speech was not unlike that of Ireland to-day, and that modern American may owe its nasal intonation to its Puritan origin. Whether broadcasting will standardise pronunciation or make us bi-dialectal, remains to be seen.

In an English dictionary we find that only about 28 *per cent. of the words are of Teutonic origin*, while at least 56 *per cent. are of Romance origin.* From this fact, we might be led to infer that English was a Romance rather than a Teutonic tongue. But this dictionary estimate is entirely misleading. While only 28 per cent. of the words in a dictionary are Teutonic, not less than 70 per cent., and sometimes nearly 90 per cent. of the words in the works of the leading English writers are of Teutonic origin.

This difference between what is called the *dictionary estimate* and the *currency estimate* is due to the fact (1) that the words most commonly used are Teutonic, viz., the name of familiar objects and link-words; (2) that these words are repeated again and again.

Indeed, while it is possible to write many sentences without using a word of Romance origin, it is not possible to write a sentence without using words of Teutonic origin. The grammar also is essentially Teutonic, hence *English of to-day is a Teutonic language.*

## *THE DIFFERENT ELEMENTS IN ENGLISH*

### OLD ENGLISH ELEMENT

(1) The purely English words in our language include:—

1. Demonstrative Adjectives.
2. The Pronouns.
3. The Numerals.
4. Prepositions.
5. Conjunctions.
6. Strong, Auxiliary and Defective Verbs.
7. Adverbs of Time and Place.
8. Adjectives of Irregular Comparison.
9. Nouns with Mutation Plurals.
10. Most Monosyllabic Words.

(2) Old English Place Names :—

1. **Burgh, bury,** a fort : Edin*burgh*, Salis*bury*.
2. **Burn,** a stream : Black*burn*.
3. **Dale,** a valley : Clydes*dale*.
4. **Ey,** an island : Angles*ey*.
5. **Field**, a clearing : Shef*field*.
6. **Law,** a hill : Sid*law*.
7. **Mere,** a lake : Winder*mere*.
8. **Stead,** a place : Hamp*stead*.
9. **Stan,** a stone : *Stan*ton.
10. **Stock,** a place : *Stock*port.
11. **Ton,** an enclosure : Pres*ton*.

### THE CELTIC ELEMENT

Celtic origins have already been discussed. Crossing from the Continent, between the 6th and 3rd centuries

B.C., Celts absorbed and replaced the Iberians in these islands. The earlier invaders have their descendants in Scotland, Ireland and the Isle of Man, while the later invaders found refuge from their English foes in Wales, Cornwall and Brittany. How much original Iberian is contained in modern Celtic cannot be assessed but the Scots and Irish are believed to contain more Iberian than Celtic stock. The marked variety in dialects is due to the long years of oral transmission while the fact that modern English contains so few Celtic words shows the completeness of the English displacement in the 5th and 6th centuries.

The Celtic element entered the language at three different periods :—

(1) During the Saxon invasion and conquest of Britain, many Celtic words were adopted into the English language. These words are divided into two classes :—

**Common Words,** such as *bannock, basket, barrow, cradle, darn.*

**Place Names.**

1. **Aber,** a river mouth : *Aber*deen.
2. **Avon,** water : the *Avon.*
3. **Ben,** a mountain : *Benmore.*
4. **Car** or **Cær,** a fortress : *Car*lisle.
5. **Kil,** a church : *Kil*chattan, *Kil*marnock.
6. **Dal,** a field (used as a prefix) : *Dal*ry.
7. **Dun,** a hill fort : *Dum*barton.
8. **Innis** or **Inch,** an island : *Inch*marnock.
9. **Inver,** a river mouth : *Inver*ness.
10. **Mul,** a round hill : *Mull* of Galloway.
11. **Strath,** a wide valley : *Strath*clyde.
12. **Usk** or **Esk,** water : *Usk.*

(2) Many Celtic words were introduced by the Norman French :—as *baggage, basin, budget, cloak, quay, rogue.* These words were taken by the Norman-French from the Celtic inhabitants of Brittany.

(3) Since the middle of the 18th century, Celtic words have been borrowed from the Scottish Highlanders and from the Irish :—as *clan, plaid, kilt, brogue, shamrock.*

The 20th century has seen a Celtic revival, especially in Ireland and Scotland, which may eventually enrich modern English.

## THE FIRST LATIN ELEMENT

Before the Nordic invasion of England, the Britons or Celts had been for nearly four hundred years under the rule of Romans who came not to exterminate but to colonise. The conquered Celt did not surrender his language ; he became bi-lingual (like the native town-dweller in India to-day) and dropped Latin when the Romans left Britain. The English, arriving 40 years later, learned no new Latin words from the Celts, save those which denote military roads, camps and harbours constructed by the Romans. They are :—

**Castra,** a camp : Lan*caster*, *Chester*.
**Fossa,** a ditch : *Fos*bridge.
**Colonia,** a colony : Lin*coln*.
**Portus,** a harbour : *Ports*mouth.
**Strata,** paved roads : *Strat*ford.
**Vallum,** a rampart : *Wall*send.

## THE SECOND LATIN ELEMENT

The Romans left two permanent legacies : roads and Christianity. The former became the possession of the English, the latter of the Celts in Wales and Cornwall and later in Ireland through Patricius. Latin therefore lingered on among the Britons, but there was no infusion into English from this source, so fierce was the hatred between Welsh and Teuton. But England was not unprepared for the introduction of Roman Christianity into Kent by Augustine, and the conversion of Saxon England led to the addition of many new Latin words to English. Many of these were naturally *Church Terms*, but as a considerable intercourse arose between Rome and Britain through the presence of Italian monks, the Latin and Greek *names of many articles of commerce* previously unknown were introduced.

The existence of Latin and Celtic Christianity side by side did much to purify and promote both sects, but the acceptance at Whitby of the Roman form in 664 brought England in close touch with the Continent and merchandise and ideas poured into England to enrich both people and language.

Among the Church terms are :—*angel*, *bishop*, *monk*, *priest*, *psalter*, *disciple*, *altar*, *candle*, *creed*, *font*.

Among the commercial terms are :—*butter*, *candle*, *lettuce*, *pepper* and *turtle*.

This stage marks the transition from archæological to written history.

## THE SCANDINAVIAN ELEMENT (Second Nordic Invasion)

The Vikings who invaded England and Ireland, came from Denmark ; Scotland and Wales were invaded from Norway. They brought a much-needed vitality to English life ; town life commenced and Englishmen took to the sea once more. The Danes quickly surrendered their customs, religion and tongue but their absorption was the " most considerable quickening force in our national character." Their influence on the language was strongest in the north (Danelaw).

Many Danish words were added or adapted to the English language :—

1. **Place Names.**

**By,** a town : Grims*by*.
**Fell,** a hill : Goat *Fell*.
**Tarn,** a lake : *Tarn*syke.
**Beck,** a brook : Wans*beck*.
**Ness,** a headland : Skip*ness*.
**Toft,** a farm : Lowes*toft*.
**Thorpe,** a village : Al*thorpe*.
**Fiord,** an inlet : Mil*ford*.

2. **Common Words** :—*are*, *blunt*, *dairy*, *fellow*, *flee*, *flit*, *ill*, *kirk*, *odd*, *plough*, *sky*, *ugly*.

(1) The *pronunciation* of the language was affected in those districts where the Danes settled, thus producing dialects and doublets ; as *church*, *kirk* ; *evil*, *ill*. Even to-day harder sounds prevail in Scotland and the north-east of England owing to this influence.

(2) Many *inflections* were lost during this period. Englishmen and Danes, having many roots in common, neglected the inflections in their intercourse with each other.

## THE THIRD LATIN ELEMENT

After the Norman Conquest in 1066, English practically ceased to be a written language for nearly 300 years. Norman-French was spoken at school and college, church and court, while English was left to the serf ; and in this way English was affected both in grammar and vocabulary. When English again became the written language of England, it was divided into three dialects of which the Midland became the parent of Modern English.

(1) The Norman-French invasion brought a number of new words into the language, which relate to :—

1. **Feudalism and War**—

Chivalry : baron, squire.
Fealty : tournament, joust, courtesy.
Homage : siege, lists, herald, duke.
Captain : prince, castle, fief, serf.

2. **Government and Law**—

Parliament : assize, session.
Judge : plaintiff, danger, jury.
Court : justice, vassal, sue.

3. **Church and Architecture**—

Pilgrim : penance.
Friar : pardon, charity, conscience.
Palace : tonsure, relic, prior, mercy, pity.
Chapel :

4. **Hunting and Cookery**—

Venison : allure, bay, brace.
Quarry : catch, chase, couple.
Beef : forest, retrieve, venison, rabbit.
Veal : mutton, pullet.

(2) The influx of Norman-French words pushed out of use many English words, but in some cases the English word and the new French word remained, and thus we have in our language to-day many synonyms, one being an English, the other a French word. This is called **Bi-lingualism,** and it has greatly added to the variety and grace of modern English. We find many of those synonyms still used in pairs, such as *will and testament, humble and lowly, acknowledge and confess.* These survivals are evidence of the practice of using the two languages to an audience consisting of both French and English.

(3) **Doublets** and **Hybrids** were also results of this mixed vocabulary. *Doublets are different forms of the same word.* These different words may or may not have the same meaning, but in general, however widely they may differ in meaning, the underlying notion is the same. The Norman French, unable to pronounce the English letter *w*, substituted *gu*, hence we have the doublets *ward, guard*; *wise, guise*; *wile, guile. A Hybrid is a derivative, the different parts of which come from different languages. e.g.*—

Bicycle: Lat. *bi* (*bis*), twice; Gk. *kuklos*, a circle.
Wondrous: Eng. *wonder*; Lat. *osus*, full of.
Goddess: Eng. *god*; Low Lat. *issa*, a fem. suffix.
Perhaps: Lat. *per*, through; Eng. *hap*, chance.

(4) The **pronunciation** of English was also strongly affected by this French influence. Harsh or guttural sounds were either dropped altogether or were greatly modified. This can be seen in the pronunciation of such a word as *slaughter*, the guttural sound of which is still preserved in some of the dialects of Scotland; *ch* was turned either into *k* or softened, *e.g. church, kirk.*

(5) As we have seen, *many Old English words were lost* or pushed out of use by French intruders during this period. This was due to the fact that the language had ceased to be written, and was used only by the poor and illiterate. Hence we find that natural and homely objects have retained their English names; while abstract terms and words relating to Art and Science, have been introduced. The relative position of the Norman-French and the English is strikingly illustrated by the fact that the words referring to animals while living are in the majority of cases English, while the flesh of these animals served up for food has a French name. Thus we have *ox, beef*; *calf, veal.*

(6) The loss of vocabulary was also accompanied by *the loss or modification of many inflections.*

*Note.*—Among those changes we find (1) Plural endings reduced to two: viz., *-en* and *-es*; (2) *-es* the usual Genitive ending; (3) the omission of the dual forms of Pronouns; (4) the ordinary Infinitive, with *to* before it; (5) the Present Participle ending in *-inge*; (6) the Passive Participle dropping the prefix *i* (*ge*); (7) *arn* = are, introduced; (8) the inflections of Adjectives reduced to *-e.*

(7) *The power or habit of forming compound words,* which is one of the characteristics of Teutonic languages, was also lost, although within recent years there seems to have arisen a revival of that practice. *e.g. streamlining.*

## THE ROMANCE ELEMENT

The influence of the Norman invasion on the language was of a destructive character rather than constructive. The words added to the language were few in number, and it was only whon English was again asserting itself as the language of Englishmen that there was a considerable addition of French words to our vocabulary. Indeed, more words were introduced into the language by Chaucer than by the Norman Conquest. Chaucer, however, was not the first writer to leaven English in this way, although he was the most important. And not only did those words pour into the language through the medium of writers like Chaucer and Gower, but our intercourse with France and Italy led to the introduction of many new words.

The Romance element therefore (so called because the words came from languages derived from Latin, such as French, Italian, Spanish, etc.), came into the language and literature, not only through books, but also through commercial intercourse, and while it added to our vocabulary, it modified our pronunciation, and gave a new grace and lightness to our literature.

*Note.*—The leading distinctions between the three dialects—Northern, Midland, Southern, are: (1) The Northern dialect had its Present Indicative Plural in *-es*, the Midland in *-en*, and the Southern in *-eth*. (2) The East Midland and the Southern dialects had the same forms for the Present Indicative Singular: *hop*e, *hop*st, *hop*eth; while the Northern dialect had *hop*e, *hope*s, *hop*es. (3) The Southern retained the prefix *ge* or *i* before Passive Participles: this was never used in the North. (4) The Northern dialect had the Present Participle ending *-ande*; the Midland and the Southern dialects had *-inde*. (5) The Northern dialect had many Scandinavian forms not found in the other dialects:—as *nefe* for *fist*; *low* for *ley* = *flame*; *gar* for *do*. (6) The Southern Plural ending most commonly used was *-en*, *e.g.* *kun* for *kine*; while the Northern was *-er*, *e.g.* *brether* for *brethern*. (7) The Northern dialect had the Pronominal forms *thai*, *thair*, *thaim*; the Midland and the Southern dialects had *hi*, *heore*, *heom*. (8) There were also considerable differences in spelling. Thus, while the letters *f*, *s*, *i* were found in words of the Northern dialect, in the corresponding words of the Southern dialect, the letters *v*, *z*, *u* were used.

## THE FOURTH LATIN ELEMENT

This element was introduced into the English language through **the Revival of Learning,** the influence of which was more widely felt owing to **the Invention of Printing.**

Constantinople, the capital of the Byzantine Empire, had been the centre of a short-lived revival of Greek culture. The capture of this city by the Turks in 1453 drove many of its most learned inhabitants with their manuscripts to Italy. Their presence caused a new interest to be taken in the works of the leading Latin and Greek writers, an interest which spread to France, Germany, and England. The invention of printing made the gratification of this new love of the classics possible, and the writings of many English authors of this period were filled with Latin and Greek words, most of which, however, were unable to retain their position in the language. Sir Thomas Browne's *Hydriotaphia* is an example of a work filled with Latin words which failed to become naturalised citizens of English, *e.g. diuturnity, pupulosity, lacrymatories, exenteration, ponderation, ferity, transcorporating.*

John Lyly's *Euphues* contains not only an excessive number of words of Classic origin, but also many Classic constructions and far-fetched conceits. This style, which was fashionable in Queen Elizabeth's reign, has been called **Euphuism,** from the name of Lyly's book.

The words of the Fourth Latin Element were taken directly from Latin and Greek, and hence we have in English a great many **Latin and Greek Doublets,** one form of the root having come to us *through French*, the other having come directly.

**Latin Doublets**

Example, sample; fact, feat; fragile, frail; fidelity, fealty; legal, leal, loyal; secure, sure; potion, poison; pauper, poor; radius, ray; tract, trait.

**Greek Doublets**

Balsam, balm; blaspheme, blame; dactyl, date; presbyter, priest; paralysis, palsy.

## THE RESTORATION ELEMENT

Charles II, on his return from exile in 1660, brought with him a love for French customs and manners, but this love of things French had a greater influence on the literature than on the language. Light comedy, light essays, attention to the dramatic unities, and the substitution of the heroic couplet for blank verse were the principal results, but a few French words were also introduced, and these words can be distinguished from the earlier words by their pronunciation or accent. The

Restoration word still retains its French accent or pronunciation, while the words introduced at an earlier period have now taken an English sound. The following are the leading Doublets which have thus been formed :—

Critic, critique ; dragon, dragoon ; suit, suite ; corpse, corps.

## MISCELLANEOUS ELEMENTS

(1) **Dr. Samuel Johnson** in the eighteenth century had a fondness for words of Latin origin as well as for Latin constructions. This did not lead to any change in the language, although it had an important influence on the style of writing of the period.

(2) **The French Revolution** had a greater influence on thought than on language, but indirectly and along with German influence, it led to a taste for simpler words. especially those of Teutonic origin.

(3) **Our colonial development,** our intercourse with other nations, and our sea-faring habits have caused us to take words from nearly every language in the world :—

**African** : canary, giraffe, guinea, oasis.

**American** : canoe, moccasin, tomahawk, wigwam.

**Australasian** : kangaroo, taboo, tattoo.

**Arabic** : alcohol, algebra, coffee, sofa.

**Chinese** : china, tea, typhoon.

**Dutch** : boom, golf, smack, waggon (*see below*).

**French** (Modern) : débris, début, etiquette, souvenir

**Hebrew** : amen, cherub, Sabbath, Messiah.

**Hindustani** : Brahmin, bungalow, calico.

**Italian** : alert, balcony, canto, opera.

**German** (Modern) : quartz, meerschaum, morganatic poodle.

**Malay** : amuck, bamboo, bantam, guttapercha.

**Persian** : bazaar, caravan, dervish, shawl.

**Portuguese** : albatross, castle, cocoa, fetish.
**Slavonic** : polka, sable, slave, steppe.
**Spanish** : alligator, cargo, cigar, negro.

(4) **Influence of Crusades** :—Arabic and Persian words : azure, saffron, scarlet, damask, cotton, sugar, orange, assassin, hazard, caravan, mattress.

(5) **Dutch** :—

(*a*) 14th Century (Edward III) Dutch weavers settled in East of England : curl, spool, hawker, huckster, tub, tug, pack, botch.

(*b*) 16th and 17th Century : during time of Elizabeth and Stuarts : (nautical terms) : deck, cruise, keel, yacht, hoist, skipper, boom, sloop, holland(s), buoy, hogshead, landscape, yawl, cashier, drill, furlough.

(*c*) South African Dutch : 2nd half 19th Century and Boer War (1899-1902) : —laager, kraal, trek, commandeer.

(6) Main channels by which new words have entered English :—

1. By foreign invasion, *e.g.* from Latin, Scandinavian, Norman-French.

2. By commerce, *e.g.* Dutch, Chinese, Spanish, Arabic.

3. By influence of religion, literature, music and the great arts : Greek, Latin, Hebrew, Modern French, Italian.

4. By coinage, *i.e.* the making of words to express new ideas in philosophy or science :—*e.g.* Eurasian, folklore, hypnotism, cyclone.

Newton : centripetal, centrifugal.
Jeremy Bentham : international.
Macaulay : constituency.
Whewell : scientist.
Milton : Pandemonium, Satanic, obdurate, mysterious.

Shakespeare: articulate, deracinate, fantastical, impartial, opposition, nurture, epithet, government, luxurious.

Burke: colonial, colonisation, diplomacy, financial, expenditure, municipality.

(7) Many scientific and technical words have been added during recent years. These words, in many cases, are of Greek origin:—

Telephone, telegraph, gramophone, electrocution, cinematograph.

## Words Derived from Names of Places

Arras (Arras), attic (Attica), babel (Babel), bayonet (Bayonne), bedlam (St. Mary of Bethlehem, London), calico (Calicut), cambric (Cambrai), copper (Cyprus), currant (Corinth), damask (Damascus), florin (Florence) gin (Geneva), guinea (Guinea Coast), magnet (Magnesia in Thessaly), meander (Maeander in Asia Minor), muslin (Mosul), palace (Palatine in Rome), parchment (Pergamum), pheasant (Phasis in Asia Minor), sherry (Xeres), spaniel (Spain), tawdry (St. Audrey's Fair), worsted (Worstead in Norfolk).

## Words Derived from Names of Persons

Academy (Academia), atlas (Atlas), bessemer (Bessemer, d. 1898), boycott (Boycott, d. 1897), burke (Burke, d. 1829), cardigan (Lord Cardigan of Crimean War), cicerone (Cicero), dunce (Duns Scotus, d. 1308), epicure (Epicurus, the Athenian), fuchsia (Fuchs, 16th century), guillotine (Guillotin, 18th century), hermetically (Hermes), jeremiad (Jeremiah), jovial (Jupiter), macadamise (McAdam, d. 1836), martinet (Martinet, 17th century), maudlin (Mary Magdalene), pasteurise

(Pasteur, d. 1895), petrel (St. Peter), philippic (Philip of Macedon), platonic (Plato), sandwich (Earl of Sandwich, d. 1792), shrapnel (General Shrapnel of Peninsular War), spoonerism (Spooner, d. 1930), tantalise (Tantalus)

## SOME IMPORTANT DATES IN THE HISTORY OF THE LANGUAGE

410. Romans leave Britain (First Latin Period).
449. First English Invasion.
597. Conversion of Saxons to Christianity (Second Latin Period).
787. Danish Invasion.
1066. Norman Conquest (Third Latin Period).
1204. Loss of Normandy.
1258. Parliament proclaimed in English.
1348. English first taught in schools.
1362. English used in Law Courts.
1453. Capture of Constantinople (beginning of Fourth Latin Period).
1477. Printing introduced into England by Caxton.
1603. Union of Crowns.
1611. Authorised Version of the Bible issued.

---

# CHAPTER XI

## THE DICTIONARY AND ITS USES

"The student without a dictionary is as helpless as a ship without a compass."

"There is as much romance in one column of a dictionary as lies between the boards of '*Treasure Island*.'"

"A dictionary is not a book, it is a habit."

The history of the language shows us the ancestry of words and it must be the aim of every student to "possess" as many significant words as possible. He must not be content with sensing the meaning of a new or rare word; he must be able to use it in its context.

Few realise the full value of a good English dictionary which :—

(*a*) provides the accepted spelling;

(*b*) shows the accent or stressed syllable;

(*c*) sounds the vowels and, where possible, the consonants;

(*d*) indicates the grammatical parts of speech;

(*e*) defines, sometimes by quotation (as in the best dictionaries);

(*f*) traces the history;

(*g*) includes variants, where they exist, to the above.

The alphabetical arrangement of words and the use of key-words at the head of each column facilitate references, and practice brings speed.

Here is a list of common roots. A knowledge of these enables us not only to recognise families of words but to trace, with little aid from a dictionary, the word-history. Use this knowledge to discover other examples of derived words and check by means of your dictionary. Only one derivative is given from each root.

**Latin Roots (Nouns and Pronouns)**

| | | | |
|---|---|---|---|
| 1 | aedes | *house* | edifice. |
| | aevum | *age* | primeval. |
| | ager | *field* | agriculture. |
| | agger | *heap* | exaggeration. |
| | alter | *one of two* | altruist. |
| | amicus | *friend* | amicable. |
| | anima | *soul* | magnanimous. |
| | annus | *year* | perennial. |
| | aqua | *water* | aqueous. |

| No. | Latin | Meaning | Derivative |
|---|---|---|---|
| 10 | arbiter | *judge* | arbitration. |
| | arbor | *tree* | arbour. |
| | arcus | *bow* | arch. |
| | arma | *arms* | armament. |
| | ars | *art* | artist. |
| | astrum | *star* | disaster. |
| | avis | *bird* | aviation. |
| | barba | *beard* | barber. |
| | bellum | *war* | belligerent. |
| | brachium | *arm* | amphibrach. |
| 20 | campus | *plain* | camp. |
| | canis | *dog* | canine. |
| | caput | *head* | recapitulate. |
| | caro | *flesh* | incarnation. |
| | causa | *cause* | accusative. |
| | centrum | *centre* | concentrate. |
| | civis | *citizen* | civil. |
| | clivus | *slope* | declivity. |
| | cor | *heart* | encourage. |
| | corpus | *body* | corporal. |
| 30 | crimen | *charge* | incriminate. |
| | crux | *cross* | crucifix. |
| | culpa | *fault* | exculpate. |
| | cura | *care* | curator. |
| | dens | *tooth* | dentrifice. |
| | deus | *god* | deity. |
| | dies | *day* | journal. |
| | dominus | *lord* | predominate. |
| | domus | *house* | domicile. |
| | dux | *leader* | duke. |
| 40 | eques | *horseman* | equestrian. |
| | equus | *horse* | equine. |
| | ens | *being* | nonentity. |
| | facies | *face* | deface. |
| | fama | *report* | infamy. |
| | fames | *hunger* | famine. |
| | fauces | *throat* | suffocate. |
| | ferrum | *iron* | ferrule. |
| | festum | *feast* | festal. |
| | filius | *son* | affiliate. |
| 50 | filum | *thread* | enfilade. |
| | finis | *end* | infinite. |
| | flos | *flower* | flourish. |
| | focus | *hearth* | fuel. |
| | foedus | *treaty* | confederate. |
| | folium | *leaf* | folio. |

| | | | |
|---|---|---|---|
| | fons | *spring* | fountain. |
| | forma | *shape* | formation. |
| | fors | *chance* | fortunate. |
| | frater | *brother* | friar. |
| 60 | furor | *madness* | infuriate. |
| | fumus | *smoke* | fumigate. |
| | gelu | *frost* | congeal. |
| | gens | *nation* | gentile. |
| | genus | *kind* | degenerate. |
| | gloria | *glory* | glorify. |
| | grex | *flock* | gregarious |
| | gradus | *step* | gradually. |
| | heres | *heir* | heritable. |
| | homo | *man* | human. |
| 70 | hospes | *guest* | hospitable. |
| | hostis | *enemy* | hostile. |
| | humus | *ground* | humble. |
| | ignis | *fire* | ignition. |
| | initium | *beginning* | initiate. |
| | insula | *island* | insulate. |
| | iter | *journey* | itinerant. |
| | janua | *gate* | janitor. |
| | jus | *law* | jurisprudence. |
| | juvenis | *youth* | rejuvenate. |
| 80 | laqueus | *noose* | lace. |
| | lex | *law* | legislate. |
| | liber | *book* | library. |
| | limen | *threshold* | preliminary. |
| | lingua | *tongue* | linguist. |
| | litera | *letter* | literal. |
| | locus | *place* | dislocate. |
| | lumen | *light* | illuminate. |
| | luna | *moon* | lunar. |
| | lux | *light* | pellucid. |
| 90 | magister | *master* | magistrate. |
| | manus | *hand* | manufacture. |
| | mare | *sea* | maritime. |
| | mater | *mother* | matricide. |
| | medius | *middle* | Mediterranean. |
| | mens | *mind* | mentality. |
| | merx | *goods* | merchandise. |
| | miles | *soldier* | militant. |
| | modus | *measure* | accommodate. |
| | mons | *mountain* | amount. |
| 100 | mors | *death* | mortal. |
| | musa | *song* | muse. |

| | | | |
|---|---|---|---|
| | navis | *ship* | navigate. |
| | nervus | *sinew* | nervous. |
| | nomen | *name* | nominal. |
| | norma | *standard* | enormous. |
| | nox | *night* | nocturnal. |
| | nota | *mark* | notice. |
| | numerus | *number* | enumerate |
| | oculus | *eye* | oculist. |
| 110 | odor | *smell* | odoriferous. |
| | omen | *token* | ominous. |
| | onus | *burden* | exonerate. |
| | opus | *work* | co-operate. |
| | orbis | *circle* | exorbitant. |
| | ordo | *rank* | ordination. |
| | os | *mouth* | oral. |
| | os | *bone* | ossify. |
| | ovum | *egg* | oval. |
| | panis | *bread* | pantry. |
| 120 | pars | *part* | particle. |
| | pater | *father* | patrimony. |
| | pax | *peace* | pacify. |
| | pecus | *cattle* | peculiar. |
| | pes | *foot* | expedition. |
| | pluma | *down* | plumage. |
| | poena | *punishment* | repent. |
| | pondus | *weight* | ponderous. |
| | pons | *bridge* | pontoon. |
| | populus | *people* | populate. |
| 130 | praeda | *booty* | predatory. |
| | pretium | *price* | depreciate. |
| | puer | *boy* | puerile. |
| | pullus | *chicken* | pullet. |
| | quies | *rest* | acquiesce. |
| | radius | *ray* | radiate. |
| | radix | *root* | eradicate. |
| | ratio | *reason* | ratiocinate. |
| | res | *thing* | reality. |
| | rete | *net* | reticule. |
| 140 | rex | *king* | regal. |
| | rivus | *river* | rival. |
| | robur | *strength* | robust. |
| | rota | *wheel* | rotation. |
| | rus | *country* | rustic. |
| | salus | *health* | salutary. |
| | sanguis | *blood* | sanguine. |
| | senex | *old man* | senility. |

| | | | |
|---|---|---|---|
| | signum | *mark* | significant. |
| | sol | *sun* | solar. |
| 150 | somnus | *sleep* | somnolent. |
| | stella | *star* | constellation. |
| | summa | *summit* | summary. |
| | tempus | *time* | contemporary. |
| | terminus | *end* | terminal. |
| | terra | *earth* | territory. |
| | testis | *witness* | testament. |
| | turba | *crowd* | turbulent. |
| | umbra | *shadow* | umbrella. |
| | unda | *wave* | inundate. |
| 160 | urbs | *city* | suburb. |
| | vacca | *cow* | vaccinate. |
| | vallis | *valley* | vale. |
| | velum | *covering* | veil. |
| | ver | *spring* | verdant. |
| | verbum | *word* | verbal. |
| | vestis | *garment* | investiture. |
| | via | *way* | deviate. |
| | villa | *farm* | village. |
| | vir | *man* | virtue |
| 170 | vita | *life* | vital. |
| | vitium | *fault* | vicious. |
| | vox | *voice* | vocal. |
| | vulgus | *common people.* | vulgarity. |
| | vulnus | *wound* | invulnerable. |

## Latin Adjectives

| | | | |
|---|---|---|---|
| 1 | aequus | *equal* | equation. |
| | alacer | *cheerful* | alacrity. |
| | altus | *high* | altar. |
| | aptus | *fit* | aptitude. |
| | antiquus | *old* | antique. |
| | arduus | *steep* | arduous |
| | asper | *rough* | exasperate. |
| | audax | *bold* | audacity. |
| | bis | *twice* | biscuit. |
| 10 | bonus | *good* | bounty. |
| | brevis | *short* | abbreviate. |
| | cavus | *hollow* | excavate. |
| | celer | *swift* | accelerate. |
| | clarus | *clear* | clarify. |
| | decem | *ten* | December. |
| | dexter | *right* | ambidextrous. |

| | | | |
|---|---|---|---|
| | dignus | *worthy* | dignity. |
| | duo | *two* | dual. |
| | durus | *hard* | obdurate. |
| 20 | facilis | *easy* | facilitate. |
| | felix | *happy* | felicitate. |
| | firmus | *firm* | confirm. |
| | fortis | *strong* | fortify. |
| | gratus | *joyful* | gratify. |
| | gravis | *heavy* | grief. |
| | inanis | *empty* | inane. |
| | latus | *broad* | latitude. |
| | levis | *light* | levity. |
| | liber | *free* | liberate. |
| 30 | magnus | *great* | magnitude. |
| | malus | *bad* | malefactor. |
| | maturus | *ripe* | premature. |
| | medius | *middle* | intermediate. |
| | memor | *mindful* | commemorate |
| | minor | *less* | diminish |
| | miser | *poor* | misery. |
| | mollis | *soft* | mollify. |
| | multus | *many* | multiply. |
| | novus | *new* | novice. |
| 40 | nudus | *naked* | denudate. |
| | nullus | *none* | nullify. |
| | omnis | *all* | omniscient. |
| | par | *equal* | umpire. |
| | pauper | *poor* | poverty. |
| | peritus | *skilful* | expert. |
| | pius | *religious* | pious. |
| | planus | *level* | plane. |
| | plus | *more* | plural. |
| | potis | *able* | potent. |
| 50 | primus | *first* | primitive. |
| | probus | *honest* | approval. |
| | proprius | *one's own* | property. |
| | proximus | *next* | approximate. |
| | quatuor | *four* | quadrate. |
| | rigidus | *stiff* | rigid. |
| | sacer | *holy* | desecrate. |
| | sanctus | *holy* | sanctify. |
| | sanus | *sound* | sane. |
| | satis | *enough* | satisfy. |
| 60 | salvus | *safe* | salvation. |
| | septem | *seven* | septennial. |
| | severus | *strict* | severity. |

| | | | |
|---|---|---|---|
| | similis | *like* | simile. |
| | solum | *alone* | solitude. |
| | unus | *one* | unity. |
| | vanus | *empty* | vanity. |
| | varius | *different* | variety. |
| | verus | *true* | aver. |
| | vetus | *old* | veteran. |
| 70 | viridis | *green* | verdure. |

## Latin Verbs

| | | | |
|---|---|---|---|
| 1 | aestimo | *value* | estimate |
| | ago | *act* | action. |
| | alo | *nourish* | alimony. |
| | ambulo | *walk* | somnambulist. |
| | amo | *love* | amiable. |
| | aperio | *open* | April. |
| | ardeo | *burn* | arson. |
| | augeo | *increase* | auction. |
| | bibo | *drink* | imbibe. |
| 10 | cado | *fall* | cascade. |
| | caedo | *cut* | excise. |
| | candeo | *shine* | candidate. |
| | cano | *sing* | chant. |
| | capio | *take* | captor. |
| | caveo | *take care* | caution. |
| | cedo | *yield* | succession. |
| | cerno | *discern* | discreet. |
| | cingo | *surround* | precinct. |
| | clamo | *shout* | proclaim. |
| 20 | claudo | *shut* | cloister. |
| | colo | *till* | cultivate. |
| | coquo | *cook* | biscuit. |
| | credo | *believe* | credible. |
| | cresco | *grow* | crescent. |
| | cubo | *lie down* | recumbent. |
| | curro | *run* | chariot. |
| | desidero | *long for* | desiderate. |
| | dico | *say* | verdict. |
| | dirigo | *lay straight* | direct. |
| 30 | do | *give* | date. |
| | doceo | *teach* | docile. |
| | dormio | *sleep* | dormitory. |
| | duco | *lead* | conduct. |
| | emo | *buy* | redemption. |
| | eo | *go* | exit. |

| | | | |
|---|---|---|---|
| | esse (sum) | *be* | essence. |
| | facio | *make* | factor. |
| | fallo | *deceive* | fallacious. |
| | fendo | *ward off* | defence. |
| 40 | fero | *bear* | refer. |
| | ferveo | *boil* | effervescence. |
| | fido | *trust* | confidence. |
| | flagro | *blaze* | conflagration. |
| | flecto | *bend* | reflect. |
| | fligo | *strike* | conflict. |
| | fluo | *flow* | confluence. |
| | for | *speak* | infant. |
| | fodio | *dig* | fossil. |
| | formido | *dread* | formidable. |
| 50 | frango | *break* | fracture. |
| | frigeo | *to be cold* | frigid. |
| | fruor | *enjoy* | fruit. |
| | fugio | *flee* | refugees. |
| | fundo | *pour* | confusion. |
| | furo | *rage* | fury. |
| | gero | *bear* | belligerent. |
| | gradior | *walk* | progress. |
| | habito | *dwell* | inhabitant. |
| | haereo | *stick* | adhere. |
| 60 | halo | *breathe* | exhale. |
| | haurio | *drain* | exhaust. |
| | horreo | *tremble* | horrify. |
| | impero | *command* | empire. |
| | jacio | *throw* | conjecture. |
| | jungo | *join* | conjunction. |
| | laudo | *praise* | laudable. |
| | lego | *gather* | collect. |
| | levo | *raise* | lever. |
| | ligo | *bind* | religion. |
| 70 | linguo | *leave* | relinquish. |
| | liqueo | *melt* | liquid. |
| | loquor | *speak* | colloquial. |
| | luceo | *shine* | translucent. |
| | ludo | *play* | elusive. |
| | luo | *wash* | deluge. |
| | mando | *consign* | mandate. |
| | maneo | *dwell* | mansion. |
| | memoro | *remind* | commemorate. |
| | mereo | *deserve* | merit. |
| 80 | mergo | *plunge* | submerge. |
| | metior | *measure* | immense. |

| No. | Latin | Meaning | Derivative |
|---|---|---|---|
| | miror | *wonder at* | mirror. |
| | misceo | *mix* | mixture. |
| | mitto | *send* | emissary. |
| | moneo | *warn* | monument. |
| | monstro | *show* | demonstrate. |
| | moveo | *move* | emotion. |
| | muto | *change* | commute. |
| | nascor | *am born* | natal. |
| 90 | necto | *tie* | connect. |
| | noceo | *harm* | innocent. |
| | nosco | *know* | notable. |
| | numero | *count* | enumerate. |
| | nuntio | *announce* | pronounce. |
| | nutrio | *nourish* | nurse. |
| | orno | *equip* | ornate. |
| | oro | *pray* | inexorable. |
| | pando | *spread* | expansive. |
| | pango | *agree on* | compact. |
| 100 | pareo | *appear* | apparition. |
| | pasco | *feed* | pasture. |
| | paro | *prepare* | comparison. |
| | patior | *suffer* | passion. |
| | pello | *drive* | propel. |
| | pendeo | *hang* | pendant. |
| | penetro | *enter* | penetrate. |
| | peto | *seek* | petition. |
| | placeo | *please* | complacent. |
| | plaudo | *clap* | applause. |
| 110 | plecto | *twixt* | perplex |
| | pleo | *fill* | complete. |
| | plico | *fold* | multiply. |
| | pono | *place* | opposite. |
| | porto | *carry* | support. |
| | precor | *pray* | deprecate. |
| | prehendo | *seize* | comprehend. |
| | premo | *press* | print. |
| | privo | *take away* | privacy. |
| | probo | *prove* | probable. |
| 120 | pugno | *fight* | pugnacious. |
| | pungo | *prick* | puncture. |
| | puto | *think* | compute. |
| | quaeso | *seek* | request. |
| | queror | *complain* | querulous. |
| | rapio | *snatch* | rapid. |
| | rego | *rule* | regulation. |
| | rideo | *laugh* | deride. |

| No. | Latin | Meaning | English |
|---|---|---|---|
| | rodo | *gnaw* | rodent. |
| | rogo | *ask* | interrogate. |
| 130 | rumpo | *break* | rupture. |
| | salio | *leap* | sally. |
| | sano | *cure* | sanitorium. |
| | sapio | *am wise* | sapient. |
| | scando | *climb* | ascend. |
| | scio | *know* | science. |
| | scribo | *write* | scripture. |
| | seco | *cut* | insect. |
| | sedeo | *sit* | session. |
| | sentio | *feel* | sensation. |
| 140 | sequor | *follow* | consecutive. |
| | servio | *serve* | servitude. |
| | servo | *preserve* | conserve. |
| | sisto | *stand* | insist. |
| | solvo | *loose* | solution. |
| | specio | *see* | spectacle. |
| | spero | *hope* | despair. |
| | spiro | *breathe* | inspire. |
| | spondeo | *promise* | respond. |
| | statuo | *set up* | statue. |
| 150 | sto | *stand* | station. |
| | stringo | *bind* | stringent. |
| | struo | *build* | structure. |
| | suadeo | *persuade* | dissuade. |
| | sumo | *take* | resume. |
| | surgo | *rise* | resurrection |
| | tango | *touch* | contact. |
| | tego | *cover* | detect. |
| | tendo | *stretch* | tent. |
| | teneo | *hold* | retain. |
| 160 | tero | *rub* | attrition. |
| | terreo | *frighten* | terror |
| | tento | *assail* | attempt. |
| | texo | *weave* | textile. |
| | timeo | *fear* | timid. |
| | tingo | *dip* | tincture. |
| | tolero | *endure* | tolerate. |
| | tono | *thunder* | astonish |
| | torqueo | *twist* | torture. |
| | torreo | *burn* | torrid. |
| 170 | traho | *draw* | traction. |
| | tribuo | *give* | tribute. |
| | trudo | *thrust* | intrude. |
| | unguo | *anoint* | unction. |

| | | | |
|---|---|---|---|
| | utor | *use* | utility. |
| | valeo | *am strong* | valiant. |
| | veho | *carry* | vehicle. |
| | vereor | *fear* | reverence. |
| | venio | *come* | convention. |
| | verto | *turn* | convert. |
| 180 | video | *see* | vision. |
| | vinco | *conquer* | victor. |
| | vivo | *live* | revival. |
| | voco | *call* | convocation. |
| | volo | *fly* | volley. |
| | volo | *wish* | benevolent. |
| | volvo | *roll* | revolver. |
| | voveo | *vow* | devotion. |

## Greek Nouns

| | | |
|---|---|---|
| agon | *contest* | agony. |
| anthropos | *man* | anthropology. |
| arctos | *bear* | arctic. |
| astron | *star* | astronomy. |
| atmos | *vapour* | atmosphere. |
| baros | *weight* | barometer. |
| biblion | *book* | bible. |
| bios | *life* | biology. |
| cheir | *hand* | surgeon. |
| chronos | *time* | chronometer. |
| demos | *people* | democracy. |
| eikon | *image* | iconoclast. |
| gamos | *marriage* | monogamy. |
| ge | *earth* | geology. |
| helios | *sun* | heliograph. |
| hippos | *horse* | hippodrome. |
| hudor | *water* | hydraulic. |
| kuklos | *wheel* | cycle. |
| logos | *word* | geology. |
| metron | *measure* | thermometer. |
| ode | *song* | prosody. |
| pathos | *feeling* | sympathy. |
| phos | *light* | phosphorescent |
| polis | *city* | cosmopolitan. |
| techne | *art* | technical. |
| theos | *god* | atheist. |
| therme | *heat* | thermostat. |
| zoon | *animal* | zoology. |

### Greek Verbs

| | | |
|---|---|---|
| chrio | *anoint* | Christ. |
| grapho | *write* | telegraph. |
| luo | *loosen* | analysis. |
| phileo | *love* | philanthropy. |
| rheo | *flow* | rhetoric. |
| skopeo | *see* | telescope. |
| stello | *send* | apostle. |
| trepo | *turn* | tropic. |

### Greek Adverbs and Adjectives

| | | |
|---|---|---|
| eu | *well* | euphony. |
| monos | *alone* | monotony. |
| poly | *many* | polygamy. |
| tele | *afar* | telephone. |

### Old English Verbs

| | | |
|---|---|---|
| beorgan | *shelter* | harbour. |
| bugan | *bend* | bough. |
| biddan | *pray* | bead. |
| bindan | *bind* | band. |
| buan | *dwell* | neighbour. |
| cunnan | *know* | cunning. |
| deman | *judge* | doom. |
| faran | *go* | farewell. |
| gangan | *go* | gangway. |
| grafan | *dig* | grave. |
| scieran | *cut* | share. |
| tellan | *count* | teller. |
| witan | *know* | witness. |
| wyrcan | *work* | wright. |

### Old English Nouns

| | | |
|---|---|---|
| aecer | *field* | acre. |
| ceorl | *man* | churl. |
| eage | *eye* | daisy. |
| here | *army* | harbour. |
| hlaf | *loaf* | lady. |
| hus | *house* | husband. |
| mere | *lake* | marsh. |
| mona | *moon* | month. |
| spell | *message* | gospel. |

Most of these roots may have their meanings enlarged or restricted by the addition of affixes. An affix is usually understood to be either a prefix or a suffix. A prefix precedes the root and has an adverbial or adjectival meaning in relation to the root. A suffix has a variety of functions :—

(*a*) Used to form a noun, it means agent, instrument or state ; it may also be used to suggest diminution or augmentation.

(*b*) Used to form a verb, it means " to make " or " to do " ; it may also add emphasis to the original root meaning.

(*c*) Used as an adjective, it means " having the quality of " or " having a tendency to."

(*d*) Used as an adverb, it denotes place, direction or manner.

Affixes in English are inherited from Greek, Latin (sometimes in French form) and Old English.

## PREFIXES

### English (or Teutonic)

**a-**, a form of *on*, asleep, aweary
**after-**, afternoon
**be-**, behalf, behoof
**down-**, downfall
**for-**, 1. *not*, forbid; 2. *utterly*, forlorn
**fore**, *before*, foretell, forebode.
**gain-**, *against*, gainsay
**in-**, **im-**, **en-**, **em-**, inborn, endear
**mis-**, *wrongly*, mistake
**off-**, *from*, offspring
**on-**, onward
**out-**, *from*, outset
**over-**, oversee, overwise
**to-**, *this*, to-morrow
**un-**, 1. *not*, unclean; 2. *back*, undo
**under**, understand
**up-**, upstart
**wan-**, *without*, wanton
**with-**, 1. *against*, withstand; 2. *again*, withdraw

## Latin Prefixes

ab-, a-, abs-, *from*, abuse
ad-, *to*, adore, advise
ambi-, *around*, ambition
ante-, *before*, antecedent
bis-, *twice*, biped
circum-, *around*, circumlocution
con-, *together*, conduct
contra-, *against*, contradict
de-, *down*, denote
ex-, e-, *out of*, extort
in-, *into*, invade
in-, *not*, innocent
inter-, *between*, interfere
ob-, *against*, oppose
pene-, *almost*, peninsula
per-, *through*, perform
post-, *after*, postpone
prae-, pre-, *before*, prevent
pro-, *before*, proceed
re-, *back*, redound
se-, *apart*, seclude
sine-, *without*, sinecure
sub-, *under*, subdue
super-, *over*, supernatural
trans-, *across*, transgress
vice-, *instead of*, viceroy

*Note.*—The final consonant of a prefix is frequently assimilated with the succeeding consonant for the sake of Euphony—pleasing sound :—as *oppose* for ***obpose***.

## Greek Prefixes

a-, an-, *not*, anarchy
amphi-, *on both sides*, amphibious
ana-, *up*, analysis
anti-, *against*, antipathy
apo-, *from*, apostrophe
cata-, *down*, catastrophe
di-, *two*, dissyllable
dia-, *through*, diameter
en-, em-, *in*, emporium
epi-, *upon*, epitaph
hyper-, *over*, hyperbole
hypo-, *under*, hypocrite
meta-, *after*, metaphor
para-, *beside*, paraphrase
peri-, *round*, perimeter
pro-, *before*, prophet
pros-, *towards*, prosody
syn-, *together*, syntax

# SUFFIXES

## English Suffixes

(1) *Denoting the agent* :— **-er, -ar, -or, -ster.**
*worker, beggar, spinster.*

(2) *Denoting state, action, or condition* :— **-dom, hood, -ing, -ness, -red, -ship, -th.**
*kingdom, manhood, hatred, friendship, truth.*

(3) *Denoting diminution* (*Diminutives*) :— **-en, -ing, -ling, -kin, -ock.**
*chicken, duckling, lambkin, hillock.*

(4) *Adjectival* :— **-ed, -en, -ful, -like, -less, -some.**
*wicked, wooden, godless, winsome.*

(5) *Adverbial* :— **-ly, -wards, -wise, -way.**
*surly, upwards, likewise, straightway.*

(6) *Frequentative* :— **-k, -le, -l.**
*stalk, startle, kneel.*

(7) *Causative* :— **-en, -se, -er.**
*fatten, cleanse, falter.*

**Latin, Greek, and French Suffixes**

(1) *Denoting the agent* :— **-ain, -an, -ee, -eer, -ier, -or, -trix, -ant, -ent.**
*tenant, captain, doctor, engineer.*

(2) *Denoting state, condition* :— **-age, -ance, -ence, -ess, -tion, -sion, -lence, -our, -ery, -ry, -ty.**
*nonage, distance, honour, verity.*

(3) *Diminutives* :— **-aster, -et, -le, -icle, -cule, -ule, -et, -let, -ette, -ot.**
*poetaster, ballot, rivulet, particle.*

(4) *Adjectival* :— **-al, -an, -ain, -ane, -ant, -ate, -able, -ese, -esque, -ile, -ian, -ine, -ive, -ose, -ous.**
*loyal, ignorant, picturesque, grandiose.*

(5) *Causative* :— **-fy, -ish, -ise (-ize).**
*magnify, flourish, minimise.*

## THE FORMATION OF NOUNS

I.—Nouns are formed from Nouns—

(1) By a change in the word itself :—as font, *fount*; stick, *stake*; rod, *rood*; head, *hood.*

(2) By a prefix :—as **re***action*, **in***gratitude*, **mis***statement*.
(3) By a suffix :—as *king***dom**, *maid***en**, *boy***hood.**

II.—Nouns are formed from Adjectives—

(1) By a change in the word itself :—as hot, *heat* ; proud, *pride*.
(2) By a suffix :—as wise, *wis***dom** ; safe, *safe***ty** ; good, *good***ness.**

III.—Nouns are formed from Verbs—

(1) By a change in the word :—as bear, *birth* ; live, *life* ; dig, *ditch*.
(2) By a prefix :—as **off***spring*, **down***fall*.
(3) By a suffix :—as marry, *marri***age** ; deny, *deni***al**

## THE FORMATION OF ADJECTIVES

I.—Adjectives are formed from Nouns by a suffix :—as wood, *wood***en** ; grace, *graci***ous** ; success, *success***ful.**

II.—Adjectives are formed from Adjectives—

(1) By a prefix :—as noble, **ig***noble* ; regular, **ir***regular*
(2) By a suffix :—as white, *whit***ish** ; four, *four***th.**

III.—Adjectives are formed from Verbs by a suffix :—as charm, *charm***ing** ; elude, *elus***ive.**

## THE FORMATION OF VERBS

I.—Verbs are formed from Nouns—

(1) By a change in the word :—as half, *halve* ; proof, *prove* ; sit, *seat*.
(2) By a prefix :—as **be***head*, **un***mask*.
(3) By a suffix :—as *length***en**, *typ***ify.**

II.—Verbs are formed from Adjectives—

(1) By a change in the word :—as safe, *save* ; hale, *heal*.

(2) By a prefix :—as be*dim*, re*new*.

(3) By a suffix :—as *civil*ise, *bright*en.

III.—Verbs are formed from Verbs—

(1) By a change in the word :—rise, *raise* ; lie, *lay* ; fall, *fell*.

(2) By a prefix :—as gain*say*, fore*see*.

(3) By a suffix :—as *tal*k (*tell*), *shov*el (*shove*).

**Cognates** are words which are derived from the same root :—as *sing*, *song*.

**Patronymics** are derivatives formed by adding a prefix or suffix to denote sonship :—as *Macleod*, *Johnson*, *O'Connor*, *Fitzgerald*.

An **Augmentative** is a derivative formed by a suffix denoting increase. The chief Augmentative suffixes are *ard*, *oon*, *one*, *ery* :—as *drunkard*, *balloon*, *trombone*, *rookery*.

A **Diminutive** is a derivative formed by a suffix denoting decrease :—as *rivulet*, *bullock*, *ballot*.

A **Frequentative** is a derivative formed by a suffix denoting repetition :—as *sparkle*, *talk*.

The following are the leading changes which are made in words :—

(1) **Aphæresis** or the omission of a letter or a syllable from the beginning of a word :—as *sample*, *example*.

(2) **Syncope** or the omission of one or more letters from the middle of a word :—as *o'er*, *over*.

(3) **Apocope** or the omission of a letter or a syllable from the end of a word :—as *o'* for *of*.

(4) **Prosthesis** or the addition of a letter to the beginning of a word :—as *newt*, *ewt*.

(5) **Epenthesis** or the insertion of a letter in the middle of a word :—as *tender*, from Lat. *tener*.

(6) **Tmesis** or the separation of a word into two for the purpose of inserting another word between the separated parts :—as " from *what* quarter *soever*."

(7) **Epithesis** or **Paragoge** the addition of a letter to the end of a word :—as *climb*, *clim*.

(8) **Metathesis** or the transposition of a letter in a word :—as *bird*, *brid*.

(9) **Mutation** or **Umlaut** the change of vowel-sound, owing to the influence of the vowel i in the following syllable :—as *kernel*, *corn* ; *kitten*, *cat*.

(10) **Vowel-Gradation** or **Ablaut** is the name given to the change of vowel-sound in Strong Verbs :—as *write*, *wrote*, *written*.

## EXERCISE I

1. **Form Nouns from the following :—**

Wise, Pope, earl, Christian, deacon, great, cave, please, judge, sell, friend, child, long, stoop, greet, grow, simple, depart, abound, brilliant, enchant, felon, marry, sublime, steal, merry, chick, monstrous.

2. **Form Adjectives from the following :—**

Please, hand, girl, silk, delight, loyal, five, teach, glad, lovely, grief, America, offend, exact, hero, poison, shadow.

3. **Form Verbs from the following :—**

Dim, light, clear, civil, gold, Christian, sweet, paralysis, length, weak, clean, long, low, grass, food, hear, sit.

## EXERCISE II

**Point out the Prefixes and Suffixes in the following words, giving their meaning and stating whether taken from English, Latin, or Greek :—**

Syllogism, priesthood, paddock, codling, ballot, lambkin, drunkard, doctor, spinster, diagonal, contradict, gainsay, antecedent, antagonist, education, truth, verity, interrupt, besprinkle, subtract, untie, forlorn, forsake, forenoon, insecure, innate, withstand, withdraw, childlike, human, catalogue, kitten, sparkle, marriage, punish, magnify, criticise, cleanse, lengthen, tenant, talk, poetaster, baptise, labour, describe, mishap, correct, ossify, seclude, credibility, infidel, forego, forearm.

### EXERCISE III

1. **Form words with the following prefixes :—**

Apo, ante, anti, a (English), a (Greek), per, peri, syn, con, with, contra, gain, di, pro, dia, post, fore, for, up, out, un, in, ex, trans, hypo, meta, se, sub.

2. **Form words with the following suffixes :—**

Ock, ot, ard, ee, ane, ish, fy, se, en, kin, let, less, le, able, ous, ose, ian, ive, wise, ful, al, ese, ise, th, ty, hood, dom, our, age, ster, ar, eer, tion, ant, ling.

3. **Give instances of Corresponding Prefixes in English derived from Anglo-Saxon, Latin, and Greek.**

## DICTIONARY PRACTICE

Find the etymology of the following words—(an eight-week course) :—

1. Days of the week, months of the year, jovial, mercurial, saturnine, lunatic, volcano, quixotic, milliner, copper, sardine, nightingale, dirge, rhubarb, antimacassar, guinea, sterling, atlas, stipulation, curfew.

2. Lumber, sign, clerk, calculation, volume, paper, influence, sardonic, journey, decimate, panic, bank, eavesdropper, charwoman, farthing, garden, walnut, butcher, wassail, heaven.

3. Ledger, lord, lady, halibut, marquee, teller, country-dance, corporal, rime, beldam, impertinent, silly, adder, apron, salary, mass, florin, boulevard, Charing Cross, Rotten Row.

4. Nave, some, candidate, compassion, trivial, Bible, Scripture, surname, pagan, heathen, caprice, heliotrope, hydropathic, canter, rent, Passover, ask, music, cathedral, madam.

5. Sanguine, gin, thimble, tantalise, jolly-boat, posthumous, primrose, sand-blind, daisy, mob, van, cab, bus, chap, legend, supercilious, dexterity, sinister, porpoise.

6. Samphire, coward, doll, puzzle, infantry, livery, furlong, constable, steward, comrade, chum, antler, lug-sail, sentry, humble pie, umpire, starboard, larboard, foreign, money.

7. Bonfire, pantry, gaffer, grocer, tailor, heavy, offal, rubbish, cambric, calico, nostril, harbinger, lukewarm, ferret, piebald easel, bronze, bugle, cubit, elbow.

8. Bombast, alarm, denizen, gauntlet (to run), counterpane, grammar, broker, cauliflower, briar, anon, meadow, island, bird, tattoo, quarry, deuce, fee, villain, pamphlet, libel.

## IDIOMS OR PHRASES WITH A HISTORY

The English Language is rich in its allusiveness. One aim of literature is to record appropriately the wisdom of the ages; this wisdom is often condensed into a proverb or idiom, many of which have passed into current speech. Below are some common phrases; their origins (sometimes a matter of conjecture) have been added :—

**A1** :—In the first class; excellent. Used by Lloyd's Registry of Shipping, the letter referring to the condition of the hull, the number to that of the equipment of the vessel.

**Heel of Achilles** :—The weak or vulnerable part of a thing or argument. Achilles, held by the heel, was submerged by his mother in the river Styx; his whole body with the exception of the heel, became as a consequence, invulnerable to attack from mortals.

**Arcadian** :—Belonging to the Golden Age, ideal, simple, rustic. A fertile district of southern Greece, surrounded by mountains.

**Armageddon** :—A great conflict to decide a final issue. The final conflict involving the destruction of the world (Revelations xvi. 16).

**Attic Salt** :—Conversation seasoned (or salted) with the choicest wit. The Athenian (or Attic) dialect was the most literary of the Greek dialects.

**Babel** :—A confusion of speech or noise. The tower of Babel was erected on the plain of Shinar (Genesis xi.).

**Badger** (verb) :—To worry or molest unceasingly. The badger after continuous baiting by dogs, eventually left its lair.

**Bag and Baggage** :—Personal possessions ; the two words are brought together by their alliterative association.

**Bandy** (words) :—To interchange quickly ; to indulge in smart repartee. The bandy was a stick used in hockey or shinty.

**Bedlam** :—Utter confusion. The hospital of St. Mary, Bethlehem was abolished as a priory by Henry VIII, and later used as a lunatic asylum in London.

**Bee-line** :—Direct course, shortest way. The bee with its full load of pollen is reputed to fly straight to its hive.

**Blackguard** :—Ruffian (by degeneration). Originally one who guarded the kitchen utensils and was perhaps blackened by contact.

**To go by the board** :—To discard without hope of compensation. Ships threatened with danger at sea jettisoned their cargo (board : side of ship).

**To draw a bow at a venture** :—To achieve a greater success than was expected. To hit the mark (with an arrow) by accident.

**To draw the long bow** :—To exaggerate. As no doubt the English long-bowmen did after Crecy and Agincourt.

**Bowdlerise** :—To erase all objectionable passages Thomas Bowdler expurgated Shakespeare's plays.

**Bricks without straw** :—To achieve the impossible (Exodus v. 18).

**Bumbledom** :—Unnecessary assumption of authority. The practice of Mr. Bumble in "Oliver Twist."

**Burn one's Boats** :—To compel decisive action by cutting off every possibility of escape. Cortez, having arrived in Mexico, destroyed his boats.

**Caviare to the General** :—That which is beyond the appreciation of the general public. Sturgeon roe is an acquired taste.

**Cock and Bull story** :—An incredible story. As untruthful as the fables of Æsop which contain dialogues between birds and animals.

**Haul over the coals** :—To submit to critical examination and censure. The Mediæval ordeal by fire compelled a suspect to walk blindfolded across heated iron bars.

**Cut and Dried** :—Prepared in advance. It was the practice of herbalists to cut and dry their leaves or flowers before distilling them.

**Devil's Advocate** :—Adviser of less honourable course. It is the duty of the prosecuting (or devil's) advocate to present the case of the accused in the worst light.

**Horns of a Dilemma** :—The choice of an alternative, neither of which is desirable. The unhappy choice of being impaled on one or the other horn.

**Doric** :—Any rustic dialect but usually applied to the Scots vernacular. Doris was a district in ancient Greece.

**El Dorado** :—A golden land ; a place of fabulous wealth. A region containing great wealth between the Orinoco and the Amazon, said to have been discovered by one of Pizarro's officers.

**White Elephant** :—A possession costly and useless. A white elephant, held sacred in the East, might be neither killed nor employed.

**Epicurean** :—A connoisseur of what is best in eating, drinking, art, etc. Originally a follower of Epicurus, a Greek philosopher, whose teaching is now misunderstood to mean that the highest good is self indulgence.

**Fat in the Fire** :—Unexpected catastrophe, such as the overflow of fat from a pan into the fire.

**Feather in one's cap** :—Any mark of distinction. Probably from the practice of a successful archer at the popinjay who pinned a feather into his hat.

**Show the white feather** :—To betray evidence of cowardice. In cock-fighting, it was thought that a bird with a white feather in its tail would not fight to the end.

**Feather one's nest** :—To become rich at the expense of others. From the habit of certain birds which use the feathers of others to build their nests.

**Flash in the Pan** :—A promising effort which achieves nothing. The powder in the pan of the musket sometimes ignited without sufficient force to eject the bullet.

**Flesh Pots of Egypt** :—The material things of the world as opposed to the ideal. The Israelites who escaped from Egypt were prepared to barter their new-found liberty for meat and drink.

**French Leave** :—Any unauthorised departure. The large number of guests at an 18th century French salon rendered impossible the usual courtesy of saying farewell to the hostess.

**Gilbertian situation** :—A grotesquely ironic or impossible situation, such as W. S. Gilbert conceived in his operas written in conjunction with Arthur Sullivan.

**Halcyon Days** :—The golden days of youth. The halcyon (probably the kingfisher) was believed to hatch its young in a nest floating on the water which remained calm for fourteen days at the winter solstice.

**Mad as a Hatter** :—Mad (vindictive) as an atter or adder.

**Hobson's Choice** :—No choice at all (Hobson's or none). Hobson's livery stable at Cambridge hired horses in strict rotation. The student must accept that next the door or none.

**By hook or by crook** :—By any means available. The shepherd to rescue his lamb would normally use his crook; failing that, he would use any other implement such as a hooked stick.

**Look a gift-horse in the mouth** :—To appreciate a present for its value. A horse's age may be known from its teeth.

**Job's Comforter** :—One who aggravates grief in attempting to give comfort. Job's friends did their utmost to persuade him to curse God.

**Johnsonese** :—Pedantic or Latinised English. Dr. Johnson, especially in his earlier works, was a master of sententious expression.

**Jonah** :—One believed to bring bad luck or misfortune to a party or cause. Jonah, believed to be an evil influence, was cast overboard.

**Knuckle under** (verb) :—To surrender. To knuckle is to kneel, a token of submission.

**Smell of the Lamp** (verb) :—To suggest laborious composition; to lack spontaneous expression. The lamp probably suggests late rather than deep study.

**At Loggerheads** (verb) :—To be continuously quarrelling. Probably from the quarrelsome life of the young "tar-boys" who would use their loggerheads as weapons when necessary.

**Rift in the Lute** :—A flaw discovered in something otherwise perfect. A crack in the lute destroyed the purity of the tone.

**Machiavellian** :—Perfidious; without political morality. Machiavelli was a Florentine diplomat of the 15th century and taught that in politics, the end justified the means.

**Malapropism** :—Confusion of words different in meaning but similar in sound. Mrs. Malaprop is an illiterate character in Sheridan's "Rivals."

**Beside the Mark** :—Irrelevant; impertinent; not to the point—as an arrow or bullet just missing the target.

**Martinet** :—A strict disciplinarian. Martinet was an exacting officer in the army of Louis XIV.

**Draw it Mild** :—Cease exaggeration. Strong ale drawn from a barrel could be diluted till it became mild.

**Nemesis** :—Fortune; that which is predestined. Nemesis was the goddess of vengeance.

**P's and Q's** :—Manners; rules of etiquette. Probably from pints and quarts in an ale reckoning; or from pieds and queues.

**Parthian Shot or Shaft** (N.B., not "parting") :—A witty or bitter remark on the eve of departure or to end an argument. The Parthians in battle used to feign flight, then turning in their saddle, deliver an unexpected volley of arrows.

**Cast Pearls before Swine** (verb) :—To bestow riches or kindness on people who are unappreciative. Sermon on the Mount.

**Hoist with his own Petard** :—To be the victim of his own ingenuity. " Hamlet " (Act iii, sc. 4).

**Philistine** :—One insensitive to good breeding ; one lacking culture. The term adapted from the German was used by Matthew Arnold.

**Philippic** :—A speech delivered with bitter invective against an individual—such as Demosthenes delivered against Philip of Macedon.

**Eat Humble Pie** (verb) :—To apologise ; to acknowledge superiority. The umbles (numbles) were the entrails of the hunted deer and were eaten by the lower servants.

**Plain as a Pikestaff** :—Self-evident ; obvious. Probably packstaff, the long staff carried by the professional beggar in Scotland.

**Take Pot-luck** :—To eat without formality. To be content with whatever may be in the pot.

**Beg the Question** :—To take for granted that which requires proof. Probably from the debates of the school men to whom a question or theme was set for oral answering.

**Cross the Rubicon** :—To make a bold decision. Cæsar by crossing the Rubicon, passed from his own territory and so committed an act of war against Pompey.

**Grain of Salt (with a)** :—With modification. A comment on a highly seasoned story.

**Scot-free** :—Unharmed. Originally, free of tax or levy ; but to pay " scot and lot " was to pay according to assessment.

**Shibboleth** :—A test word to confirm origin; a rallying cry of a party, sometimes used in a contemptuous sense (Judges xii, 6).

**Catch a Tartar** (verb) :—To encounter unexpected resistance. The Tartars were both savage and elusive.

**Skin of one's Teeth (to escape)** :—By a very small margin; narrowly. A figurative expression.

**On Tenter hooks** (verb) :—To be very anxious; to be on the rack with excitement. Stretching-hooks (*tendere* = to stretch) were used to stretch the woven cloth to prevent its shrinking.

**Through Thick and Thin** :—In spite of all difficulties; overcoming every obstacle—as a pioneer cuts his way through a jungle whether it be dense or thin.

**Ultima Thule** :—Any remote place. As the islands (probably the Shetlands) north of Britain were to the Romans.

**Utopia** :—Any ideal or impossible condition or place. Sir Thomas More described such an island in his book "Utopia."

**Vandalism** :—Wanton destruction—such as the Vandals were responsible for in North Africa.

**Sail close to the Wind** :—To succeed by taking a hazardous risk. The more closely a sailing vessel is hauled into the wind, the greater is the risk of capsizing.

**Wild Goose Chase** :—A vain pursuit. The wild goose is elusive, and when caught, not worth eating.

**Wire-pulling** :—Securing by unfair influence the help of another. Marionettes were puppets worked by wires pulled from behind; hence, wire-pulling is now a common method of receiving profit or promotion.

## EXERCISE

Give accurately the meaning of each of the following expressions or words. Use each correctly in a sentence *so as to bring out its meaning*. If possible, give the origin of each (it may originate in the Bible, in English, classical or other literature, in history, or in sports, or it may be metaphorical or proverbial) :—

1. A Titanic struggle.
2. Original sin.
3. To bell the cat.
4. A Benedict (Benedick).
5. A Gasconade.
6. A modern Maecenas.
7. The olive branch.
8. A Pyrrhic victory.
9. A sop to Cerberus.
10. To kill the fatted calf.
11. A snake in the grass.
12. To pour oil on troubled waters.
13. A Herculean task.
14. To spoil the Egyptians.
15. A scapegoat.
16. To buy a pig in a poke.
17. A Procrustean bed.
18. The cloven hoof.
19. A Pharisee.
20. The sword of Damocles.
21. A Gargantuan appetite.
22. Laodicean zeal.
23. The handwriting on the wall.
24. A Judas kiss.
25. A palpable hit.
26. Crocodile tears.
27. To exact one's pound of flesh.
28. A wet blanket.
29. An Ishmaelite.
30. To cut the Gordian knot.
31. A round robin.
32. To enter the lists against.
33. To be a square peg in a round hole.
34. A bone of contention.
35. A blue stocking.
36. The curse of Cain.
37. A labour of Sisyphus.
38. To paint the lily.
39. Castles in Spain.

40. Dutch courage.
41. To bury the hatchet.
42. The lion's share.
43. A whited sepulchre.
44. A swan song.
45. To fight like Kilkenny cats.
46. To cleanse the Augean stables.
47. A Jeremiad.
48. To throw up the sponge.
49. To cut the painter.
50. To pull chestnuts out of the fire.
51. Dead Sea fruit.
52. The Greek calends.
53. Greek fire.
54. The fiery cross.
55. To meet one's Waterloo.
56. Like the laws of the Medes and Persians.
57. Below the salt.
58. A modern Crœsus.
59. A Dorcas society.
60. To burn the candle at both ends.
61. To have an axe to grind.
62. To be in high feather.
63. Simony.
64. To tilt at windmills.
65. To kick the bucket.
66. A wolf in sheep's clothing.
67. A son of Anak.
68. To heap coals of fire.
69. The Slough of Despond.
70. To turn king's evidence.
71. To have a rod in pickle for.
72. A Sybarite.
73. A Hedonist.
74. To out-Herod Herod.
75. A Quixotic scheme.
76. A Barmecide Feast.
77. A Stoic.
78. A stalking Horse.
79. Our withers are unwrung.
80. An unlicked cub.
81. A storm in a tea-cup.
82. To wear one's heart on one's sleeve.
83. A busman's holiday.
84. Fabian tactics.
85. Draconian legislation.

86. The old Adam in us.
87. The Scylla and Charybdis of.
88. The Midas touch.
89. To toe the line.
90. Below the belt.
91. To hold a brief for.
92. To hide one's light under a bushel.
93. To be on one's high horse.
94. To beg the question.
95. It never rains but it pours.
96. A Greek gift.
97. The worship of Mammon.
98. To strain at a gnat and swallow a camel.
99. It's the last straw that breaks the camel's back.
100. A straw will show the way the wind blows.
101. One swallow does not make a summer.
102. To look for a needle in a haystack.
103. You can take a horse to the water but you cannot make it drink.
104. People in glass houses should not throw stones.
105. Flotsam and jetsam.
106. Between wind and water.
107. To run with the hare and course with the hounds.
108. It's an ill wind that blows nobody any good.
109. To blackball a person.
110. To black-list a person.

## WORDS LIABLE TO BE CONFUSED

**Synonyms** are words which have a similar but not an identical meaning:—pride and arrogance; antique, archaic and obsolete.

**Antonyms** are pairs of words, each meaning the opposite of the other:—height and depth; jovial and sullen; clergy and laity.

**Homonyms** are words which have the same form and sound but are unrelated in root and meaning:—hue (colour or tint) and hue (outcry). Quail (a bird) and quail (to flinch).

Words are frequently confused through a mistaken

association of ideas :—oculist and optician ; collusion and collision.

Only by careful observation of such words as they are used by the best authors, and by frequent reference to a dictionary may their exact meaning be learned. Here are

(*a*) some words differentiated in meaning,

(*b*) some words for practice and dictionary reference.

(*a*) **Discover and Invent** :—

Discover : to find some thing, place or principle that has always existed.

Invent : to devise, usually mechanically.

Radium was discovered ; the steam engine was invented.

**Liberty and Freedom** :—

Liberty : a state following confinement or control.

Freedom : independence.

The prisoner is now at liberty; others enjoy their freedom.

**Character and Reputation** :—

Character : what a man's qualities are.

Reputation : what they are believed to be.

"The character of Titus Oates differed from his reputation."

**Temporal and Temporary** :—

Temporal : limited time as opposed to limitless time or eternity ; lay, as opposed to spiritual.

Temporary : confined to present time ; as opposed to permanent.

Lords Temporal ; a temporary delay.

**Delightful and Delicious** :—

Delightful : giving pleasure to the mind and the senses, except taste.

Delicious : giving pleasure to the sense of taste.
A delightful cruise ; delicious food.

**Optician and Oculist :—**

Optician : one who provides lenses or spectacles ; one who studies optics.

Oculist : one skilled in the diseases of the eye.

**Continual and Continuous :—**

Continual : rarely ceasing.

Continuous : without intermission of any kind.

It rained continually all February ; it rained continuously for two hours.

**Ingenious and Ingenuous :—**

Ingenious : skilful, inventive.

Ingenuous : ready to believe the best ; simple, easily deceived.

James Watt was ingenious ; St. Francis of Assisi was ingenuous.

**Deprecate and Depreciate :—**

Deprecate : to pray strongly against ; to regret, to protest.

Depreciate : to diminish in value ; to disparage.

We deprecate the violation of treaties.
A falling share depreciates ; a rising share appreciates.

**Imperial and Imperious :—**

Imperial : pertaining to an empire.

Imperious : with authority ; aggressive or haughty.

An imperial conference ; an imperious ruler.

**Verbal and Oral :—**

Verbal : of, or in, words.

Oral : of, or with, the mouth ; by word of mouth.

The examination was both written and oral.
The instructions were merely verbal, both written and spoken.

**Council and Counsel** :—

Council : an assembly convened to deliberate.
Counsel : advice.

**Stimulus and Stimulant** :—

Stimulus : an incentive.
Stimulant : a means to re-create energy (*e.g.* oxygen).

A prize is a stimulus to effort ; brandy is administered as a stimulant.

**Imaginary and Imaginative** :—

Imaginary : pertaining to the fancy, poetic or supernatural ; existing only in the mind.

Imaginative : having the quality of one given to "make-believe."

Sir J. M. Barrie was imaginative ; he created many imaginary situations in his plays.

**Eminent and Imminent** :—

Eminent : outstanding, illustrious.
Imminent : impending, threatening.

An eminent writer ; an imminent disaster.

**Irritate and Aggravate** :—

Irritate : to provoke, to make angry.

Aggravate : to intensify, to make more angry one already angry.

His callousness irritated the judge.
His indifference to reproof aggravated his offence.

**Practice and Practise** :—

Practice (like advice and licence) : used only as a noun.

Practise (like advise and license) : used only as a verb.

**Presumptive and Presumptuous** :—

Presumptive : based on probable evidence.

Presumptuous: arrogant, wilful, going beyond authority, unreasonably confident.

The heir presumptive; the presumptuous officer was censured.

**Euphemism and Euphuism :—**

Euphemism: substitution of a pleasant for an offensive expression.

Euphuism: the style of writing affected by John Lyly in his "Euphues," 1579.

**Luxuriant and Luxurious :—**

Luxuriant: abundant and profuse of growth (especially of vegetation).

Luxurious: excessively comfortable, self-indulgent.

Luxuriant vegetation in the Tropics. Luxurious furniture.

## EXERCISE

(b) Distinguish the meanings of the following words and use each word in a significant sentence :—

wisdom, prudence; stationary, stationery; reverend, reverent; confidant, confident; dependant, dependent; centre, middle; construct, construe; ellipse, ellipsis; accent, emphasis; fact, truth; mutual, common; presentment, presentiment; sanitary, sanatory; similar, identical; indict, indite; millenary, millinery; elusive, illusive; exercise, exorcise; literal, littoral; collusion, collision; credulity, credibility; human, humane; gaol, goal; sleight, slight; shear, sheer; moat, mote; fort, forte; draft, draught; cue, queue; cord, chord; eligible, illegible; aesthetic, ethic; monitory, monetary; elicit, illicit; emigrant, immigrant; prescription, proscription; vial, viol; statue, statute; German, germane; accelerate, expedite; sensual, sensuous; defer, differ; pertinent, pertinacious; economic, economical; nebulous, nebular; consequent, consequential; expedient, expeditious; laudable, laudatory; observance, observation; purport, purpose; exceptionable, exceptional; childish, childlike; ascetic, acetic; choral, chorale; decry, descry; prodigy, progeny; fortuitous, fortunate; dual, duel; censor, censure.

## SOME COMMON ABBREVIATIONS

**Ab init.** (*ab initio*). From the beginning.
**A.D.** (*anno domini*). Of the Christian Era.
**Ad inf.** (*ad infinitum*). To the end.
**Ad lib.** (*ad libitum*). At pleasure.
**A.M.** (*ante meridiem*). Before noon.
**Anon.** Anonymous.
**A.R.A.** Associate of the Royal Academy.
**A.V.** Authorised version.
**B.A.** Bachelor of Arts.
**B.B.C.** British Broadcasting Corporation.
**B.C.** Before Christ.
**B.L.** Bachelor of Law.
**B.Sc.** Bachelor of Science.
**C.A.** Chartered Accountant.
**Cantab.** (*Cantabrigiensis*). Of Cambridge.
**Cantuar.** (*Cantuaria*). Canterbury.
**Cet. par.** (*ceteris paribus*). Other things being equal.
**Cf.** (*confer*). Compare.
**Circ.** (*circiter*). About.
**C.O.D.** Cash on delivery.
**Colloq.** Colloquially.
**Cur. or curt.** Current—this month.
**Cwt.** Hundredweight.
**D.D.** Doctor of Divinity.
**D.F.** (*defensor fidei*). Defender of the Faith.
**Do.** (*ditto*). The same.
**D.P.H.** Department of Public Health.
**D.S.O.** Distinguished Service Order.
**d.t.** Delirium tremens.
**D.V.** (*Deo volente*). God willing.
**Etc.** (*et cetera*). And others.
**Et seq.** (*et sequens*). And the following.
**E. and O.E.** Errors and omissions excepted.
**fcp.** Foolscap.
**F.E.I.S.** Fellow of Educational Institute of Scotland.
**F.R.A.S.** Fellow of Royal Astronomical Society.
**F.R.C.P.** Fellow of Royal College of Physicians.
**F.R.C.S.** Fellow of Royal College of Surgeons.
**G.M.T.** Greenwich mean time.
**Hon.** Honorable or honorary.
**Ib. or Ibid.** (*ibidem*). In the same place.
**i.e.** (*id est*). That is.
**I.H.S.** (*Greek I.H.C.*). The first three letters of "Jesus."
**Incog.** (*incognito*). Avoiding recognition.
**Infra dig.** (*infra dignitatem.*) Beneath the dignity of.
**In loc.** (*in loco*). In the place (of).
**Inst.** Instant—the current month.
**K.C.** King's Counsel.
**L.C.C.** London County Council.
**LL.B.** Bachelor of Laws.
**LL.D.** Doctor of Laws.
**L.S.D.** (*librae, solidi, denarii*) Pounds, shillings, pence.
**M.A.** Master of Arts.
**M.B.E.** Member of British Empire.
**M.D.** (*medicinæ doctor*). Doctor of Medicine.

**Mldle. or Mlle.** Mademoiselle.
**MS(S).** Manuscript.—manuscripts.
**Mus.B.** Bachelor of music.
**N.B.** (*nota bene*). Note carefully.
**Né(e).** Born.
**Nem. con.** (*nemine contradicente*). Unanimous.
**Non seq.** (*non sequiter*). It does nor follow.
**O.B.E.** Order of the British Empire.
**Ob.** (*obiit*). Died.
**Per an.** (*per annum*). Yearly.
**Pro tem.** (*pro tempore*). For the time being.
**Prox.** (*proximo*). Next.
**P.S.** (*post scriptum*). Written after.
**P. & O.** Peninsular and Oriental Company.
**Q.E.D.** (*quod erat demonstrandum*). Which was to be shown.
**Q.E.F.** (*quod erat faciendum*). Which was to be done.
**Q.V.** (*quod vide*). Which see or consult.
**R.I.P** (*requiescat in pace*). May he rest in peace.
**R.S.V.P.** (*répondez s'il vous plaît*). Reply, if you please.
**Sc. Sculp.** (*sculpist*). He engraved it.
**S.D.** (*sine die*). Without date—indefinitely adjourned.
**Ut sup.** (*ut supra*). As above.
**Vid.** (*vide*). See.

---

## CHAPTER XII

## PROSODY

**Prosody** (*Gr. pros-odia, lit. a song sung to an instrument*) deals with the laws of metre.

English verse is regulated by the recurrence of accent, *i.e.* it is *accentual.* (*Note.*—Latin metre is *quantitative*—*i.e.* it depends on *quantity.* Syllables in Latin are divided into *short* and *long*: these adjectives refer to the *time* the voice dwells on the syllables.)

English scansion depends on the stress or emphasis (in sound) with which we pronounce a syllable (*i.e.* a sound which must contain a vowel but which may also contain consonants). *e.g.* in the word *ad-ver-tise* we stress the syllable *aa-*, *i.e.* we accent the first syllable.

**Rhythm** (*Gr. rhuthmos, measured flow or motion*) is the regular, recognisable sequence of accented and unaccented syllables forming a definite group—a regular pattern of syllables, in so far as the succession of accents is concerned. These groups of syllables are called *feet.*

Some passages in prose (*e.g.* in Kingsley's "*Westward Ho!*") are capable of being arranged into such groups—*i.e.* they have rhythm. This rhythm may not be entirely definite—we may call it a loose rhythm. In poetry, when the rhythm is regular and capable of being *scanned, i.e.* of having the syllables assessed as stressed, unstressed or common (neither stressed nor unstressed), *so as to give a definite pattern, a succession of the same foot,* we say it is in metre.

Many modern poems do not possess a regular metre—these may be termed *dithyrambic.*

**Rhyme** (*Anglo-Saxon, rim*), described by Milton as "the invention of a barbarous age, to set off wretched matter and lame metre," should be spelled rime but it has been confused with the Greek rhuthmos.

Rhyme is a similarity of sound between the endings of two or more words, usually found at the ends of lines. *This similarity of ending sound should begin at the accented vowel and continue to the end of the word, and the consonants preceding the rhyming sounds should be different to form a perfect rhyme, e.g.* :—

> When Ruth was left half deso*late,*
> Her father took a second *mate.*

It should be noted that in rhyme it is the *sound* that is to be considered, irrespective of the spelling: the effect on the *ear*, not on the *eye*. In these lines :—

> That deep-brow'd Homer ruled as his *demesne* :
> Yet did I never breathe its pure se*rene.*

we have a perfect rhyme. Yet, in *peace* and *seize* we have an imperfect rhyme, as it does not satisfy the ear. Such imperfect rhyme, *i.e.* rhyme in respect only of the vowel sounds or of the consonantal sounds, is termed **Assonance** Example :—

With which, like flowers that mock the corse *beneath*
He had adorned and hid the coming bulk of *Death*.

We have different types of rhyme. Rhyme is usually of *one* syllable ; this type is termed *masculine* (or single) rhyme, *e.g. bell, dell*. When the rhyme consists of two syllables it is termed *feminine* (or double) rhyme, *e.g. lending, bending*. When the rhyming sounds are more than two, we have *polysyllabic rhyme*. This type of rhyme is used chiefly in humorous verse, *e.g.* Butler's "*Hudibras*" (Burlesque).

Call fire, and sword, and *desolation*,
A godly thorough *Reformation*. BUTLER.

And it seemed as if a voice
(Sweeter far than by harp or by *psaltery*
Is breathed) called out, Oh rats, rejoice !
The world is grown to one vast *drysaltery* !
So munch on, crunch on, take your *nuncheon*,
Breakfast, supper, dinner, *luncheon*.

"*Pied Piper of Hamelin.*"

**Middle Rhyme** (sometimes called Leonine) is found in lines in which an accented sound in the middle of a line corresponds with the sound at the end, *e.g.* :—

Perfume and *flowers* fall in *showers*.—TENNYSON.
The splendour *falls* on castle *walls*.—TENNYSON.
Come uppe *Whitefoot*, come uppe *Lightfoot*.—J. INGELOW.

**Identical Rhyme** consists in using exactly the same sound twice. It is unusual, *e.g.* :—

All close they met again, before the *dusk*
Had taken from the stars its pleasant *veil*,
All close they met, all eves, before the *dusk*
Had taken from the stars its pleasant *veil*.

KEATS'S "*Isabella.*"

**Eye Rhyme** is found when the rhyme exists *for the eye* but *not for the ear, e.g. dough* does not rhyme with *cough* although it appears to do so; nor does *quay* rhyme with *day*.

**Alliteration** is the recurrence of the same sound in closely situated words. It should be noted that this recurrence of the same sound is not invariably confined to the initial syllables of words. The alliteration of initial syllables is invariably found in Old English poetry: this type of alliteration is called Head Rhyme. Chaucer, who used the end type of rhyme introduced by the Normans, scoffingly called the old head rhyme "rim-ram-roff."

Here is an example of the use of alliteration in Old English poetry:—

> In a *s*omer *s*eson whan *s*oft was the *s*onne
> I *sh*ope me in *sh*roudes as I a *she*pe were.
>
> LANGLAND'S "*Piers Plowman.*"

Other examples:—

> *D*are the unpastured *d*ragon in his *d*en.
>
> —SHELLEY'S "*Adonais.*"
>
> *R*uin seize thee *r*uthless king.—GRAY.

Study the following examples:—

> Five *m*iles *m*eandering with a *m*azy *m*otion.—COLERIDGE.
> The *mil*d-eyed *mel*ancho*l*y *L*otus-eaters ca*m*e.—TENNYSON.
> The *mo*ping *o*wl d*o*th to the *m*oon co*m*plain.—GRAY.

**Vowel Music** is the varying of vowel sounds so as to produce a pleasing, euphonious effect; the contrasted vowels are usually in the accented syllables.

Consider the effect of the sound values in:—

> Charmed magic casements opening on the foam
> Of perilous seas in faery lands forlorn.
>
> KEATS.

O my Luve's like a red, red rose
  That's newly sprung in June:
O my Luve's like the melodie
  That's sweetly play'd in tune.

BURNS.

Count the number of "l's" in Collins's "*Ode to Evening*" and study the effects produced.

A **Verse** (*L. vertere—to turn*) is correctly used of *one line*, but it is commonly used for a number of lines of poetry forming a definite stanza. Verse is sometimes used as a term to distinguish the form in which language is written, *e.g.* verse as distinguished from prose. It should be remembered that the word poetry properly refers to the spirit of the language and treatment of the theme. (See page 345, Ch. XV.)

**Cæsura** (*L. caedere—to cut*).—In English prosody this term means the pause of the voice when speaking lines of poetry, especially in the longer metres, *e.g.* pentameter and hexameter. In scansion, it is indicated by a caret ‸.

O Prince, ‸ O Chief of many throned Powers
That led the embattled Seraphim to war ‸
Under thy conduct, ‸ and, in dreadful deeds
Fearless, ‸ endangered Heaven's perpetual King, ‸
And put to proof his high supremacy, ‸
Whether upheld by strength, ‸ or chance, ‸ or fate. ‸

MILTON'S "*Paradise Lost.*"

Writers of good blank verse give their lines great flexibility and variety by varying the position of the cæsura.

This is the forest primeval. ‸ The murmuring pines ‸ and the hemlocks, ‸
Bearded with moss, ‸ and in garments green, ‸ indistinct in the twilight, ‸
Stand like Druids of old, ‸ with voices sad and prophetic. ‸

LONGFELLOW'S "*Evangeline.*"

**Blank Verse** is unrhymed verse. The term blank verse can be applied to lines of poetry using any kind of metre but because most blank verse is written in iambic pentameter, that is usually what is meant when the term is used.

A **Foot** is the unit of metre in verse.

TWO SYLLABLE FEET

| *Name* | *Adjective* | *Composed of* | *Designated by* |
|---|---|---|---|
| Iambus (iamb). | Iambic. | unaccented + accented. | ⏑ — or *xa* |
| Trochee. | Trochaic. | accented + unaccented. | — ⏑ or *ax* |
| Spondee. | Spondaic. | Two accented | — — or *aa* |
| Pyrrhic. | Pyrrhic. | Two unaccented syllables. | ⏑ ⏑ or *xx* |

THREE SYLLABLE FEET

| *Name* | *Adjective* | *Composed of* | *Designated by* |
|---|---|---|---|
| Anapæst. | Anapæstic. | Two unaccented + one accented. | ⏑ ⏑ — or *xxa* |
| Dactyl. | Dactylic. | One accented + two unaccented. | — ⏑ ⏑ or *axx* |
| Amphibrach. | Amphibrachic. | Unaccented + accented + unaccented. | ⏑ — ⏑ or *xax* |

Of the above feet the commonest in English verse are :—iambic, trochaic, anapæstic, dactylic.

The best way to remember these feet, and to realise the metrical effect of each different foot is to commit to memory a few lines of each kind of metre. Some of these feet are seldom used as normal feet in lines of English poetry.

**Iambic Metre** is commonest in our speech and poetry : it is the normal metre in a play of Shakespeare's.

You call | me mis|believ|er, cut-|throat dog, |
And spit | upon | my Jew|ish gab|erdine. ||

SHAKESPEARE'S "*Merchant of Venice.*"

**Trochaic Metre.**—

Crabbed | Age and | Youth |
Cannot | live to|gether. ||

Queen and | Huntress | chaste and | fair, |
Now the | sun is | laid to | sleep, |
Seated | in thy | silver | chair, |
State in | wonted | manner | keep. ||

B. JONSON.

**Anapæstic Metre**:

See the fur|ies arise, |
See the snakes | that they rear |
How they hiss | in their hair |
And the spar|kles that flash | from their eyes.||

DRYDEN'S "*Alexander's Feast.*"

But he lay | like a Warr|ior tak|ing his rest |

C. WOLFE

**Dactylic Metre**:

Merrily, | merrily | shall I live | now |
Under the | blossom that | hangs on the | bough. ||

SHAKESPEARE'S "*Tempest.*"

Bird of the | wilderness, |
Blithesome and | cumberless. ||

HOGG'S "*Skylark.*"

The metre of a line of poetry is described in terms of (1) the kind of foot used, and (2) the number of feet in the line.

In order to find out this information we *scan* the line, *i.e.* we assess the value of each syllable (accented or stressed or long: or unaccented or unstressed or short: or common—neither definitely stressed nor unstressed) and then we divide the line into *feet*. This operation is called **Scansion**. We then designate the lines in accordance with the number of feet they contain.

| | | | | | |
|---|---|---|---|---|---|
| Monometer | is a | line of | one foot | | |
| Dimeter | ,, | ,, | two feet. | | |
| Trimeter | ,, | ,, | three feet. | | |
| Tetrameter | ,, | ,, | four | ,, | |
| Pentameter | ,, | ,, | five | ,, | |
| Hexameter | ,, | ,, | six | ,, | (Alexandrine.) |
| Heptameter | ,, | ,, | seven | ,, | (Fourteener.) |
| Octometer | ,, | ,, | eight | ,, | |

When scanning a line give each syllable the value it has *when you pronounce it.* If the poetry which you are scanning is archaic, it should be remembered that pronunciation may have altered, *e.g.* in Shakespeare's time "persevere" was pronounced per-*sev*-er. This alteration of pronunciation affects rhyme, *e.g.* in Pope's "*Rape of the Lock*"—

Hear thou, great Anna, whom three realms *obey*
Dost sometimes counsel take—and sometimes *tea.*

And again, in his "*Essay on Criticism*,"

From the same foes, at last, both felt their *doom*,
And the same Age saw Learning fall, and *Rome*.

Do not expect to find all lines of poetry entirely regular, having a definite number of feet and each foot the same. In the verses of the eighteenth century poets, we do have an almost unbroken regularity of metre. Such metre is often condemned on account of its unvarying regularity, the effect of which is monotonous. Most poets avoid the monotony by:—

(1) **Aberrations**: the substitution of a different foot for the normal foot used, *e.g.* a spondee for an iambus.

The qual|ity | of mer|cy is | not strain'd | (Spondee for iambus.)

Damn'd as | thou art, | thou hast | enchant|ed her.| (Trochee for iambus.)

**Equivalence** is a term used to indicate the substitution of a three syllable foot for a two syllable foot, or vice versa. It can be considered as being included under the more comprehensive term of aberration.

(2) Adding an extra unaccented syllable to the normal length of the line, thus making the line *hypermetrical*, *i.e.* beyond the requirements of the scheme of feet used, *e.g.*—

O thou | foul thief, | where hast | thou stow'd | my daugh||ter? ||

(3) Having a syllable short of the normal length, thus making the line *catalectic* (*Gr. katalektikos—incomplete*), *e.g.*—

*Portia*: Thus hath | the can|dle singed | the moth.||
"*Merchant of Venice*" (one foot short).

(4) Having a syllable short at the beginning of the line, *e.g.*—

1. While | the cock | with live|ly din |
Scatters | the rear | of dark|ness thin |
3. And to | the stack | or the | barn door |
Stout|ly struts | his dames | before.|

Such lines as 1 and 4 are termed *truncated* lines.

**Examples of Various Metres.**—Scan the Examples.

**Dimeter.**

Sceptre and crown
Must tumble down. SHIRLEY.

Bird of the wilderness
Blithesome and cumberless. HOGG.

### Trimeter.

Crabbed Age and Youth
Cannot live together. SHAKESPEARE.

Toll for the Brave!
The brave that are no more!
All sunk beneath the wave
Fast by their native shore. COWPER.

Fair Daffodils, we weep to see
You haste away so soon:
As yet the early-rising Sun
Has not attain'd his noon. HERRICK.

### Tetrameter.

When Britain first at Heaven's command
Arose from out the azure main. THOMSON.

The way was long, the wind was cold,
The minstrel was infirm and old. SCOTT.

### Pentameter.

Beside yon straggling fence that skirts the way,
With blossom'd furze unprofitably gay. GOLDSMITH

Had it pleas'd Heaven
To try me with affliction, had they rain'd
All kinds of sores and shames on my bare head,
Steep'd me in poverty to the very lips,
Given to captivity me and my utmost hopes,
I should have found in some place of my soul
A drop of patience. SHAKESPEARE.

### Hexameter.

Four times the sun had risen and set; and now on the fifth day
Cheerily called the cock to the sleeping maids of the farm-house.
Soon o'er the yellow fields, in silent and mournful procession,
Came from the neighbouring hamlets and farms the Acadian women,
Driving in ponderous wains their household goods to the seashore. LONGFELLOW'S "*Evangeline.*"

*N.B.*—In "*Evangeline*" metre, the first four feet may be spondees or trochees or dactyls, the fifth is nearly always a dactyl and the sixth a spondee or trochee.

**Doggerel** is the name given to verse which is imperfect in metre and faulty in rhyme. It is sometimes applied to worthless verse, in contempt.

### Special Metres and Stanzas

**A Stanza** (*It. stanza*) is a group of lines or verses of poetry having a definite pattern—a fixed sequence as regards length of line and metrical form, usually having a rhyme scheme. A stanza is frequently called a verse. The term is also loosely applied to divisions in a poem (corresponding to paragraphs in prose), *e.g.* as in "*Lycidas.*"

**Heroic Couplet**: consists of two lines of iambic pentameter which rhyme. It is so-called because it has been much used in translating epic and heroic poetry.

> That's my last Duchess painted on the wall,
> Looking as if she were alive; I call
>
> BROWNING.

When the *sense* is completed in the couplet it is generally termed a *closed couplet* or a Popean couplet, since Pope's couplets usually are closed.

> True ease in writing comes from art, not chance,
> As those move easiest who have learn'd to dance.
>
> POPE.

Sometimes Pope and Dryden use three rhyming lines instead of the heroic couplet. These three lines are bracketed and termed *triplets*.

> But as the slightest sketch if justly trac'd,
> Is by ill-colouring but the more disgrac'd,
> So by false learning is good sense defac'd.

When the voice has to pause at the end of a line, whether there is any punctuation or not, the line is termed *end-stopt*.

When the voice cannot pause at the end of a line, it is termed a *run-on* line. In such lines we have examples of *enjambment* (*Fr. striding over*).

I have done nothing but in care of thee, (end-stopt)
(Of thee, my dear one, thee my daughter !) who (run-on or enjambed)
Art ignorant of what thou art, nought knowing ,, ,,
Of whence I am ; nor that I am much better ,, ,,
Than Prospero, master of a full poor cell, (end-stopt)
And thy no greater father.

SHAKESPEARE.

**Ballad Metre.**—The commonest ballad stanza is one of four lines but these lines may vary in length, and the rhyme schemes may also vary. The authentic ballad contains many aberrations and many ballads written by modern poets imitate these crudenesses of the old ballad and their archaic diction.

Examples of ballad stanzas :—

That man hath perfect blessedness *a.*
Who walketh not astray *b.*
In counsel of ungodly men, *c.*
Nor stands in sinners' way. *b.*

Ye Highlands and ye Lowlands, *a.*
O where hae ye been ? *b.*
They hae slain the Earl of Murray, *c.*
And hae laid him on the green. *b.*

O well is me, my gay goshawk, *a.*
That you can speak and flee ; *b.*
For you can carry a love-letter *c.*
To my true Love from me. *b.*

O listen, listen, ladies gay ! *a.*
No haughty feat of arms I tell ; *b.*
Soft is the note and sad the lay, *a.*
That mourns the lovely Rosabelle. *b.*

**The In Memoriam stanza** (so-called from Tennyson's

use of it in his poem of that name) is a four-lined stanza of iambic tetrameters rhyming *abba*.

There rolls the deep where grew the tree. *a.*
O earth what changes hast thou seen. *b.*
There where the long street roars, hath been *b.*
The stillness of the central sea. *a.*

**Elegiac Stanza.**—If there is any recognised elegiac stanza in English it is that used by Gray in his "*Elegy Written in a Country Churchyard.*" It is a four-line stanza of iambic pentameter rhyming *abab*.

The boast of heraldry, the pomp of pow'r, *a.*
And all that beauty, all that wealth e'er gave— *b.*
Awaits alike th' inevitable hour; *a.*
The paths of glory lead but to the grave. *b.*

There are many famous elegies in the English language, *e.g.* Shelley's "*Adonais*," Milton's "*Lycidas*," and in them different stanzas are used.

**Burns Stanza.**—As implied in the name, this is the favourite stanza of Burns, rhyming *aaabab*.

Wee, sleekit, cowrin, tim'rous beastie, *a.*
O, what a panic's in thy breastie! *a.*
Thou need na start awa sae hasty, *a.*
  Wi' bickering brattle! *b.*
I wad be laith to rin an' chase thee, *a.*
  Wi' murd'ring pattle! *b.*

**Rhyme Royal.**—This stanza is so-called on account of its being used by James I of Scotland in his "*King's Quhair*"; it is used by Chaucer in the "*Clerk's Tale*" and by W. Morris in the "*Earthly Paradise.*"

The lines are iambic pentameter, rhyming *ababbcc*.

Then smiling did he turn to leave the place, *a.*
But with his first step some new fleeting thought *b.*
A shadow cast across his sun-burnt face; *a.*
I think the golden net that April brought *b.*
From some warm world his wavering soul had caught; *b.*
For, sunk in vague sweet longing, did he go *c.*
Betwixt the trees with doubtful steps and slow. *c.*

"*Atalanta's Race*"—W. MORRIS.

**Ottava Rima**: Ottava is the Italian for octave (eight)—the number of lines in such a stanza. Byron uses it in "*Don Juan*" and Keats in "*Isabella.*" It is composed of 8 iambic pentameter lines rhyming *abababcc.*

For them the Ceylon diver held his breath, *a.*
And went all naked to the hungry shark; *b.*
For them his ears gush'd blood; for them in death *a.*
The seal on cold ice with piteous bark *b.*
Lay full of darts; for them alone did seethe *a.*
A thousand men in troubles wide and dark: *b.*
Half-ignorant, they turn'd an easy wheel, *c.*
That set sharp racks at work, to pinch and peel. *c.*

KEATS'S "*Isabella.*"

**Spenserian Stanza**: This stanza, used by Spenser, in his "*Faerie Queene,*" is a 9-lined rhyming stanza, the first 8 lines iambic pentameter, the ninth an alexandrine rhyming *ababbcbcc.* This stanza is used in Burns's "*Cottar's Saturday Night,*" Shelley's "*Adonais,*" Keats's "*Eve of St. Agnes.*" It is Chaucer's eight-line stanza with an alexandrine, rhyming with the last line, added.

Eftsoons they heard a most melodious sound, *a.*
Of all that might delight a dainty ear, *b.*
Such as at once might not on living ground, *a.*
Save in this paradise, be heard elsewhere: *b.*
Right hard it was for wight which did it hear, *b.*
To read what manner music that might be; *c.*
For all that pleasing is to living ear *b.*
Was there consorted in one harmony: *c.*
Birds, voices, instruments, winds, waters, all agree. *c.*

SPENSER'S "*Faerie Queene.*"

**Sonnet** (See under Ch. 15: Literary Forms).—The sonnet is a poem of fourteen lines of iambic pentameter having a definite rhyme scheme. There are two forms with some possible variations.

### I.—Italian, Petrarchan or Classical Type

|  |  | | |
|---|---|---|---|
| When I consider how my light is spent | a. | Quatrain | Octave |
| Ere half my days in this dark world and wide, | b. | | |
| And that one talent which is death to hide | b. | | |
| Lodg'd with me useless, though my soul more bent | a. | | |
| To serve therewith my Maker, and present | a. | Quatrain | |
| My true account, lest He returning chide— | b. | | |
| " Doth God exact day-labour, light deni'd ? " | b. | | |
| I fondly ask : but Patience, to prevent | a. | | |
| *Volta or Turn of Thought* | | | |
| That murmur, soon replies, " God doth not need | c. | Tercet | Sestet |
| Either man's work, or His own gifts ; who best | d. | | |
| Bear His mild yoke, they serve Him best ; His state | e. | | |
| Is kingly ; thousands at His bidding speed, | c. | Tercet | |
| And post o'er land and ocean without rest ; | d. | | |
| They also serve who only stand and wait." | e. | | |

Milton's Sonnet "*On His Blindness.*"

It should be noted that this type consists of an octave and a sestet, with a pause and volta (turn of thought) occurring at or near the end of the octave. There are 5 rhyming sounds. The rhymes of the sestet may vary ; other schemes are :

| | | |
|---|---|---|
| *c. d. c.* | and | *c. d. e.* |
| *d. c. d.* | | *d. c. e.* |

### II.—A. Surrey or Shakespearean Type B. Spenserian Type

|  |  | |
|---|---|---|
| A. Let me not to the marriage of true minds | a. | Three Quatrains |
| Admit impediments. Love is not love | b. | |
| Which alters when it alteration finds, | a. | |
| Or bends with the remover to remove— | b. | |
| O no ! it is an ever-fixed mark | c. | |
| That looks on tempests and is never shaken ; | d. | |
| It is the star to every wandering bark, | c. | |
| Whose worth's unknown, although his height be taken. | d. | |
| Love's not Time's fool, though rosy lips and cheeks | e. | |
| Within his bending sickle's compass come ; | f. | |
| Love alters not with his brief hours and weeks, | e. | |
| But bears it out ev'n to the edge of doom. | f. | |

If this be error, and upon me proved, *g*. } Rhyming
I never writ, nor no man ever loved. *g*. } Couplet

SHAKESPEARE.

*Note.*—This type consists of 3 unlinked quatrains, rhyming alternately, and a concluding couplet. It has 7 rhyming sounds.

B. One day I wrote her name upon the strand; *a*.
But came the waves and washed it away: *b*.
Again I wrote it with a second hand, *a*.
But came the tide and made my pains his prey. *b*.

"Vain man!" said she, "that dost in vain assay *b*.
A mortal thing so to immortalise; *c*.
For I myself shall like to this decay, *b*.
And eke my name be wiped out likewise." *c*.

"Not so," quoth I, "let baser things devise *c*.
To die in dust, but you shall live by fame: *d*.
My verse your virtues rare shall eternise, *c*.
And in the heavens write your glorious name— *d*.

(THREE QUATRAINS, LINKED)

Where, when as death shall all the world subdue *e*. } Rhyming
Our love shall live, and later life renew." *e*. } Couplet

SPENSER.

*Note.*—This type consists of 3 quatrains, *linked*, rhyming alternately, and a final couplet. The last rhyming sound of the first two quatrains is used as the first rhyming sound of the next. Thus there are 5 rhyming sounds.

**Christabel Metre.**—In Old English poetry each line may be regarded as being divided into two parts, the first part containing two stressed syllables, the second part at least one, the accented syllables being alliterated, *e g.*—

*G*rendel *g*ongan *G*odes yrre baer.

As *stress* and not quantity is the basis of English metre, the unstressed syllables are the least important.

Coleridge, in order to escape the close confinement of orthodox poetic feet, in his poem "*Christabel*" arranges his lines in such a manner that, so long as each has *four* stressed syllables, the unstressed syllables have little significance as regards their number, *e.g.* he has lines varying from *four* stressed syllables only to lines of *fourteen* syllables, *four* of which are stressed.

> Tu-whit.—Tu-whoo.
> And didst bring her home with thee in love and in charity.

When scanning the lines of this poem, we discover the basic foot to be the iambus but many anapæstic feet are to be found, *e.g.*

> On the topmost twig that looks up at the sky.

Scott, similarly, uses considerable freedom in his metre as in "*Marmion*."

**Parallelism.**—This term is sometimes used to indicate systematic arrangement of lines in stanzas, *e.g.* there is a parallel development in most songs (study the arrangement in "Blow, blow, thou winter wind," etc.). In this song we notice (1) the stanzas are constructed similarly; (2) there is a parallel development of theme also. But the term "parallelism" is probably best restricted to a type of verse in which successive lines repeat the idea of the previous one, that is, the lines are repetitive of the idea first expressed. The writer is not concerned so much with the length of his line as with repetition of the idea in various ways. This feature of parallelism is particularly prominent in Hebrew literature.

*Psalm* 142.

> I cried unto the Lord with my voice;
> with my voice unto the Lord did I make my supplication.
> I poured out my complaint before him;
> I shewed before him my trouble.
> When my spirit was overwhelmed within me, then thou knewest my path.
> In the way wherein I walked have they privily laid a snare for me.

I looked on my right hand, and beheld, but there was no
  man that would know me:
refuge failed me;
no man cared for my soul.
I cried unto thee, O Lord: I said,
Thou art my refuge and my portion in the land of the living.
Attend unto my cry; for I am brought very low:
deliver me from my persecutors, for they are stronger than I.

**Vers Libre** (*Fr. free verse*).—As the name implies, this type of verse is unrestricted in respect of the usual, or formerly accepted, rigid verse forms. It is unrestricted in length of line, in the poetic foot used, in stanzaic form and in its use of rhyme. It is verse entirely arbitrary—dependent on the individuality, whim and caprice of the poet. Perhaps the fact that the post-war attitude towards the arts has been iconoclastic explains the popularity of vers libre with many of our modern poets.

Although vers libre is popular at present, it must not be understood that it is merely a recent discovery. In "*Christabel*" Coleridge attains a certain freedom from current prosodic practice. Matthew Arnold in his "*Forsaken Merman*" uses a great deal of freedom.

Call her once before you go.
  Call once yet.
In a voice that she will know:
"Margaret! Margaret!"
Children's voices should be dear
(Call once more) to a mother's ear;
Children's voices wild with pain—
Surely she will come again.
Call her once and come away;
This way, this way!
"Mother dear, we cannot stay."
The wild white horses foam and fret.
Margaret! Margaret!

Walt Whitman (1819-1892), the American poet, also

used vers libre in his poems, *e.g.* in "*Out of the Cradle Endlessly Rocking.*"

Out of the cradle endlessly rocking,
Out of the mocking-bird's throat, the musical shuttle,
Out of the Ninth-month midnight,
Over the sterile sands, and the fields beyond, where the child, leaving his bed, wander'd alone, bare-headed, barefoot,
Down from the shower'd halo,
Up from the mystic play of shadows, twining and twisting as if they were alive,
Out from the patches of briers and blackberries,
From the memories of the bird that chanted to me,
From your memories, sad brother—from the fitful risings and fallings I heard,
From under that yellow half-moon, late-risen, and swollen as if with tears.
From those beginning notes of sickness and love, there in the transparent mist,
From the thousand responses of my heart, never to cease,
From the myriad thence-aroused words,
From the word stronger and more delicious than any,
From such, as now they start, the scene revisiting,
As a flock, twittering, rising, or overhead passing,
Borne hither—ere all eludes me, hurriedly,
A man—yet by these tears a little boy again,
Throwing myself on the sand, confronting the waves,
I, chanter of pains and joys, uniter of here and hereafter,
Taking all hints to use them—but swiftly leaping beyond them,
A reminiscence sing.

It should also be remembered that in many of the irregular odes, *e.g.* in Dryden's "*Alexander's Feast,*" there are many of the features which characterise vers libre.

**Anaphora** is a device of arrangement in which successive lines or sentences are made to begin with the same word or group of words, *e.g.* :—

Have I not had to wrestle with my lot?
Have I not suffer'd things to be forgiven?
Have I not had my brains sear'd, my heart riven?

BYRON'S "*Childe Harold.*"

## EXERCISES IN PROSODY

1. By altering the order of the following words, write them in a quatrain of iambic pentameter, rhyming *a.a.b.a.*

For about, below, above, in and out 'tis a Magic Shadow-show nothing but in a box played whose candle is the Sun which we Phantom figures come and go round.

2. By altering the order of the following words, write a quatrain rhyming *a.b.a.b.* The metre is iambic pentameter, lines 1 and 3 being hypermetrical.

The infinite fierce chorus I even hear now the endless groan the cries of agony which reach our own in long reverberations through the ages that have gone before us.

3. By altering the order of the following words, write them in a quatrain of iambic tetrameter, rhyming alternately.

Twenty of Roslin's bold barons there are within that proud chapelle lie buried the holy vault doth hold each one but holds the sea lovely Rosabelle !

4. Without altering the order of the words, write the following as a rhyming stanza of six lines, correctly punctuated.

Alone aloud in the raptured ear of men we pour our dark nocturnal secret and then as night is withdrawn from these sweet-spring meads and bursting boughs of May dream while the innumerable choir of day welcome the dawn.

5. Write the following as iambic pentameter, blank verse.

*A*. All these and more came flocking ; but with looks downcast and damp yet such wherein appeared obscure some glimpse of joy to have found their Chief not in despair, to have found themselves not lost in loss itself ; which on his countenance cast like doubtful hue.

*B*. Thither, if but to pry, shall be perhaps our first eruption —thither, or elsewhere ; for this infernal pit shall never hold Celestial Spirits in bondage, nor the Abyss long under darkness cover. But these thoughts full counsel must mature.

*C*. But he who reigns Monarch in Heaven till then as one secure sat on his throne, upheld by old repute, consent or custom, and his regal state put forth at full, but still his strength concealed—which tempted our attempt, and wrought our fall.

*D*. (*N.B.*—The opening words do not begin a line.) :—

Not Babylon nor great Alcairo such magnificence equalled in al' their glories, to enshrine Belus or Serapis their gods, or seat their kings, when Egypt with Assyria strove in wealth and luxury.

*E.* Without altering the order of the words, write the following in iambic pentameter blank verse. Punctuate them properly. The initial words do not necessarily begin a line :—

All things invite to peaceful counsels and the settled state of order how in safety best we may compose our present evils with regard of what we are and where dismissing quite all thoughts of war.

*F.* Rewrite in blank verse :—

He ceased ; and next him Moloch, sceptred king, stood up—the strongest and the fiercest Spirit that fought in Heaven, now fiercer by despair. His trust was with the Eternal to be deemed equal in strength, and rather than be less cared not to be at all.

## EXERCISES IN PROSODY

Scan the following passages ; name the metres used.

1. Each thought on the woman who loved him the best
And the children stood watching them out of the town.

2. Ere frost-flower and snow-blossom faded and fell, and the splendour of winter had passed out of sight,
The ways of the woodlands were fairer and stranger than dreams that fulfil us in sleep with delight ;
The breath of the mouths of the winds had hardened on tree-tops and branches that glittered and swayed.

3. Welcome, wild North-easter.
Shame it is to see
Odes to every zephyr ;
Ne'er a verse to thee.

4. Whither, midst falling dew,
While glow the heavens with the last steps of day,
Far through their rosy depths dost thou pursue
Thy solitary way ?

5. Now strike the golden lyre again :
A louder yet, and yet a louder strain !
Break his bands of sleep asunder
And rouse him like a rattling peal of thunder.
Hark ! hark ! the horrid sound
Has raised up his head ;
As awaked from the dead
And amazed he stares around.

Revenge, revenge, Timotheus cries,
See the furies arise!
See the snakes that they rear
How they hiss in their hair,
And the sparkles that flash from their eyes!

6. Their glittering tents he passed, and now is come
Into the blissful field, through groves of myrrh,
And flowering odours, cassia, nard, and balm;
A wilderness of sweets; for Nature here
Wantoned as in her prime, and played at will
Her virgin fancies, pouring forth more sweet,
Wild above rule of art, enormous bliss.

7. Not proud, nor servile; be one poet's praise,
That, if he pleas'd, he pleas'd by manly ways:
That flatt'ry, ev'n to Kings, he held a shame,
And thought a lie in verse or prose the same.

8. Still, as of yore, Queen of the North!
Still canst thou send thy children forth.
Ne'er readier at alarm-bell's call
Thy burghers rose to man thy wall,
Than now, in danger, shall be thine
Thy dauntless voluntary line.

9. Thou, in bewitching words, with happy heart,
Did'st chaunt the vision of that Ancient Man,
The bright-eyed Mariner, and rueful woes
Did'st utter of the Lady Christabel;
And I, associate with such labour, steeped
In soft forgetfulness the livelong hours,
Murmuring of him who, joyous hap, was found,
After the perils of his moonlight ride,
Near the loud waterfall; or her who sate
In misery near the miserable Thorn.

10. Take wings of foresight; lighten thro'
The secular abyss to come,
And lo, thy deepest lays are dumb
Before the mouldering of a yew;
And if the matin songs, that woke
The darkness of our planet, last,
Thine own shall wither in the vast,
Ere half the lifetime of an oak.

11. Thus robed in russet I romed aboute
All a somer season, for to seke Dowel,
And freyned full oft of folke that I mette,
If any wight wist wher Dowel was at inne.

12. He waiteth, if by word or countenance,
That she to hym was changed of corage;
But never koude he fynde variance.
She was ay oon in herte and in visage,
And ay the forther that she was in age
The moore trewe, if that were possible,
She was to hym in love and more penyble.

13. At last he came unto a gloomy glade
Covered with boughes and shrubs from heaven's light,
Whereas he sitting found in secret shade
An uncouth salvage, and uncivile wight
Of griesly hew and fowle ill favoured sight:
His face with smoke was tand, and eies were bleared,
His head and beard with sout were ill debight,
His cole blacke hands did seeme to have been seard
In smythes fire-spitting forge, and nayles like clawes appeared.

14. Joy of my life, full oft for loving you
I blesse my lot that was so lucky placed;
But then the more your own mishap I rew,
That are so much by so meane love embased.
For, had the equall hevens so much you graced
In this as in the rest, ye mote invent
Some hevenly wit, whose verse could have enchased
Your glorious name in golden moniment.
But since you deigned so goodly to relent
To me your thrall, in whom is little worth,
Tha little that I am, shall all be spent
In setting your immortall prayses forth:
Whose lofty argument, uplifting me,
Shall lift you up unto an high degree.

15. As an unperfect actor on the stage
Who with his fear is put besides his part,
Or some fierce thing replete with too much rage,
Whose strength's abundance weakens his own heart.
So I for fear of trust, forget to say
The perfect ceremony of love's rite,
And in mine own love's strength seem to decay,
O'ercharged with burden of mine own love's might.
O, let my books be then the eloquence
And dumb presagers of my speaking breast,
Who plead for love and look for recompense
More than that tongue that more hath more expressed,
O, learn to read what silent love hath writ;
To hear with eyes belongs to love's fine wit.

16. While thus he spake, th' angelic squadron bright
Turned fiery red, sharp'ning in moonéd horns
Their phalanx, and began to hem him round
With ported spears, as thick as when a field
Of Ceres, ripe for harvest, waving, bends
Her bearded grove of ears, which way the wind
Sways them.

17. Not louder shrieks to pitying heaven are cast,
When husbands, or when lapdogs, breathe their last.

18. Such is the fate of simple bard,
On life's rough ocean luckless starr'd!
Unskilful he to note the card
Of prudent lore,
Till billows rage, and gales blow hard,
And whelm him o'er!

19. O'er rough and smooth she trips along
And never looks behind,
And sings a solitary song
That whistles in the wind.

20. Deep graved in every British heart,
O never let those names depart.
Say, to your sons—"Lo, here his grave,
Who victor died on Gadite wave."

21. Some have accused me of a strange design
Against the creed and morals of the land,
And trace it in this poem every line;
I don't pretend that I quite understand
My own meaning when I would be very fine;
But the fact is I have nothing planned,
Unless it were to be a moment merry,
A novel word in my vocabulary.

22. But in my spirit will I dwell,
And dream my dream, and hold it true;
For though my lips may breathe adieu,
I cannot think the thing farewell.

23. This is the forest primeval: but where are the hearts that beneath it
Leaped like the roe, when he hears in the wood the voice of the huntsman?

## CHAPTER XIII

## FIGURES OF SPEECH

A Figure of Speech is a departure from the literal, *i.e.* the plain and ordinary use of words, to secure some special effect, *e.g.* to embellish, emphasise, make significant some particular idea: such a use of words adds clearness, beauty or force and may do all these at one and the same time.

Figures of Speech may be classified under :—

1. Comparison, based on the perception of Resemblance.

Figures of Resemblance :—

(1) Simile (and Homeric or Epic Simile).
(2) Metaphor (and Confused or Mixed Metaphor).
(3) Personification.
(4) Parable, Fable (Apologue), Allegory.

2. Contrast, based on the perception of Difference.

Figures of Contrast :—

(1) Antithesis.
(2) Epigram, Paradox.
(3) Oxymoron.
(4) Pun (Paronomasia).
(5) Condensed Sentence (Zeugma).

3. Association of Ideas, based on Contiguity or Relationship.

Figures of Contiguity :—

(1) Metonymy.
(2) Synecdoche.
(3) Transferred Epithet (Hypallage).
(4) Antonomasia.

4. Figures based on Arrangement.

(1) Climax.
(2) Anti-climax (Bathos).
(3) Inversion.
(4) Interrogation (Rhetorical Question).
(5) Exclamation.
(6) Chiasmus.

5. Miscellaneous Figures :—

*(1) Irony (and Sarcasm).
*(2) Innuendo, Insinuation.
(3) Apostrophe.
(4) Vision (Historic Present).
*(5) Hyperbole.
*(6) Meiosis.
(7) Litotes.
*(8) Euphemism.
(9) Circumlocution (Periphrasis).
(10) Prolepsis.
(11) Hendiadys.
(12) Anacoluthon.
(13) Aposiopesis.
(14) Asyndeton.
(15) Polysyndeton.
(16) Onomatopœia.
(17) Alliteration.
(18) Essential Epithet.

* Irony, Innuendo, Hyperbole, Meiosis, Euphemism may also be treated under Contrast (2).

*N.B.*—Many of the above so-called figures of speech are not correctly described as figures of speech ; rather are they devices of style.

## 1. SIMILE

Byron, in the first line of his poem, "*The Destruction of Sennacherib*," wrote :—

> " The Assyrian came down *like a wolf on the fold.*"

"*Like a wolf on the fold*" is a simile. Byron uses this comparison to illustrate his meaning, to show the merciless nature of the Assyrian.

*The first function of the simile is to give information.*

This is an example of a simple simile, such as might be used in prose or even in conversation. In speech or in writing, if the speaker or writer is merely endeavouring to illustrate his meaning, he is usually content to use simple similes. But the poet, and the prose writer who is aiming at giving something more than mere meaning, usually uses elaborate and extended similes, for they strive to produce something beautiful in itself.

> " Then felt I like some watcher of the skies
> When a new planet swims into his ken ;
> Or like stout Cortez, when with eagle eyes
> He stared at the Pacific—and all his men
> Look'd at each other with a wild surmise—
> Silent ; upon a peak in Darien."
>
> " *On First Looking into Chapman's Homer.*"—KEATS.

Here we have two elaborate similes. In the poem, the poet compares his joy with that of (1) some watcher of the skies ; (2) stout Cortez ; but in both examples he tells us why each of these is full of unbounded elation and the joy of discovery—which he considers to be akin to that of his own in discovering Chapman's translation of Homer's "*Iliad.*"

We have a still more elaborate and extended simile in that type known as the Epic or Homeric simile—

so called from its frequently being used in Homer's epics, "*The Iliad*" and "*The Odyssey.*"

" As when some hunter in the spring hath found
A breeding eagle sitting on her nest,
Upon the craggy isle of a hill lake,
And pierced her with an arrow as she rose,
And follow'd her to find out where she fell
Far off ;—anon her mate comes winging back
From hunting, and a great way off descries
His huddling young left sole ; at that, he checks
His pinion, and with short uneasy sweeps
Circles above his eyry, with loud screams
Chiding his mate back to her nest ; but she
Lies dying, with the arrow in her side,
In some far stony gorge out of his ken,
A heap of fluttering feathers : never more
Shall the lake glass her, flying over it ;
Never the black and dripping precipices
Echo her stormy scream as she sails by :—
As that poor bird flies home, nor knows his loss—
So Rustum knew not his own loss, but stood
Over his dying son, and knew him not."

" *Sohrab and Rustum.*"—M. ARNOLD.

The following is an extract from Pope's "*Essay on Criticism*" :—

" Fir'd at first sight with what the Muse imparts,
In fearless youth we tempt the heights of Arts,
While from the bounded level of our mind,
Short views we take, nor see the lengths behind ;
But more advanc'd, behold with strange surprise
New distant scenes of endless science rise !
So pleas'd at first the tow'ring Alps we try,
Mount o'er the vales, and seem to tread the sky,
Th' eternal snows appear already past,
And the first clouds and mountains seem the last ;
But, those attained, we tremble to survey
The growing labours of the lengthen'd way,
Th' increasing prospect tires our wand'ring eyes,
Hills peep o'er hills, and Alps on Alps arise ! "

From "*So,*" we have another example of an extended and elaborated simile. Dr. Johnson, criticising it, states,

" the comparison of a student's progress in the sciences with the journey of a traveller in the Alps, is perhaps the best that English poetry can show. A simile, to be perfect, *must both illustrate and ennoble the subject;* must show it to the understanding in a clearer view, and display it to the fancy with greater dignity, but either of these qualities may be sufficient to recommend it. In didactic poetry, of which the great purpose is instruction, a simile may be praised which illustrates, though it does not ennoble; in heroics, that may be admitted which ennobles, though it does not illustrate. That it may be complete, it is required to exhibit, independently of its references, a pleasing image; for a simile is said to be a short episode."

We may define a simile shortly as a statement of some point of resemblance which the writer conceives between two things which are different in other respects: the statement or simile is usually introduced by like, as, or so.

It should be noted carefully that the two things compared must differ in kind; otherwise, we have a true and real comparison in which not merely one point, but a great many points of resemblance can be discovered.

## 2. METAPHOR

A Metaphor may be defined as a momentary identification of one thing with another; in it, we put one thing in place of another because of some imagined resemblance. Thus a metaphor is really an implied simile and may be extended into one by stating the resemblance fully.

*He was a lion in the fight.* In this, momentarily, we identify the man with the lion. He was *like* a lion in the fight—in this we have the simile stated fully.

We frequently use **Personal Metaphor** (Personification) when we attribute to inanimate objects the qualities which are associated with people, *e.g.* the *thirsty* ground, a *treacherous* calm. Byron describes the grasshopper :—

" He is an *evening reveller,* who *makes*
*His life an infancy,* and *sings* his fill."

**Examples of Metaphor** :—

" I still had hopes my latest hours to crown,
Amidst these humble bowers to lay me down ;
*To husband out life's taper at the close,*
*And keep the flame from wasting by repose.*"

GOLDSMITH

" Awake ! for Morning *in the Bowl of Night*
Has flung the Stone that puts the Stars to flight :
And Lo ! *the Hunter of the East has caught*
The Sultan's Turret in a *Noose of Light.*"

FITZGERALD.

" Such harmony is in immortal souls ;
But while *this muddy vesture of decay*
Doth grossly close it in, we cannot hear it."

SHAKESPEARE

Frequently we have examples of extended or sustained metaphor, *e.g.* :—

THE LESSONS OF NATURE

" Of this fair volume which we world do name,
If we the sheets and leaves could turn with care,
Of Him who it corrects, and did it frame,
We clear might read the art and wisdom rare ;
Find out this power which wildest powers doth tame,
His providence extending everywhere,
His justice which proud rebels doth not spare,
In every page, no period of the same.
But silly we, like foolish children, rest
Well pleased with colour's vellum, leaves of gold,
Fair dangling ribbons, leaving what is best,
On the great Writer's sense ne'er taking hold ;
Of if by chance we stay our minds on aught
It is some picture on the margin wrought."

W. DRUMMOND.

When using extended metaphor in particular, care must be exercised to avoid **Mixed Metaphor.** Mixed Metaphor results from confusion of images, *e.g.* :—

Behind that harsh face there breathes a heart full of love.

To *water* the *spark* of grace.

The *white face* of the British soldier is the *backbone* of the Indian army.

We can have succession of metaphor without confusion, *e.g.* :—

" Life's but a walking shadow ; a poor player
That struts and frets his hour upon the stage,
And then is heard no more : it is a tale
Told by an idiot, full of sound and fury,
Signifying nothing."

SHAKESPEARE.

Remember, when criticising simile and metaphor, that :—

1. There should be only **one** point of resemblance between the things compared or momentarily identified.

2. This resemblance should be clear—not obscure or too far-fetched as is often the case in the extravagant similes and metaphors of these poets called by Dr. Johnson " The Metaphysical " poets, *e.g.* Donne, Cowley, Crashaw. Such far-fetched, strained similes are termed *Conceits.*

3. Simile and metaphor should both illustrate and ennoble—especially so in poetry. In unassuming prose, these figures should at least illustrate clearly.

4. Simile and metaphor will best perform their desired function when some abstract thought is illustrated by means of some concrete parallel, *e.g.* examples quoted from Keats's " *Chapman's Homer.*"

5. Simile and metaphor should in all respects be apposite and appropriate.

**Decayed Metaphor.**

Throughout the course of time, many words which have been used in a metaphorical sense have lost their original literal sense, so that the words now live merely in their acquired, *i.e.* metaphorical sense.

In the Parable of the Talents, for example, the word *talent* means a coin ; to-day, the word means a faculty, any natural or special gift, a special aptitude.

Here is a list of words that have undergone a similar development. Find out their original, literal meanings—and, if you are unaware of them, their present meanings.

| Nouns | Adjectives |
|---|---|
| Root (of the trouble). | Golden (opinion). |
| Cynosure. | Glowing (report). |
| Gall. | Iron (Duke). |
| Fustian. | Frowning (cliff). |
| Bombast. | Warm (welcome). |
| Clue. | |

As language is a living growth, such processes still continue : it is obvious that there will be a stage in the decay of a metaphor when it is extremely difficult to state whether the metaphorical use has supplanted the literal use or not. Both meanings of the word may be alive—*e.g.* we speak of the height of a building (literal), and the height of nonsense (metaphorical).

It should be noted that our language is enriched by decay of metaphor. One word, originally having one, literal meaning has often had other meanings attached to it. Originally *free* meant a person who was not a slave. Refer to a good dictionary and note the multiplicity of meanings the word free now has.

## 3. PERSONIFICATION

Personification consists in imagining inanimate objects to be endowed with human attributes. (Compare with Personal Metaphor.)

Often writers are induced to adopt Personification when they identify their image with some type of person, *e.g. lean Hunger*. When an artist depicts Time, it is as an old man, holding an hour glass in his hand, with a prominent forelock of hair, and a scythe. The artist is symbolising what we connect with the conception of time—its inexorable, fleeting nature. Frequently abstract ideas are personified and they are given capital letters ; but apart from the capital letter to indicate that the idea is personified, there is often little other guide. Many examples of this almost artificial type of personification are to be found, especially in the work of the Augustan Age of English poetry, *e.g.* Pope, Gray. In Gray's "*Elegy*" we find :—

"Let not *Ambition* mock their useful toil,
Their homely joys and destiny obscure;
Nor *Grandeur* hear with a disdainful smile
The short and simple annals of the Poor."

"Can *Honour's* voice provoke the silent dust
Or *Flattery* soothe the dull cold ear of *Death* ?"

It will be seen that the examples given above are, at best, very simple examples of Personification. The poet has not worked out the analogy between the idea and a person sufficiently far. Such examples, we feel, are scarcely adequate when we compare them with fuller analogies in which the identification of the idea with a person is elaborated and made complete. Contrast Gray's examples with that of Shakespeare below :—

"Blow, blow, thou winter wind:
Thou art not so *unkind*
As man's ingratitude;

Thy *tooth* is not so keen
Because thou art not seen,
Although *thy breath* be rude.
Freeze, freeze, thou bitter sky,
That dost not *bite* so nigh
As benefits forgot;
Though *thou the waters warp*,
Thy *sting* is not so sharp
As friend remembered not."

Here is a beautiful example of personification in prose from R. D. Blackmore's "*Lorna Doone*."

"The spring was in our valley now; creeping first for shelter shyly in the pause of the blustering wind. There the lambs came bleating to her, and the orchis lifted up, and the thin dead leaves of clover lay, for the new ones to spring through. Then the stiffest things that sleep, the stubby oak and the stunted beech, dropped their brown defiance to her, and prepared for a soft reply. While her over-eager children (who had started forth to meet her, through the frost and shower of sleet), catkined hazel, gold-gloved withy, youthful elder, and old woodbine, with all the tribe of good hedge-climbers (who must hasten, while haste they may)—was there one of them that did not claim the merit of coming first?"

It should be noted that the mere writing of a capital letter at the beginning of a word, which signifies some passion or idea, does not constitute a good example of personification.

Ruskin deprecates in poets the attributing to inanimate Nature the capacity to sympathise with human affairs: he calls their doing so the **Pathetic Fallacy.** Study the following example:—

"They rowed her in across the rolling foam—
The *cruel, hungry* foam, etc.

KINGSLEY'S "*Sands of Dee.*"

### 4. PARABLE. FABLE (APOLOGUE). ALLEGORY

These are all based on Resemblance.

Parable is based on simile. As opposed to Apologue, parable is limited by strict rules of probability, its story being concerned with facts of familiar or common occurrence.

Fable is based on personification.

Allegory is based on metaphor.

All these forms in literature present a surface or superficial story but the main intention is to enforce a secondary meaning. These forms in literature have been used either to present some abstract moral truth in a simple manner to rudimentary intellects or to sugar coat the pill—the sugar coating being the attractive surface narrative, the pill being the lesson or moral.

In "*Æsop's Fables*" beasts and birds are made to act, think and speak as men. The term Apologue is more particularly applied to this type of fable.

Christ used Parables to simplify and make attractive His spiritual meanings to His audiences—simple fisher and rustic folk. Study the Parable of the Sower (St. Luke).

The Allegory is the most sustained form of this type of writing.

Some of our best examples are (in verse) :—Spenser's "*Faerie Queene*," Dryden's "*Absalom and Achitophel.*" In prose, we have excellent examples in Addison's "*Vision of Mirza*" and Bunyan's "*Pilgrim's Progress.*"

## FIGURES OF CONTRAST

### 1. ANTITHESIS

In Antithesis we set down terms that are contrasted with each other: we oppose the one term to the other.

Examples :—

> Better to *reign* in *Hell* than *serve* in *Heaven.*—MILTON.

> Ill fares the land, to hast'ning ills a prey,
> Where *wealth accumulates* and *men decay.*
>
> GOLDSMITH.

> Some books are to be *tasted*, others to be *swallowed*, and some few to be *chewed* and *digested*.—BACON.

A style of writing based on Antithesis is frequently used by writers, *e.g.* Bacon, Johnson. (See Chapter XIV on Style.)

## 2. EPIGRAM AND PARADOX

**Epigram** "is an apparent contradiction in language, which, by causing a temporary shock, rouses our attention to some important meaning underneath." (BAIN.) Originally an epigram was a metrical inscription on a monument. It is a pithy, pointed saying in which the words appear to be contrasted but the contrast is not real as in true antithesis. Epigram is frequently applied to a smart saying containing some incongruity.

Examples :—

> Fools are more hard to conquer than persuade.—DRYDEN
>
> Great wits are sure to madness near allied.—DRYDEN.
>
> Deign on the passing world to turn thine eyes,
> And pause awhile from letters to be wise.
> JOHNSON.
>
> Brevity is the soul of wit.—SHAKESPEARE.

**Paradox** :—In this form the epigram assumes a definite contradiction.

Examples :—

> The *child* is *father* of the man.—WORDSWORTH.
>
> A *favourite* has no *friend*.—GRAY.
>
> In *solitude*, where we are *least alone*.—BYRON.
>
> He was *conspicuous* by his *absence*.

## 3. OXYMORON

Oxymoron is a condensed antithesis in which two words—most frequently an adjective and noun, though sometimes an adverb and adjective—are made to oppose each other.

Examples :—

Parting is such *sweet sorrow.*—SHAKESPEARE.

*fiend-angelical !*
*Dove-feather'd raven ! wolfish-ravening lamb !*—
A *damn'd saint*, an *honourable villain !*

SHAKESPEARE.

At length with love and wine at once opprest
The *vanquish'd victor* sunk upon her breast.

DRYDEN.

*Idly busy.*

## 4. PUN (PARONOMASIA)

This figure consists in using the same word in different senses ; or in playing on two words which have the same sound but different meanings. It is chiefly used for the purpose of humour, yet at best it is superficial. In earlier writings we sometimes find pun used in unexpected places, *e.g.* in "*Othello.*"

" Put out the light and then put out the light."

Examples :—

They went and *told* the sexton,
And the sexton *toll'd* the bell.

HOOD.

Ben Battle was a soldier bold
  And used to war's alarms,
A cannon ball shot off his *legs*
  So he laid down his *arms*.

HOOD.

## 5. CONDENSED SENTENCE. (ZEUGMA)

Condensed Sentence consists in bringing together, under one predicate, two or more ideas that are different and incongruous.

Examples :—

He gave a sigh and a sixpence.
She went home in a flood of tears and a taxi.
He lost his temper and his train.

Zeugma (*Gr. zeugnunai—to yoke*). " A figure by which an adjective or verb which agrees with a nearer word is, by way of supplement, referred also to another more remote, whether grammatically corresponding or not " (*Chambers's Dictionary*), is usually classified with Condensed Sentence.

## FIGURES OF CONTIGUITY

### 1. METONYMY

**Metonymy** (*literally a change of name, Gr. meta -onoma*). **In this figure we refer to a thing by using something closely related to it and associated with it.**

Examples :—

*Sceptre* and *crown*
Must tumble down,
And in the dust be equal made
With the poor crooked *scythe* and *spade*.

SHIRLEY.

And all *Arabia* breathes from yonder box.
The *tortoise* here and *elephant* unite,
Transformed to combs, the speckled and the white.

POPE.

### 2. SYNECDOCHE

Synecdoche may be classified as a species of metonymy in which we mention a part when the whole is to be understood, or the whole for a part. It should be noted that the part is always *significant*.

Examples :—

He employs five hundred *hands*.
He had not a *roof* to shelter him.
My ventures are not in one *bottom* trusted.—SHAKESPEARE.

## 3. TRANSFERRED EPITHET (HYPALLAGE)

In this figure we apply an adjective, which is properly associated with one idea, to another.

Examples :—

The prisoner was put into the *condemned* cell.
He laid his head on a *sleepless* pillow.
They had an *anxious* day awaiting the decision.

But let my due feet never fail,
To walk the *studious* cloister's pale.

MILTON.

## 4. ANTONOMASIA

In this figure the name of some outstanding historical character or character in literature is substituted for the quality or qualities which is or are associated with the person.

Examples :—

A *Daniel* come to judgment!

He was a *Machiavelli* in policy.

Some village-*Hampden*, that with dauntless breast
The little tyrant of his fields withstood,
Some mute inglorious *Milton* here may rest,
Some *Cromwell*, guiltless of his country's blood.

GRAY'S "*Elegy*."

# FIGURES BASED ON ARRANGEMENT

## 1. CLIMAX

Climax (*Gr. klimax—a ladder*), as the derivation implies, is the enumerating of ideas in ascending order of importance. By so arranging the ideas, emphasis is given to the culminating one ; consequently, this device of arrangement is frequently found in oratory. Climax is not confined only to sentences ; it may be traced in paragraphs also.

Examples :—

" As Caesar loved me, I weep for him ; as he was fortunate, I rejoice at it ; as he was valiant, I honour him ; but, as he was ambitious, I slew him."—SHAKESPEARE.

Sometimes a writer employs intentional climax for the sake of humour :—

Men, monkeys, lap-dogs, parrots, perish all.
Not louder shrieks to pitying heaven are cast,
When husbands, or when lap-dogs breathe their last.

POPE.

## 2. ANTI-CLIMAX

In Anti-climax the order of arranging the ideas is *not reversed* but the least important idea is placed last. Frequently this device is used for humour, but sometimes a writer may *inadvertently* place the least important item last. It is then called **Bathos** (*Gr. meaning depth*). The writer is striving for impressiveness and fails to achieve it. Bathos is most frequently met with in fine writing.

Example :—

Here thou, great Anna ! whom three realms obey,
Dost sometimes counsel take—and sometimes tea.

POPE.

## 3. INVERSION

**Inversion** consists of a change in the normal order of words. This device is frequently used to give emphasis to a word or phrase. In the poetry of the XVIIIth century, poets, we often conclude, used this device for facilitating rhyme. Sometimes this device leads to ambiguity, *e.g.* " And all the air a solemn stillness holds." Gray's " *Elegy.*"

Examples :—

Sweet are the uses of adversity.—SHAKESPEARE.
Ill fares the land.—GOLDSMITH.
Succeeding sports the mirthful band inspired.—GOLDSMITH.
Bliss was it in that dawn to be alive.—WORDSWORTH.

## 4. INTERROGATION. (RHETORICAL QUESTION)

**Interrogation** is not merely the ordinary question in which the speaker or writer is seeking an answer. The answer is obvious, so the question is put as a rhetorical device, or to make emphatic the idea dealt with.

Examples :—

Can the Ethiopian change his skin, or the leopard his spots ?

What is this life, if full of care,
We have no time to stand and stare? W. H. DAVIES.

Which of us, by taking thought, can add one cubit unto his stature ?

## 5. EXCLAMATION

**Exclamation,** indicated by an exclamation mark, is used to indicate some strong emotion, not fully or accurately described. It is chiefly found in rhetoric where a listener is pre-supposed.

Example :—

O, what a fall was there, my countrymen!

## 6. CHIASMUS

**Chiasmus** (*Gr.—two lines crossed* as in the letter X) is a contrast by parallelism in reverse order.

Examples :—

Do not *live* to *eat*
×
But *eat* to *live.*

Others on earth o'er human race preside,
*Watch* all her *ways* and all their *actions guide.*
POPE.

**Chiasmus** may be defined as one phrase followed by another in which the order of the terms is reversed.

## MISCELLANEOUS FIGURES

### 1. IRONY AND SARCASM

**Irony** (*Gr. eironeia—dissimulation*) is a mode of expression which enables the writer or speaker to convey his meaning with greater force by means of a contrast between the thought which he evidently designs to express and that which his words properly signify. He states, superficially the opposite of what he intends. He *dissimulates* his meaning.

When spoken, irony is usually easily discernible, *e.g.* if an elaborate experiment was spoiled through a boy's clumsiness and his science master turned on him and exclaimed, " You're a fine fellow ! ", the culprit would be in no doubt of his master's meaning.

When irony is used in writing, when there is no inflection of the voice to guide one, it is liable to be missed.

(Compare what happened to Daniel Defoe after writing his *The Shortest Way with the Dissenters*).

(*a*) Study the following examples of irony.

" It is ful fair to been yclept ' ma dame,'
And goon to vigilyes al bifore,
And have a mantel royalliche ybore."

Chaucer, feigning approval, laughs at the petty ambitions of the bourgeoisie.

(*b*) By an extension of meaning, irony may also suggest a *mocking discrepancy between promise and fulfilment*, or *between appearance and reality*. *e.g.* :—

" A manly man, to been an abbot able,
Ful many a deyntee hors hadde he in stable."

The second line is an ironic comment on the monk vowed to poverty and holy works but whose avocations are those of the wealthy, leisured class.

Chaucer's "*Pardoner*":—

> But of his craft, fro Berwick unto Ware,
> Ne was there swich another pardoner.
> For in his male he had a pilwe-beer,
> Which that, *he seyde*, was our lady veyl.

Irony is sometimes used in a playful way for the purpose of humour, chiefly in mock-heroic writings, *e.g.* Pope's "*Rape of the Lock*," Lamb's "*Dissertation on Roast Pig.*"

Irony may be used for sarcastic effect though it should be noted that in **Sarcasm,** (*Gr. sarkasmos—tearing flesh like dogs*) the writer states what he means but in such a way as to imply ridicule, disapproval or contempt. Sarcasm is more intended to inflict pain than irony; it may also be used for humour.

**Satire** originally was a literary composition in verse which aimed at holding up to ridicule and scorn: it usually was a criticism of a man and his works.

A satire generally aims at amending morals and manners and its chief means of doing so are by using irony, sarcasm, invective, wit and humour.

**Tragic** or **Dramatic** irony is that type of irony which the Greeks introduced in their drama. To the audiences the plots of the Greek plays were known. Apparently trivial remarks spoken by the players (who as actors were not supposed to know the plot) were fraught with impending tragic import for the audience that knew the plot. The actors were supposed to know only the surface meaning: the audience knew the underlying import of the words. In Shakespeare's "*Macbeth*" we have examples of tragic irony. After the murder of Duncan, Lady Macbeth says, "A little water clears us of this deed." Those who know the plot realise the ironic contrast between this statement and that made later by Lady Macbeth, namely :—

" Here's the smell of blood still : all the perfumes of Arabia will not sweeten this little hand."

There is tragic or dramatic irony in King Duncan's praising the situation of the castle which the audience knows is to be the scene of his murder.

" This castle has a pleasant seat : the air
Nimbly and sweetly recommends itself
Unto our gentle senses."

Note that irony, sarcasm, satire have their distinctions although they are difficult to define. It is useful to try to remember the aim of each type of writing.

**Irony** presupposes an understanding audience or reader, otherwise it is in danger of missing its mark : it aims at establishing a bond of meaning between the writer or speaker and those for whose benefit the words are written or spoken.

**Sarcasm** aims at inflicting pain or at least heaping scorn and ridicule on some thing or person.

**Satire** aims at amending faults—frequently those of a writer or other prominent person.

These terms are by no means always exclusive.

## 2. INNUENDO. INSINUATION.

**Innuendo** (*Latin*, *innuere—to nod*), **Insinuation** (*Latin*, *insinuare*). These differ from irony proper in that in both, the underlying meaning—usually some fault or shortcoming—is nodded at, hinted at, *i.e.* the meaning is conveyed by indirect means, *e.g.* " Yes," replied the Doctor, " cold baths are all right. Many people can't stand them, and those that can don't need them ! "

" There are two times in a man's life when he should not speculate—when he cannot afford it, and when he can."—MARK TWAIN.

## 3. APOSTROPHE.

**Apostrophe** (*Gr.—a turning away*). In this, a species of exclamation, a speaker or writer suddenly breaks off from the theme of his speech or narrative to address, in the second person, some person or thing, usually absent or inanimate.

Examples :—

Frailty ! thy name is woman !—SHAKESPEARE.

O my love ! my wife !
Death, that hath suck'd the honey of thy breath,
Hath had no power yet upon thy beauty.
SHAKESPEARE.

## 4. VISION. HISTORIC PRESENT.

In **Vision** the writer or speaker describes something past or to come in the present tense instead of in the past or future tense. By so doing, he makes it appear as if it were actually happening and he were witnessing it. Accordingly, the use of Vision (Historic Present) helps to make a description more dramatic.

Examples :—

" Behold a ghastly band, each a torch in his hand."
DRYDEN.

" When Athens armies fell at Syracuse,
And fetter'd thousands bore the yoke of war,
Redemption rose up in the Attic Muse,
Her voice the only ransom from afar.
See ! as they chant the tragic hymn, the car
Of the o'ermastered victor stops, the reins
Fall from his hands."
BYRON.

## 5. HYPERBOLE.

**Hyperbole** (*Gr.—exaggeration*). In this figure, for the sake of emphasising his meaning, a writer or speaker purposely exaggerates his statement. Note that there is no desire to convey an untrue meaning—merely a desire to heighten the desired effect. The contrast between the literal truth and the hyperbole should not amount to a conceit, it should be congruous.

Examples :—

All the perfumes of Arabia will not sweeten this little hand.
SHAKESPEARE.

Hell grew darker at their frown.—MILTON.

If the hyperbole is too far fetched, it becomes inappropriate.

Examples :—

The sky shrunk upward with unusual dread,
And trembling Tiber dived beneath his bed.
DRYDEN.

If by your art, my dearest father, you have
Put the wild waters in this roar, allay them :
The sky, it seems, would pour down stinking pitch,
But that the sea, mounting to the welkin's cheek,
Dashes the fire out.
SHAKESPEARE.

## 6. MEIOSIS.

**Meiosis** (*Gr.—lessening*) is a kind of inverted hyperbole in which the truth is understated, not to deceive, but to emphasise the impression made by the words. A schoolboy uses it when he says, " He can't half run ! "

Examples :—

Exposing what is mortal and unsure
To all that fortune, death and danger dare,
Even *for an egg-shell.*
HAMLET.

mute
The camel labours with the heaviest load,
And the wolf dies in silence—not bestow'd
In vain should such examples be : if they,
Things of ignoble or of savage mood,
Endure and shrink not, we of nobler clay
May temper it to bear—*it is but for a day.*
BYRON.

## 7. LITOTES.

**Litotes** (*Gr.—frugality*) is an affirmation made indirectly by the negation of its contrary.

Examples :—

> A citizen of no mean city.
> Not bad!
> Not a few.

## 8. EUPHEMISM.

**Euphemism** (*Gr. eu—well* and *phemi*—I speak). In this type of expression something which is harsh or disagreeable is softened or rendered more favourably by the use of mild, or vague or periphrastic language.

Examples :—

> He slept with his fathers.
> He is a stranger to the truth.

N.B.—Euphemism is sometimes confused with Euphuism. Euphuism is derived from the title of a book, "*Euphues*," by John Lyly. It was written in a highly artificial style based on antithesis, abounding in conceits, alliterative, and containing many illustrations from a false natural history. (See under Style p. 312.)

## 9. CIRCUMLOCUTION. (PERIPHRASIS)

**Circumlocution** (*L. circum—about, loquor—I speak*) or **Periphrasis** (*Gr. peri—about, phrasis—a speaking*) consists in stating something in a roundabout way. It is used frequently in euphemism (see above) and for the purpose of humour. It was often used in the poetry of the XVIIIth century and came under the censure of Wordsworth as "gaudy and inane phraseology."

Examples :—

Slight lines of hair surprise the finny prey.—POPE.
oft from out it leaps
The finny darter with the glittering scales,
Who dwells and revels in thy glassy deep.
BYRON.

## 10. PROLEPSIS

**Prolepsis** (*Gr. pro—before, lambanein—to take*). In this the writer or speaker anticipates an event and treats it as if it had already happened.

Examples :—

I am dead, Horatio.—*Hamlet*.

So the two brothers and their *murder'd man*
Rode past fair Florence.
KEATS'S "*Isabella*".

## 11. HENDIADYS.

**Hendiadys** (*Gr. hen dia dyoin—literally one through two*). In this a compound notion is expressed by its two constituent parts as though they were independent of each other : they are joined by *and* but the one should be subordinated to the other. It is chiefly found in Greek and Latin poetry.

Example :—

I shall try *and* come.

## 12. ANACOLUTHON.

**Anacoluthon** (*Gr. an—negative, akolouthos—following*). In this there is a lack of sequence in the construction of a sentence. the latter part does not agree grammatically with the first part.

Example :—

So, all smile—
I shuffle sideways with my blushing face.
"*Fra Lippo Lippi.*"—BROWNING.

## 13. APOSIOPESIS.

**Aposiopesis** (*Gr. apo-siopa-ein—falling silent*). In this the speaker or writer fails to complete the sense of his statement, but enough of the sense is expressed to indicate what should have followed.

Example :—

He took careful aim and fired——.

## 14. ASYNDETON.

**Asyndeton** (*Gr. a—negative, syndetos—bound together*) consists in the omission of conjunctions for the sake of effect.

Examples :—

" To spend too much time in studies, is sloth ; to use them too much for ornament, is affectation : to make judgment wholly by their rules, is the humour of a scholar."—Bacon

The sun's rim dips : the stars rush out :
At one stride comes the dark.

Coleridge.

## 15. POLYSYNDETON.

**Polysyndeton** is a figurative repetition of connectives or conjunctions.

Example :—

Nor son nor wife, nor limb nor life,
In the brave days of old.

Macaulay.

## 16. ONOMATOPŒIA.

**Onomatopœia** (*Gr. onoma—a name, poiein—to make*) consists in a correspondence between sound and sense, so that the sound suggests the sense. Sometimes words are made so that they resemble the sounds of which they are the names, *e.g.* cuckoo, crash, boom.

In his "Essay on Criticism" Pope wrote :—

"'Tis not enough no harshness gives offence,
*The sound must seem an echo to the sense.*
Soft is the stream when Zephyr gently blows,
And the smooth stream in smoother numbers flows ;
But when loud surges lash the sounding shore,
The hoarse, rough verse should like the torrent roar."

Examples :—

Breaking the *s*ilence of the sea*s*,
Among the farthe*s*t Hebride*s*.

WORDSWORTH.

The *moan* of doves in i*mmem*orial el*ms*,
The *m*ur*m*uring of i*nnum*era*b*le *b*ees.

TENNYSON.

Study Tennyson's "*Brook*" for splendid examples. It should be noted that onomatopœia effect may be produced by **rhythmic arrangement**—the sense is conveyed by both rhythm and sound. (See under Prosody.)

Examples :—

A needless Alexandrine ends the song,
*That like a wounded snake, drags its slow length along.*

POPE.

And ten low words oft creep in one dull line.—POPE.

I galloped, Dirck galloped, we galloped all three.—

BROWNING.

And like a downward smoke, the slender stream
Along the cliff to fall and pause and fall did seem.

TENNYSON.

Onomatopœic effect is not confined merely to poetry : stylists in prose often use the device.

## 17. ALLITERATION.

**Alliteration** consists in a systematic repetition of the same sound (letter, letters or syllables) : this repetition of sound is most frequently found at the beginnings of words but may occur throughout a stanza or sentence. (See under Prosody.)

Examples :—

Ruin seize thee ruthless king!—GRAY.

Nor cast one *l*onging *l*ingering *l*ook behind.—GRAY.

I hear the *f*ar-o*ff* cur*f*ew sound,
Over *s*ome *w*ide-*w*atered *s*hore,
*S*winging *sl*ow with *s*u*ll*en roar.
MILTON.

## 18. ESSENTIAL EPITHET.

**Essential Epithet.**—The practice of Latin and Greek writers of invariably coupling a particular adjective with the name of a character (*e.g.* pius Aeneas) has been continued by English writers. This adjective—the essential epithet—points out the outstanding, or what is generally accepted as being the outstanding, feature of the character.

Examples :—

The *Iron* Duke. The *Merry* Monarch.
The *impecunious* Micawber.

The essential epithet is very frequently used in Ballads : gold is invariably referred to as "guid red gowd" : hand, as "lily-white."

### EXERCISES ON CHAPTER XIII

(*a*) Name the figures of speech and other literary devices contained in the following ; (*b*) criticise their use in the examples given :—

1. To them his heart, his love, his griefs were given.
But all his serious thoughts had rest in Heaven.
As some tall cliff, that lifts its awful form,
Swells from the vale, and midway leaves the storm,
Though round its breast the rolling clouds are spread,
Eternal sunshine settles on its head.

2. In my youth's summer I did sing of One,
The wandering outlaw of his own dark mind.

3. As when, upon a tranced summer-night,
Those green-rob'd senators of mighty woods,
Tall oaks, branch-charmed by the earnest stars,
Dream, and so dream all night without a stir,
Save from one gradual solitary gust
Which comes upon the silence, and dies off,
As if the ebbing air had but one wave.

4. Life, like a dome of many-coloured glass,
Stains the white radiance of Eternity,
Until Death tramples it to fragments.

5. Whether 'tis nobler in the mind to suffer
The slings and arrows of outrageous fortune,
Or to take arms against a sea of troubles
And by opposing end them?

6. A daring pilot in extremity,
Pleased with the danger, when the waves went high
He sought the storms; but, for a calm unfit,
Would steer too nigh the sands to boast his wit.

7. Brevity is the soul of wit.

8. A youth of labour with an age of ease.

9. "Toast any girl but her," he said,
With every other flutter,
"But I'll have none but Annie Bread,
And won't have any but her!"

10. Then to the well-trod stage anon,
If Jonson's learnéd sock be on,
Or sweetest Shakespeare, Fancy's child,
Warble his native wood-notes wild.

11. But, O grief,
Where hast thou led me?

12. The hungry judges soon the sentence sign,
And wretches hang that jurymen may dine.

13. O blest retirement! friend to life's decline.

14. Saint Peter sat by the celestial gate:
His keys were rusty, and the lock was dull.

15. We have had enough of action, and of motion we,
Roll'd to starboard, roll'd to larboard, when the surge was seething free,
Where the wallowing monster spouted his foam-fountains in the sea.

16. Why, man, he doth bestride the narrow world
Like a Colossus, and we petty men
Walk under his huge legs and peep about
To find ourselves dishonourable graves.

17. Venice—
The revel of the earth, the masque of Italy.

18. Proceed, illustrious youth,
And Virtue guard thee to the throne of Truth!
Yet should thy soul indulge the gen'rous heat
Till captive Science yields her last retreat;
Should Reason guide thee with her brightest ray,
And pour on Misty Doubt resistless day.

19. Then, not unequal to the Florentine (Dante)
The Southern Scott (Ariosto), the minstrel who call'd forth
A new creation with his magic line,
And, like the Ariosto of the North (Scott),
Sang ladye-love and war, romance and knightly worth.

20. As some fair female unadorn'd and plain,
Secure to please while youth confirms her reign,
Slights every borrow'd charm that dress supplies,
Nor shares with art the triumph of her eyes;
But when those charms are pass'd, for charms are frail,
When time advances, and when lovers fail,
She then shines forth, solicitous to bless,
In all the glaring impotence of dress.

21. A noise like of a hidden brook
In the leafy month of June,
That to the sleeping woods all night
Singeth a quiet tune.

22. When Athens' armies fell at Syracuse,
And fetter'd thousands bore the yoke of war,
Redemption rose up in the Attic Muse,
Her voice their only ransom from afar;
See! as they chant the magic hymn, the car
Of the o'ermaster'd victor stops, the reins
Fall from his hands, his idle scimitar
Starts from his belt—he rends his captive's chains,
And bids him thank the bard for freedom and his strains.

23. Yet once more, O ye Laurels, and once more
Ye Myrtles brown, with Ivy never-sear,
I come to pluck your berries harsh and crude,
And with forc'd fingers rude,
Shatter your leaves before the mellowing year.

24. No surly porter stands in guilty state
To spurn imploring famine from the gate.

25. A man severe he was, and stern to view;
I knew him well, and every truant knew.

26. Their lean and flashy songs
Grate on their scrannel pipes of wretched straw.

27. Break his bands of sleep asunder
And rouse him like a rattling peal of thunder.

28. The one red leaf, the last of its clan,
That dances as often as dance it can,
Hanging so light, and hanging so high,
On the topmost twig that looks up at the sky.

29. Dos'n't thou 'ear my 'erse's legs, as they canters awaay?
Proputty, proputty, proputty—that's what I 'ears 'em saay.

30. He bolted the door—and his dinner.

31. But whose best flowers are daughters.

32. O'er which To-day bends sad and sees his face.

33. Thou had'st a voice whose sound was like the sea.

34. For now sits Expectation in the air.

35. But O! my country's wintry state,
What second spring shall renovate?

36. The Germans in Greek are sadly to seek,
All save only Herman, and Herman's a German.

37. Where the Norweyan banners flout the sky,
And fan our people cold.

38. Some mute inglorious Milton here may rest.

39. Who, too deep for his hearers, still went on refining,
And thought of convincing, while they thought of dining.

40. When can their glory fade?

41. Fifty thousand horse and foot bound for Table Bay.

42. His jarring discord, and his discord dulcet.

43. Nothing went unrewarded but desert.

44. No sleep till morn when Youth and Pleasure meet.

45. The lightning flashed, the thunder roared, the rain fell like anything.

46. The chain of artistic descent does indeed lose itself in the very fountain-head of Art.

47. And frequent cups prolong the rich repast.

48. . . . Weep your tears
Into the channel, till the lowest stream
Do kiss the most exalted shores of all.

49. Truly, sir, all that I live by is with the awl.

50. . . . But 'tis a common proof
That lowliness is young ambition's ladder.

51. . . . Mischief, thou art afoot,
Take thou what course thou wilt.

52. . . . I rather choose
To wrong the dead, to wrong myself and you,
Than I will wrong such honourable men.

53. I know not, gentlemen, what you intend,
Who else must be let blood.

54. The Puritan hated bear-baiting, not because it gave pain to the bear, but because it gave pleasure to the spectators.

55. There is a fire in that dark eye, under which the insolence of condescension cannot thrive.

56. Are his Harolds and Giaours, we would ask, real men?

57. Rescued the Black Prince, that young Mars of men.

58. Many lives will be written, and, for the gratification of innocent curiosity, ought to be written, and read and forgotten.

59. Will all great Neptune's ocean wash this blood
Clean from my hand? No: this my hand will rather
The multitudinous seas incarnadine,
Making the green—one red.

60. So the two brothers with their murdered man rode past fair Florence.

61. That whistle garrisoned the glen.

62. The admiral with twenty sail attacked a fleet of twice that number.

# CHAPTER XIV.

## STYLE.

Style may be defined as the personality of the writer appearing in his writings. Buffon, the great French critic, defined style in the statement, " Style is the man." The manner in which the writer expresses his thoughts may serve as a working definition of style from which we can begin a survey of the subject.

If a writer's style is his personality, a clear and comprehensive definition of it may escape us, but we can at least examine the material which he uses. A writer uses **words.** He uses these words in **sentences,** and he groups his sentences in **paragraphs.**

## THE WORD

There are certain principles which govern the choice of words. Since the primary purpose of all speech and writing is to convey meaning, it seems reasonable to use simple diction. This will be a guarantee that the meaning will be conveyed to the largest number of people. This principle is called the Law of Simplicity.

The following observations should be remembered. Simple words are frequently short words, *i.e.* words of few syllables. Ornate words are frequently polysyllabic. Simple words are often of English origin ; polysyllabic words are often derived from the classical tongues.

The Authorised Version of the Bible and Bunyan's "*Pilgrim's Progress*" contain a large preponderance of simple Anglo-Saxon words. Nearly all great prose writers admit thir indebtedness to the Authorised Version. Accordingly, we should accept their judgment as valid—they admit the excellence of the choice of simple words.

Read what Dean Swift states—"If it were not for the Bible and Common Prayer Book in the Vulgar Tongue, we should hardly be able to understand anything that was written among us an hundred years ago, which is certainly true, for those books, being perpetually read in Churches, have proved a kind of standard for language, especially to the common people. And I doubt whether the alterations since introduced have added much to the beauty or strength of the English Tongue, though they have taken off a great deal from that *Simplicity which is one of the greatest perfections in any language.*"

A simple style is not arrived at merely by choosing simple words. In addition, simple phrases and simple structure of sentences must be used to attain simplicity of style.

It is quite possible to have an involved sentence in which the words are simple.

Although the principle of simplicity of diction should generally be observed in writing, there are certain occasions when the law should not be rigorously applied.

There are occasions when we desire our language to possess dignity. When we are dealing with elevated thought we require our language to be in keeping with that thought. Such subjects as *e.g.* the Immortality of the Soul, cannot be dealt with in merely simple words, for the subject is by no means simple.

We should invariably aim at a diction *commensurate and in keeping with the subject.* When judging the diction of a passage apply this rule.

When a language is at an early stage of development, most of its words are the names of concrete things. As a language grows throughout the course of time its vocabulary increases and many terms for abstract thoughts are introduced.

If the diction of a passage is unnecessarily ornate or elaborate it offends against the Law of Simplicity. This constitutes a fault. Diction that offends because it is obviously too ornate for the occasion affords examples of :—

**Bombast.** (*Low Latin, bombax—cotton used for* stuffing).

**Pomposity.**

**Rhodomontade** from a character in Ariosto's "*Orlando Furioso,*" who uses pompous language).

On some occasions a writer is eager to produce an imposing effect but fails to do so : when this occurs, we have **Bathos.**

The above faulty styles are frequently classed as **Fine-writing.**

**Poetic Diction** is the term applied to that choice of words which, in particular, the 18th century poets indulged in, *e.g.* Fish became *denizens of the deep* or *members of the finny tribe*, verse becomes *numbers.*

**Johnsonese** is a term applied to that style of writing Dr. Johnson used, characterised by a choice of words of classical origin rather than words of Anglo-Saxon origin. It is a highly Latinised style not only in regard to diction but also to constructions, phrases and sentences. It should be noted that Dr. Johnson is never ambiguous or difficult to those who possess as wide a vocabulary as he did. His style is suitable when the subject is commensurate with the language used. It was scarcely commensurate when he referred to a hill as "a considerable protuberance."

Other considerations in addition to that of simplicity of diction must be taken into account when making our choice of words. We must ensure that our words describe our meaning accurately, that they are the best words in our vocabulary to express our meaning closely and fully, and that they are the proper words for the occasion. The principle governing the selection of proper diction is the **Law of Propriety.**

There are various groups of words that offend against the Law of Propriety, *i.e.* words that constitute impropriety of diction.

**Malaprops** or **Malapropisms** are words wrongly used which resemble in sound the words which should have been used. The use of Malapropisms results from ignorance (*cf.* Mrs. Malaprop in Sheridan's "*The Rivals*") and from an endeavour to display learning which is not possessed. Naturally, it is chiefly with polysyllabic words that the confusion occurs. The use of Malapropisms is often intentionally adopted for the purpose of creating mirth (*cf.* Shakespeare's Dogberry and Launcelot Gobbo).

Example from "*The Rivals*"; Mrs. Malaprop—"I would by no means wish a daughter of mine to be a progeny (prodigy) of learning. But I would send her, at nine years old, to a boarding school . . . . Then, sir, she should have a supercilious (superficial) knowledge in accounts, and as she grew up, I would have her instructed in geometry (geography) that she might know something of the contagious (contiguous) countries."

When applying the Law of Propriety to our diction we discover that there are a great many pairs and groups of words which closely resemble each other in meaning. These words are called **Synonyms.** The derivation of this word implies "one word having the same meaning with another," but it is found in practice that it is very doubtful if there are pairs or groups of words which have on all occasions the same meaning. Define synonyms as *words which closely resemble each other in meaning.*

When we wish to express a meaning, and there are several words which appear to be suitable, we shall almost invariably find one word to be more suitable than the others.

**Synonyms.** Distinguish the meanings and uses of the words in the following groups :—

Moderation, mildness, sobriety, remission, leniency, temperance
Inertia, passiveness, torpidity, quiescence, inactivity.
Plain, simple, natural, pure, even, flat, manifest, easy, evident, smooth, clear, obvious, homely, unsophisticated, artless, open, unadorned.
Animosity, hatred, antipathy, aversion, dissension, acrimony, feud, strife, acerbity, bitterness, hostility.
Change, alter, vary, modify, diversify, qualify, transmute, shift, fluctuate, veer, exchange.

When choosing our diction we should avoid using expressions that have become hackneyed and threadbare through too frequent use. The use of over-worked expressions, which lack freshness and individuality, detracts from a writer's style. Hackneyed expressions are often termed **Stereotypes** or **Clichés.** (Consult a dictionary for the meaning of these terms).

**Journalese** is the term applied to that style of writing often used in our daily press by the poorest kind of reporters. It is characterised by the excessive use of clichés, hackneyed expressions and over-worked allusions. It is essentially a tawdry and cheap style and should be avoided. It offends against both the Law of Simplicity and the Law of Propriety.

Here is an exaggerated example of Journalese. Remove all the faults.

At the psychological moment the referee blew his whistle, just as the custodian of the home team propelled the leathern sphere into mid-field. A mighty conclamation of voices made the welkin ring ! Despite the best efforts of Jupiter Pluvius, the home team had triumphed. A sensational climax to a truly hectic contest. For the remainder of the evening, Bacchus reigned supreme in the case of most of the supporters, who evinced their enthusiasm by breaking windows and having a regular orgy of licence.

## EXTENSION, LIMITATION, AMELIORATION AND DETERIORATION OF MEANINGS OF WORDS.

Words suffer changes throughout the course of time A certain word may be used with propriety in one age and its use in another age may be an impropriety, *e.g. extravagant* in the time of Shakespeare meant *wandering*. ("*Hamlet*," Horatio speaking—

> " The *extravagant* and *erring* spirit hies
> To his confine ").

Nowadays, *extravagant* applies almost exclusively to wandering in expenditure, beyond one's income; erring usually means wandering from the path of rectitude—committing some fault.

Some words *extend* their meanings in the course of time, *e.g. influence.* This word, originally a term in astrology, meant the power or virtue of the stars upon men and things.

Some words *change* their meaning through the metaphorical meaning ousting the literal meaning, *e.g. talent* (originally a coin); *scruple* (originally used only of a certain small weight); *eccentric* (orig. used only of figures not having the same centre).

Some words *limit* their meaning, *e.g. extravagant*; *censure* (orig. merely opinion, *cf.* "*Hamlet*," Polonius, "Take each man's *censure*").

*Accident*, orig. any occurrence, usually unforeseen, nowadays, frequently limited to an occurrence in which some damage is sustained.

Some words *better* their meaning, *e.g. knight* (orig. a boy servant).

Some words *deteriorate* in their meaning, *e.g. vagabond* (orig. a wanderer, now frequently a rascal as well); *villain* (orig. merely a serf).

Good prose writers, and poets in particular, exercise a nice choice in words. In Shakespeare's "*Romeo and Juliet*," Mercutio, describing the effects of Queen Mab visiting the soldier in his sleep, says,

> "And then anon
> Drums in his ear, at which he starts and wakes,
> And, being frighted, *swears* a prayer or two,
> And sleeps again."

Milton writes: "While birds of calm sit *brooding* on the charmed wave."

Keats writes, in his "Ode to Autumn": "For summer has o'erbrimmed their *clammy* cells."

The words in italics express a great wealth of meaning. If we try to substitute a single word for each of them, we find our substitute very inadequate in comparison with the poet's choice. The poet's words are *irreplaceable.*

A third principle in the selection of diction is that words should not offend against the **Law of Purity.** This law imposes on our selection certain limitations regarding the purity of words. Words that are not acceptable in this respect are called Barbarisms. Such words are not sanctioned in literary English for one reason or another. The following are classes of **Barbarisms**:—

**Provincialisms** (Dialect Terms) are open to condemnation because they are not current throughout the land—they are used only in particular localities; *to sort* (Scotticism—to mend); *glaur* (Scot.—mud); to *threep* (Scot.—to urge). For other examples, see Burns's poems; Tennyson, "Northern Farmer" (old style).

**Obsolete Terms** (Archaisms) are words that are no longer current. Note that in works of a former age the use of terms that are no longer current would not constitute a fault unless they were obsolete at the time of writing. Examples :—*uprist* (uprose), *yclept* (called), *eftsoons* (soon afterwards), *wight* (creature or person), *wanhope* (despair).

**Technical Terms,** unless used in some technical publication, should be avoided as their meanings are not generally known. Examples :—*heterodyne, œsophagus* (gullet), *pleistocene, epistemological.*

**Foreign Terms.**—Many words and phrases from foreign languages have come to be used in English. Some of these are ultimately adopted. Examples :—Americanisms (N.B. these must be regarded as foreign terms) ; *debunk getaway, eats, boost, muscle in.*

Other examples from foreign tongues :—*parvenu, cause célèbre, dolce far niente, sturm und drang, entente, détente.*

**Coinages** (Neologisms) are words that have been invented—you will not find them in a dictionary. Perhaps poets may occasionally have justification for a coinage but it is a practice to be condemned. Perhaps only for words to denote inventions can the practice be upheld.

Examples :—to *jollify, enthuse, intrigue* (in such a use as " I was greatly intrigued by, etc."), *plusage, delouse, stagger* (holidays).

**Colloquialisms, Slang, Vulgarisms.**—Because of their similarity these may be classed together.

Colloquialisms are words and expressions used in familiar conversation, but should be limited to it. Examples :—*shan't, won't, jiffy, a tip.*

Slang consists of words and phrases current within a limited group, or class, or profession—" shoptalk," *e.g. swag, crib* (with burglars).

**Vulgarisms** are words or expressions used frequently in

conversation, but are more debased and even less reputable than colloquialisms. Vulgarisms should be avoided. Examples :—*half a mo'*, *clink* (gaol), *quod* (gaol), *tight*, *get the breeze up*.

These last three groups offend against good taste.

It should be noted that there are occasions when the use of Barbarisms can be upheld; indeed, there are occasions when their use is necessary. A novelist or dramatist dealing with the conversation of characters must use many colloquialisms to make the conversations true to life. If their characters are uneducated people, they must make their conversation reflect their lack of education (*cf.* the conversation of Sairey Gamp in "*Martin Chuzzlewit*.")

Some Barbarisms come in course of time to be accepted in literary or reputable English. It is difficult to discover when a Barbarism has graduated into literary English. Perhaps it is unfortunate that, unlike the French, we have no Académie to legislate in these matters. Until you find foreign terms, technical terms, provincialisms, coinages and colloquialisms used by reputable writers, you are well advised to avoid their use. Notice that the final tests of the use of such words depend on

(1) their being in general currency,
(2) their being sanctioned in literary or reputable English.

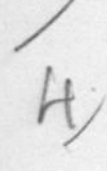

## BREVITY

A writer should aim at expressing his thoughts in as few words as possible consistent with lucidity. A diffuse style is a wasteful one and may well lead to obscuring the meaning which the words are meant to convey. In a diffuse style, attention is apt to be drawn to unessential words.

On the other hand, to be too brief—to apply the Law of Brevity too rigorously—is apt to lead to obscurity, which must be avoided at all costs. It should also be remembered that we do not wish to be over terse, for the resulting style is apt to be jejune—unattractive and devoid of interest. (*cf.* Bacon's style in his "*Essays*").

The chief offences against brevity are :—

**Tautology,** a needless repetition of the meaning in different words.

**Pleonasm,** the use of more words than are necessary to express the meaning.

**Redundancy,** a general term to denote anything superfluous either in words or in repetition of ideas.

There are occasions when the Law of Brevity cannot be applied without loss of effect and intention. Writers frequently indulge in **Repetition** for the sake of emphasis or other purposes. Dryden intentionally repeats the word "fallen" in Alexander's Feast :—

"Fallen, fallen, fallen, fallen,
Fallen from his high estate."

See also E. A. Poe's poem, "The Bells."

Here are some examples of Redundancy.

He bought the *entire* monopoly for salt.
He made a *new* invention.
He wrote his *own* autobiography.
The volunteers gave their services *willingly*.
It brings happiness to all classes, *high and low*.
The modern newspaper *of to-day* is a marvel.
*As a rule* we are usually introduced to the principal character in the first scene.
I was *all alone* and *by myself*.

**Verbosity** consists in using unnecessary words.

**Prolixity** consists in giving unnecessary details thereby obscuring the important facts. Often uneducated people are guilty of being prolix through failing to appreciate the essential facts. Frequently prolixity is indulged in for the sake of humour (*cf.* Sairey Gamp).

Example: (Betsy Prig has expressed the conviction that Mrs. Harris, to whom Mrs. Gamp is continually alluding, does not exist.) Mrs. Gamp, speaking to Mr. Westlock, "Don't I know as that dear woman is expecting of me at this minnit, Mr. Westlock, and is a-lookin' out of window down the street, with little Tommy Harris in her arms, as calls me his own Gammy, and truly calls, for bless the mottled little legs of that there precious child (like Canterbury Brawn, his own dear father says, which so they are) his own I have been, ever since I found him, Mr. Westlock, with his small red worsted shoe a-gurglin' in his throat, where he had put it in his play, a chick, wile they was leavin' of him on the floor a-looking for it through the 'ouse and him a-choakin' sweetly in the parlour! Oh, Betsey Prig, what wickedness you've showed this night, but never shall you darken Sairey's doors agen, you twining serpaint!"

## MELODY AND EUPHONY

In addition to the principles already enumerated, good writing *should please the ear*. It should sound pleasing, it should be euphonious. This requirement is specially necessary in poetry but it also should have consideration in prose writings. Sometimes words offend because of their sound, sometimes on account of their lack of rhythm, for good prose has a rhythm although it is not rigorous as it usually is in verse. There should be a pleasing flow in good writing and an attractive elegance. Avoid awkward groupings of words and cacophonous effects unless they are intentional.

To sum up (bearing in mind the exceptional circumstances when such rules should not be applied at all, or rigorously)—

Choose words that are *simple*, *short*, that most adequately express your meaning with accuracy and are pleasing to the ear. Avoid all stereotypes and barbarisms and use no more words than are necessary.

## THE SENTENCE

Apart from grammatical considerations, a sentence should possess unity of thought. Unrelated thoughts should not be included in one sentence—for no longer is it a true sentence (a number of words containing a complete thought). It should be noted that this rule applies to all kinds of sentences, whether short or long. A short sentence can offend against the law of Unity as well as a long one.

Example:—I had an egg for breakfast and it was raining.

This sentence is not likely to occur in anyone's composition, the law is so flagrantly ignored. But there are many sentences in which the offence is not so easily noticed and these require scrutiny. (See under Errors in Composition, Ch. VI.)

Observance of the Law of Unity demands a very restricted use of parentheses, as these contain thoughts additional to, and sometimes separated from, that of the sentence.

Kinds of sentences—(from the point of view of structure).

A **Periodic** sentence is one whose meaning is incomplete until we reach the end of it (the period).

A **Loose** sentence is one in which the principal thought is complete before the period; a subordinate clause follows or subordinate clauses follow. In this type of sentence, grammatical completeness has been reached before the end of it.

Example of **Periodic Sentence**:—The man, who had been released from gaol the previous week, and had again broken into several shops, was arrested.

Example of **Loose Sentence**:—The man was arrested, who had been released from gaol the previous week, and had again broken into several shops.

It will be noticed that a periodic sentence can be converted into a loose sentence, and vice versa.

The relative advantages of these types of sentences are :—

The periodic sentence sustains the interest : in it the mind is kept in suspense until the end.

The loose sentence is apt to fail in retaining the interest once the main idea has been grasped. In such, the sentence is, sometimes to our disappointment, prolonged beyond our expectation.

It will be deduced that the periodic sentence is likely to be favoured by orators as they will try to maintain interest.

When you examine the examples of different styles of writing, take note of the type of sentences used. You will soon realise that no author keeps rigorously to one type of sentence although one type will probably predominate.

The **Balanced Sentence** is one in which one part is antithetically placed against another. The commonest type of balanced sentence contains two main statements contrasted.

Examples :—

"Man eats to live ; not lives to eat."

*Coriolanus.* "I speak this in hunger for bread, not in thirst for revenge."

"You may as well strike at the heaven with your staves as lift them against the Roman state."

Often a balance of ideas is maintained among three groups, *e.g.*,

"Some books are to be tasted, others to be swallowed, and some few to be chewed and digested."

"Reading maketh a full man ; conference a ready man ; and writing an exact man."

BACON.

A succession of balanced sentences gives an impression of artificiality—and such a succession is apt to cause our interest to flag.

All obviously mannered styles seem forced and unnatural.

Study the following extract of a mannered style, largely dependent on balanced statements, from LYLY'S "*Euphues, The Anatomy of Wit.*"

"This young gallant of more witte than wealth, and yet of more wealth than wisdom, seeing himself inferior to none in pleasant conceits, though himself superior to all in honest conditions, insomuch that he thought himself so apt to all things that he gave himself almost to nothing but practising of those things commonly which are incident to those sharp wittes, fine phrases, smooth quippes, merry taunts, using jesting without meane (moderation) and abusing mirth without measure. As therefore the sweetest Rose hath his prickell (thorn), the finest velvet his bracke (flaw), the fairest flower his branne (husk), so the cheapest wit hath his wanton will, and the holiest head his wicked way. And true it is that some men write and most men believe, that in all perfect shapes a blemish bringeth rather a lyking every way to the eyes, than a loathing anyway to the mind. Venus had hir mole in hir cheeke, which made hir more amiable. Helen hir scarre in hir chinne, which Paris called Cos Amoris, the whetstone of Love."

## THE PARAGRAPH

There is a close analogy between the sentence and the paragraph. Like the sentence, the paragraph must have a *unity* of effect.

Errors in paragraphing can be divided into :—

1. The inclusion in one paragraph of ideas that are not relevant—*i.e.* which are not closely enough connected with the theme.

2. The failure to include ideas that are relevant and connected—*i.e.* the putting into two or more paragraphs ideas that should be included in one paragraph.

Each paragraph should contain all ideas that have to

do with one aspect of the subject. If, for example, we were writing a composition on "Our Navy," and were describing the various kinds of craft which comprise it, we should probably devote one paragraph to each craft, *e.g.* dreadnoughts, cruisers, destroyers, etc. We should not confuse our observations on each type of vessel but should keep them separate.

As a rule each paragraph contains, near the beginning of it, a sentence which gives the topic of the paragraph—called the **Topic or Key Sentence.** This might be said to correspond to the principal clause in a sentence, the following sentences corresponding to the subordinate clauses.

The sentences in a well constructed paragraph cohere—they follow each other in an orderly and logical manner. There should be nothing disjointed in the sentences of a paragraph.

Let us examine the first two paragraphs of Bacon's Essay "*Of Studies.*"

Studies serve for delight, for ornament, and for ability. Their chief use for delight, is in privateness and retiring; for ornament, is in discourse; and for ability, is in the judgment and disposition of business; for expert men can execute, and perhaps judge of particulars one by one; but the general counsels, and the plots and marshalling of affairs, come best from those that are learned.

To spend too much time in studies, is sloth; to use them too much for ornament, is affectation; to make judgment wholly by their rules, is the humour of a scholar; they perfect nature, and are perfected by experience; for natural abilities are like natural plants, that need pruning by study; and Studies themselves do give forth directions too much at large, except they be bounded in by experience. Crafty men contemn studies, simple men admire them, and wise men use them; for they teach not their own use; but that is a wisdom without them and above them, won by observation.

**Diction.**—The paragraphs contain examples of archaisms, *e.g. privateness* and *retiring*. Many words are obviously not used in their modern sense. *e.g. expert* here means professional men, skilled and practised in particular business; in modern times it frequently means adroit, skilful; *affectation* here means pedantry; *admire* here means to wonder at; *humour* here means oddity or peculiarity.

Words of Latin origin predominate, *e.g. studies, serve, delight, ornament, ability*—all of Latin origin in the first sentence.

**Sentences.**—The sentences are balanced, usually holding a threefold balance, *e.g.* "*Studies serve for delight, for ornament, and for ability.* This threefold balance is maintained throughout paragraph one, and is continued in paragraph two, *e.g.* "*To spend too much time in studies is sloth, to use them too much for ornament is affectation, to make judgment wholly by their rules, is the humour of a scholar, etc.*" The same balance can be traced to the end of paragraph two.

Several of the sentences we would divide into two or more sentences, *e.g.* sentence two, paragraph one. We would begin a new sentence at "For expert men, etc."

The sentences are jerky chiefly on account of the absence of connecting words (Asyndeton).

**Style** in general. The diction is archaic nowadays, but it would not be considered so when Bacon wrote. The style is balanced, at times it is elliptical (*e.g. for ornament, is in discourse*). It is terse, even laconic to a degree. It is epigrammatical, even paradoxical. (*To spend too much time in studies, is sloth*). The writing is full of meaning: it suffers at times from a too rigorous economy of words with the result that it is difficult to grasp the meaning. It is a bare style and unattractive, it demands rather more concentration than the average reader is prepared to grant, especially if he is reading for pleasure as well as for information.

There is merely an appeal to the intellect in this style of writing: it is a tribute to the logicality of the writer's mind but can scarcely be commended as attractive.

Judging Bacon from modern standards of attainment in writing, we may be able to criticise his writing adversely, but we must remember that he lived from 1561-1626. He "did rather drive at a masculine and clear expression than at any fineness or affectation of phrases."

Let us compare his sentences, artificially arranged in balanced ideas as they are, with the two opening sentences of Milton's "*Areopagitica.*"

"They who to States and Governours of the Commonwealth direct their speech, High Court of Parliament, or wanting such accesse in a private condition, write that which they foresee may advance the public good, I suppose them, as at the beginning of no meane endeavour, not a little alter'd and mov'd inwardly in their mindes; some with doubt of what will be the successe, others with feare of what will be the censure; some with hope, others with confidence of what they have to speake. And me perhaps each of these dispositions, as the subject was whereon I enter'd, may have at other times variously affected, and likely might in these foremost expressions now also disclose which of them sway'd most, but that the very attempt of this addresse thus made, and the thought of whom it hath recourse to, hath got the power within me to a passion, farre more welcome than incidentall to a Preface."

The sentences here are long and involved—the style heavy and cumbersome.

In contrast with the above, let us examine a passage from Dryden, 1631-1700.

"But I have descended, before I was aware, from Comedy to Farce which consists principally of grimaces. That I admire not any comedy equally with tragedy, is, perhaps, from the sullenness of my humour; but that I detest those farces, which are now the most frequent entertainments of the stage, I am sure I have reason on my side. Comedy consists, though of low persons, yet of natural actions and characters; I mean such humours, adventures and designs, as are to be found and met with in the world. Farce, on the other side, consists of forced humours, and unnatural events. Comedy presents us with the imperfections of human nature. Farce entertains us with what is monstrous and chimerical. The one causes laughter in those who can judge of men and manners, by the lively representation of their folly or corruption; the other produces the same effect in those who can judge of neither, and that only by its extravagances. The first works on the judgment and fancy; the latter on the fancy only. There is more of satisfaction in the former kind of laughter, and in the latter more of scorn. But, how it happens that an impossible adventure should cause our mirth, I cannot so easily imagine. Something there may be in the oddness of it, because on the stage it is the common effect of things unexpected to surprise us into a delight; and that is to be ascribed to the strange appetite, as I may call it, of the fancy; which, like that of a longing woman, often runs out into the most extravagant desires; and is better satisfied sometimes with loam, or with the rinds of trees, than with the wholesome nourishments of life. In short there is the same difference betwixt Farce and Comedy, as betwixt an empiric and a true physician: both of them may attain ends; but what the one performs by hazard, the other does by skill. And as the artist is often unsuccessful, while the mountebank succeeds; so farces more commonly take the people than comedies. For to write unnatural things is the most probable way of pleasing them, who understand not Nature. And a true poet often misses of applause, because he cannot debase himself to write so ill as to please his audience."

We can see from the above example of Dryden's style that it is clear and vigorous, it is happily phrased, embodying a colloquial ease which never descends to the level of being undignified. It is essentially **modern prose.**

Here is a criticism of Dryden's style by Dr. Johnson. You will notice that it is not so typically Johnsonese as the passage quoted on page 330. Perhaps Johnson was influenced by his subject. The dominant features of his own style—"the formality of a settled style, in which the first half of the sentence betrays the other. The clauses are balanced, the periods modelled"—are absent in Dryden's style.

"Criticism, either didactic or defensive, occupies almost all his (Dryden's) prose, except those pages which he has devoted to his patrons; but none of his prefaces were ever thought tedious. They have not the formality of a settled style, in which the first half of the sentence betrays the other. The clauses are never balanced, nor the periods modelled; every word seems to drop by chance, though it falls into its proper place. Nothing is cold or languid; the whole is airy, animated, and vigorous; what is little, is gay; what is great, is splendid. He may be thought to mention himself too frequently; but while he forces himself upon our esteem, we cannot refuse him to stand high in his own. Everything is excused by the play of images, and the spriteliness of expression. Though all is easy, nothing is feeble; though all seems careless, there is nothing harsh; and though, since his earlier works, more than a century has passed, they have nothing yet uncouth or obsolete."

Balance :— Johnson

Here is a passage from Johnson's "*Life of Dryden*," in which the features of Johnson's style are abundantly present.

"1. Of dramatic immortality he did not want examples among his predecessors, or companions among his contemporaries; but in the meanness and servility of hyperbolical adulation I know not whether, since the days in which the Roman emperors were deified, he has been ever equalled, except by Afra Behn in an address to Eleanor Gwyn. 2. When once he has undertaken the task of praise, he no longer retains shame in himself nor supposes it in his patron. 3. As many odiferous bodies are observed to diffuse perfumes from year to year without sensible diminution of bulk or weight, he appears never to have impoverished his mint of flattery by his expenses, however lavish. 4. He had all the forms of excellence, intellectual and moral, combined in his mind, with endless variation; and when he had scattered on the hero of the day the golden shower of wit and virtue, he had ready for him whom he wished to court on the morrow new wit and virtue with another stamp. 5. Of this kind of meanness he never seems to decline the practice, or lament the necessity; he considers the great as entitled to encomiastic homage, and brings praise rather as a tribute than a gift, more delighted with the fertility of his invention than mortified by the prostitution of his judgment. 6. It is indeed not certain that on these occasions his judgment much rebelled against his interest. 7. There are minds which easily sink into submission, that look on grandeur with undistinguishing reverence, and discover no defect where there is elevation of rank and affluence of riches."

**Diction.**—Johnson's diction is largely of classical origin, *e.g. servility of hyperbolic adulation, diminution, encomiastic homage.* In place of many of such words shorter and more homely terms could have been chosen with advantage, *e.g.* praise for *adulation*, lessening for *diminution*, praise for *encomiastic homage.*

**Sentences.**—They are chiefly of the balanced type. The opposite of what he wrote of Dryden's style might almost be quoted against him—" The clauses are balanced, the periods modelled, every word does *not* drop by chance." As an example of balanced sentence, study sentence, 5, "*Of this kind of meanness, etc.*" Many of his sentences are in halves, the second half being introduced by either a cumulative conjunction or by an adversative conjunction, *e.g.* in the first sentence, " *but in the meanness, etc.*" ; in sentence 4 beginning, "*He had all the forms of excellence, etc.*," " *and when he had scattered, etc.*" He frequently omits any conjunction, *e.g.* sentence 5, the second half of the sentence implementing the first.

**Style.**—Johnson's style is pedantic, pompous, elaborate and highly Latinised on account of his choice of diction and type of sentences. We feel he is not natural. He can be natural, and when he is, his style is different (*cf.* his style in his letter to Lord Chesterfield). There is dignity and high-sounding quality in this extract *but* it seems needlessly artificial and not commensurate with the subject.

In his Preface to the Lyrical Ballads, Wordsworth quotes two passages, one from Dr. Johnson and one from the Authorised Version of the Bible. Johnson's passage he calls " this hubbub of words," and asks us to contrast it with the simple words of the Bible. Wordsworth was attacking the poetic diction so frequently adopted by XVIIIth century poets.

"Turn on the prudent Ant thy heedless eyes,
Observe her labours, Sluggard, and be wise;
No stern command, no monitory voice,
Prescribes her duties, or directs her choice;
Yet, timely provident, she hastes away
To snatch the blessings of a plenteous day;
When fruitful Summer loads the teeming plain,
She crops the harvest, and she stores the grain.
How long shall sloth usurp thy useless hours,
Unnerve thy vigour, and enchain thy powers?
While artful shades thy downy couch enclose,
And soft solicitation courts repose,
Amidst the drowsy charms of dull delight,
Year chases year with unremitting flight,
Till Want now following, fraudulent and slow,
Shall spring to seize thee, like an ambush'd foe."

"Go to the Ant, thou Sluggard, consider her ways, and be wise: which having no guide, overseer, or ruler, provideth her meat in the summer, and gathereth her food in the harvest. How long wilt thou sleep, O Sluggard? when wilt thou arise out of thy sleep? Yet a little sleep, a little slumber, a little folding of the hands to sleep. So shall thy poverty come as one that travelleth, and thy want as an armed man."—PROVERBS, Ch. 6.

Read the following paragraphs carefully. They are from Macaulay's Essay on Milton.

"We would speak first of the Puritans, the most remarkable body of men, perhaps, which the world has ever produced. The odious and ridiculous parts of their character lie on the surface. He that runs may read them; nor have there been wanting attentive and malicious observers to point them out. For many years after the Restoration, they were the theme of unmeasured invective and derision. They were exposed to the utmost licentiousness of the press and of the stage, at the time when the press and the stage were most licentious. They were not men of letters; they were, as a body, unpopular; they could not defend themselves; and the public would not take them under its protection. They were therefore abandoned, without reserve, to the tender mercies of the satirists and dramatists. The ostentatious simplicity of their dress, their sour aspect, their nasal twang, their stiff posture, their long graces, their

Hebrew names, the Scriptural phrases which they introduced on every occasion, their contempt of human learning, their detestation of polite amusements, were indeed fair game for the laughers. *But it is not from the laughers alone that the philosophy of history is to be learnt.* And he who approaches this subject should carefully guard against the influence of that potent ridicule which has already misled so many excellent writers.

"Those who roused the people to resistance, who directed their measures through a long series of eventful years, who formed, out of the most unpromising materials, the finest army that Europe had ever seen, who trampled down King, Church and Aristocracy, who, in the short intervals of domestic sedition and rebellion, made the name of England terrible to every nation on the face of the earth, were no vulgar fanatics. Most of their absurdities were mere external badges, like the signs of freemasonry, or the dresses of friars. We regret that these badges were not more attractive. We regret that a body to whose courage and talents mankind has owed inestimable obligations had not the lofty elegance which distinguished some of the adherents of Charles the First, or the easy good-breeding for which the court of Charles the Second was celebrated. But, if we must make our choice, we shall, like Bassanio in the play, turn from the spacious caskets which contain only the Death's head and the Fool's head, and fix on the plain leaden chest which conceals the treasure."

These two paragraphs are typical of Macaulay. In the first he deals with the external appearance and idiosyncrasies of the Puritans, and, in the second, he gives us their sterling qualities.

Clear, orderly sequence of thought is a marked feature of Macaulay's paragraphing. He strictly adheres to their unity. In his paragraphs, the topic sentence is first in both paragraphs.

His sentences are full of significant illustrations. He makes a judicious choice of long and short sentences. Notice the telling effect of the short sentence No. 9 ("*But it is not from the laughers, etc.*") coming after the long periodic No. 8. The type of sentence chiefly used by him is the periodic.

His style is clear, vivid, picturesque and full of illustrations. He appeals to the intelligence of the reader rather than to his imagination. His metaphors and similes are concrete and extremely effective, *e.g.* "*Most of their absurdities were mere external badges like the signs of freemasonry, or the dresses of the friars.*"

Here are two examples of Oratory. When we consider the occasion of Lincoln's address, and the people to whom the words were addressed, we realise that the simple diction and style coupled with the directness of appeal are eminently suitable.

In the extract from Burke's Speech "On Conciliation with America," we have an example of striking eloquence which is never commonplace.

### Address at the Dedication of the National Cemetery at Gettysburg.

November, 1863. (During American Civil War.)

"Fourscore and seven years ago our fathers brought forth upon this continent a new nation, conceived in liberty, and dedicated to the proposition that all men are created equal.

Now we are engaged in a great civil war, testing whether that nation, or any nation so conceived and so dedicated, can long endure. We are met on a great battle-field of that war. We have come to dedicate a portion of that field as a final resting-place for those who here gave their lives that that nation might live. It is altogether fitting and proper that we should do this.

But in a larger sense we cannot dedicate, we cannot consecrate, we cannot hallow this ground. The brave men, living and dead, who struggled here, have consecrated it far above our power to add or detract. The world will little note nor long remember what we say here, but it can never forget what they did here. It is for us, the living, rather, to be dedicated here to the unfinished work which they who fought here have thus far so nobly advanced. It is rather for us to be here dedicated to the great task remaining before us; that from these honoured dead we take increased devotion to that cause for which they gave the last measure of devotion; that we here highly resolve that these dead shall not have died in vain; that this nation, under God, shall have a new birth of freedom; and that government of the people, by the people, and for the people, shall not perish from the earth."

## Extract from Burke's Speech "On Conciliation with America."

"As to the wealth which the colonies have drawn from the sea by their fisheries, you had all that matter fully opened at your bar. You surely thought these acquisitions of value, for they seemed even to excite your envy; and yet the spirit by which that enterprising employment has been exercised, ought rather, in my opinion, to have raised your esteem and admiration. And, pray, Sir, what in the world is equal to it? Pass by the other parts, and look at the manner in which the people of New England have of late carried on the whale fishery. Whilst we follow them among the tumbling mountains of ice, and behold them penetrating into the deepest frozen recesses of Hudson's Bay and Davis's Straits, whilst we are looking for them beneath the arctic circle, we hear that they have pierced into the opposite regions of polar cold, that they are at the antipodes, and engaged under the frozen serpent of the south. Falkland Island, which seemed too remote and romantic an object for the grasp of national ambition, is but a stage and resting-place in the progress of their victorious industry. Nor is the equinoctional heat more discouraging to them, than the accumulated winter of the poles. We know that whilst some of them draw the line and strike the harpoon on the coast of Africa, others run the longitude, and pursue their gigantic game along the coast of Brazil. No sea but what is vexed by their fisheries. No climate that is not witness to their toils. Neither the perseverance of Holland, nor the activity of France, nor the dexterous and firm sagacity of English enterprise, ever carried this most perilous mode of hardy industry to the extent to which it has been pushed by this recent people; a people who are still, as it were, but in the gristle, and not yet hardened into the bone of manhood. When I contemplate these things; when I know that the colonies in general owe little or nothing to any care of ours, and that they are not squeezed into this happy form by the constraints of watchful and suspicious government, but that, through a wise and salutary neglect, a generous nature has been suffered to take her own way to perfection; when I reflect upon these effects, when I see how profitable they have been to us, I feel all the pride of power sink, and all the presumption in the wisdom of human contrivances melt and die away within me. My rigour relents. I pardon something to the spirit of liberty."

Here is an example of markedly individualistic style from Thomas Carlyle's "*French Revolution*," describing the assassination of Marat by Charlotte Corday.

It is yellow July evening, we say, the thirteenth of the month; eve of the Bastille day—when 'M. Marat,' four years ago, in the crowd of the Pont Neuf, shrewdly required of that Besenval Hussar-party, which had such friendly dispositions, 'to dismount, and give up their arms, then'; and became notable among Patriot men. Four years: what a road he has travelled; and sits now, about half-past seven of the clock, stewing in slipper-bath; sore afflicted; ill of Revolution Fever—of what other malady this History had rather not name. Excessively sick and worn, poor man; with precisely elevenpence halfpenny of ready-money, in paper; with slipper-bath; strong three-footed stool for writing on, the while; and a squalid—Washerwoman, one may call her; that is his civic establishment in Medical School Street; thither and not elsewhither has his road led him. Not in the reign of Brotherhood and Perfect Felicity; yet surely on the way towards that?—Hark, a rap again! A musical woman's voice, refusing to be rejected: it is the Citoyenne who would do France a service. Marat, recognising from within, cries, Admit her. Charlotte Corday is admitted.

"Citoyen Marat. I am from Caen the seat of Rebellion, and wished to speak with you.—Be seated, Mon enfant. Now what are the Traitors doing at Caen? What Deputies are at Caen?—Charlotte names some Deputies. 'Their heads shall fall within a fortnight,' croaks the eager People's friend, clutching his tablets to write: Barbaroux, Pétion, writes he with bare shrunk arm, turning aside in the bath: Pétion and Louvet, and—Charlotte has drawn her knife from the sheath: plunges it, with one sure stroke, into the writer's heart. 'A moi, chère amie, Help, dear!' no more could the Death-choked say or shriek. The helpful Washerwoman running in, there is no Friend of the People, or Friend of the Washerwoman left; but his life with a groan gushes out indignant, to the shades below.

Here is a criticism of Carlyle's style quoted from "*Beauchamp's Career*."

A favourite author was one writing of Heroes, in a style resembling either early architecture or utter dilapidation, so loose and rough it seemed, a wind-in-the-orchard style, that tumbles down here and there an appreciable fruit with uncouth bluster; sentences without commencement running to abrupt endings and smoke, like waves against a sea-wall, learned dictionary words giving a hand to street-slang, and accents falling on them haphazard like slant rays from driving clouds; all the pages in a breeze, the whole book producing a kind of electrical agitation in the mind and the joints.

A Note on Style by Washington Irving, well worth studying:—

"Figures and metaphors should, upon no occasion, be scattered with too profuse a hand; and they should never be incongruous with the train of our sentiment. Nothing can be more unnatural than for a writer to carry on a process of reasoning, in the same kind of figurative language which he would employ in description. When he reasons, we look only for perspicuity; when he describes, we expect embellishment; when he divides or relates, we desire plainness and simplicity. One of the greatest secrets in composition is to know when to be simple. This always lends a heightening to ornament, in its proper place. The judicious disposition of shade makes the light and colouring strike the more. He is truly eloquent who can discourse of humble subjects in a plain style, who can treat important ones with dignity, and speak of things which are of a middle nature in a temperate strain. For one who upon no occasion can express himself in a calm, orderly, distinct manner, but begins to be on fire before his readers are prepared to kindle along with him, has the appearance of a madman raving among persons who enjoy the use of their reason, or of a drunkard reeling in the midst of sober company."

The following adjectives will be found useful as a vocabulary of critical terms when criticising Style:—

*Terse*, concise, curt, laconic, direct.
*Bare*, bald, jejune.
*Clear*, perspicuous, lucid.
*Vigorous*, forceful, nervous, virile.
*Grand*, sublime, elevated, dignified, weighty.
*Graceful*, elegant, delicate.
*Pompous*, inflated, magniloquent, bombastic, turgid.
*Conceited*, precious, frigid.
*Animated*, racy, vivacious.
*Diffuse*, prolix, verbose, languid.

*Pedantic.*
*Colloquial*, conversational.
*Graphic*, picturesque,
*Ornate*, laboured, elaborate, florid.
*Obscure.*
*Mannered.*
*Journalese.*
*Colourless.*
*Euphuistic.*
*Bathetic.*

Point out the salient features of the styles in which the following extracts are written:—

1. "It (cricket) must be rather a warm pursuit in such a climate," observed Mr. Pickwick.

"Warm!—red hot—scorching—glowing. Played a match once—single wicket—friend the colonel—Sir Thomas Blazo—who should get the greatest number of runs. Won the toss—first innings—seven o'clock a.m.—six natives to look out—went in; kept in—heat intense—natives all fainted—taken away—fresh half-dozen ordered—fainted also—Blazo bowling—supported by two natives—couldn't bowl me out—fainted too—cleared away the colonel—wouldn't give in—faithful attendant—Quanko Samba—last man left—sun so hot, bat in blisters, ball scorched brown—five hundred and seventy runs—rather exhausted—Quanko mustered up last remaining strength—bowled me out—had a bath, and went out to dinner."

"*Pickwick Papers*"—DICKENS.

2. On they swept, gaining fast on the Spaniard.

"Call the men up, and to quarters; the rain will be over in ten minutes." Yeo ran forward to the gangway, and sprang back again with a face white and wild.

"Land right ahead! Port your helm, sir! For the love of God, port your helm!"

Amyas, with the strength of a bull, jammed the helm down, while Yeo shouted to the men below.

She swung round. The masts bent like whips; crack went the foresail like a cannon. What matter? Within two hundred yards of them was the Spaniard; in front of her, a huge dark bank rose through the dense hail, and mingled with the clouds; and at its foot, plainer every moment, pillars and spouts of leaping foam.

"What is it?—Morte? Hartland?"

It might be anything for thirty miles.

"Lundy!" said Yeo. "The south end! I see the head of the Shutter in the breakers! Hard a-port yet, and get her close-hauled as you can, and the Lord may have mercy on us still! Look at the Spaniard!"

Yes, look at the Spaniard!

On their left hand, as they broached-to, the wall of granite sloped down from the clouds toward an isolated piece of rock some two hundred feet in height. Then a hundred yards of roaring breaker upon a sunken shelf, across which the race of the tide poured like a cataract; then, amid a column of salt smoke, the Shutter, like a huge black fang, rose waiting for its prey; and between the Shutter and the land, the great galleon loomed dimly through the storm.

He, too, had seen his danger, and tried to broach-to. But his clumsy mass refused to obey the helm. He struggled a moment, half hid in foam, fell away again, and rushed upon his doom.

"Lost! lost! lost!" cried Amyas madly, and throwing up his hands let go the tiller. Yeo caught it just in time.

"Sir! sir! what are you at? We shall clear the rock yet."

"Yes!" shouted Amyas in his frenzy; "but he will not!"

Another minute. The galleon gave a sudden jar, and stopped. Then one long heave and bound, as if to free herself. And then her bows lighted clean upon the Shutter.

An awful silence fell on every English soul. They heard not the roaring of wind and surge; they saw not the blinding flashes of the lightning; but they heard one long ear-piercing wail to every saint in heaven rise from five hundred human throats; they saw the mighty ship heel over from the wind, and sweep headlong down the cataract of the race, plunging her yards into the foam, and showing her whole black side even to her keel, till she rolled clean over, and vanished for ever and ever.

"Shame!" cried Amyas, hurling his sword far into the sea," to lose my right, my right! when it was in my very grasp! Unmerciful!"

A crack which rent the sky, and made the granite ring and quiver; a bright world of flame, and then a blank of utter darkness, against which stood out, glowing red-hot, every mast, and sail, and rock, and Salvation Yeo as he stood just in front of Amyas, the tiller in his hand. All red-hot, transfigured into fire; and behind, the black, black night.

*"Westward Ho!"*—KINGSLEY.

3. The tremendous sea itself, when I could find sufficient pause to look at it, in the agitation of the blinding wind, the flying stones and sand, and the awful noise, confounded me. As the high watery walls came rolling in, and, at their highest, tumbled into surf, they looked as if the least would engulf the town. As the receding wave swept back with a hoarse roar, it seemed to scoop out caves in the beach, as if its purpose were to undermine the earth. When some white-headed billows thundered on, and dashed themselves to pieces before they reached the land, every fragment of the late whole seemed possessed by the full might of its wrath, rushing to be gathered to the composition of another monster. Undulating hills were changed to valleys, undulating valleys (with a solitary storm-bird sometimes skimming through them) were lifted up to the hills; masses of water shivered and shook the beach with a booming sound; every shape tumultuously rolled on, as soon as made, to change its shape and place, and beat another shape and place away; the ideal shore on the horizon with its towers and buildings, rose and fell; the clouds flew fast and thick; I seemed to see a rending and upheaving of all nature.

"*David Copperfield*"—DICKENS.

4. Looked at broadly, one would say they had been an eminently pious people. It is a part of the complaint of modern philosophers about them, that religion, or superstition, or whatever they please to call it, had too much to do with their daily lives. So far as one can look into that commonplace round of things which historians never tell us about, there have rarely been seen in this world a set of people who have thought more about right and wrong, and the judgment about them of the upper powers. Long-headed, thrifty industry—a sound hatred of waste, imprudence, idleness, extravagance—the feet planted firmly upon the earth—a conscientious sense that the worldly virtues are, nevertheless, very necessary virtues, that without these, honesty for one thing is not possible, and that without honesty no other excellence, religious or moral, is worth anything at all—this is the stuff of which Scotch life was made, and very good stuff it is. It has been called gloomy, austere, harsh, and such other epithets. A gifted modern writer has favoured us lately with long strings of extracts from the sermons of Scotch divines of the last century, taking hard views of human short-comings and their probable consequences and passing hard censures upon the world and its amusements. Well, no doubt amusement is a very good thing; but I should rather infer from

the vehemence and frequency of these denunciations that the people had not been in the habit of denying themselves too immoderately; and, after all, it is no very hard charge against those teachers that they thought more of duty than of pleasure. Sermons always exaggerate the theoretic side of things; and the most austere preacher, when he is out of the pulpit, and you meet him at the dinner-table, becomes singularly like other people. We may take courage, I think, we may believe safely that in those minister-ridden days, men were not altogether so miserable; we may hope that no large body of human beings have for any length of time been too dangerously afraid of enjoyment. Among other good qualities, the Scots have been distinguished for humour—not for venomous wit, but for kindly, genial humour, which half loves what it laughs at—and this alone shows clearly enough that those to whom it belongs have not looked too exclusively on the gloomy side of the world. I should rather say that the Scots had been an unusually happy people. Intelligent industry, the honest doing of daily work, with a sense that it must be done well, under penalties; the necessaries of life moderately provided for; and a sensible content with the situation of life in which men are born—this through the week, and at the end of it the "Cottar's Saturday Night"—the homely family, gathered reverently and peacefully together, and irradiated with a sacred presence—Happiness! such happiness as we human creatures are likely to know upon this world, will be found there, if anywhere.

*"The Influence of the Reformation on the Scottish Character"*—
FROUDE.

5. I am disgusted with the affectation of men of letters, who complain that they have renounced a substance for a shadow, and that their fame (which sometimes is no insupportable weight) affords a poor compensation for envy, censure, and persecution. My own experience, at least, has taught me a very different lesson; twenty happy years have been animated by the labour of my *History*, and its success has given me a name, a rank, a character in the world to which I should not otherwise have been entitled. The freedom of my writings has indeed provoked an implacable tribe; but, as I was safe from the stings, I was soon accustomed to the buzzing of the hornets; my nerves are not tremblingly alive, and my literary temper is so happily framed that I am less sensible of pain than of pleasure. The rational pride of an author may be offended, rather than flattered, by vague indiscriminate praise; but he cannot, he should not, be indifferent to the fair testimonies of private and

public esteem. Even his moral sympathy may be gratified by the idea that now, in the present hour, he is imparting some degree of amusement or knowledge to his friends in a distant land; that one day his mind will be familiar to the grandchild of those who are yet unborn. I cannot boast of the friendship or favour of princes; the patronage of English literature has long since been devolved on our booksellers, and the measure of their liberality is the least ambiguous test of our common success. Perhaps the golden mediocrity of my fortune has contributed to fortify my application.

"*Autobiography*"—GIBBON.

6. Some slight abstraction I thus attempt of my oriental dreams, which filled me always with such amazement at the monstrous scenery, that horror seemed absorbed for a while in sheer astonishment. Sooner or later came a reflux of feeling that swallowed up that astonishment, and left me not so much in terror, as in hatred and abomination of what I saw. Over every form and threat, and punishment, and dim sightless incarceration, brooded a killing sense of eternity and infinity. Into these dreams only it was, with one or two slight exceptions, that any circumstances of physical horror entered. All before had been moral and spiritual terrors. But here the main agents were ugly birds, or snakes, or crocodiles, especially the last. The cursed crocodile became to me the object of more horror than all the rest. I was compelled to live with him; and (as was always the case in my dreams) for centuries. Sometimes I escaped, and found myself in Chinese houses. All the feet of the tables, sofas, etc., soon became instinct with life; the abominable head of the crocodile, and his leering eyes, looked out at me, multiplied into ten thousand repetitions, and I stood loathing and fascinated. So often did this hideous reptile haunt my dreams that many times the very same dream was broken up in the very same way; I heard gentle voices speaking to me (I hear everything when I am sleeping), and instantly I awoke; it was broad noon, and my children were standing, hand in hand, at my bedside, come to show me their coloured shoes, or new frocks, or to let me see them dressed for going out. No experience was so awful to me, and at the same time so pathetic, as this abrupt translation from the darkness of the infinite to the gaudy summer air of highest noon, and from the unutterable abortions of miscreated gigantic vermin to the sight of infancy, and innocent *human* natures.

"*Confessions of an English Opium Eater*"—DE QUINCEY

## EXERCISE XXXVII

Read these two poems: then answer the questions that follow :—

(*a*) "O Youth ! for years so many and sweet
'Tis known that thou and I were one,
*I'll think it but a fond conceit*—
It cannot be that thou are gone !
Thy vesper bell hath not yet toll'd :—
And thou wert ay a masker bold !
What strange disguise hast thou put on
To make believe that thou art gone ?
*I see these locks in silvery slips,*
*This drooping gait, this alter'd size* :
But Springtide blossoms on thy lips,
And tears take sunshine from thine eyes !
Life is but thought : so think I will
That Youth and I are housemates still."

COLERIDGE.

(*b*) " I long have had a quarrel set with Time
Because he robbed me. Every day of life
Was wrested from me after bitter strife :
I never yet could see the sun go down
But I was angry in my heart, nor hear
The leaves fall in the wind without a tear
Over the dying summer. I have known
No truce with Time nor Time's accomplice, Death.
*The fair world is the witness of a crime*
*Repeated every hour.* For life and breath
Are sweet to all who live ; *and bitterly*
*The voices of these robbers of the heath*
*Sound in each ear* and chill the passer-by.
What have we done to thee, thou monstrous Time ?
What have we done to Death that we must die ? "

BLUNT.

(1) Both poets deal with Time.

(*a*) Give briefly the substance of Coleridge's thought. Indicate two apt figures which he has used to illustrate his thought.

(*b*) Discuss the nature of Blunt's " quarrel set with Time." Show how the original metaphor is sustained throughout his poem.

(*c*) What is the final attitude of each poet to Time ? Which do you prefer ? Justify your preference.

(2) Paraphrase the four phrases in italics.

*N.B.*—All the exercises on Interpretation (Chapter VII, page 146) are very suitable for analysis of Style.

See Exercises in Prosody, page 277. Discuss the style of each extract. See also, Exercises on Précis, page 189.

---

# CHAPTER XV

## LITERARY FORMS

### Prose and Poetry

At the outset, it should be noted that the terms prose, poetry and verse are not terms that exclude each other on all occasions. Writings in prose are writings that are direct, in straightforward arrangement of words, an arrangement that is free from conscious, regular metre. Prose is derived from *Latin*—*prorsus*—straightforward.

Poetry is usually in metrical arrangement—an arrangement that can claim some regularity of pattern in metrical feet. But there are passages written in prose which, because of the treatment of the theme, can claim true poetic spirit. Their authors have not been primarily concerned with *merely giving information*—and that is usually the first purpose of the writer in prose. The spirit of true poetry may be, and is, found in prose writings. (Study the passage from R. D. Blackmore on *Spring*. See Chapter on Figures of Speech under Personification, page 290). If you examine the following extract from Conrad's "*Mirror of the Sea*," you will realise that Conrad is giving us much more than mere information about the West Wind.

"The West Wind reigns over the seas surrounding the coasts of these kingdoms; and from the gateways of the channels, from promontaries as if from watch-towers, from estuaries of rivers as if from postern gates, from passage-ways, inlets, straits, firths, the garrison of the Isle and the crews of the ships going and returning look to the westward to judge by the varied splendours of his sunset mantle the mood of that arbitrary ruler. The end of the day is the time to gaze at the kingly face of the Westerly Weather, who is the arbiter of ships' destinies. Benignant and splendid, or splendid and sinister, the western sky reflects the hidden purposes of the royal mind. Clothed in a mantle of dazzling gold or draped in rags of black clouds like a beggar, the might of the Westerly Wind sits enthroned upon the western horizon with the whole North Atlantic as a footstool for his feet and the first twinkling stars making a diadem for his brow. Then the seamen, attentive courtiers of the weather, think of regulating the conduct of their ships by the mood of the master. The West Wind is too great a king to be a dissembler: he is no calculator plotting deep schemes in a sombre heart; he is too strong for small artifices; there is passion in all his moods. even in the soft mood of serene days, in the grace of his blue sky whose immense and unfathomable tenderness reflected in the mirror of the sea embraces, possesses, lulls to sleep the ships with white sails. He is all things to all oceans; he is like a poet seated upon a throne—magnificent, simple, barbarous, pensive, generous, impulsive, changeable, unfathomable—but when you understand him, always the same. Some of his sunsets are like pageants devised for the delight of the multitude, when all the gems of the royal treasure-house are displayed above the sea. Others are like the opening of his royal confidence, tinged with thoughts of sadness and compassion in a melancholy splendour meditating upon the short-lived peace of the waters. And I have seen him put the pent-up anger of his heart into the aspect of the inaccessible sun, and cause it to glare fiercely like the eye of an implacable autocrat out of the pale and frightened sky."

Wordsworth in his famous Preface to the *Lyrical Ballads*, states:—

"I here use the word 'Poetry' (though against my own judgment) as opposed to the word Prose, and synonymous with metrical composition. But much confusion has been introduced into criticism by this contradistinction of Poetry and Prose, instead of the more philosophical one of Poetry and Matter of Fact, or Science. The only strict antithesis to Prose is Metre; nor is this, in truth, a *strict* antithesis, because lines and passages of metre so naturally occur in writing prose, that it would be scarcely possible to avoid them, even were it desirable."

From a consideration of the above, it will be realised that we should pay attention to the *treatment* of the theme as well as to the *form* before we decide whether we are dealing with poetry or prose.

## PROSE WRITINGS

### The Essay

An essay, from its derivation, means a trial, an attempt. The term *essay* is applied to a great many varieties of composition, *e.g.* Pope's "*Essay on Criticism*" (in verse), Locke's "*Essay on the Human Understanding*" (a philosophical treatise), Macaulay's long examination of historical and literary themes ("*Essays on Clive,*" "*Milton,*" etc.). It is also used of schoolboys' compositions. The term seems too comprehensive to be sufficiently distinctive.

Perhaps the outstanding quality of an essay is its originality ; the quality of mind of the essayist makes the essay. Of the Essay, Sir E. Gosse writes, "The style of it must be confidential as well as a model of current, cultivated ease of expression and a mirror of the best conversation."

In its revelation of personality, the essay closely resembles the lyric.

Unlike most literary forms such as history, drama, epic, idyll, lyric, which have come down to us from the Greeks, the essay, like the novel, is of comparatively modern origin. It was a Frenchman, le Sieur de Montaigne, who died in 1569, who first wrote "Essais." In his Preface, "Here, Reader," he writes, "is an honest book. It warns you at the front door that my aim is purely private and domestic. . . . My book is devoted to the particular purposes of my friends and relatives ;

that when they have lost me (which they must do before long) they may find in it some characteristic touches of my temperament and mood, and so keep more complete and more living whatever knowledge they had of me. . . . But my wish is to be seen simply in my own fashion, natural and ordinary, unstudied and without artifice; *for it is myself that I am painting.*"

"The great merit of Montaigne," writes Hazlitt, "was, that he may be said to have been the first who had the courage to say as an author what he felt as a man."

### The Novel

This literary form is the most popular of our times. Pope wrote, "The proper study of mankind is man," and the popularity of the novel seems to prove the truth of his statement.

It might be claimed that the novel is the loosest form of literary art. It has the greatest flexibility and freedom of movement. The author can interpose himself and his thoughts between the reader and the story: he may hold up the action to give a detailed picture of the setting or background of the story; the length of the novel is practically unlimited—its limits are really the patience and interest of its readers.

The very looseness of its form makes clear definition difficult; the comprehensive title novel includes so many kinds and types that one would almost require a definition for each type to ensure exactness.

"A prose narrative chiefly dealing with imaginary characters and events" might serve as a general definition.

The elements of the novel may be summed up as:— **Plot**; **Character**; **Dialogue**; **Style**; **Setting** (background in time and place); and the **Philosophy of Life** exposed by the author.

Certain of these elements will receive special attention in different types of novel. If the novel is a detective story, the plot will most probably be the most important element. If the plot is loose, poorly constructed, perhaps the type of novel is meant to emphasise character, and the plot loose as it is, may be sufficient for the purpose the author intends. (Consider the plots of "*Pickwick Papers*" and "*David Copperfield*".)

Characterisation will generally be admitted to be the most important element of the novel. You must have character before you can have action and dialogue, or a plot. Our recollections of our greatest novels are chiefly those of character. Think of the Dickens's novels and we think of "*Micawber*," "*Peggotty*," "*Steerforth*," "*Mark Tapley*," "*Betsy Trotwood*." The details of the plots escape us, but the characters remain.

There are two chief methods used in portraying character :—

1. **The Analytical method,** in which the author dissects the character, explains his motives, supplies all information and often passes judgment on him. He *psychologises* the character, lays bare his soul, motives and impulses. The Ultra Modern novelists (the psycho-analysts) chiefly explore the workings of the mind—the stream of consciousness.

2. **The Dramatic method.**—The characters drawn by this method explain themselves, reveal their personalities by their actions and speech, as in drama.

**Dialogue** should be natural and suitable, and is of great importance in revealing character, its passions, impulses and opinions. Dialogue should be an integral part of the story ; it should contribute to the movement of the plot and the elucidation of the characters and their relationships.

**Setting or background** in time and place should have our attention. We notice in which country, or in which part of a country the action takes place. We get a picture of the people then living, their interests, costumes, habits. In some novels, for example in historical novels, the background will be of great importance especially if the action takes place in a remote period. But apart from historical novels, the background may assume an importance equally as great as that of character. (Study Hardy's "*The Return of the Native*" and Emily Bronte's "*Wuthering Heights*," in which novels the authors associate inanimate nature with the human action.)

**The Style** in which a novel is written deserves our attention. Style is more than mere diction—choice of words and expression—it is the man himself. We all use, more or less, the language of our time, but the man of genius "subjects such language to his own purposes, and moulds it according to his own peculiarities," as Cardinal Newman has written. Careful examination of a man's style will reveal much of his education, of influences that have left their mark on him. All that goes to the making of the man will be at least partially revealed in his style.

The last and most comprehensive element in the novel is the author's philosophy of life or criticism of life. "Directly or indirectly," as W. H. Hudson states, "whether the writer is conscious of it or not, every novel must present a certain view of life and of some of the problems of life." Since the subject of the novelist is life, *quidquid agunt homines*, it is impossible for him not to give either expressly (as do Mr. G. B. Shaw and Mr. H. G. Wells) or by implication, some suggestion at least, of the impression that life makes upon him. It may be unintentional, but it is there.

In criticising a novel, we must take into account what

aim and purpose the novelist has in mind. To condemn a novel because it has a weak plot is unfair unless a well-knit, complicated plot is essential in that particular type of novel. In a detective novel, a clever, complicated plot is necessary, and if we have that, we will be ready to excuse some weakness in portrayal of character.

**The Historical Novel** is one whose plot is connected with historical events and characters. The plan most frequently adopted is for the author to choose as his hero some fictitious character or some obscure historical character and connect him with authentic historical happenings and characters, *e.g.* in "*Ivanhoe,*" Scott connects Ivanhoe with King Richard (The Black Knight) and the Crusades. By so doing, the writer of an historical novel secures more scope and freedom. If he chose an important historical character, many details of his or her life would be well known to the readers and the author would find himself compelled to keep to these well-known historical facts.

The best historical novels are written about periods that are interesting and not too obscure or remote. (Apply this to G. Eliot's "*Romola.*")

It should be kept in mind that the writer of an historical novel is not under contract to be correct in every historical detail; and on the other hand, we do not expect to be misled about important historical facts. A good historical novel often gives such a reliable picture of the period that it fills in many blanks which have of necessity to be left out in small text books on history. As an example, consider Thackeray's "*Henry Esmond*"; our knowledge of the period of the War of the Spanish Succession is enhanced by the reading of it. This historical novel is outstanding in respect of its style. Thackeray, who had made a complete and thorough study of the period with a view to delivering lectures on it (see the *English Humorists*), became so familiar with the language of that time that he was able to use it in his novel describing the period. (Compare the style of the alleged *Spectator* number in the novel with that of Addison.)

Scott, to give an air of old-worldliness to his novels, uses a number of archaisms in his dialogue, but they are by no means accurate for the period represented. It has been said, and at times with some justification, that Scott's great historical knowledge and love of antiquarian lore was a hindrance rather than a help to him when writing his Waverley novels. An historical novel that is overloaded with historical detail is apt to pall. After all, an historical novel is primarily a novel. Scott frequently avoids tiring the reader with historical or antiquarian lore by putting his information in notes at the end of the volume. If such detail appears to hold up the action, this annoys readers—especially youthful readers—who want to get on with the story.

## THE SHORT STORY

The short story, largely owing to the number of magazines in modern times, has become very popular. It has many features in common with the novel and yet it differs from it. It is not merely a condensed novel.

A short story produces a singleness of effect denied to the novel.

"As a novel cannot be read at one sitting," writes E. A. Poe, "it denies itself of the immense force derivable from totality. In the brief tale the author is enabled to carry out the fulness of his intention, be what it may. During the hour of reading the reader is at the writer's control. A skilful literary artist has constructed a tale. If wise he has not fashioned his thoughts to accommodate his incidents: but having conceived with deliberate care, a certain unique or single *effect* to be wrought out, he then invents such incidents as may best aid him in establishing this preconceived effect. In the whole composition there should be no word written of which the tendency, direct or indirect, is not to the one pre-established design. The idea of the tale has been presented unblemished, because undisturbed : and this is an end unattainable by the novel."

There is room in the novel for leisurely movement—for comment, for philosophy and at times extensive psychology. Details of life, character and setting, which the novelist may paint with minute detail, must be delineated by a few deft strokes. "The miniature painter," as Prof. Walker states, "is not greater than the portrait painter, but his work must necessarily be finer. Hence the importance of avoiding divagation and irrelevancy in the short story."

Above all, the short story should have unity of impression, a single predominating incident and a single pre-eminent character. The plot must necessarily suffer compression.

The single effect aimed at in the short story is usually one of these three :—

1. To reveal character, *e.g.* "*Markheim,*" R. L. Stevenson.

2. The solution of a clever plot, *e.g.* "*The Gold Bug,*" E. A. Poe.

3. The influence of the setting on the characters, *e.g.* "*The Fall of the House of Usher,*" E. A. Poe.

## History

History records what has happened to the human race, or sections of the human race, throughout the ages. History is usually written in prose, although there have been attempts to write history in verse (*e.g.* Daniel's "*History of the Civil Wars*"), and it should be remembered that many of the epics and epic fragments contain material for the historian.

Apart from the title of a history, which gives the clue to what subject is treated (*e.g.* "*History of Rome*"), the nature of the *treatment* of the subject is of great importance. A history may be a very bare recital of events in chronological order; such is usually termed a **Chronicle** (*e.g.* "*The Anglo-Saxon Chronicle*"). The term **Annals** is often similarly used (events concisely recorded under the dates of their occurrence).

But we expect more from an historian than a bare record of events. We want to have reasons advanced for occurrences and conclusions drawn from them. We expect the historian to assess the values of events and deal with their significance and importance. A history which attempts to show the causes and assess the results of events is termed a **Philosophical** History (*e.g.* Gibbon's "*Decline and Fall of the Roman Empire*"; Buckle's "*History of Civilisation in England*"). A **Constitutional** History is one which traces the origin and development of the system of government in a country (*e.g.* Hallam's "*Constitutional History*").

A **Church** or **Ecclesiastical** History deals with the events in the life of a church (*e.g.* Fuller's "*Church History of Britain*").

(Note that **Natural History** deals with Biology—an account of the origin and classification of the various kinds of animals.)

It is an obvious essential that the historian should have studied the period about which he writes as thoroughly as means permit. He should present facts *impartially*—but here arises a difficulty. Although complete impartiality may be aimed at, is it really capable of achievement? If we imagine an historian, who is a believer in Free Trade, writing on the subject of Free Trade and Protection, it is almost impossible for him not to indicate his preference in some way or other. If a history merely impartial could be achieved, would it be interesting? It would scarcely be a human performance.

If we know the bias or political outlook of an historian, we can make allowance for it. An historian dealing with a cause he supports and believes in will warm to it, be enthusiastic about it. For example, Macaulay was a Whig; if we desire to have the Whig point of view on the Civil War, we are sure of finding it in his "*History of England.*" If we want the Tory point of view, as a corrective, we can consult a history from that point of view, *e.g.* Clarendon's "*History of the Great Rebellion.*"

## Biography

Biography may be regarded as a branch of history, for if a suitable choice of subject is made by the writer, we shall frequently find that the person chosen is important in history—even although it is a specialised type of history, such as that of literature, exploration and discovery, invention or social reform.

Friends or relatives of great men often write their biographies. They have had special opportunities of coming into contact with these great personalities and accordingly have the requisite knowledge of them and their achievements.

Yet, as in history proper, we have the right to expect an honest assessment of the character chosen and his achievements. A biography should be no uncritical eulogium. The life, character and achievements of the subject of biography should be of sufficient importance and interest. In the finest biographies we find there is something akin to hero-worship in the mind of the writer, but not entirely blind hero-worship which will see no faults or shortcomings. Some splendid examples of Biography in our literature are:—Boswell's "*Life of Samuel Johnson*" Lockhart's "*Life of Scott*" Forster's "*Life of Dickens.*"

## Autobiography

It may be assumed that only famous men should write their autobiographies. Unless a man's life is likely to be of interest to his fellow men, it is not likely to be a suitable subject for autobiographical treatment. This interest may be of any kind—the writer may be a great politician, a great engineer, a great war leader. The writer has to be careful that what he relates will interest his readers. He must be frank and honest, and avoid distorting the facts of his life in an endeavour to give merely a favourable account of his career and achievements.

## Prose or Verse

There are several literary forms which may be written in prose or verse, *e.g.* Drama, Satire, Parody (Burlesque).

## Drama

Aristotle laid down the principle governing drama when he stated that drama "*proceeds by action and not by narration.*" In a novel, the author describes everything—characters, plot, background, etc. In a drama, the scene is before our eyes or we are supposed to imagine it, often assisted, as in Shakespeare's time when there was little scenery, by descriptions from the mouths of the players.

The two main divisions of drama are tragedy and comedy, although many other classifications have been attempted. Shakespeare in "*Hamlet*," writes of "tragedy comedy, history, pastoral, pastoral-comical, historical-pastoral, tragical-historical, tragical-comical," satirising the stupid sub-divisions of some dramatists.

**Tragedy.**—Aristotle defined tragedy as, "*An imitation of some action that is serious, entire and of some magnitude—in the way, not of narration, but of action, effecting* *through pity and terror the correction and refinement of such passions.*"

**Classical** drama observed the THREE UNITIES OF TIME, PLACE and ACTION. Of these, by far the most important is the unity of ACTION. This laid down the principles that :—A. There should be one main plot and no sub-plots. B. There should be unity of effect—no admixture of tragedy with comedy or comedy with tragedy.

The unity of TIME meant that the action of the plot should be confined to twenty-four hours (" a single revolution of the sun ").

The unity of PLACE meant substantially that the action was confined to one place.

Since tragedy should evoke our pity, it follows that the character of the tragic hero should be one with which we can sympathise. The character of the tragic hero, according to Aristotle, should be " *That of a person neither eminently virtuous or just, nor yet involved in misfortune by deliberate vice or villainy, but by some error of human frailty.*"

Dramas which observe the dramatic unities are called Classical, *e.g.* Addison's " *Cato.*" Shakespeare did not observe any of the unities unless it suited his purpose ; dramas resembling Shakespeare's plays in this respect are called **Romantic.** In "*Macbeth,*" the time of the action exceeds twenty-four hours ; there is an element of comedy in it, although of a grim kind (in the Porter scene). There are sub-plots in Shakespeare's plays.

It should be noted carefully that a certain unity of action must be preserved in any drama, whether classical or romantic, otherwise the play would appear disjointed and incoherent. Detached incidents and unconnected episodes would never supply a plot—" *a contexture of events.*" Although unity, in the strict Aristotelian sense, is not to be found in Shakespeare's plays, we do find an *effective* unity. For example, the main plot in "*King Lear*" deals with the ingratitude of King Lear's daughters, Regan and Goneril, to their father; the sub-plot deals with the ingratitude of Edmund, son of the Earl of Gloster, to his father. The sub-plot echoes the main plot and adds to the general cumulative effect of the tragedy of Lear as a whole.

## Comedy

Plays that end happily we term comedies. Of comedy Aristotle states—"*Comedy is an imitation of characters inferior, not with respect to every sort of vice, but to the ridiculous only.*" Comedies are written principally to amuse us. Such a comedy as Goldsmith's "*She Stoops to Conquer*" seems to have no other purpose. Many comedies, while amusing to us because they appeal to our sense of the ludicrous, have a didactic purpose. Sheridan's comedies draw our attention to faults and weaknesses in society. Ben Jonson's comedies perform the same purpose. They have the same purpose as the "*Spectator*" essays—to reform human society by ridiculing its shortcomings. It is interesting to note that Hazlitt, writing of Shakespeare's comedies, states, "The fault, then, of Shakespeare's comic Muse is, in my opinion, that it is too good-natured and magnanimous—it does not take the highest pleasure in making human nature look as mean, as ridiculous, and contemptible as possible" "The most pungent ridicule, is that which is directed to mortify vanity, and to expose affectation."

As already stated, drama may be written in prose or verse. Shakespeare uses verse—iambic pentameter, unrhymed (blank verse), in the majority of his lines, but there is more prose in his comedies than in his tragedies.

Prose is held to be more in keeping with comedy for, as already emphasised, comedy is regarded as inferior to tragedy.

The high seriousness and dignity of tragedy have been found to be best maintained by the use of blank verse. At parts in the tragedies of Shakespeare where there are humorous passages, we find them in prose ; and we find the same where menial characters are speaking. In such places the characteristic vein of tragedy is absent and the language is in keeping with the inferior occasion and characters.

### The Masque (Mask)

This form of entertainment flourished chiefly in the reigns of Elizabeth, James I and Charles I, and was extremely popular at court and among the nobility. It was a combination of poetry, song, music and dance, and appealed to the audience *largely as a spectacle*. No expense was spared in the production of masques and frequently the services of great artists of the period were secured, *e.g.* the famous architect Inigo Jones was employed for stage decoration in the reign of James I ; Henry Lawes, a noted musician, composed the music for Milton's Masque "*Comus*."

The dancers in the Masque acted as mummers. The plot was slight and of little importance, the characters were simple. The most important literary feature of the masques was the lyrics they contained. Many of the best lyrics of the period are to be found in them, especially in the masques of Ben Jonson. The nature of the masque may be gathered from the short masque which Shakespeare introduces in "*The Tempest*" in order that Prospero may, as he says,

"Bestow upon the eyes of this young couple (Ferdinand and Miranda) some vanity of my art."

## Satire.

**Satire** is a literary composition the prime aim of which is *censure.* It aims at amending morals and manners, usually by accentuating the faults which the author desires to have improved. The writer of satire frequently uses humour, wit, sarcasm, invective and irony. (*See* Chapter XIII on Figures of Speech.)

**Personal Satire** attacks vice or weakness in some person, *e.g.* Pope's attack on Addison, in his "*Letter to Dr. Arbuthnot*":—

> "Peace to all such (inferior scribblers), but were there One whose fires
> True Genius kindles, and fair Fame inspires;
> Blest with each talent and each art to please,
> And born to write, converse, and live with ease:
> Should such a man, too fond to rule alone,
> Bear, like the Turk, no brother near the throne;
> View him with scornful, yet with jealous eyes,
> And hate for arts that caus'd himself to rise;
> Damn with faint praise, assent with civil leer,
> And without sneering, teach the rest to sneer;
> Willing to wound, and yet afraid to strike,
> Just hint a fault, and hesitate dislike;
> Alike reserv'd to blame, or to command,
> A tim'rous foe, and a suspicious friend.
> Dreading ev'n fools, by flatterers besieg'd,
> And so obliging, that he ne'er oblig'd;
> Like 'Cato,' give his little Senate laws,
> And sit attentive to his own applause;
> While Wits and Templars ev'ry sentence raise,
> And wonder with a foolish face of praise:—
> Who but must laugh, if such a man there be?
> Who would not weep, if *Atticus* were he? (Atticus for Addison.)

Unless personal satire is restrained and good-humoured, it is apt to descend to scurrility.

An example of satire on national prejudices and peculiarities is to be found in Addison's "*Sir Roger de Coverley Essays.*" An example of satire on a religious sect is had in Butler's "*Hudibras.*" In Dryden's "*Absalom and Achitophel*" we have an example of satire of a political party (Earl Shaftesbury and the Exclusionists).

When satire becomes too bitter it becomes distasteful. Swift, in satirising man's desire to live long in his "*Gulliver's Travels,*" portrays the Struldbrugs as a most repulsive set of creatures. We feel he has overstepped the bounds of all legitimate satire and we agree with Thackeray when he states, "As for the moral (of '*Gulliver's Travels*') I think it is horrible, shameful, unmanly, blasphemous; and giant and great as this Dean is, I say we should hoot him."

### Burlesque (Parody or Travesty)

A burlesque is a ludicrous representation of something (*e.g.* it may be a manner of speaking, or acting). Parody is an imitation of a poem or literary work but changed in such a way as to produce a humorous effect. Travesty is defined as something having the vesture or appearance of another thing, which disguised is thereby made to appear ridiculous. We find these terms used interchangeably.

In good burlesque or parody certain features are essential to make it a success.

We should be able to recognise a likeness to the original work parodied. This likeness may be discovered in the treatment of the theme, in the style and also in the actual form (*e.g.* the same stanza and metre used in a poem). Max Beerbohm's "*A Christmas Garland*" parodies the styles of several well-known authors, such as Kipling, Galsworthy; but he also parodies their characteristic outlook on life and their treatment of themes.

The method of the parodist is that of the caricaturist —he seizes upon some dominant feature in the original work and exaggerates it until by distortion it becomes humorous.

Wit and humour are essential qualities of good parody. A mock-heroic or mock-epic poem, such as Pope's "*Rape of the Lock*," parodies the real epic in respect of its characteristic elevated theme, style and treatment, by according the dignified style of the epic to some trivial happening—in Pope's poem, the loss of a lock of hair.

Lamb parodies the epic style and treatment in his "*Dissertation upon Roast Pig*." Gay writes a travesty of Italian opera in his "*Beggar's Opera*," in which the inmates of Newgate prison replace the characters of typical high opera.

Clever and amusing examples of Parody are to be found in :—

"*Rejected Addresses*," by John and Horace Smith.

"*Tricks of the Trade*," by Sir John Squire.

"*Peter Bell, a Lyrical Ballad*," by John Hamilton Reynolds, a parody of Wordsworth at his worst.

## Literary Forms in Poetry.

### Narrative Poetry.

**The Epic Poem.**—Writing of the epic, Aristotle stated that "*epic poetry agrees so far with tragic as it is an imitation of great characters and actions by means of verse; but in this it differs, that it makes use of only one kind of metre throughout, and that it is narrative; the time of epic action is indefinite.*"

Arnold's definition of epic is contained in these words, "*An epic poem treats of one great complex action in a grand style and with fulness of detail.*"

To any one who knows Homer's "*Iliad*" and

"*Odyssey*," perhaps the best definition is "a poem written in imitation of Homer."

Another contrast with tragedy lies in the fact that the epic hero should be successful—he should triumph over circumstances.

In character, action, setting and style, the epic should be elevated, lofty and sublime. Nothing trivial should enter into epic treatment. All elements should be in keeping to produce a sublime effect.

The achievement of writing a successful epic has been attempted by many of our poets, but few can be said to have succeeded to any great extent. Our greatest *authentic* epic (*i.e.* an epic dealing with historical events, or events believed to be historical in the early history of a people) is Beowulf. Its author is unknown.

Our greatest *literary* epic is undoubtedly Milton's "*Paradise Lost*," in which he attempts to "assert Eternal Providence,

And justify the ways of God to men."

The Homeric or epic simile is an outstanding feature of his "grand style."

The **Epic Machinery,** as Pope defines it in his introductory letter to his "*Rape of the Lock*," is "a term invented by the Critics, to signify that part which the Deities, Angels or Demons are made to act in a Poem."

### The Ballad

The ballad (*derived from Low Latin—ballare, to dance*) was originally a song sung to a dance. As one old woman said of the ballads after they were collected, "They were made for singing and no' for reading."

The ballad often took the form of question and answer ; frequently it had a refrain.

In modern times the ballad has become a narrative poem in ballad metre. (*See* Chapter XII on Prosody.)

The original or authentic ballad was anonymous. It has been well defined as "a tale telling itself," as we gather nothing of the personality of the author. The modern ballad imitates many of the features of the authentic ballad.

**Features of the Ballad.**—It has directness, concreteness, simplicity and objectivity; it is told in a vigorous manner. (Contrast it with the leisurely treatment in epic poetry.) There is nothing reflective in the ballad. Its language is crude and archaic. Its metre lacks smoothness and the rhymes are frequently false. It has characteristic phrases and diction (*milk-white* hand; *cherry* cheeks; *guid red* gowd). The ballad often proceeds by "incremental repetition," "a lingering and leaping," as Prof. Gummere has defined it. Some additional information is given with each repetition, *e.g.*:—

> The *first* line that Sir Patrick read,
> A loud lauch lauched he;
> The *next* line that Sir Patrick read,
> The tear blinded his e'e.

Coleridge, in his "*Rime of the Ancient Mariner*," illustrates many of these features, *e.g.*:—

archaic language: "*eftsoons, uprist*"
false rhymes: *hear—Mariner.*
*cold—emerald.*

## Lyrical Poetry

To the Greeks the lyric was a poem designed for being sung by a single voice to the accompaniment of a lyre. One feature of lyric poetry is outstanding—*its essential connection with music*. This musical element may be supplied by an external musical accompaniment, as in a *vocal* song lyric, or by the inherent music of the words used in a *literary* song lyric. In both types of song lyric music is present.

In the development of the lyric in English, it will be found that in early times, when the language was crude and the theme usually comparatively unimportant, an external musical accompaniment was almost essential. On the other hand—for example, in the exquisite lyrics of Shelley, Keats and Tennyson—the latent music of the words, their euphony, the onomatopœic effects and happy rhythms, all supply an effect so fascinating in itself that the presence of an external musical accompaniment is generally superfluous.

**Features of Lyrical Poetry.**—Its *subjectivity*. In contradistinction to ballad poetry which is objective, lyrical poetry is subjective. As we learned when dealing with the ballad, it was "a tale telling itself." The personality of the author is not reflected in his writing. Stories of battles and supernatural happenings are among their chief topics. Something outside of themselves supplies the stimulus to the writers. In lyrical poetry the individuality of the writer is displayed. He tells of the reaction of some stimulus on himself. He relates an *experience*. He displays his personality, his judgment, his thought, his mood, his emotion. The lyric is so characteristic of its writer that we can feel almost sure that lines of poetry are those of a certain poet if we are acquainted with his characteristic or individual treatment. (Consider the description of Arnold as "an elegiac poet.") Lyrical poetry is the work of a *conscious* artist.

Its *unity*. Professor Palgrave, in his preface to "*The Golden Treasury*," states that the term *lyrical* implies "that each poem shall turn on some *single* thought, feeling or situation." When writing a lyric the poet is emotionalised, his being is excited by some stimulus—perhaps some beautiful sight or some inspiring experience such as are described by Wordsworth in his "*Daffodils*" and "*On Westminster Bridge.*" Some critics, such as E. A. Poe, hold that a long lyric cannot exist because emotion cannot be maintained over a long period. Wordsworth admits that good lyrical poetry may be written as the result of "*emotion recollected in tranquillity.*"

**Its Structure.**—Most lyrics are divisible into three sections, namely :—

1. Motive : that which acts as stimulus to emotionalise the poet.

2. Thoughts arising from the motive.

3. The poet's conclusion on the matter.

(Divide Wordsworth's "*Daffodils*" in the above sections and proceed to more difficult poems.)

Lyrical poetry is found in the following forms :— 1. The Song Lyric. 2. The Sonnet. 3. The Ode. 4. The Elegy. 5. The Idyll.

1. The **Song Lyric.**—As already noted, this form may be divided into Vocal and Literary Song Lyrics. The literary song lyrics will be found to possess sufficient inherent music to dispense with an external musical accompaniment. The relative importance of words to music in any vocal lyric is too big a subject to discuss here. The popularity which a song owes to its association with some political or religious or other cause must be remembered when this question is under consideration. A lyric suitable for a musical setting will generally possess these qualities :—

A. The subject will be capable of being understood in one audition ; the theme will not be very difficult of comprehension.

B. Open vowels and liquid consonants, on which the singer can linger, will predominate.

C. There will be regularity of metre to correspond with regularity of beat in the music.

D. There will be regularity of stanzaic form to correspond with the musical setting (*e.g.* Shakespeare's song, "*Blow, blow, thou winter wind*").

2. The **Sonnet.**—The forms of the sonnet have already been dealt with in Chapter XII on Prosody. The Sonnet, owing to its severely limited length, has a severity of unity imposed upon it even greater than that of the other lyrical forms. Yet, as Wordsworth states in his sonnet "*On the Sonnet*":—

> "In truth, the prison unto which we doom
> Ourselves, no prison is: and hence to me,
> In sundry moods, 'twas pastime to be bound
> Within the Sonnet's scanty plot of ground,
> Pleased if some souls (for such there needs must be)
> Who have felt the weight of too much liberty,
> Should find short solace there, as I have found."

D. G. Rossetti, writes:—

> "A Sonnet is a moment's monument—
> Memorial from the soul's eternity
> To one dead deathless hour."

3. **The Ode.**—This is the most elevated and majestic of the lyrical forms. Its theme is one which is lofty and meditative (*e.g.* Wordsworth's "*Odes to Duty and Intimations of Immortality*"). The treatment accorded to it by the poet is dignified and in keeping with the theme. If the theme is trivial, it will be for burlesque effect as in Burns's "*To a Haggis.*"

Odes may be divided into:—

A. Regular Odes, and B. Irregular Odes.

A. Regular Odes.—These maintain a regular stanza throughout, *e.g.* Shelley's "*Skylark*" and Keats's "*Ode to Autumn.*"

The Pindaric ode, which imitates the structure of the odes of Pindar, consists of nine stanzas divisible into three parts. The first three stanzas form the *Strophe* or *Turn*; the second three stanzas form the *Antistrophe* or *Counter-turn*; the last three, the *Epodos* or *After Song*. The first, second and third stanzas of each part correspond in structure, *i.e.* stanzas one, four, seven; two, five, eight; three, six, nine, have the same metrical arrangement and rhyme scheme.

B. Irregular Odes.—At first sight, the irregular ode seems to have its metre altered in an arbitrary manner. But a closer examination of an irregular ode will reveal that changes have been made by the poet for some sufficient reason—usually a change in thought or emotion. The changes are not the result of mere caprice on the part of the poet. Examine the changes of metre in Dryden's "*Alexander's Feast*" (Note that its alternative title is "*The Power of Music*") and you will notice that the poet changes the metre to be in keeping with the emotion which Timotheus, through his music, induces in Alexander.

4. The **Elegy.**—In English poetry the classification of elegies depends on the subject matter of poems. In Greek poetry, a poem written in elegiac metre was called an elegy, irrespective of its subject matter.

The subject of elegy is most frequently the death of a friend; but even when a poem is mournful, serious and melancholy, it is often called an elegy, or at least, elegiac.

There is no distinctive structure or metre in the elegy. (Study the metre of Cowper's "*On Receipt of my Mother's Picture*," Milton's "*Lycidas*," Gray's "*Elegy written in a Country Churchyard*.")

On account of the great popularity of Gray's "*Elegy*" the quatrain which he used (*see* Chapter XII on Prosody) has come to be regarded as the elegiac quatrain.

The following features of elegy are usually discernible :—

A. The sense of grief for the departed friend, although serious, is not harrowing in nature.

B. The writer is usually reminiscent, dealing with places and incidents associated with his departed friend.

C. Usually towards the end of the elegy a note of hope for the future is expressed, *e.g.* in "*Lycidas*" we find :—

"Weep no more, woful shepherds, weep no more,"

and in Shelley's "*Adonais*" :—

"He lives, he wakes—'tis Death is dead, not he :
Mourn not for Adonais——"

D. Frequently, characters are given the names of characters in **Pastoral** poetry, as in Milton's "*Lycidas*" and Arnold's "*Thyrsis.*" Such elegies are termed pastoral elegies.

*Note.*—Some elegies are so long that they violate the general rule in lyrical poetry, namely that it should be short, *e.g.* Tennyson's "*In Memoriam.*"

5. The **Idyll.**—From its derivation, an idyll is simply "a little picture" or, it may be a series of pictures. The idyll, accordingly, we shall find to be a comparatively short poem and mainly descriptive in nature. Narrative may find a place in the idyll but it will be a subsidiary one.

Crabbe's poetry is too realistic to allow of its being termed idyllic. He wrote :—

"I sing the cot,
As truth will paint it, and as bards will not."

The descriptions must be imaginative. Wordsworth realised this essential when he wrote in his Preface to "*The Lyrical Ballads,*" "The principal object, then, proposed in these Poems, was to choose incidents and situations from common life, and to relate or describe them, throughout, as far as was possible in a selection of language really used by men, and, at the same time, to throw over them *a certain colouring of imagination . . .*" Simplicity of subject (usually a rustic scene and characters) and a simple, direct, yet attractive style are features of the idyll.

Largely as a result of the necessity for simplicity of subject, we frequently find the *pastoral* element in the idyll. Theocritus may be regarded as the father of pastoral poetry. He depicted what may well be the ideal conditions for a shepherd's life in the delightful climate of his home, Sicily. Other poets, such as Spenser, Jonson, Pope, in English poetry, continued the accepted pastoral tradition, and so pastoral poetry in English is often highly conventional, and far removed from reality. Characters are frequently given the names of shepherds and shepherdesses and their occupations imagined to be of a pastoral nature.

It should be remembered that there is a genuine pastoral poetry, *e.g.* Wordsworth's "*Michael*," Allan Ramsay's "*Gentle Shepherd*" and, perhaps less so, Burns's "*Cottar's Saturday Night.*"

*Note.*—We may have an idyll in prose, *e.g.* Goldsmith's "*Vicar of Wakefield.*"

---

## CHAPTER XVI

## LITERARY APPRECIATION

**Literary appreciation** is a systematic attempt to estimate the merits and defects of a certain work of literature. It is based on a sense of taste and is therefore not a mere mechanical process to be taught by a set of rules, but this taste is itself derived from familiarity with great authors whose works furnish a standard to the critic. It is not therefore a matter of lavish praise or of petty fault-finding, but of sound personal judgment working by definite and well-established rules.

The work in question must be thoroughly studied. Read it over rapidly to obtain a general impression of the theme. Then read it slowly and carefully (at least once) with the following ideas in mind.

1. Consider thoroughly what the author has tried to tell and be able to *summarise* his *meaning* intelligently.

2. Consider fully the method employed. Is the form used, that of novel, essay, biography, letter, speech or any other? If poetry, is the form lyrical, narrative or dramatic—lyric, sonnet, elegy, ode, dramatic monologue? If it is a drama, is it a tragedy, comedy, farce, burlesque, history, pastoral or melodrama?

3. Consider how far it reveals the characteristics of the form chosen. In what ways is it defective? Would another form, say drama rather than novel, have been more suitable?

4. Consider the author's use of words, figures of speech, etc. If the work is in verse, consider the metre, stanza, form, etc.

5. Consider the treatment. Does the author give the feeling of sincerity? Does the work present a noble and wholesome view of life and of human nature? Is there a definite unity of impression or do any details introduce a jarring note?

From these general hints on Literary Appreciation let us pass to the appreciation of a poem, a novel, a play, an essay.

**Appreciation of a Poem.**

It is well to remember that a poem is the expression of the joy of the poet and that the whole evolution of the poem is determined by his desire to communicate that joy to his readers or listeners as fully as possible. Let the reader then approach each poem as something the primary purpose of which is to give a sense of satisfaction. A poem may tell a story, or create characters and make them act and talk as in a play, or again, it may express directly the poet's own opinions, experiences, desires, regrets or aspirations. Of course the poet may use any or all of these methods to strip away the veils that obscure the essential nature of his subject from the ordinary man. So much has he to help the reader to see the unusual, that at times his method seems unnecessarily repetitive to the plain man who asks why he uses strange, roundabout expressions when he has at hand simple and direct words or phrases. The reason is that the poet has often to express ideas *outwith ordinary experiences.* This he can do only by the use of words, though all language is derived from the *general experience* of ordinary men.

The poet, by his method of combining or associating words, must make them express unsuspected meanings since, in his poem, he is revealing a mood which has been aroused in him by some subject or cause—a flower, a song, a landscape, workmen digging in the street, a battle, etc.—and *which is peculiarly his own.* This mood he wishes to communicate to his readers. To do so he must select those aspects of the subject which he feels to be *significant* and reveal them to the reader in that rhythmical pattern of words we call metre.

The effect of rhythm in music is widely understood and applied. It helps to maintain the regular march of a regiment of men as they step out to the music of the regimental band. It explains why seamen hauling on a rope to a sea chanty obtain a unity of effort. *This same rhythm* is used by the poet to secure *unity of feeling*, the *sympathy* of the reader, and in poetry finds expression in definite metres, stanza forms, poetic forms, figures of speech, etc.

**Outline** :—

(*a*) **Statement of theme.**

(*b*) **Summary of poem,** tracing in detail the development of the main idea. (Very briefly.)

(*c*) **Style** :—

1. **Type of poem**—how far does it reveal the characteristics of the lyric, sonnet, ode or elegy, etc. ?

2. **Metre and stanza form,** with a comment on any variations.

3. **Use of Figures of Speech,** word-pictures, sound effects, etc. How far is it adequate or appropriate ?

4. **Language**—vivid, simple, archaic, ordinary, etc.

(*d*) **Treatment**—is the point of view or motive of poet sincere, admirable, desirable, etc. ?

## EXERCISE I

Select the most *striking word* or *words* in the following quotations and discuss the *effect* produced :—

1. Then felt I like some watcher of the skies
   When a new planet swims into his ken.
2. I wish the wind may never cease
   Nor fashes in the flood.
3. Our noisy years seem moments in the being
   Of the eternal silence.
4. Yellow and black, and pale and hectic red,
   Pestilence-stricken multitudes.
5. Finish, good lady, the bright day is done
   And we are for the dark.

6. Around the ancient track marched rank upon rank,
The army of unalterable law.
7. By the struggling moonbeam's misty light
And the lantern dimly burning.
8. Face to face they gaze,
Their eyes shining, grave with a perfect pleasure.
9. He has torn the cataracts from the hills
And they clanked at his girdle like manacles.
10. All in a hot and copper sky.
11. Bare ruined choirs where late the sweet birds sang.
12. On a lone winter night when the frost
Has wrought a silence.

## EXERCISE II

*Assonance, alliteration, onomatopœia, repetition, cacophony, euphony* are among the effects illustrated here. State the *device* used in each extract and discuss the *effect* produced by it:—

1. The lustre of the long convolvuluses
That coiled around the stately stem.
2. Trusty, dusky, vivid, true,
With eyes of gold and bramble-dew
Steel-true and blade-straight,
The great artificer
Made my mate.
4. Myriads of rivulets hurrying thro' the lawn,
The moan of doves in immemorial elms.
And murmuring of innumerable bees.
5. Approach thou like the rugged Russian bear
The armed rhinoceros or Hyrcan tiger.
6. The double, double, double beat
Of the thundering drum.
7. And when he rood men myght his brydel heer
Gynglen in a whistlying wynd als clere
And eek as loude as doth the chapel belle.
8. Take but this Poesy that now followeth
My clayey hest with sullen, sullen breath.
9. I heard the ripple washing in the reeds
And the wild water lapping on the crag.
10. Which like a wounded snake drags its slow length along.
11. Perhaps it is the owlet's scritch
For what can ail the mastiff bitch?
12. Hame, hame, hame, O hame fain wad I be—
O hame, hame, hame to my ain countrie.

### EXERCISE III

1. Quote *six* lines of poetry that appeal to you and point out what their *beauty* depends upon.

2. State *five* common topics of poetry. Give one example of *each* from your reading, name the author and then summarize the poem.

3. Name *four* poems which describe particular places and show in *each* case (*a*) how much you learn of the actual appearance of the place, (*b*) the feelings aroused by it in the poet.

4. Name *four* poems dealing with love of one's country. Compare and contrast the methods employed by the poets and consider how far they have been successful.

5. Wordsworth, Shelley and Hogg have written poems on the skylark. What differences do you find in their methods of treatment? Which poem appeals to you most?

6. Write a brief summary of *three* poems dealing with death. Show how the effect of grief is produced in each.

7. Name *three* poems which give felicitous descriptions of the *sea*. Give quotations or references to justify your choice.

8. Write an appreciation of your favourite poem.

9. Write a critical appreciation of the following poems:—

 "*Rosabelle.*"—SCOTT.
 "*The Donkey.*"—CHESTERTON.
 "*The Vagabond.*"—STEVENSON.
 "*Grantchester.*"—BROOKE.
 "*Roundabouts and Swings.*"—CHALMERS.
 "*The Rape of the Lock.*"—POPE.
 "*Ode on Alexander's Feast.*"—DRYDEN.
 "*Tam o' Shanter.*"—BURNS.
 "*St. Agnes' Eve.*"—KEATS.
 "*Morte d'Arthur.*"—TENNYSON.

10. Compare and contrast Milton's "*L'Allegro*" and "*Il Penseroso.*"

## Appreciation of an Essay.

The essay, it has been stated, is a revelation of the writer's personality, but an appreciation is not merely a comment on the portraiture. Yet, because of the personal nature of the essay, the first purpose of the appreciation should be not only the discovery of the main theme but also the author's point of view. After this the student naturally considers the ideas given and the plan of selection. From that he will go to an examination of the diction and sentence-structure, and distinctive characteristics of the writing.

**Outline** :—

(*a*) A **brief statement** of the theme or topic of the essay.

(*b*) A short **summary** of the subject matter. This, in practice, may often be built up from the topic sentences.

(*c*) **Style.**—Diction, type of sentence used. Note any peculiarities, such as use of Latinisms, archaisms, etc. Comment on special qualities in the structure, noting specially beginning or ending.

(*d*) **The author's tastes, prejudices, etc.?** What kind of personality is revealed?

(*e*) **Literary qualities,** *e.g.* **humour, pathos.**

**Appreciation of an Essayist.**

The appreciation of an essayist demands a more general view. It will normally contain fewer quotations from a single essay and say more about the essayist's characteristics and range of interests. It will tell something of his choice of subjects and perhaps refer to the influences which helped in his development as an essayist.

**Outline** :—

(*a*) **Brief sketch of origin** and **history** of the essays.

(*b*) **Purpose of the author,** *e.g.* for moral or educational purposes, or merely for pleasure. In practice there is generally a combination of two or more purposes.

(*c*) **Range of essays** giving a number of titles. From these make a selection as varied as possible and give the theme of each in a sentence.

(*d*) **Detailed analysis** of a typical essay. This may be done more or less briefly, according to the time at the student's disposal.

(*e*) **Statement** of what we learn of the author's opinions, interests, prejudices, whims, *e.g.* attitude to travel, country-life, sport, wealth, reading, etc.

(*f*) **Treatment and methods** of author. Discuss diction, sentence structure, use of humour, pathos, satire, sentiment.

(*g*) **Conclusion,** as to his place among essayists, *e.g.* the most humorous, interesting, vivid, etc.

*Note.*—The method suggested above may be applied after the necessary adjustments, to a novelist, a dramatist or a poet.

## EXERCISE IV

1. The following are the introductory paragraphs of essays by Bacon, Jefferies and E. V. Knox. *Compare* and *contrast* the ideas expressed, and the methods employed :—

(*a*) God Almighty first planted a garden ; and, indeed, it is the purest of human pleasures ; it is the greatest refreshment to the spirits of man ; without which buildings and palaces are but gross handyworks : and a man shall ever see, that, when ages grow to civility and elegancy, men come to build stately, sooner than to garden finely ; as if gardening were the greater perfection. I do hold it in the royal ordering of gardens, there ought to be gardens for all the months in the year, in which, severally, things of beauty may then be seen in season. For December, and January, and the latter part of November, you must take such things as are green all winter : holly, ivy, bays, juniper, cypress-trees, yew, pineapple-trees ; fir-trees, rosemary, lavender ; periwinkle, the white, purple and the blue ; germander, flags, orange-trees, lemon trees, and myrtles, if they be stored ; and sweet marjoram, warm set.

—" *Of Gardens.*"

(*b*) A July fly went sideways over the long grass. His wings made a burr about him like a net, beating so fast that they wrapped him round with a cloud. Every now and then, as he flew over the trees of grass, a taller one than common stopped him, and there he clung, and then the eye had time to see the scarlet spots—the loveliest colour—on his wings. The wind swung the bennet and loosened his hold, and away he went again over the grasses, and not one jot did he care if they were Poa or Festuca, or Bromus or Hordeum, or any other name. Names were nothing to him ; all he had to whirl was his scarlet pots about in the brilliant sun, rest when he liked and go on again. I wonder whether it is a joy to have bright scarlet spots, and to be clad in the purple and gold of life; is the colour felt by the creature that wears it? The rose, restful of a dewy morn before the sunbeams have topped the garden wall, must feel a joy in its own fragrance, and know the exquisite hue of its stained petals. The rose sleeps in its beauty.—*The July Grass.*

(*c*) In reviewing my garden after a year's tenancy, I am aware that there should be, according to vulgar taste, a good many more flowers in it. I still notice a complete absence of Kniphofia nobilis and Eupatorium purpurem, Coreopsis grandiflora makes no great show, and Solidago canadense has not flowered, unless that funny little thing down by the potting shed is it. People, whose gardens are a positive mass of bloom, come and ask me about mine. "Why isn't your garden a positive mass of bloom?" they say crossly, and I have to apologise.

But in my heart I am content; for there are in my garden, as they say in the French exercise books, some apples, some pears, and some plums. And when I say that I consider these to be the most important product of the flower-garden in late August and early September, I am not alone in my opinion. I have the best literary judgment on my side. Remember what the great essayist and philosopher, Bacon, wrote about gardens. Or, if you don't remember, look it up, like me in the book.—*Bacon and My Garden.*

2. What do we learn of the *appearance, tastes, whims, prejudices* and *purpose* in the writing of the authors of the following autobiographical essays?

(*a*) *Of Myself* . . . . . *Cowley.*
(*b*) *The Spectator* . . . . *Steele.*
(*c*) *The Man in Black* . . . *Goldsmith.*

3. *Compare* and *contrast* the treatment of *travel* in the following essays:—

(*a*) *Of Travel* . . . . . *Bacon.*
(*b*) *On going a Journey* . . . *Hazlitt.*
(*c*) *Walking Tours* . . . . *Stevenson.*

4. Discuss the treatment of *sport* in the following essays:—

(*a*) *Cricket* . . . . . *Charles Whitley.*
(*b*) *The Charms of Golf* . . . *A. A. Milne.*
(*c*) *The Truth about Sport* . . . *A. St. John Adcock.*

5. Criticise the essays on *Will Wimble, Beau Tibbs, Dick Minim the Critic* and *Mrs. Battle's Opinions on Whist* as *pen-portraits.*

6. Name *one* essay (giving the author), dealing with each of the following topics: Prejudice, Death, Superstition, Holidays, Murder, Dogs or other Pets, Idling, School Stories, Early Rising, A Country Sunday. Write a *brief* account of the theme of each.

7. Give some account of the part played by Bacon, Addison, Lamb and Chesterton in the development of the essay.

8. "To *banish vice and ignorance.*" Name *three* Spectator essays which seem to fit this purpose. Summarize them in such a way as to show the methods employed.

9. Consider how far it is true that the modern essay deals with trivial subjects in a light fashion. Illustrate your answer by reference to the work of contemporary essayists.

10. Write a critical appreciation of the most *instructive* or most *humorous* or most *personal* essay you have read.

11. Write a critical appreciation of the following:—

(*a*) *Of Studies* . . . . *Bacon.*
(*b*) *Of Greatness* . . . . *Cowley.*
(*c*) *The Spectator Club* . . . *Steele.*
(*d*) *Death of Sir Roger* . . . *Addison.*
(*c*) *The Advantage of Living in a Garret* . . . . *Johnson.*
(*f*) *A City Night Piece* . . . *Goldsmith.*
(*g*) *Christ's Hospital* . . . *Lamb.*
(*h*) *The Indian Jugglers* . . . *Hazlitt.*
(*i*) *My Books* . . . . *Leigh Hunt.*
(*j*) *The Ideal House* . . . *Stevenson.*
(*k*) *On a Distant View of a Pig* . . *Alpha of the Plough.*
(*l*) *Dandy: the Story of a Dog* . . *W. H. Hudson.*

12. Write an appreciation of your favourite essayist.

## Appreciation of a Novel.

The attraction of most novels depends mainly upon the fascination of the story and the liveliness of the characterisation, though later novels insist more and more upon the purpose of the author and his outlook on life. So in writing a description or appreciation of a novel, the writer will naturally deal with the plot, though it is a mistake to attempt a complete summary of a very long novel, such as "*Henry Esmond.*" In such an instance a brief outline of the main themes is sufficient.

He must consider if the details of the plot seem natural and probable. He must consider how far the people in the novel have become real and lifelike to him, and he must describe briefly their significance in the story according to the part they play in it and the qualities of heart and mind they reveal. Again, he must consider how far the novel helps him to understand life better here or elsewhere, in the past or the present. He must discuss the theories of life set forth and his agreement with, or dislike of, them. Then again, he must consider the method of telling the story and how far it is the most suitable for the purpose of the author. This will involve a discussion of the diction, the form of narrative, whether in the first or third person, or the use of letters.

**Outline** :—

(*a*) **General statement** dealing with the purpose of the novel and what it does. Brief reference to the author and his work.

(*b*) **Brief summary** of the plot or, if the novel is too long, a brief outline of the main topics, with a few leading incidents.

(*c*) **Description** of chief characters giving the part they play in the story and the qualities they reveal.

(*d*) **Description** of the setting with special reference to its importance in the plot, and

(*e*) **Description** of the style, diction, etc. (This is specially important in an historical novel.)

(*f*) **Point of view,** attitude to life, etc. Is the author a humorist, a satirist? Is he prejudiced in any way? Has he any definite purpose in view, an abuse to attack, a reform to commend?

(*g*) **Final impression** made upon the reader.

## EXERCISE V.

1.

| Novel. | Character. | Habitual Saying or Action. |
|---|---|---|
| *David Copperfield* | Uriah Heep | " I'm so very 'umble." |
| *A Tale of Two Cities* | Mrs. Cruncher | " Always flopping." |
| *Hard Times* | Gradgrind | " Fact, fact, fact, I want fact." |
| *Martin Chuzzlewit* | Mark Tapley | " Showing a jolly disposition." |
| *Pickwick Papers* | Tony Weller | " Beware of widders." |

What quality or experience is revealed by the above characteristic behaviour? What saying or action do you associate with Sarah Gamp, Sam Weller, Captain Cuttle, Scrooge, Miss Mowcher?

2. In which novels of Scott do the following *types* appear? State briefly the part played by them in the story :—

A Covenanter; A Soldier of Fortune; A Crusader; A Highland Freebooter; A Border Farmer; A Scottish Lawyer; A Scottish Beggar; An English Squire; A Smuggler; An English Outlaw.

3. Describe fully the *duel* scenes in :—

(*a*) *The Master of Ballantrae.*
(*b*) *Henry Esmond.*
(*c*) *Rob Roy.*

4. Give some account of *country life* and *customs* as revealed in *Cranford, The Vicar of Wakefield, Under The Greenwood Tree.*

5. Write a description of a novel which deals with the adventures of a *boy* or *girl* such as *Tom Sawyer, Oliver Twist, Tom Brown's Schooldays, The Mill on The Floss, Lorna Doone, Jane Eyre, Stalky and Co., The Hill.*

6. Give some account of the treatment of *history* in a novel by Charles Reade, Scott or Thackeray.

7. The plot of many novels such as *Tom Jones, Kidnapped, Humphrey Clinker,* is based upon a *journey* undertaken by the chief character. Write a *summary* of such a novel and discuss the convenience of this device for developing plot, characterisation, setting.

8. Discuss the skill of the following novelists in depicting *humble* or *middle-class* life. Name three characters from each of their works and show by *quotation* or *reference* your opinion of the author's treatment of them :—

Dickens, Jane Austen, Trollope, Bennett, H. G. Wells.

9. Write a critical appreciation of any *humorous* or *satirical* novel you have read.

10. How far is it possible for a novelist to be a social *reformer*? Illustrate your answer by reference to the works of Dickens, Thackeray, Kingsley, G. Eliot, H. G. Wells or John Galsworthy.

11. Write a critical appreciation of the following novels :—

| | |
|---|---|
| *Evelina* . . . . . . | *Francis Burney.* |
| *Northanger Abbey* . . . . | *Jane Austen.* |
| *The Antiquary* . . . . | *Scott.* |
| *Bleak House* . . . . . | *Dickens.* |
| *Pendennis* . . . . . | *Thackeray.* |
| *Shirley* . . . . . . | *Charlotte Brönte.* |
| *Alton Locke* . . . . . | *Kingsley.* |
| *Diana of the Crossways* . . . | *Meredith.* |
| *Barchester Towers* . . . . | *Trollope.* |
| *Adam Bede* . . . . . | *George Eliot.* |
| *Catriona* . . . . . . | *Stevenson.* |
| *The Old Wives' Tale* . . . | *Arnold Bennett.* |
| *The Rover* . . . . . | *Joseph Conrad.* |
| *The Forsyte Saga* . . . . | *John Galsworthy.* |
| *The Return of The Native* . . | *Thomas Hardy.* |
| *Tono Bungay* . . . . . | *H. G. Wells.* |

12. Write an appreciation of the work of your favourite novelist.

## Appreciation of a Play

The appreciation of a play does not differ very much from that of a novel except perhaps that the setting, manners, customs and description of nature are much less important. Here also the plot is significant and some idea of it, however lacking in detail, should be given, with special reference to arresting incidents or scenes. The closely-knit structure of a play, whether comedy or tragedy, lends itself to such analysis or summary more easily than the novel. The writer should in his summary lay special emphasis on the situation from which develops the crisis and make scant reference to sub-plots. The chief interest in the greatest plays is that of character-study and the clash and conflict of chief characters should be described in addition to the statement of their qualities and the part they play. The type and form of the play, its origin and setting, its structure and metre, these must all be included, as well as comments on the use of rhyme, prose or blank verse. Here may be discussed the use of dramatic devices such as suspense, tension, relief and dramatic irony. Consider next the dramatist's philosophy of life, his outlook, whether romantic or realistic, pessimistic or optimistic. Finally show the importance of this play in the body of work written by the dramatist.

**Outline :—**

(*a*) **Central idea** on which the play is based.

(*b*) **Brief summary of plot,** leading to the crisis.

(*c*) **Description of chief characters,** the part they play, and their relations with one another.

(*d*) **Description of the type of play,** the diction, metre, use of figures of speech.

(*e*) **Literary devices** used in the play.

(*f*) **View of life** the dramatist expresses in the play.

(*g*) **Comparison of this play with others of the same author.**

## EXERCISE VI

1. Here are the *first* lines of speeches of some Shakespearean characters. What information do these lines give regarding them ?

(*a*) Orsino :—
If music be the food of love, play on.

(*b*) Antonio :—
In sooth I know not why I am so sad.

(*c*) Falstaff (drinking sack) :—
Now, Hal, what time of day is it, lad ?

(*d*) Hamlet :—
A little more than kin and less than kind.

(*e*) Caliban :—
As wicked dew as e'er my mother brush'd
With raven feather from unwholesome fen
Drop on you both.

2. Explain the following passages and indicate the circumstances in which they were spoken :—

(*a*) Merchant of Venice :—

Hath a dog, money ? Is it possible
A cur can lend three thousand ducats ?

(*b*) Hamlet :—

I would have such a fellow whipped for o'erdoing Termagant : it out-Herods Herod.

(*c*) Macbeth :—

If it were done when 'tis done, then 'twere well
It were done quickly.

(*d*) Midsummer Night's Dream :—

Sometimes lurk I in a gossip's bowl
In very likeness of a roasted crab.

(*e*) King Lear :—

The gods are just, and of our pleasant vices
Make instruments to plague us.

(*f*) Twelfth Night :—

I take these wise men that crow so at these set kind of fools, no better than fools' zanies.

3. Mention *one* play of Shakespeare the scene of which is chiefly laid in :—

(*a*) London ; (*b*) An enchanted island ; (*c*) A forest ; (*d*) Venice ; (*e*) Scotland ; (*f*) Rome ; (9) Illyria ; (*h*) Denmark ; (*i*) Athens ; (*j*) Egypt.

State briefly what we learn of the setting.

4. In what plays do the following characters occur ? State briefly the part played by *each* of them :—

Cordelia, Macduff, Dame Quickly, Orsino, Celia, Hubert, Nerissa, Fluellen, Hermia, Bolingbroke.

5. Write a brief summary of the following *sub-plots* and show their connection with the *main theme* :—

(*a*) The Elopement . . . *The Merchant of Venice.*
(*b*) The Mousetrap Play . . *Hamlet.*
(*c*) The Masque . . . *The Tempest.*
(*d*) Pyramus and Thisbe . . *Midsummer Night's Dream.*
(*e*) The Gadshill Robbery . *Henry IV, Part I.*
(*f*) The Blinding of Arthur . *King John.*

6. Consider the *first scenes* of the following plays and discuss the methods employed by Shakespeare to catch the interest of his audience :—

*Hamlet; As You Like It; Julius Cæsar; The Tempest; Macbeth; Coriolanus.*

7. Write *one* sentence about the relations of the following with the other characters in the play in which they are found :—

Olivia, Caliban, Portia, Theseus, Rosalind, The Prince (Henry IV).

8. Outline briefly the *plot* of *Julius Cæsar* and prepare a *diagram* of events to show the rising action, turning point and falling action. (An inverted V forms a suitable figure.)

9. Distinguish between Romantic Comedy, Comedy of Humours and Comedy of Manners by a comparison of *The Tempest, Volpone, The Rivals.*

10. Select *one* scene from a play with which you are familiar and write out in full the stage directions for each speech.

11. Analyse the plots of *The Merchant of Venice* and *King Lear,* showing the connection of the various stories of which the plot is composed.

12. Write an appreciation of the work of your favourite dramatist.

## CONTEXT QUESTIONS.

This type of exercise is not a mere test of accurate reading and a good memory. The quotation selected nearly always requires a sound understanding of the work in which it is found ; this means describing the ideas preceding it, and generally the ideas immediately following. Usually the passage furnishes difficulties in the shape of allusions or of obscure language which require explanation. Some comment on the style, force or importance of the passage is also essential. It is clear that the annotation usually requires discussion of allusions, linguistic and grammatical difficulties, points of diction, figures of speech and versification. In addition, the significance of a quotation which marks a crisis or reveals character must be shown. This seems a formidable and lengthy exercise but, as about only one half of these suggestions is generally to be considered, the annotation should normally be about eight lines long. Less than six is not likely to be satisfactory. When referring to the context, avoid going too far forward or too far back and do not write out the quotation unless specially asked to do so.

**Outline** :—

(*a*) **State briefly** where the passage occurs and name the *author*. If the work is part of a longer work, for example, a song in a play, the name of the longer work should be given.

(*b*) **State significance** of the passage where necessary by referring it to its context, as it reveals character of speaker, etc.

(*c*) **Explain difficulties** of grammar, classical allusion, etc.

(*d*) **Comment on points of style,** such as choice of diction, figures of speech.

(*e*) **Write a brief note** on the prosody if the passage is in *verse*.

(*f*) **Write a brief note on the spirit or tone** of the passage.

*Example* :—

Then to the well-trod stage anon
If Jonson's learned sock be on
Or sweetest Shakespeare, Fancy's child,
Warble his native wood-notes wild.

*Annotation* :—This is an extract from *L'Allegro* by Milton and describes how the poet in the city finds pleasure in the comedies of Jonson and Shakespeare.

*Well-trod* refers to the high standard of contemporary drama. *Jonson's learned sock*—the sock or soccus was worn in classical comedy, and symbolises comedy here. Jonson was a great classical scholar. The poet further suggests that Shakespeare was a natural genius and gave his comedies an open-air atmosphere. The metre is in rhyming couplets of iambic tetrameter with the first foot occasionally a trochee, a device which adds quickness of movement to the rhythm. The passage reveals the delight of the poet in drama.

## EXERCISE VII

*Annotate* the following passages :—

1. And Frenssh she spak ful faire and fetisly
After the scole of Stratford-atte-Bowe.
For Frenssh of Parys was to here unknowe

2. At length they all to mery London came,
To mery London, my most Kyndly Nurse,
That to me gave this Life's first native source.

3. Full many a glorious morning have I seen
Flatter the mountain-tops with sovereign eye,
Kissing with golden face the meadows green,
Gilding pale streams with heavenly alchemy.

4. For if such holy Song
Enwrap our fancy long,
Time will run back, and fetch the age of gold

5. The trumpet's loud clangour
Excites us to arms
With shrill notes of anger
And mortal alarms.

6. Here thou, great Anna ! whom three realms obey,
Doth sometimes counsel take—and sometimes tea.

7. In full-blown dignity, see Wolsey stand,
Law in his voice, and fortune in his hand.

8. Ill fares the land, to hast'ning ills a prey
Where wealth accumulates, and men decay ;
Princes and lords may flourish, or may fade,
A breath can make them, as a breath has made.

9. Some village-Hampden that with dauntless breast
The little tyrant of his fields withstood ;
Some mute inglorious Milton here may rest,
Some Cromwell guiltless of his country's blood.

10. Thou, as a gallant bark from Albion's coast
(The storms all weather'd and the ocean cross'd)
Shoots into port at some well-haven'd isle
Where spices breathe and brighter seasons smile.

11. Ramsay and famous Ferguson
Gied Forth and Tay a lift aboon
Yarrow an' Tweed, to mony a tune,
Owre Scotland rings,
While Irwin, Lugar, Ayr an' Doon
Naebody sings.

12. The sounding cataract
Haunted me like a passion : the tall rock,
The mountain, and the deep and gloomy wood,
Their colours and their forms, were then to me
An appetite.

13. And now 'twas like all instruments,
Now like a lonely flute :
And now it is an angel's song,
That makes the heavens be mute.

14. Where rose the mountains, there to him were friends ;
Where roll'd the ocean, thereon was his home ;
Where a blue sky, and glowing clime, extends,
He had the passion and the power to roam.

15. Chorus hymeneal
Or triumphal chaunt
Matched with thee, would be all
But an empty vaunt.

16. Cold Pastoral !
When old age shall this generation waste,
Thou shalt remain, in midst of other woe
Than ours, a friend to man, to whom thou say'st,
" Beauty is truth, truth beauty "—that is all
Ye know on earth, and all ye need to know.

17. The old order changeth, yielding place to new,
And God fulfils himself in many ways
Lest one good custom should corrupt the world.

18. Do you feel thankful, ay or no,
For this fair town's face, yonder river's line,
The mountains round it and the sky above,
Much more the figures of man, woman, child,
These are the frame to ?

19. But the majestic river floated on
Out of the mist and hum of that low land,
Into the frosty starlight, and there mov'd,
Rejoicing, through the hush'd Chorasmian waste,
Under the solitary moon.

20. They say the lion and the lizard keep
The Courts where Jamshyd gloried and drank deep ;
And Bahram, that great Hunter—the Wild Ass
Stamps o'er his Head, and he lies fast asleep.

21. This be the verse you grave for me ,
Here he lies where he longed to be ;
Home is the sailor, home from sea,
And the hunter home from the hill.

22. A dust whom England bore, shaped, made aware,
Gave, once, her flowers to love, her ways to roam,
A body of England's, breathing English air,
Washed by the rivers, blest by suns at home.

MILTON?

23. We have no waters to delight
Our broad and brookless vales—
Only the dewpond on the height
Unfed, that never fails.

24. He saw the grey little church across the park,
The mounds that hid the loved and honoured dead;
The Norman arch, the chancel softly dark,
The brasses black and red.

25. We skated on stream and pond; we cut
The crinching snow
To Doric temple and Arctic hut;
We laughed and sang at nightfall, shut
By the fireside glow.

26. I have seen the lady April bringing the daffodils,
Bringing the springing grass and the soft warm April rain.

---

# CHAPTER XVII

## COMMON LITERARY TERMS AND PHRASES

**Alexandrine**:—A line consisting of six iambic feet, so called from French poems on Alexander the Great or from the French poet, Alexandre Paris.

*e.g.* With pangs | unfelt | before | unpit | ied and | alone. |
GRAY.

**Allegory**:—A story told by means of a sustained metaphor or a series of metaphors, which has two or more meanings, one of which is explicit, the other being implicit.

*e.g.* "*Pilgrim's Progress*," "*Faerie Queen*."

**Alliteration** :—The repetition of a stressed sound, generally consonantal, in closely successive words to emphasize their meaning, or increase their euphony.

*e.g.* The fair breeze blew, the white foam flew,
The furrow followed free.

**Antistrophe** :—"Counter-turn." The part of a Greek ode in reply to the strophe and similar in form, sung by the chorus as they returned to their former place before the altar.

*e.g.* Gray, "*The Bard.*"

**Anachronism** :—The post-dating or ante-dating of the existence of any thing.

*e.g.* As cannons overcharged with double cracks. ("*Macbeth.*")

**Archaism** :—A word or phrase which belongs to an earlier period and is no longer in common use.

*e.g.* Nathless, wot, varlet.

**Assonance** :—A term generally applied to the similarity of vowel sounds.

*e.g.* Blunder, number.

**Augustan** :—The name usually given to the period of Queen Anne's reign when literature was distinguished by clarity and common sense.

*e.g.* *Spectator* Essays, Pope's Poetry.

**Ballad** :—Originally a song sung to dancing; now a simple song or, more commonly, a simple narrative poem dealing with a well-known subject and written in the ballad metre.

*e.g.* "*Sir Patrick Spens,*" "*The Wife of Usher's Well.*"

A common ballad stanza :—

Annan Water's wading deep,
And my Love Annie's wond'rous bonny;
And I am loath she shall wet her feet,
Because I love her

**Bathos** :—An unintentional anti-climax in which there is a sudden fall in dignity and importance in the last expression of a series rising in force and dignity.

*e.g.* You jeered at the man, you threatened him, you thrust him against a window so violently that the man was fatally injured and the window broken.

**Blank Verse** :—Any unrhymed verse, but generally applied to verse of unrhymed iambic pentameter.

*e.g.* Will all great Neptune's ocean wash this blood
Clean from my hand ? No : this my hand will rather
The multitudinous seas incarnadine.

**Bombast** :—An inflated style in which high-sounding words are employed to express ideas which are simple and commonplace.

*e.g.* Floral tributes, the matutinal ablutions.

**Bowdlerize** :—To expurgate : to remove words which are improper. Thomas Bowdler prepared an edition of Shakespeare in 1818 in which "Those words are omitted which cannot with propriety be read to a family."

**Burlesque** :—A ludicrous imitation of a work, generally a drama or part of a drama, for the purpose of ridicule.

*e.g.* Bottom's play in "*A Midsummer Night's Dream.*"

**Cæsura** :—" Cutting." A break or pause in the metre, generally about the middle, common in the longer metres.

*e.g.* But do not use it oft, let me entreat you.

**Catalectic** :—The name applied to the metre of a line when the unaccented syllable of the last foot is missing ; if two are missing, the line is called hypercatalectic.

But rapture | and beauty | they cannot | recall. |

**Classical** :—An adjective used to describe the art of the great Greek and Roman periods, sometimes applied to the Augustan Age, and in a wider sense to any national art which possesses the qualities of clarity, simplicity and grandeur and deals with the permanent aspects of human experience.

*e.g.* Nothing is here for tears, nothing to wail
Or knock the breast, no weakness, no contempt,
Dispraise or blame—nothing but well and fair,
And what may quiet us in a death so noble.

SAMSON AGONISTES.

**Cliché** :—Word or phrase which is hackneyed or stale. Sometimes called a Stereotype.

*e.g.* " to sink into the arms of Morpheus " for " to sleep."

**Cognates** are words, not necessarily in the same language, which are derived from the same original root.

*e.g.* mater, mère, mother.
skirt, shirt.

**Cognate Object** :—A noun or pronoun which contains the same meaning as the verb which it follows.

*e.g.* I have fought the good fight.

**Colloquialism** :—A word or phrase used in ordinary conversation or in written dialogue, but not in dignified speech or in ordinary writing.

*e.g.* This looks quite alright.

**Conceit** :—A far-fetched or strained simile or metaphor.

*e.g.* But thou thereon didst only breathe,
And sent'st it back to me ;
Since when it grows, and smells, I swear,
Not of itself, but thee !

**Dénouement** :—The term used to describe the clearing up or disentangling of the complication of the plot, generally found in the fourth act of a play. Also used of the end of a novel or short story. The terms Resolution, Falling Action are also used.

Most plays of Shakespeare, especially the tragedies, show the Denouement in the fourth act; in the comedies it may be found later.

**Dialect** :—The term applied to the form of language peculiar to any province or district of a country.

*e.g.* Loon (Aberdeenshire—a boy);
Jannock (Lancashire—excellent).

**Didactic** :—A term applied to any form of writing in verse or prose which instructs, or instils a moral.

*e.g.* Pope's "*Essay on Man.*"
Addison's "*Vision of Mirza.*"

**Elegy** :—A mournful, plaintive and generally reflective poem, usually a lament for the dead or a longing for what is absent.

*e.g.* Gray's "*Elegy*"; Milton's "*Lycidas.*"

**Elision** :—The omission of a vowel or syllable in pronunciation especially when it immediately precedes another vowel.

*e.g.* All pains the immortal spirit must endure,
*Scan.* All pains | th' immor | tal spir | it must | endure. |

**Enjambment** :—The continuation or overflow of a sentence or phrase beyond the end of one line of verse into the next.

*e.g.* These are the chief; to number o'er the rest
And stand, like Adam, naming every beast
Were weary work.

**Epic** :—A great narrative poem generally consisting of twelve books, and dealing with the adventures of great soldiers or heroes, whose deeds are part of the history of a nation. It is written in the grand style.

*e.g.* "*The Iliad,*" "*Paradise Lost.*"

**Ethic Dative** :—A pronoun used to refer to a person indirectly concerned. The use is almost archaic.

*e.g.* Heat me these irons hot.

**Euphemism** :—The substitution of a pleasing expression for a coarse or harsh expression.

*e.g.* Your explanation convinces me that you are a stranger to the truth.

**Euphony** :—Pleasing sound due to the harmonious flow of words.

*e.g.* Eftsoons they heard a most melodious sound
Of all that mote delight a daintie eare.

**Euphuism** :—A term derived from the romance, "*Euphues*" by John Lyly whose affected style was marked by

(*a*) an excessive use of antithesis and alliteration, and

(*b*) constant allusion to mythology and natural history, the latter often inaccurate.

*e.g.* Knowest thou not that as the almond tree beareth most fruit when he is old, so love hath greatest faith when it groweth in age.

**Grub Street** :—The name of a former London street which, according to Dr. Johnson, was "much inhabited by writers of small histories, dictionaries and temporary poems," whence any mean production is called Grub Street.

**Homonym** :—A word which has the same form as another but a different meaning.

*e.g.* From his case he took the papers concerning the case.

**Hybrid** :—A word composed of elements belonging to two or more languages.

*e.g.* bicycle, macadamized.

**Irony** :—A mode of speech in which the meaning is contrary to the words as the speaker pretends to adopt another's point of view for the purpose of ridicule.

*e.g.* Verily ye are the people and wisdom shall die with you.

**Irish Bull** :—A blunder or unconscious contradiction of terms. The Irish are considered, doubtless without cause, to be partial to this device.

*e.g.* I am never at peace unless I have a good fight on hand.

**Johnsonese** :—The style of writing practised by Dr. Johnson, and characterised by Latinisms and ponderous expressions.

**Journalese** :—A term applied to the style of writing more or less common in the poorer newspapers, and distinguished by the use of pompous words and periphrases.

*e.g.* Despite the constant attendance of Jupiter Pluvius, the two and twenty modern gladiators pursued the leather sphere with unabated zeal.

**Lake Poets** :—The name applied, at first in derision, to the poets Wordsworth, Coleridge and Southey who lived in the Lake District and there sought inspiration in nature.

**Lampoon** :—Orig. a drinking song. From " lampons," let us drink. Now a bitter and coarse personal satire.

**Macaronic Verse** :—A term applied to verse, generally humorous, written in two or more languages.

*e.g.* cantant (ne saevi, magne policeman).
Noctem in Old Kent Road. Sic transit gloria Monday.

**Masque** :—A dramatic work consisting of songs, dialogue and music presented with elaborate stage-settings.

*e.g.* the masque in "*The Tempest*," "*Comus.*"

**Metathesis** :—The interchange of successive sounds letters in a word.

*e.g.* gars, grass.

**Melodrama** :—Orig. a play interspersed with songs. Now a play of simple powerful characters and exciting incidents, in which the good and bad characters are suitably rewarded.

**Miracle and Mystery Plays** :—Plays dating from the tenth century based on stories from the Bible or incidents in the lives of Saints. The parts were taken by members of the trading and merchant gilds (mysteries).

*e.g.* " Abraham and Isaac," from "*The Chester Pageant.*"

**Morality Plays** :—These plays succeeded the above, and are stories in which the characters are personified virtues and vices.

*e.g.* " Everyman."

**Neologism** :—A new word or coinage not yet established in general use.

*e.g.* Sorority, swing music.

**Onomatopœia.**—Formation of words or names suggested by sounds peculiar to the action or object named.

*e.g.* Quack-quack, cuckoo, swish.
By zig-zag paths and juts of pointed rock.

**Ottava Rima** :—An eight-lined stanza of iambic pentameters, with rhyme-scheme a b a b a b c c, originating in Italy.

See Chapter on Prosody.

**Palindrome** :—A word, phrase or sentence that reads the same backwards or forwards.

*e.g.* Hannah, minim.

**Parody** :—An imitation of a serious work where the style is the same but the theme, in order to arouse ridicule, is ludicrously different.

**Pastiche** :—A deliberate imitation of a certain form of composition but not intended as a parody.

*e.g.* "*Henry Esmond*" is written in the manner of the "*Spectator Essays.*"

**Pathetic Fallacy** :—The attribution of personal emotion to Nature.

*e.g.* " The cruel crawling foam."

**Picaresque** :—A term applied to fiction which describes the adventures of a clever and amusing rogue.

*e.g.* "*Humphrey Clinker.*"

**Poetic Licence** :—A liberty allowed to poets but not to prose writers in the use of archaisms, ellipses and distortion of facts.

*e.g.* Youth's a stuff will not endure.

**Rhetoric** :—A term applied to eloquent speech or writing, such as is found in a peroration, which appeals to the emotions rather than the intellect.

**Rhetorical Question** :—A question put not to elicit information but to emphasize a statement of the opposite meaning.

*e.g.* Shall not the Judge of all the world do right ?

**Romantic** :—A term applied to art which deals with what is strange, describes atmosphere rather than form, and appeals to the emotions rather than the reason.

*e.g.* For old, unhappy far-off things,
And battles long ago.

**Saga** :—Originally a Scandinavian story in prose dealing with the fortunes of a family. Since the writing of Galsworthy's "*Forsyte Saga*" the term is used to describe a novel or a series of novels dealing with the fortunes of a family in one or more generations.

**Slang** :—The mode of speech peculiar to one class of society, educated or uneducated, but not accepted as standard language. It is often applied to the terms peculiar to a trade or profession.

*e.g.* Take the count, Show the white feather.

**Solecism** :—A departure from the idiom, grammar, etc., of the language.

*e.g.* You ain't ; the use of the gelatine in the French Revolution aroused universal horror.

**Spenserian Stanza** :—A stanza consisting of nine lines, rhyming a b a b b c b c c, the first eight being iambic pentameters and the last an alexandrine. First used by Spenser in "*The Faerie Queen.*"

See Chapter on Prosody.

**Split Infinitive** :—The term applied to the insertion of an adverb or adverbial phrase between the " to " and the verb of the infinitive.

*e.g.* I want you to in every possible way assist me.

**Spoonerism** :—A transposition of initial letters of spoken words, generally unintentional, causing a humorous effect.

*e.g.* There is a half-warmed fish in my breast.

**Strophe** :—The part of a Greek ode sung by the chorus as they moved from the altar to one side of the scene.

*e.g.* Gray, "*The Bard.*"

**Umlaut** :—A vowel change due originally to the influence of a following vowel, still seen in certain plurals.

*e.g.* man, men ; goose, geese.

**Unities** :—The three dramatic unities which Aristotle derived from Greek drama are the unities of time, place and action.

(*a*). The unity of time—that the time occupied by the play should not exceed one day.

(*b*) The unity of place—that the action should be confined to one place or within such distance as might be covered in one day.

(*c*) The unity of action—that there should be one main plot.

**Vers Libre** :—" Free Verse." Verse which follows no definite rules of prosody and is generally unrhymed.

*e.g.* This is the dead land
This is cactus land
Here the stone images
Are raised.

SHELLEY.

**Verse** (Dramatic Lyric or Monologue).

The dramatic lyric or monologue is a poem with no characteristic metre, created during the dearth of ordinary drama in the nineteenth century by Tennyson and fully developed by Browning. It reveals the emotions, actions, motives and attitude to life of a narrator, historical or imaginary, to an audience of one or more persons.

*e.g.* *" Ulysses," " My Last Duchess," " Fra Lippo Lippi."*

# INDEX


A

ABBREVIATIONS, 256.
Aberration, 264.
Ablaut (vowel gradation), 239.
Adjectives, formation of, 237.
  kinds, 44.
Adverb, 57.
Adverbial phrase, 59.
Agreement, rules of, 110.
  adjective, 117.
  conjunction, 118.
  noun, 113.
  preposition, 117.
  pronoun, 113.
  verb, 114.
Alexandrine, 264, 388.
Allegory, 281, 290, 388.
Alliteration, 260, 282, 306, 389.
Ambiguity, 122.
Amphibrach, 262.
Anachronism, 122, 389.
Anacoluthon, 282, 304.
Anapaest, 262.
Anaphora, 275.
Anglo-Saxon, 205.
Annals, 353.
Anti-climax (bathos), 282, 296, 390.
Antistrophe (counter-turn), 367, 389.
Antithesis, 281, 291.
Antonomasia, 281, 295.
Antonyms, 251.
Aphaeresis, 238.
Apocope, 238.
Apodosis, 14, 52.
Apologue, 281, 290.
Aposiopesis, 282, 305.
Apostrophe, 282, 301.
Apostrophe (punctuation), 36, 66.
Appreciation of essay, 374.
  essayist, 375.
  novel, 378.
  poem, 371.
  play, 381.
Archaism (obsolete term), 120, 318, 389.
Aryan, 200.
Assonance, 259, 389.
Asyndeton, 282, 305.
Augmentative, 238.
Augustan, 387.
Autobiography, 355.
Auxiliary verb, 51.

B

BALLAD, 362, 389.
Ballad metre, 268, 389.
Barbarism, 120, 318, 320.
Bathos (anti-climax), 282, 296, 314.
Biography, 354.
Bilingualism, 213.
Bombast, 314, 390.
Bowdlerise, 390.
Brevity, 320.
Bull, Irish, 394.
Burlesque, 259, 360, 390.

C

CAESURA, 261, 390.
Caricature, 101.
Celtic, 201.

Celtic element, 208.
Character sketch, 99.
Chiasmus, 282, 297.
Circumlocution (periphrasis), 125, 282, 303.
Classical, 391.
Clause, adjective, 11.
  adverbial, 13.
  noun, 8.
Cliché (stereotype), 316, 391.
Climax, 282, 295.
Cognate object, 36, 391.
Cognates, 238, 391.
Coinage (neologism), 121, 219, 319, 395.
Colloquialism, 120, 319, 391.
Colon, 65.
Comedy, 357.
Comma, 64.
Comparison, adjectives, 46.
  adverbs, 60.
Conceit, 287, 391.
Conditional subjunctive, 52.
Conjunction, 62.
Conjunctive adverb, 60.
Couplet closed (heroic), 267.

D

Dactyl, 262.
Dative, ethic, 35, 393.
Demonstrative adjective, 44.
  pronoun, 42.
Descriptive adjective, 45
Dénouement, 391.
Dialect, 318, 392.
Dialogue, 96.
  in novel, 348.
Diction, 314, 326.
  poetic, 314.
Dictionary practice, 240.
Dimeter, 265.
Diminutive, 238.
Doggerel, 267.
Doublet, 214.
  Greek, 217.
  Latin, 217.
Drama, 355.
  classical, 356.
  romantic, 356.

E

Elegy, 367, 392.
Elision, 392.
Ellipsis, 13, 121.
Emphatic pronoun, 41.
End-stopt lines, 267.
English, early, 205.
  element, 208.
  middle, 206.
  modern, 206.
  old, 205.
  old (verbs), 233.
  (nouns), 233.
Enjambment, 268, 392.
Epenthesis, 239.
Epic, 361, 392.
  machinery, 362.
Epigram, 281, 292.
Epithesis, 239.
Epithet, essential, 307.
  transferred (hypellage), 295.
Epodos (after-song), 367.
Equivalence, 265.
Essay, 346.
  argumentative, 88.
  beginning, 73.
  body, 76.
  descriptive, 82.
  ending, 76.
  expository, 84.
  narrative, 79.
  reflective, 86.
Essay writing, 72.
Euphemism, 257, 282, 303, 393.
Euphony, 322, 393.
Euphuism, 217, 255, 303, 393.
Exclamation, 282, 297.
Exclamation mark, 66.

## F

FABLE, 290.
Fallacy, pathetic, 290, 396.
Factitive object, 35.
Farce, Dryden on, 325.
Figures of Speech, arrangement, 282.
  association, 281.
  contrast, 281.
  miscellaneous, 282.
  resemblance, 281.
Fine writing, 122, 314.
Foot, poetic, 262.
Fourteener, 204.
Frequentative, 238.

## G

GERUND, 48.
Gerundive infinitive (dative), 53.
Grammar, laws of, 110.
Greek, 201.
Greek roots, 232.
Grub street, 393.

## H

HENDIADYS, 304.
Hexameter, 266.
History, 352.
Homonyms, 251, 393.
Hybrid, 214, 393.
Hyphen, 67.
Hypallage (transferred epithet), 295.
Hyphen, 67.
Hyperbole, 282, 301.

## I

IAMBUS, 262.
Idioms (phrases with a history), 241, 248.
Idyll, 368.
Imperative mood, 53.
Impropriety, 121.
Indefinite pronoun, 42.
Infinite verb, 47, 52
Infinitive, split, 397.
Innuendo, 282, 300.
Insinuation, 282, 300.
Interjection, 63.
Interrogation (rhetorical question), 68, 282, 397.
Interrogative, adjective, 44.
  adverb, 60.
  pronoun, 42.
Interpretation, hints for, 134.
Invasion, English, 203.
Inversion, 282, 296.
Inverted commas, 67.
Irony, 282, 298, 300, 393.
  dramatic (tragic), 299.

## J

JOHNSONESE, 122, 314, 394.
Journalese, 122, 316, 394.

## L

LAMPOON, 394.
Language, analytic, 205.
  making, 200.
  synthetic, 205.
Latin, 200.
Latin element, first, 210.
  fourth, 216.
  second, 210.
  third, 212.
Latin roots, 222.
Laws of brevity, 312.
  simplicity, 312.
  propriety, 315.
  purity, 318.
  unity, 323.

Learning, Revival of, 216.
Letters, business, 92.
  formal, 95.
  personal, 91.
Licence, poetic, 396.
Litotes, 282, 303.
Lyric, features of, 364.

M

Malapropism, 121, 315.
Masque, 358, 394.
Material, adjectives of, 45.
Meiosis, 282, 302.
Melody, 322.
Metaphor, 281, 285.
  decayed, 288.
  mixed, 287.
  personal, 286.
Metonymy, 281, 294.
Metre, anapaestic, 263.
  ballad, 268, 389.
  Christabel, 272.
  dactylic, 263.
  Evangeline, 266.
  iambic, 262.
  trochaic, 263.
Miscellaneous elements, 218.
Misrelated participle, 34, 116.
Mood, 52.
Mutation (umlaut), 239.

N

Neologism (coinage), 319, 395.
Nominative case, 33.
Novel, historical, 349.
  plot, 348.
  setting, 349.
Numeral adjective, 45.
  pronoun, 42.

O

Obsolete Terms, 120, 318.
Objective case, 34.
Octave, 271.
Ode, 366.
Onomatopœia, 282, 305, 395.
Optative subjunctive, 52.
Oratory, 334.
Ottava rima, 270.
Oxymoron, 281, 292.

P

Palindrome, 395.
Parable, 281, 290.
Paradox, 281, 292.
Paragoge, 239.
Paragraph, 325.
Parallelism, 273.
Parody, 360, 395.
Participle, 47.
Pastiche, 396.
Patronymic, 238.
Pedantry, 122.
Pentameter, 266.
Pen portrait (character sketch), 99.
Period, 63.
Periphrasis (circumlocution), 125, 282, 303.
Personal pronoun, 40.
Personification, 289.
Picaresque, 396.
Plays, miracle, 395.
  mystery, 395.
Pleonasm, 321.
Poetry, lyrical, 363.
  narrative, 361.
  pastoral, 368.
Poets, Lake, 394.
Polysyndeton, 282, 305.
Pomposity, 314.
Possessive adjective, 44.
  case, 36.

Potential subjunctive, 52.
Précis, hints for, 182.
Prefixes, English (Teutonic), 234.
Greek, 235.
Latin, 235.
Preposition, 60.
Printing, Invention of, 216.
Prolepsis, 282, 304.
Pronouns, kinds of, 40.
Proper adjectives, 45.
Propriety, law of, 315.
Prose and poetry, distinguished, 345.
Prosthesis, 238.
Protasis, 14, 52.
Provincialisms (dialect terms), 318.
Pun (paronomasia), 281, 293.
Pyrrhic, 262.

Q

Quality, adjective of, 45.
Question, rhetorical (interrogation), 297, 396.

R

Redundancy, 321.
Reflexive pronoun, 40.
Relative pronoun, 41.
Restoration element, 215.
Repetition, 321.
Rhetoric, 296.
Rhodomontade, 314.
Rhyme, 258.
eye, 260.
feminine, 259.
identical, 259.
masculine, 259.
middle, 259.
royal, 269.
Rhythm, 258.
Romance element, 215.
Romantic, 396.
Run-on lines (enjambment), 268, 392.

S

Saga, 396.
Sarcasm, 282, 299.
Satire, 299, 359.
Scandinavian element, 211.
Scansion, 257, 264.
Scotticism, 121.
Semicolon, 61.
Sentence, 323.
adversative, 8.
balanced, 324.
complex, 8.
compound-complex, 16.
copulative, 8.
condensed (zeugma), 294.
disjunctive, 8.
illative, 8.
loose, 323.
periodic, 323.
topic (key), 326.
Sequence of tense, 56.
Sestet, 271.
Simile, 281, 283.
epic (Homeric), 283.
Slang, 122, 319, 396.
Solecism, 397.
Song lyric, 365.
Sonnet, 270, 366.
classical (Petrarchan), 270.
Shakespearean, 271.
Spenserian, 272.
Spoonerism, 397.
Spondee, 262.
Stanza, 267.
Burns, 269.
elegiac, 269.
In Memoriam, 268.
Spenserian, 270, 397.
Stereotype (cliché), 316.

Story, short, 351.
Strong verb, 48, 50.
Strophe (turn), 367.
Style, errors of, 120.
Subjunctive mood, 52.
Suffixes, English, 235.
French, 236.
Greek, 236.
Latin, 236.
Syllable, 257.
Syncope, 238.
Synecdoche, 294.
Synonyms, 251, 315.
Synthesis, methods of, **28**.

T

TAUTOLOGY, 124, **321**.
Tense, 56.
Terms, obsolete (archaisms), 318, 389.
technical, 121, **319**.
stylistic, 327.
Tetrameter, 266.
Teutonic, 203.
Tmesis, 239.
Transitive verbs, **51**.
Tragedy, 355.
Travesty, 360.
Trimeter, 266.
Triplet, 267.
Trochee, 262.
Truncated lines, **265**.

U

UMLAUT (mutation), 239, **397**.
Unities, dramatic, 356, **397**.

V

VERBS, conjugated, 54.
formation of, 237.
of incomplete predication 34.
voice, 51.
Verbosity, 321.
Vers libre, 274, 398.
Verse, 261.
blank, 261, 390.
macaronic, 394.
Vision (historic present), **301**.
Volta, 270.
Vowel gradation (umlaut), **239**.
music, 260.
Vulgarism, 319.

W

WEAK verb, 48.
Words, amelioration, **317**.
arrangement, **126**.
confused, 251.
deterioration, 317.
extension, 317.
limitation, 317.
selection, 120.

Z

ZEUGMA (condensed sentence), 281, 293.